Changing

Psychology, social regulation and subjectivity

Julian Henriques Wendy Hollway
Cathy Urwin Couze Venn
Valerie Walkerdine

METHUEN LONDON AND NEW YORK

First published in 1984 by
Methuen & Co. Ltd
11 New Fetter Lane,
London EC4P 4EE

Published in the USA by
Methuen & Co.
in association with Methuen, Inc.
733 Third Avenue, New York,
NY 10017

Typeset in Great Britain by
Scarborough Typesetting Services
and printed at the
University Press, Cambridge

British Library Cataloguing in Publication Data

Changing the subject.
1. Psychology
I. Henriques, Julian
150 BF121

ISBN 0-416-34560-3
ISBN 0-416-34570-0 Pbk

Library of Congress Cataloging in Publication Data

Changing the Subject
Bibliography: p.
Includes index.
Contents: Fitting work, psychological assessment in organizations/Wendy Hollway – Social psychology and the politics of racism/Julian Henriques – The subject of psychology/Couze Venn – Developmental psychology and the child-centred pedagogy, the insertion of Piaget into early education/ Valerie Walkerdine – Gender difference and the production of subjectivity/Wendy Hollway – Power relations and the emergence of language/Cathy Urwin
1. Psychology – methodological and social aspects. 2. Psychology, applied – methodology. 3. Personality and culture. 4. Social control.
5. Social change.
I. Henriques, Julian.
BF38.5.C425 1984 155 84-4503

ISBN 0-416-34560-3
ISBN 0-416-34570-0 (pbk)

Contents

About the authors

In providing these biographical notes we have departed from the usual practice which, by highlighting the achievements of authors as individuals, assumes writing to be the product of unique singular minds. This practice would be inconsistent with the approach to subjectivity developed in this book.

We came to the radical and sexual politics of the late 1960s, as well as to alternative social theory, as three white women and two black men from different class and cultural backgrounds. Our involvement with psychology has thus not been the only point of departure, although we have all taught psychology in some area of higher education.

Some members of the group were involved with the journal, *Ideology and Consciousness*.

Cathy, Julian and Wendy had studied undergraduate psychology. Valerie was a primary school teacher who got a PhD in Developmental Psychology. Couze gained his PhD in the sociology and philosophy of the social sciences. Cathy taught psychology in an undergraduate department after completing her PhD and then moved to become a Research Fellow using psychoanalytic theory and practice as well as her earlier specialism in child psychology. Wendy taught social psychology in a variety of institutions, applied to education, social and community work, and later to organizations. She finished her PhD part-time while teaching and is bringing up a child. Julian studied for a PhD, and then moved into applied research at the Runnymede Trust. He now works as a television journalist. Valerie left a polytechnic teaching post in order to do full-time research. Later she moved into a sociology department and combined her interests in education and subjectivity by doing research on gender and schooling.

These fragmentary pieces of information are all relevant to what we have written. Needless to say there is much more, conscious and unconscious. No relations within a group can be limited solely to the task.

We are close friends, and have considered it important throughout the three years of writing this book to explore our own multiple, contradictory and changing subjectivities.

Julian Henriques is an assistant producer with BBC Television.

Wendy Hollway is Lecturer in the Department of Occupational Psychology, Birkbeck College, University of London.

Cathy Urwin is Lowenfeld Research Fellow at the University of Cambridge.

Couze Venn is Senior Lecturer in Cultural Studies at North East London Polytechnic.

Valerie Walkerdine is Lecturer and Research Fellow at the Institute of Education, University of London.

Acknowledgements

This book is more than a series of related chapters. It has been produced collectively. Each chapter, including those ascribed to individuals has been worked on co-operatively. First of all then we want to thank each other for the constant support, open exploration and prompting. Without this we could not have got as far as we have. We are also particularly indebted to Stuart Hall, David Ingleby and Martin Richards for much needed encouragement and helpful criticisms, and to Robin Lister for his considerable editoral effort in helping us to clarify and articulate our arguments, as well as tidying up the scripts. We thank Mary Ann Kernan for her general editorial support and patience, and Francesca Ashurst and Jane Kendrick for giving up valuable time to help with the typing and the index. Many friends have listened to what we were trying to say and helped us to say it better.

Introduction: The point of departure

Changing the Subject is about transformations. The multiple meanings in the title refer to an interplay of changes in which psychology is implicated. We explore the way it helps to create the current conceptions of individual and society and the consequent implications for strategies of change. This book works towards a theory of subjectivity which implies a different politics of transformation. The book's subtitle 'psychology, social regulation and subjectivity' reflects its three sections. The first focuses on a critique of individual–society dualism and its effects on psychological theory and practices. The second develops alternative perspectives which show psychology's part in the practices of social regulation and administration and how the very notion of 'individual' is a product of discourses which have developed through these practices. The third section takes us into retheorizing subjectivity on the foundations of the first two.

Our approach to changing the discipline of psychology is therefore double-edged. First we assert the importance of modern psychology in producing many of the apparatuses of social regulation which affect the daily lives of all of us. However, unlike previous radical critiques we do not argue that psychology is or has been a monolithic force of oppression and distortion which constrains and enchains individuals. Rather, we contend that psychology, because of its insertion in modern social practices, has helped to constitute the very form of modern individuality. Psychology is productive: it does not simply bias or distort or incarcerate helpless individuals in oppressive institutions. It regulates, classifies and administers; it produces those regulative devices which form us as objects of child development, schooling, welfare agencies, medicine, multicultural education, personnel practices and so forth. Further, psychology's implication in our modern form of individuality means that it constitutes subjectivities as well as objects. It is by producing explanations as well as identifying problems that psychology contributes to specific political positions. For example through the concept of unemployability the unemployed can become identified (and, indeed, identify themselves) as a cause of unemployment (see below, Introduction to section 2, pp. 112–13).

As a result of such psychologically reinforced explanations solutions are found which perpetuate the *status quo*: the unemployable can be trained in interpersonal skills but the number of available jobs does not increase. This theme of psychology's productivity of both subjects and objects is one that informs the chapters that follow.

A critical tool for demonstrating how the modern form of individuality is in part produced by psychology is the deconstruction of the taken-for-granted, common-sense facts about human beings and our lived experience. That deconstruction involves prising apart the meanings and assumptions fused together in the ways we understand ourselves in order to see them as historically specific products, rather than timeless and incontrovertible given facts. Such an analysis of the construction of the modern form of individuality is a prerequisite for understanding and bringing about change.

This assertion leads in to the second aspect of our approach. The left and feminism have long struggled with the problem of the relation of individual and social change in their attempts to theorize and practise a politics of transformation. Our title's play on 'subject' and 'change' also refers to this central issue. The opposition of individual and society and therefore of individual change and social change is a view of the social domain which we shall criticize (see Introduction to section 1). This opposition characterizes not only psychology, but social theory as well and our rejection of it is of central importance here. It is our contention that psychology produces individuals as objects of its theorizing and practices and in turn produces people as they act and perceive themselves. Clearly, therefore, we cannot look to the same psychology (nor by the same token, to sociology or social theory) for an understanding of subjectivity which will help us to confront the issues of the relation of individual and social change raised within feminist and socialist debate. In order to address this issue, critical for any politics of transformation, our analysis reaches beyond the reductive account of subjectivity forced by the individual–society.

Subject and subjectivity

Before proceeding with a brief introductory history of psychology today and our own relation to it, we should comment on our use of the term 'subject' and 'subjectivity'. 'The subject' is the generic term used in philosophy for what in lay terms would be 'the person', 'individual' or 'human being' and what in psychology is referred to as 'the individual'. Recently the term 'theories of the subject' has tended to refer to approaches which are critical of psychology's assumptions about individuality, theoretical approaches which emphasize the way in which the social domain constitutes subjects rather than the other way round. Much of this work has been developed in France and the fact that it is written in French creates certain terminological problems – for example, the double meaning of 'asujettir', which at the same time means 'to produce subjectivity' and 'to make subject', is impossible to convey exactly into English in a single word. We have foregone the complexity of meaning in such cases and rather than load readers with an unwieldy term like 'subjectivity/subjectification' (*asujetissement*), we have plumped for 'subjectivity'. What we mean by this term will only be fully established by the end of this book. In brief we use 'subjectivity' to refer to individuality and self-awareness – the condition of being a subject – but understand in this usage that subjects are dynamic and multiple, always positioned in relation to particular discourses and practices and produced by these – the condition of being subject. (This latter condition of subjectivity is analysed in detail in the Introduction to section 2 and chapter 3 below.)

Liberatory politics

If psychology helps to produce modern social practices, and if these social practices produce individuals, how was it that in earlier radical critiques of psychology we thought of the individual as someone who could be liberated from its oppressive power? That notion of liberation carries with it the belief that it is possible for the individual to be free from social constraints – to be a pure and untainted entity. Such a view of the individual underlay the liberatory and radical politics of the 1960s and 1970s.

In the late 1960s and early 1970s a wave of protest and revolt swept the black ghettoes and campuses of the United States and the universities and colleges of Europe and, to a certain extent, Britain. This movement produced an array of critiques and counter-courses which aimed to set psychology and the other social sciences to rights by exposing their oppressive ways.

For the authors of this book that movement was central to our formation as radicals: it helped form what we have become and our approach to psychology. It supplied us and our contemporaries with a model of liberation and individual freedom, and of resistance to the forces of oppression. The concepts which underpinned the political struggles of the time created the ground for the theories we are developing here. Humanistic formulations of the individual and consequent anti-humanist counter-positions were influential in these political struggles, particularly in the moment of individual liberation (this conceptual ground is explored in the Introduction to section 2 below).

With hindsight, we can look back at an extraordinary conjuncture of events: the heyday of Keynesian economic management, with real increases in affluence in the west; the curtain falling on colonization in its old form; an apparent surge of liberating movements expressed by a multiplication of subcultures within the larger transformation, through rock music, new writing, the new wave, 'flower power', the underground and so on, and also through the growing challenge of war-resistance, Black Power, Women's Liberation and Gay Liberation. For those caught in the prism of these events, every kaleidoscopic arrangement seemed possible. Until 1968 and beyond Eros appeared capable of undermining the civilization of oppression. By the early 1970s the privileged innocent's utopian vision of peace, love and revolution was in a state of advanced disintegration. Of course, many positive things emerged from developments of that time; our gloss necessarily simplifies. But what we want to highlight is the optimistic state of mind of many who sought to challenge what was generally referred to as the 'system'. The focus was on the individual, on doing one's own thing, on building the counter-culture. The conditions appeared to make this ambition possible.

The humanization of the human sciences

This individualistic, liberatory mood finds an echo in challenges to the dominant positivism in the human sciences. It was in the name of the individual or the person that this challenge was made. Whether in ethnomethodology, in the earlier phase of Freudo-Marxism, or in the analysis of games people play, attention turned towards a complicit listening to what people actually said. There was widespread denunciation of the inhumanity of empiricist or behaviourist psychology and the mechanical emptiness of correlations and functions. The same unspoken alliance of new humanists mocked the class reductionism of orthodox Marxist positions.

It was in this context that the skirmishes took place in the humanism–anti-humanism debates in the social sciences. And on one side of the battle-field of psychology stood the forces of administrative regulation, grinding out the norms: IQ scores; taxonomies of skills; personality inventories; assessment of potential and motivation. On the other side stood the heroes of individual development and the brigades of free expression: spontaneity; self-expression; satisfaction. Thus the assertion of the human in the radical critiques of empiricist sociology and of behaviourist psychology can be viewed as part of the resistance, both inside and outside the social sciences, to the positivists' claims to speak the truth of society, human beings and human relations.

Perhaps we should emphasize that the 1960s and early 1970s witnessed an explosion in the production of social-scientific knowledge. Sociologese and psychologese filtered into every discourse of administration and management. One could say that the explosion itself was an index of the amplification of techniques and apparatuses of intervention for regulating and institutionalizing the individual in the family, at work, at play, on the street corner, at the youth club and so on. Social sciences and social administration grew in a mutually productive relationship.

To the extent that power was talked about it was the monolithic power of the system, out there. One particular effect of this perspective was that the radical humanist critique of psychology held as its logical conclusion that the only way of producing a 'non-oppressive' psychology, or for psychologists to have any positive impact on political change, was through the removal of state power – through changing the system, as the rhetoric of the late 1960s and early 1970s would have it. According to this position, there was no space for political action around or within psychology itself, even after you had removed the scales from your eyes and perceived this ideological assumption and its political effects. The only alternatives appeared to be to wait for the revolution, to drop out or cop out, or to do a bread-and-butter psychology by day and politics by night. While these politics of liberation produced positive modes of resistance, their effect was a tendency to ignore both deconstruction and reconstruction. Tackling issues within psychology or any other part of the system was reformist tinkering.

Psychology in recession

In the present context, as is the case in all areas of the social sciences, instead of debating whether psychology is bourgeois and oppressive, many academics and practitioners are having to defend themselves against the impact of spending cuts which are in danger of dismantling those very apparatuses from which they would once have dropped out. Yet the critiques of the early 1970s would lead us to assume that the wholesale dismantling of psychological services would be a politically progressive course of action. Is it not, therefore, politically correct to collude with the Tory government in this respect? The answer is not simple, demonstrating that what counts as positive action and resistance is not fixed once and for all, but depends on both the form and analysis of powers (see, in particular, 'The power/knowledge axis', in Introduction to section 2, pp. 115–18). Social changes throw up new issues which on the one hand problematize previous theorizations and courses of political action, and at the same time can clarify gaps, inconsistencies and inadequacies in previous lines of approach. In looking at the critiques of the 1970s, for example, we find that they are lacking in details which would explain how the 'conspiracy' worked between the system and for example, psychology. Demonstrating a convenient correspondence between the dominant ideology and psychology's assumptions and practices does not explain how this situation was produced. Nor does an emphasis on the hegemony of the state or some central source of power explain why psychology is particularly suited to its purposes. Until we can provide some explanations, we cannot open the discussion of whether and how things can be otherwise.

The particular circumstances of the 1960s and 1970s and the present make different forms of analysis and action necessary and possible. Opting out is an unlikely path for psychology students today who are faced with the prospect of the dole queue at the end of their academic road. The authors, on the other hand, were products of the boom period in higher education; there was no question of not being able to get jobs after three years of undergraduate study: it was more a matter of choosing amongst many available options including voluntarily dropping out. It is important to ask what form a radical questioning of the education system and the subject-matter of psychology can take under current conditions, given that in the 1960s our perspective on political change appears to have been closely tied to the kinds of freedoms available to the economically secure middle class and to the specific political circumstances of the time. There are many grounds for pessimism. The decline of student unrest in the mid-1970s was in part associated with the beginnings of the recession, felt by students who were concerned about career prospects when they first came to university and who therefore aimed to use their psychology course as a training to this end. Of course, these concerns are now being felt by academic and administrative staff within psychology departments. While psychology as a whole is concerned to assert and protect its professional status, psychology staff are seeking to demonstrate the employability of their students, particularly of that small proportion who go into the various applied fields such as clinical, educational and occupational psychology. Increasing numbers try to get into industry as fewer find places in public sector work.

The pressures that assert the need for professionalization will tend also to reassert the more traditional practices of psychology: the development of regulative tools – the normative devices of assessment and prediction, for example – and the concomitant emphasis on its respectability as a science. At the same time, the pulls to produce what is deemed socially necessary, compounded by psychology's individualist problematic, are likely to reproduce its more reactionary trends. Today's psychology offers redundancy counselling and similar practices as palliatives for individuals adjusting to the stresses and strains of society in recession. In doing so it cannot but stop short of a political and economic grasp of problems which, however unwittingly, it actually helps to produce.

Is it the case then that psychologists' moment of resistance has passed? Was the power and glory of radical psychology made possible by the economic boom? Is the economy all-determining? What we have asserted is that the economic conditions of the time made possible certain modes of resistance, such as liberatory politics, but these conditions do not cause them to happen or specify their form in any simple, linear sense. Consider, for example, that at present not all young people are rushing madly after an ever-decreasing supply of jobs. One current form of resistance is that which places itself in opposition to the traditional left's 'Right to Work' campaigns, 'Jobs not Yops' and so on, in favour of a position which argues that young people do not want boring, deadening work to fill their lives for little more pay than they receive on Social Security. Such a mode of resistance is, in the form of its individualism, not dissimilar from the opting out of the 1960s and 1970s.

It is to modes of resistance appropriate to psychological and related practices that our work is addressed. The forms and conditioning of power and resistance possible within psychology in relation to social transformation are central to this book.

Feminism: liberation and beyond

The political point of origin of the modern Women's Liberation Movement is the liberatory movement of the 1960s and 1970s. Women, like workers, had 'nothing to lose but their chains' but their freedom from the enslavement of domesticity was never allied to a form of bureaucratic politics. Isolated in the home, women were not organized in any traditional sense. Rather, liberation required women to acknowledge suburban semi-detached life as a form of oppression. The movement depended on a form of politics which privileged the awakening of personal consciousness. In doing so, against the accusations made by the traditional left that feminism was individualistic and therefore bourgeois, feminism produced a form of politics and analysis which has perhaps more than any other modern movement asserted and demonstrated the necessity of personal change. This is crucial because, unlike traditional forms of resistance, it was insisted that subjective transformation was a major site of political change. Indeed it was implied that significant political change cannot be achieved without it.

This development is one of the conditions for our current discussions. It is the impact of the Women's Movement, with an increasingly strong network of publications, which provides impetus for much recent theoretical work on subjectivity. It is to psychoanalysis that feminism has turned to theorize issues brought up by its emphasis on consciousness-change: on contradictions between what is deemed politically correct and what is desired and the consequent question of how women change their construction as feminine.

In this sense feminism has introduced into the politics of change the necessity of understanding consciousness as something produced rather than as the source of ideas and the social world – as constituted and not constitutive.

The structure of the book

In critiquing psychology and approaching the issues of individual–social change we are attempting both to stress the importance of modern psychology and to examine how those concerned with change might begin to utilize and take further certain analytic tools for addressing subjectivity.

With this in mind the book is divided into three sections broadly reflected in the subtitle, *Psychology, social regulation and subjectivity*. This tripartite division is not clear-cut. For example, the critiques in section 1 are informed by the alternative analyses which we have been developing. This is inevitable in the sense that it is only possible to mount critiques from an alternative position. But it is also helpful, we hope, because each section is familiarizing the reader in advance – and through concrete case analyses – with the perspectives and concepts to come. In section 1 we begin with the issue of individual–social dualism as it has characterized radical approaches in both psychology and sociology. By reviewing psychologists' attempts to show how the individual is made social we argue for the theoretical inadequacy of the concepts of a presocial individual and a preformed social world. By raising these issues we are distinguishing our critique from previous analyses. We exemplify this difference with case studies of two aspects of psychological theory and practice: occupational assessment and race relations.

Sections 2 opens with a discussion of themes which we suggest are necessary to move beyond critique to deconstruction and reconstruction. Such themes include the importance of historical work for understanding the production of modern forms of social organization, administration and individuality. In addition to this we tackle the central issue of the constitution and place of the 'real' or the 'material' in our analysis. Here we focus on the humanism–anti-humanism debate in an attempt to move beyond forms of simple determinism which do not leave us in the shaky terrain of either idealism or relativism. Our analysis is then developed and exemplified, first by an examination of the concept of normality as the object of the science of psychology, which traces some aspects of the history of its formation, and second by a discussion of the position of psychology in respect of the regulation of children in modern primary school practice. These studies articulate psychology's productive role and allow us to examine the constitution of the individual as an object of study, and how it becomes at the same time an object of administration and regulation.

In the final section of the book, we try to move the debate beyond the production of the individual in and through social practices towards the issues of understanding and transforming subjectivity. This shift is critical if we are to understand how a socially produced individual is not merely moulded, labelled or pushed around by external forces; but is formed by a process which treats neither society nor individual as a privileged beginning, but takes interior and exterior as problematic categories. This discussion uses recent advances in psychoanalysis, semiotics and discourse theory. In two case studies, one of heterosexual couple relations and the other of child language development, we seek to extend the use of psychoanalysis and discourse theory in conjunction with one another.

At this point we have taken the reader as far as we have travelled. Our history is not finite, our search is unfinished. We hope at least that our book will provoke enough debate and discussion to take us a stage further in our transformation.

Introduction to Section 1

From the individual to the social – a bridge too far

Our introduction has sketched the outlines of the project of this book which will begin with a critical rejection of psychology's individualistic concept of the subject. In doing so, we include in our critique those predecessors who attempted to escape the limitations of psychology. This might at first appear counter-productive. After all, it is radical and humanist psychology which stand in opposition to the dehumanization which, for example, behaviourism has perpetrated in the names of control, efficiency and the economy of human capacities.

We start therefore by reiterating that we are not simply concerned to demonstrate theoretical inadequacies. Rather our task is to examine the politics of psychology. To the extent that previous radical critiques have shared that commitment, we recognize the valuable contributions they have made. Indeed one of the conditions of possibility of our project is the unsettling of positivist psychology and the insights which this produced.

Nevertheless, it is our claim that in spite of the politically progressive effects which radical psychology has had in social practices, politics today calls for new departures. The humanist commitment of radical psychology has become part of the liberal intransigence of psychological practice inside a great variety of social institutions. For the value of individualism has become the norm. It is enshrined in child-centred progressive education, in 'objective and classless' job assessment and in studies of prejudice which advocate multi-culturalism and the interpersonal approach of social work. And in the face of the new right's attacks on the welfare state in the name of individual freedom, humanist social science can only assert the moral superiority of its own version of individualism. The force of humanist psychology (and social science) is increasingly tied to an insecure claim about who can best defend the interest of the individual.

Our focus on the individual in this Introduction is not accidental. It is our intention to demonstrate two intertwined things: that individualism is both the theoretical Achilles heel of humanist psychology and the crucial condition for the insertion of its discourse in the practices which produce the existing state of affairs.

This demonstration will proceed in two stages. In this section the focus will be on the theoretical correlate of individualism, namely individual–society dualism and its consequences for the explanation of social behaviour and practice. We shall subsequently examine the historically specific character of the subject underlying individual–society dualism. Our aim is to demonstrate that the individual is not a fixed or given entity, but rather a particular product of historically specific practices of social regulation. The implications of our analysis are, first of all, that we do not accept the innocence of theory, especially when it seeks immunity in the name of science. All theory is conditioned by historically specific circumstances and has definite effects on social existence.

For instance our question is not whether a concept such as prejudice as it occurs in social psychology's explanation of racism adequately describes racism (see chapter 2). Rather, we are concerned with the manner of its production and with interrogating the effects such a concept has for racist practices.

Similarly, we are not principally concerned with the technical sophistication or theoretical adequacy of the measurement of personalities in occupational assessment (see chapter 1). The more important questions are about the describable effects psychological discourses have on industrial practice. What matters is, the investigation of the jobs occupational psychologists do, given that their own work is always already locked into the existing complex of practices that allocate people to places in social institutions, measure their capacities, propose training programmes, define personnel problems and advise on solutions; in short that routinely participate in producing our daily existence at work.

These effects are not independent of the form the theoretical discourse takes. For example, we do not expect our theorizations in this book to be seized upon with enthusiasm in industry. So another implication of our position is that the specific discourses of psychology must be examined for the assumptions and premises which condition their utility in specific practices, their compatibility with existing power relations and, more generally, their functioning in the production of the social domain.

It is for this reason that this Introduction devotes some time to a detailed critique of the individual–society dualism that is central to the whole of the human sciences. This critique provides necessary support for the kind of analysis carried out in chapters 1 and 2. One of the claims made here is that the humanist approach in the race-relations industry and in personalizing work relations unwittingly reproduces existing power relations precisely because it fails to move out of the terrain of the dualism. It should be clear from such a claim that the arguments demonstrating the pervasiveness of the individual–society couple and our rejection of it are vital to our project. They apply to all the areas covered and are taken for granted in later chapters. But they also explain why we all have moved out of the framework offered by traditional psychology, not because we have abandoned psychology as a site for intervention, but because we have had to look elsewhere for alternative concepts and ways of thinking. In our discussion we will concentrate especially on areas within developmental psychology and social psychology which have attempted to be social and/or radical; that is, approaches which have explicitly set out to be non-reductionist and to give an account of the social formation of individuals. We shall show that the reductionism is not avoided but remains implicit in the very terms in which the problems of explaining social development or behaviour are posed.

Indeed, the problem is a wider one for the social sciences, since much of sociology has been riven by the individual–social demarcation in spite of attempts for more than a decade now to account for the subjective understanding and experience of social encounters and social relations. We shall now consider this.

Individual–society dualism

That psychology 'neglected' the social world, and was unable to bridge the individual–society divide, emerged in various attempts to rethink the relation between biology and society (Richards, 1974a; Riley, 1978); in critiques of social psychology (for example, Harré and Secord, 1972; Armistead, 1974); in various critiques of psychology's inability to account for the distinctly human aspects of persons, as opposed to rats or machines (for example, Shotter, 1974a and b); and in Ingleby's (1974a and b) and others' political critiques of psychology's implicit ideologies and its role in maintaining the *status quo*.

Many of these critiques were linked from the outset with radical perspectives. Most generally, however, the problem of social reference became less significant than the question of how to theorize the social component in psychological functioning. Here, the attempt to rework the social–individual relation has floundered because it has left the basic terms of the couple untouched. For example, 'the crisis in social psychology' (Elms, 1975), a phrase which has regularly been quoted since its initiation as a catchword for many social-psychological ills, has promoted a considerable amount of debate within the field. Though it attempts to develop new ways of thinking about social processes between individuals, the debate is circumscribed by the terms of reference of traditional psychology, and as such cannot move beyond traditional answers to how to transcend individual–society dualism. Illustrative of these impasses is the 1979 debate in the *British Journal of Social and Clinical Psychology* (Tajfel; Taylor and Brown; Moscovici).

But it is perhaps in developmental psychology rather than in social psychology that the forging of new approaches has progressed most rapidly, since, almost by definition, the study of children's development forces one up against the significance of the social world.

The social in developmental psychology

With respect to the formation of new approaches, the collection edited by Martin Richards (1974b) *The Integration of a Child into a Social World*, can be regarded as something of a landmark. Its promise lay in its recognition of the need to cut across the social–individual divide and to forge links between developmental psychology and other disciplines, notably anthropology and sociology. It pointed to methodological and conceptual inadequacies in attempts to use animal studies as a basis for studying human social development. The collection as a whole contributed to putting questions of the social formation of individuals firmly on the map.

Yet, despite its commitment, the terms of individual–society dualism are themselves retained in the way in which the problem of social formation is posed. Whether they are used implicitly or explicitly, this retention inevitably constrains the theorizing of their relationship. The dualism is implicit in Richards' introduction to the book, where he states: 'It is concerned with the process by which an infant becomes a competent member of his social community and develops the fundamental human attributes of speech, social communication, thought, self-reflection and consciousness' (p. 1).

Given the virtual impossibility of thinking outside the terms generated by the dualism, clearly the relation between the two – how society socializes the individual – is a crucial theoretical and practical question. The two terms are mutually indispensable to each other. The individual, as a concept, could not exist without its opposite number, society. In the social sciences their relation is almost universally theorized as some sort of interaction. Given that one of its major areas of study involves newborn infants, developmental psychology is particularly sensitive to the problem of how to think about the starting point of development. For Richards, the infant 'is not fully social as he is not yet a competent member of a social community'. S/he is, rather, 'a biological organism with biological propensities and organisation who becomes social through his encounters with social adults. So throughout development there is an essential tension between the biological and the social' (p. 1). This extract illustrates well how, once the terms 'individual' and 'social' are brought into play, the two entities are necessarily thought of as antithetical, as exclusive (though interacting), as separable and even as pulling in opposite directions. It also demonstrates how the individual reduces inevitably to the biological in essence once its opposite number, the social, has been posed to explain the rest. Moreover, it leaves the contribution of the infant to its own development out of account. This results in certain paradoxes in any attempt to account for the social formation of psychological functions. In these respects, Richards' account is typical of almost any formulation of development or socialization. This can be seen particularly clearly by looking at the radical humanism which emerged in both social and developmental psychology in the 1970s.

Radical humanism

One of the most systematic attempts to go beyond the terms available in theorizing the infant's entry into the social world has been John Shotter's (1974a and b) humanistic approach which is radical in its commitment. We shall discuss his account in detail because his work is influential, political and is often seen as overcoming the problems for which psychology is criticized. Indeed it has been a major influence on some of us.

Shotter's approach to psychology has itself changed dramatically and he openly acknowledges the part played by personal experience through the late 1960s in the formation of his 'new psychology'. Like several of his contemporaries within the social sciences and philosophy, he criticizes the attempt to build an account of psychology based on the methods and concepts of the natural sciences. He concentrates his critique particularly on the 'image of man' that such approaches seemed to assume, and on the 'aspects of being human' unreachable through the positivist tradition. These aspects include such phenomena as self-consciousness, responsible action, intention and the ability to participate in a society according to its prescribed rules – in other words, subjectivity. In doing so, Shotter argued that he was aligning himself with those for whom nothing less than a personal approach to human affairs is adequate (e.g. MacMurray, 1957; Hampshire, 1959; Taylor, 1966; Bannister and Fransella, 1971; Harré and Secord, 1972), and that in consequence psychology must become part of the moral sciences.

Shotter (1974b) starts from the position that 'babies born to us need to grow up to be what we think of as human' (p. 215). Nor is their development 'solely a natural process'. Rather, it is 'partly an intentional one and as such is a product of human thought and deliberation, belief and ideology'. In other words, it is a process 'in which the interests of a culture as well as the ideologies of a class can enter'. How does this process come about?

According to Shotter, infants' 'humanity seems to be transmitted to them after birth in an as yet ill-understood negotiation, a transaction between the babies and chiefly, among others, their mothers' (p. 215). From this the task of developmental psychology becomes one of discovery, or demonstrating how these negotiations contribute to the formation of the infant's own 'humanity'.

At this point, Shotter draws on G. H. Mead's (1934) theory of the social construction of the self through internalization of social interpretations of human conduct. Further, he makes a convenient link, though not an unproblematic one as we will show, between this account and Vygotsky's (1962) emphasis on the formation of individual consciousness through the internalization of language and other intermediate social processes. In addition, Shotter takes from the philosophy of action a notion of individual intention as fundamental to humanity, leading him to emphasize both that adults act with deliberate intentions in bringing up their children and that a potential for intention and responsibility is inherent in infants themselves. From this position the transition from some ill-defined but presumably prehuman state involves, firstly, the mother attributing intentions to the baby, often before he or she can be said to have them at all, and, secondly, a continuously unfolding process of 'negotiation' which contributes to the formation of 'shared understandings' increasingly relied on by the mother as she 'interprets' the social significance or meaning of the child's actions. This kind of ascription and consistent interpretation provides conditions through which the infant learns the social significance of its actions, the social definitions being internalized in a way which somehow contributes to the formation of self-consciousness, rationality and a focus of individual responsibility.

At first sight this account would seem to provide a basis for understanding the social construction of individuals. However, it is limited. Perhaps the most obvious criticism is methodological. Though Shotter's own work has been largely theoretical, it has been informed by, and has influenced, empirical studies of mother–child communication, such as those of Newson (1977 and 1978) and Treble (1972). Most studies of mother–child communication which have flourished over the decade (see, for example, Schaffer, 1977) have, by and large, involved videotaping middle-class mothers interacting with their infants in laboratory conditions. Riley (1978b) points out that this severs the studies from questions such as the effects of housing conditions on mother–child relations. However, the problem is not simply that the situation is artificial, since, in some sense, similar problems apply to any method. But we might note that the isolation of mothers and babies in this way contributes to what later (see chapter 6) we describe as the normalizing effects of such work. For example, there is a tendency for health visitors to speak of mothers' success or failure in 'meshing' with the baby – a term directly derived from this research.

A methodological focus on the mother–child pair also contributes to an analysis which translates the 'social' into 'intersubjectivity'. The concept of intersubjectivity has been an important one in attempts to bridge the individual–social divide, particularly in studies of infants' language development (see Lock, 1978, for a review). With its emphasis on meanings it goes considerably further than learning-theory paradigms to take the social domain into account. However, it sees meanings as being constructed between the mother (or other caretaker) and infant and there is a problem with the concepts of language and the social which are used (see Urwin, 1984).

The problem, therefore, is not simply how to make the work 'more social'. It is to show how individuals are constituted through the social domain. Since Shotter approaches this problem by proposing a dichotomy between the social and the individual, one is obliged to ask the question: what is the status of the infant before it 'becomes social', capable of 'responsible action', and so on? In order to make his account work, we have to assume a pregiven individual capable of processing the information contained in the interaction, or of 'internalizing' the social descriptions of its actions. As a result, this attempt at an account of the social formation of the infant's subjectivity misses its mark, since it both fails to address the social in any form other than the personal, and leaves the infant's contribution untouched and untheorized. In this empty space we are left to assume the existence of a pregiven psychological subject, a rational individual as a starting point in development.

One of the paradoxes which results from this theoretical collapse is that Shotter's position now appears remarkably close to that of Colwyn Trevarthen (1975, 1979), whose formulation is apparently the direct opposite. Whereas Shotter seeks to emphasize processes of social regulation, Trevarthen takes a strong position on infant 'predispositions' towards social action, and locates intersubjectivity as a biological capacity inherent in infants, which the supportive mother merely allows to 'unfold'. More recently, Trevarthen (1982) has replaced the emphasis on innate intersubjectivity with a catalogue of innate 'motives'. Interestingly, at a similar moment, Shotter (1978) broadened his notion of maternal interpretations to include the provision of a 'structure of motives'. As Ingleby (1980a) points out, this introduces an obvious paradox into the account, since it appears to deny any possibility of the infant having 'motives' of his or her own. Yet at the same time the account relies on some possibility of recognition on the infant's part, in order to benefit from the interpretations.

In demonstrating similarities between the positions of Shotter and Trevarthen, we are not intending to imply that they are thereby reducible to the same thing. None the less, both accounts are open to a particular set of problems which hinge on the dualism between the biological individual subject and the social domain. An attempt to get around these problems with respect to infant social development is presented in chapter 6. It is an approach which, through positing an unconscious and mechanisms of repression, works with a subject who is non-unitary, non-originating and not entirely rational.

More immediately, it is useful to point out that the paradoxes in Shotter's account are in part due to his reliance on Mead and Vygotsky. Each of these theorists poses a very different account of society as a starting point. Mead presupposes a harmonious social order regulated through symbolic systems and, inevitably from such a position, his individual, like Shotter's, is the rational, autonomous agent. In contrast, Vygotsky begins from a Marxist account of social relations. Nevertheless they both set up the problem through proposing a dualistic relation between the individual and society, and rely heavily on mechanisms of internationalization in order to account for individual consciousness, agency, rationality and other distinctly human processes. But as Giddens (1979) has pointed out with respect to Mead's theory, it is only through the introduction of the purely *ad hoc* 'I' that agency is accounted for at all.

With both Mead and Vygotsky, the mechanism of internalization through which the outside gets inside resurrects the Kantian duality of the knower and the known, a duality which is interminably difficult to transcend. Where religion provided an end point to this *reductio ad absurdum*, in the form of the soul whose existence was given by God, the external reference which could not be questioned, the intransigence of the problem led philosophy and early psychology to posit an homunculus, or a core of insight within the brain. Though the homunculus idea seems primitive to us today, it is precisely the same conceptual space which is left vacant within contemporary approaches which rely on the concept of internalization. Any attempt to resolve the problem must implicitly rely on the notion of a pregiven individual subject. In consequence, the characteristics of the individual subject gain precedence in determining the direction of development, the impact of the social becomes defused, and the question of the content of what is being internalized becomes relatively insignificant. It is for this reason that Shotter can blend together, apparently quite happily, two accounts which differ radically in their view of the nature of society. Both the implications of the assumption of the pregiven subject and the relative diffusion of the significance of content are seen clearly in the body of work concerned with child socialization.

Socialization

Since it is concerned with integrating children into society, in many ways Richards' collection can be seen as a development in socialization research. Though Richards is critical of many traditional models of socialization, it is still assumed that the concept of socialization provides an adequate account of how the infant is produced as social. In fact, research into socialization – in an eclecticism characteristic of much psychological theory – often combines different accounts in its attempts to theorize the internalization of the social world by the child, or the ways in which it is affected by it. For example:

> Socialisation is the means by which culture, including notions of appropriate sex roles, is transmitted. The agents of socialisation are primarily parents, teacher, peer-group and the media. There are four processes by which socialisation occurs. First skills, habits and some types of behaviour are learned as a consequence of reward and punishment. Second parents and others provide models for roles and behaviour which children imitate. Third the child identifies with one or both parents, a process which is more powerful than imitation through which the child incorporates and internalises the roles and values of the parent or other significant adult. Fourth, there is the part played by the growing individuals themselves. They actively seek to structure the world, to make sense and order of the environment. The categories available to the child for sorting out the environment play an important part in this process.
>
> (Weinreich, 1978, pp. 20–1)

The culture which is transmitted – the social domain – is posited at the beginning of this quotation. Further on, roles and values are also concepts which by implication refer to the social domain. Note that they are all treated as unproblematic content. The four processes, given here as if they were scientific fact, actually refer to four different frameworks within which socialization as a process has been theorized. The first two derive from a behaviourist learning paradigm which Richards criticizes for casting the individual as a passive recipient of moulding forces: either reinforcement schedules or adult socializers. As for the third process, the concept of 'identification' says very little unless it is incorporated into a psychoanalytic theory, whence it originated.

The fourth process mentioned by Weinreich stresses the infant/individual as an 'information processing system' (see chapter 2 for a critique). In developmental psychology this emphasis owes a considerable debt to Piaget's theory (see Venn and Walkerdine, 1978, and chapter 4). It contests the view of the passive individual of learning theory. In general, the notion of information processing is psychology's answer to the question of what does the internalizing, or how what is outside gets inside. From this perspective, the external world, whether it be physical objects or people, is seen as information to be processed. The aspect of individuals which is then of interest is the information-processing capacity itself, enabling them to organize the complexity of information coming from the outside world. This capacity is thus reduced to the biological material which defines the capacities of the human system (much as hardware would a computer). Though other approaches emphasize experience (whether in learning by reinforcement, Piaget's 'assimilation' and 'accommodation', Kelly's 'Man as Scientist', or attribution theory), none theorizes the content of the information as anything other than something external to the individual, to be internalized through cognitive mechanisms. Internalizing the social domain, notably through relations with adults, may be seen as a special case, in that the individual's self or identity is a product of the process. Nevertheless the basic tenets of the explanation are not modified.

Within accounts of socialization an emphasis on cognition was taken up both to bring it in line with mainstream psychology, and as a potential solution to dualism. For example: 'For socialisation theory, cognitive theory was intended to solve the problem of the relation between individual and social' (Rosenberg and Sutton Smith, 1972, p. 86). But cognitive psychology cannot solve this problem. Firstly, while the neurological and chemical features of the central nervous system must provide the boundary conditions for information processing, it is illegitimate to assume – as cognitive accounts implicity do – that structure determines content. We will mention other instances of this cognitivism, the elision between process and content, in due course. Secondly, the theoretical object of sociology, whether roles, rules or notions of social identity, cannot be incorporated into the psychological object viewed as an information-processing system. The domains do not refer to the same status of object.

The implications of ignoring these problems can be seen in how Weinreich is attempting to use the social-psychological tools available to account for how boys and girls grow up to be different. In the first place, there is no reference to the actual content of gender. Secondly, why do boys and girls take up different positions? Thirdly, why do some identify with the other-sex parent and why are differential values and powers attached to gender? None of these questions can be addressed while psychology brackets off content into the domain of the social and defines it as outside the boundaries of its theories, to fall within the domain of sociology, for example. In socialization theory it is implicitly assumed that, if they are added together, the ideas of psychology and sociology will produce a full explanation. But this assumption itself is based on the idea that the theoretical objects of the two disciplines – individual and society – are commensurable. In fact for psychology they are two different kinds of theoretical objects produced in different discourses through different disciplines, destined to bypass each other in the addition as they do in the interaction.

Theories which rely on the concept of socialization (theories which are necessarily dualistic in conception) find varying *ad hoc* formulations to bring content into the individual, for example intersubjectivity (see p. 16) or semantic universals (Chomsky, 1957 and 1965). These call on other theories which lie outside the domain of psychology (Husserl's phenomenology and structural linguistics, respectively), whose adequacy for social-psychological theory is not scrutinized. These *ad hoc* formulations get pulled into psychology's problematic of the individual and the content is not specified (nor does it retain its effects in producing subjectivity). The core, presocial individual which remains intact in these accounts still rapidly reduces to the biological.

It is sadly ironical given their opposite intentions that the conceptual frameworks of social and developmental psychologists such as Richards and Weinreich should afford such a generous toe-hold to biological accounts of, say, gender differences. Our argument is that the dualistic framework in which psychology is caught makes it impossible to theorize the individual in a radically social way. The model of interaction (however complex an interaction is asserted) leaves the idea of an unmediated biology unchallenged. So, for example, Weinreich is necessarily on the defensive: 'Undoubtedly there are sex differences which have a biological base, but many aspects of such roles do not derive directly from such differences' (1978, p. 18). She implies not only that some aspects of sex roles do have a 'biological base', but also that some derive directly from biology. The formulation betrays the extent to which the relation between the individual and society is not theorized, despite the invocation of the scientific-sounding processes of 'socialization' or 'interaction'. In an attempt to escape the reactionary implications of biological determinism, sociologists and some psychologists have fallen into the trap of denying biology altogether (it is to avoid this untenable position that Weinreich ends up with the above formulation).

The point that we are making is that whilst we should avoid founding a theory of subjectivity on a taken-for-granted biological origin, we cannot construct a position which altogether denies biology any effects. The only way to do this without granting either term of the biology–society couple the status of pregiven categories is to reconceptualize them in such a way that the implicit dualism is dissolved in favour of stressing the relational character of their mutual effects.

Let us make this clearer by considering an example. Currently in Puerto Rico hundreds of girls have started to experience an accelerated process of sexual maturation from the age of six months. There are cases of 4-year-olds showing full breast development and menstruating. This is thought to be the result of the use of oestrogen in animal feed for chickens – now the staple diet of a large number of Americanized Puerto Ricans. The effect of these biological changes is utter confusion of the children, their peers and adults regarding appropriate behaviour and expectations, so that they are caught in the limbo of child–woman. However, it is not the biological changes that have unilaterally altered the children's view of themselves or their social relations; that is, biology has not had a direct determining effect. It is because of the ways that adult women's sexuality signifies that the effects are as they are. Yet the effects of oestrogen in the diet – the biological reality – cannot be denied or disregarded (politically or theoretically). The problem is at the same time both a biological and a social one. Furthermore, the changes can be reversed with a chicken-free diet; a move contested by the corporations – mainly American – which control agribusiness there. The problem therefore is also economic and political.

Thus we have a striking case where the question of determination is shown to be a matter of a complex interrelation of conditions and effects, with no category appearing as determinant. First, the biological process itself is not a prior given, on which the social has later effects. Rather it is shown to be open to dramatic changes resulting from socioeconomic factors. Second, categories such as 'child' or 'woman' are shown to be neither biological givens nor simply social constructs. Third, it becomes impossible to think of the relationship in terms of the logic of cause and effect. In short, we have the demonstration that it is only because certain norms have become so much part of our common-sense view of reality that we are able to forget that they are the result of a production: that they have become naturalized as indisputably biological or social. The dualism is the theoretical result of that forgetting.

Now, although physical differences provide the most reliable markers for systems of social difference, biology by no means determines the content of these differences. Chapter 5 demonstrates how gender differences can be accounted for without falling into dualism. (See also Hirst and Woolley, 1982, for a very clear examination of the problems of theorizing biology and its relation to human attributes.)

Dualism within the self: roles

We have indicated how cognitive theory was meant to provide the solution to the relation between individual and society. The other concept which is used for this purpose is the idea of role: 'No other single concept would seem to offer more possibilities for exploration of the relation between persons and societies' (Holland, 1977, p. 81). Role, being originally a sociological concept, specified the content of actions or behaviours laid down by society. Banton's definition of role represents as great a consensus as one is likely to find: 'A set of norms and expectations applied to the incumbent of a particular position' (1965, p. 29)., However, the concept has not been unaffected by its take-up within psychology, reflecting the incommensurability between psychological and sociological paradigms. On the one hand, there have been structural and functional accounts of how social organization specifies roles. On the other, social psychologists (or micro-sociologists, such as Goffman) have emphasized individuals' performances. These accounts always leave untheorized a core person (though it varies as to whether it is actually called the individual, or the self, or left implied) who is the actor who takes on and performs the roles. What we are seeing here is a shift in the terrain of the dualism. The external has been welded on to the individual, but is still peripheral, able to be taken on and cast off. So for example: 'To a certain extent an individual personality is fixed and he chooses roles in the light of his predilections. But it is also true that the roles an individual takes up may influence his attitudes and his whole personality' (Banton, 1965, p. 146).

The paradigm is one of interaction, but this time the terms 'individual' and 'society' have been transposed onto 'personality' and 'role'. We are back with the same mechanisms which we found in Mead's account and the identical problems remain. We agree with Holland, therefore: 'Ironically the very divisions role theory sets out to mend in its unified theory of mind, self and society have rebounded in other forms' (1977, p. 81). That role theory should show similarities to G. H. Mead's work has to do with the fact that it is itself an offshoot of symbolic interactionism, a branch of sociology which has its basis in Mead. However, what symbolic interactionism achieved is a recognition of the importance of meaning in social relations, and it is this emphasis which has been taken up by social psychologists such as Gergen (1977) and Harré (1977). Mead recognized what Althusser was later to call the 'always-already social' (see Introduction to section 2, p. 91). Mead aimed to privilege 'the temporal and logical pre-existence of the social process to the self conscious individual' (Mead, 1934, p. 47), and in the formation of the individual through internalization of the 'me', 'the "me" is the organised set of attitudes of others which one himself has to take on' (Mead, 1934, p. 26). But as we have noted previously, this, like all functionalist sociology, on the one hand assumes a unitary social domain, and on the other hand leaves unproblematized the content and take-up of those attitudes. The same theoretical objections apply to the application of Mead's account of socialization within adult social psychology, for example in Gergen's (1977) 'socio-cognitive' theory of the self. Within this framework, an individual's cognitive representation is assumed to be a truthful representation of the external domain. Using cognition as a concept, Gergen emphasizes 'the close interdependency between cognitive process and social milieu' (Gergen, 1977, pp. 157–8). But the content of the 'social milieu' gets colonized by his theoretical framework and turned into 'rules' – part of the information-processing structure – and tied to neurology: 'We may say that the society provides a set of loosely constructed rules concerning the ways in which reality is to be interpreted if one is to function adequately within society' (ibid., p. 158). His cognitivism is complete when he hypothesizes that 'the *form* of mental processing may be the psychological counterpart of social rules' (ibid., p. 158; our italics). There is in the 'socio-cognitive' theory the unexamined assumption that the psychological and the social are commensurable and that they can be put together to add up to a coherent theory.

Even when the need for a theory of meaning is recognized, as in Harré's (1979) account, the assumptions about the nature of the individual subject have the effect of tying the theorization to the paradigm whereby the individual and the social are thought to be complementary. Harré utilizes Goffman to talk about a variety of 'selves' and the techniques of presentation of 'selves' but ultimately posits a unitary psychological being as a 'point of origin' endowed with 'basic cognitive structures' which structure and manage social action (Harré, 1977). Thus the way that the social has effects inside the individual is left problematic. He has recourse to a distinction between a 'practical order' and an 'expressive order' (Harré, 1979, p. 4), but does not begin to challenge the concept of a unitary pregiven subject.

It is this concept and the individual–social dualism which act as obstacles to a theorization of subjectivity which starts with the recognition that it is a socially constituted product. The detailed deconstruction of the subject psychology takes to be its object will be undertaken in chapter 3 to show the historical specificity of such an object.

Our critique indicates what traps must be avoided in an alternative approach: cognitivism, positing a unitary individual or a rational intentional being as a point of origin, reducing the social to intersubjective, and assuming that individual and society are commensurate as theoretical notions. A look at alternative approaches and theories used in understanding the production of psychological knowledges is the concern of sections 2 and 3. The chapters in this section, examine in more detail the specific products of psychological knowledge which stem from psychology's dualism. In these chapters we are aiming to go beyond an epistemological critique; we are not just arguing why particular positions are wrong according to some superordinate criterion of truth. In choosing to focus on the key and timely areas of employment and race we want to show how social psychology is caught within the practices that produce the social. Thus, cognitivism locates the responsibility for prejudice with particular individuals by theorizing its cause in terms of defects in the information available to, and the information-processing capacity of, the interpreting subject. Overcoming racism becomes a matter of education and information, not an economic and political issue to do with power and exploitation. Similarly, occupational psychologists might feel uneasy about shifting from helping individuals to plan and train for successful careers to helping them to accept redundancy, but, with practices which remain focused on the individual, what else can they do?

The main purpose of our critique of individual–society dualism has been to indicate how all-pervasive is its effect on psychological knowledge. We have deliberately taken examples from areas of psychology which are considered most social in the attempt to show how, despite the commitments to a social theory of the individual, as long as they are working within a dualistic framework such a theory remains elusive. In order to demonstrate this, it is important to examine both the historical production of the technologies of psychology and the formulation of certain issues in terms of an individualism which resides firmly on one side of the dualism we seek to deconstruct. Such an examination is undertaken in the two chapters which follow.

1

Fitting work: psychological assessment in organizations

Wendy Hollway

Occupational assessment is conventionally seen as one area of application of those parts of the science of psychology which measure and evaluate individuals and differentiate between them for the purposes of prediction and control of behaviour. In this chapter I want to examine occupational assessment from a rather different point of view. Analytically speaking, occupational assessment demonstrates the relations between power and knowledge (see pp. 115 ff.). Practically speaking, it shows psychology in action as a 'technology of the social'. These are perspectives drawn from Foucault's approach (which is developed fully in the Introduction to section 2). By the term 'technology of the social', I am not denoting technology in the conventional applied psychological sense of the hardware of psychological methods, with the neutrality that this implies. Rather it ties in with our emphasis – as outlined in the Introduction – on psychology's part in the processes of social regulation which are so central to modern social organization (see the Introduction to section 2, p. 106 for an elaboration of this usage within discourse theory). A technology of the social has its effects because it is legitimized by social science knowledge. Reciprocally the knowledge is a historical product of certain practices. This is what Foucault means by the mutuality of the power–knowledge relation (see the Introduction to section 2, especially pp. 100 ff.). Thus a 'knowledge' is not a body of truth as science would have it, but a historical product of certain practices, such as 'technologies of the social'. It is in this sense that I talk about the knowledges that make up psychology, rather than talking about psychology as a discipline. It is worth pointing out that power should not automatically connote something negative; something linked with oppressive practices. In a

Foucauldian analysis, power is productive of all knowledges, oppressive and liberatory.

Through a look at different occupational assessment practices – job analysis and evaluation, selection testing and interviewing, performance appraisal and the measurement of potential – I shall illustrate how applications of psychology are themselves productive of psychological knowledges and show that the latter are therefore not simply governed by considerations internal to scientific discovery, but rather by considerations based on the effectiveness of occupational assessment as a 'technology of the social'.

The difference in approach is not a matter of splitting hairs. Psychology's approach assumes that the knowledges that make up psychology are scientific. Contained in that assumption are ideas about objective progress towards absolute truth. It also assumes that there are such things as individuals and that it is just a matter of developing methods to assess them. Finally it sees applications as flowing from pure science, but only affecting scientific knowledge insofar as they provide a testing ground for 'truth'.

In contrast the second point of view sees knowledge and power as mutually productive: not just productive of changes in applications, but productive of knowledges. The knowledges which make up occupational assessment are productions of a combination of powers, sometimes pulling in the same direction, sometimes in tension. There is the power of psychology's scientific status (and thus the belief in and acceptance of it as fair and rational). There is the power of its statistical method to produce norms and thus to produce deviants. There is the institutionalized power of personnel managers, training officers, job analysts, organizational consultants and work study specialists to administer, regulate and evaluate personnel according to the needs of organizational productivity. These applications do not only produce (or fail to produce) organizational effectiveness. They also produce, modify and reproduce psychological knowledges which may or may not be consistent with each other or with the knowledges being produced in the mental hospital, or in the psychological laboratory. Through the examples of assessment practices in organizations it will become clear that progress towards 'truth' is not the simple aim or result of psychological knowledge.

A useful way into this analysis is to ask a seemingly straightforward question of occupational assessment: does it work? The question immediately begs two others. First, what is 'it'? Second, what constitutes 'working'? In answer to the first question, it can be recognized more readily that psychological assessment is not a homogeneous body of knowledge when we see it as a production in various diverse sites.

The first part of this chapter will summarize some of the recent knowledges involved in occupational assessment to illustrate this point.

A schematic answer to the second question is as follows: we shall see that there can be a discrepancy between psychology working to produce more powerful knowledges concerning people (more powerful in the sense of better understanding or prediction of their activities) and psychology working as a social technology enabling the administration and regulation of employees.

In the course of looking at how occupational assessment works, two themes will crop up regularly: one is the problem of the concept of 'individual' and the other is the scientific method. Chapter 3 provides a historical analysis of the emergence of the 'individual'. We shall see how the concept of individual is theoretically inadequate, yet works as part of a social technology. Underlying both its failure and its success is the dualism which separates it from the 'social' (see Introduction to section 1, pp. 13 ff.). Similarly with the scientific method, we shall see on the one hand its failure to produce knowledge of the complexity of people's relation to work, and on the other how it works to strengthen the powers of organizations to administer and control employees in the interests of productivity.

Sometimes the requirements of productivity pull psychological science in the direction of more powerful models: for example the glaring failure of performance appraisal methods (see pp. 52–5) to elicit the required information on which to base predictions of subsequent performance has led to at least some acknowledgement that *relations* between assessor and assessee play a part in that method (a notion that psychology is singularly ill equipped to handle). Sometimes the successful use of psychological tools drowns out theoretical criticisms. For example, the 16PF (see pp. 46–9) – an instrument to measure 'general personality' – is beloved of personnel staff dealing with management selection in many private sector organizations because 'it works' (that is, it appears to help distinguish good managers). Yet few psychologists would be prepared to defend its theoretical assumptions and thus, ultimately its validity as a selection tool.

Changing times, changing knowledges

In this part of the chapter, I shall summarize the main parameters in the history of occupational psychology. The perspective I take is one which will emphasize the production of diverse psychological knowledges and how these are an integral part of changing economic and wider cultural conditions. The summary is a 'history of the present' (see Introduction to section 2, pp. 100–5) in the sense that I am not aiming to represent all the trends and developments in psychology and its occupational applications. Rather I am concerned to illuminate the way that present practices are informed.

Two periods saw significant changes in the intensity of concern with the individual worker. In the first period, at around the turn of the century, I want to identify two themes. The first is the 'scientific management' of Taylor (1911) which was concerned to rationalize the motions entailed in labour in order to extract maximum productivity for energy expenditure by the worker. The second is the increasing size of organizations and the accompanying bureaucratic practices which required the administration of individual employees. Both produced a fairly uncomplicated managerialism (although with appropriately different emphases) which defined the position of occupational psychology as it emerged as a distinctive field.

The second epoch of significance is the economic boom period after the second world war. During this period certain problems in the traditional managerialist approach came to light (not least because of conditions of full employment and the consequent powerful position of workers). This period illustrates the relation between different psychological knowledges and the problems of organization and productivity.

Power over labour

Until the 1960s, occupational psychology was more clearly a field of application committed to helping organizations and their managers deal with the complex problems of maximizing profitability. The field of occupational psychology was summed up in the model devised by Professor Alec Roger:[1] 'fitting the man to the job and fitting the job to the man.' The first half of this definition covers the areas of occupational assessment, training and vocational guidance usually under the personnel function. The second half refers to problems of work design.

Although not called occupational psychology, Taylor's 'scientific management' of the late nineteenth century was also the expression of the concern to maximize the productivity of the worker. In this earlier capitalist view, the worker was simply treated as an 'operative' from which to extract the maximum surplus value (see chapter 3, pp. 124 and 130–2, to see how this ties in with psychology's 'subject'). 'Scientific management' consisted in the measurement – down to the finest detail – of the motions executed in the course of work. (See Braverman, 1974, for a detailed description and analysis.) The logic which saw management as maximum control over labour was the same logic which produced the work assembly-line with its rigid definition of jobs through the technology itself. Henry Ford, explaining his system of keeping workers at the bench and having stock chasers bring the materials, said, 'save ten steps a day for each of 12,000 employees and you will have saved 60 miles of wasted motion and misspent energy'. Braverman, who quoted this (1974, p. 310), comments 'that every individual needs a variety of movements and changes of routines in order to maintain a state of physical health and mental freshness and from this point of view such motion is *not* wasted'.

In more recent times, the functioning of capitalist technology in this maximization of control and productivity has acquired a new effectiveness in microelectronics technology as de Beneditti, director of Olivetti, described:

> The Taylorisation of the first factories . . . enabled the labour force to be controlled and was the necessary prerequisite to the subsequent mechanisation and automation of the productive process. . . . Information technology (microelectronics) is basically a technology of coordination and control of the labour force . . . which Taylorian organisation does not cover.
>
> (Quoted in Albury and Schwartz, 1982, p. 149)

Although some of the problems of management were solved through the division of labour, and through control via the technology of production, others were produced as a direct result of it. By the 1950s the concept of alienation had been given widespread currency through sociology. Its main application was in describing the problem of the relation of workers to blue-collar jobs. The problem of the control of labour was heightened by economic expansion and consequent full employment. Massive absenteeism and labour turnover produced problems of under-productivity, as did the consequent periods of training required before replacement workers were at peak productivity. In addition, two other factors made it necessary to consider the well-being of workers. Because of full employment, there was not a long queue of substitute workers prepared to take jobs under any conditions. If trained (and untrained) workers were to be kept, working conditions had to be considered. If one thing impressed this upon management it was the continuous sabotage of the production line which, along with turnover, absenteeism and industrial action, damaged productivity.

Organizing corporate well-being

It was in this economic context that different psychological knowledges were taken up and produced. A general humanism was ascendant in western culture in the 1960s. Concerned psychologists expressed humanistic values through a growing focus on 'the quality of working life'. Projects of job enrichment and job satisfaction mushroomed. It became a cliché that job satisfaction was not simply related to rate of pay and, similarly, that productivity was not solely dependent upon workers' skills and abilities. The question became how could employees be motivated to produce? A wider humanistic culture meant changing emphases in existing approaches to occupational assessment. For example, where selection boards had been oriented to making successful pass/fail decisions about candidates, in the 1960s and 1970s some assessment programmes changed the emphasis towards 'identification of individual development possibilities' (Stewart and Stewart, 1976). Similarly, in performance appraisal, the 'professional development' of the appraisee was seen as an important goal and this depended on feedback from colleagues – 'peer assessment' (Kilty, 1978). The 'nomothetic'[2] methods of psychometrics began to be criticized as being inappropriate for the purposes of development (Smith, Hartley and Stewart, 1978). As well as counselling, peer- and self-assessments (Kilty, 1978) and experiential methods (Smith, 1980; Golembiewski, 1980), techniques such as the repertory grid began to be applied to this end (Smith, Hartley and Stewart, 1978). The emphasis shifted from selection to training and development, as would be expected in a period which combined full employment and rapid expansion of organizations which thus needed experienced personnel to fill jobs at higher levels.

This movement did not just appear within organizational psychology.[3] The criticisms of nomothetic methods were part of a wider dissatisfaction with the lack of relevance of experimental laboratory-based methods and their objectification of people. Humanistic psychology, in contrast, stressed relating to people as people, in an egalitarian, empathic and caring mode (see for example Rogers, 1951 and 1961). People like Carl Rogers were working as therapists and producing models of the person consistent with such values, and many were applying these models in clinical psychology. Similarly group relations and interpersonal skills training for managers was also heavily influenced by these developing humanistic knowledges. Applications in the 1950s and early 1960s were much more influenced by the social psychology of groups, which had seen such a rapid expansion at that time (Back, 1979), but during the 1960s and early 1970s they became increasingly oriented to interpersonal relations and 'personal growth'.

Extremely influential in this regard was Maslow's concept of 'self-actualization' (1968), which still remains the starting-point for most humanistic approaches to organizations. Maslow's concept of a hierarchy of needs was taken up in contrast to models of economic man which assumed that workers were only interested in money. Maslow addressed the problems of alienation at a time of affluence; his hierarchy of needs specified that when material (lower-level) needs were met, individuals formed higher-level needs such as self-fulfilment. McGregor's (1960) typology of the differences between 'theory X' and 'theory Y' assumptions about people summarized these contrasting old and new knowledges, describing them exclusively from the point of view of managers. The crux of the difference between old (theory X) and new humanistic (theory Y) assumptions was whether it was believed that people disliked work – in which case they required direction, control and coercion – or whether 'the experience of physical and mental effort in work is as natural as play or rest' (Porter, Lawler and Hackman, 1976, p. 36) in which case people will be motivated to work and exercise self-responsibility (see also chapter 4 in relation to schools).

The essentialism and idealism of this latter position is striking. It does not consider the conditions of work on assembly lines and ask if there is anything 'natural' about such work. It assumes that the core characteristics of a person will be displayed whatever the work and whatever the social relations which control that person's work performance. In the context of industrial unrest, 'theory Y' was taken up as the 'correct' view of people and it was assumed that if managers were persuaded that they had been wrong to treat subordinates as if they needed to be controlled, then employee relations would improve. No one asked how managers came to hold 'theory X' assumptions in the first place, and no one recognized that it was implicit in their job function and position in the hierarchy. It is characteristic of the idealist view that people are seen as the origins of society and social relations and that therefore psychologistic interventions can succeed in changing the organization. Thus when things go wrong, groups of individuals (in this case managers) are identified as being the cause of the problem and also the case for treatment.

Organizational Development (OD) first emerged in the United States as a specific expression of this idealistic view, and flooded the western world through American multinationals, consultants and academics.[4] It was a faithful expression of this view, being concerned with training managers in interpersonal skills such as expressing feelings honestly and learning how to listen and empathize. Such managerial styles would produce, it was hoped, less conflictual relations with subordinates who would thus experience commitment to the organization and become more highly motivated, providing more and better work.

The recognition of the value of good relations with employees had been widely disseminated in the Hawthorne studies (Mayo, 1933). Training in interpersonal skills seemed to provide a technique through which this principle could be applied in any organization. It has been the technique on which management training as a function in large organizations has been built. In addition external consultants have made a living out of social skills work for nearly two decades, and the influence of this branch of humanistic psychology has been massive. (This is not to say, however, that its influence has been a reflection of its unqualified success as a social technology; see Golembiewski, 1980.)

Rowan's (1979) survey of occupational psychology in Britain supports this brief account of its history. In 1979 relatively few occupational psychologists were employed in job design and work study. The practices within the personnel function, though greatly influenced by psychology – for example through Institute of Personnel Management training courses – were not greatly favoured. Training was a preferred area. The area in which most occupational psychologists said that they would like to operate, and the direction in which they thought occupational psychology should be going, was overwhelmingly cited as organizational analysis and development, theory, research and intervention.

However, in the last four years the economic and ideological climate in most 'first-world' countries has changed rapidly. Organizational Development specialists have been some of the first white-collar personnel to be dispensed with. Freelance consultants are no longer deluged with social skills training work, these functions being relatively dispensable in recession when there is no money for development. Some of the same people are transferring their techniques to redundancy counselling.

Recession is probably not the only reason for recent changes, however. These methods have not worked in a reliable way. The effects on their interpersonal skills of a (very expensive) residential week away for middle managers tended to be very short lived when back in the organization. Similarly, training did not prove to be the panacea for organizational ills that many trainers, influenced by humanistic assumptions, believed.

The idealism of the 1960s was part and parcel of a time when affluence left room for more liberal methods of management. In sociology, the consensus model of society and organizations held sway: there was no conflict between the interests of individuals and employers (or at least not if managers' interpersonal skills could be improved). Now, with no money to foster individual development, and people unwilling to lose their jobs, organizational culture seems to be changing away from the democratic, egalitarian ideals of the 1960s and 1970s. Humanism is difficult to practice in the personnel function when the job has been transformed from hiring to firing, and from development to the evaluation of training effectiveness. A further example is the changed attitude to progressive legislation. Whereas occupational psychologists were encouraged to use the anti-discrimination legislation (1968 and 1975) as a weapon with which to influence their organizations to adopt fairer practices, now that organizations are struggling to survive there is decreasing commitment to progressive changes. Moreover, as trade unions turn their attention to fighting redundancies, their own support for minorities in the work force has diminished practically to vanishing point.

Regulating workers en masse

Whereas up to this point I have emphasized the effect of a capitalist logic – the extraction of maximum productivity from workers at all levels – a bureaucratic logic is also at work in forming the organizational issues to which psychology is applied. While the economic climate has a fairly dramatic and direct effect on such aspects of occupational psychology practice as OD and training, certain personnel functions remain essential to any organization. Indeed, with the trend towards larger organizations, they became increasingly important. While training is reduced, assessment of employees and decisions about their present and future performance remain priorities, at a time when relatively few appointments are being made.

Changes in work organization in the past few decades have been characterized by increases in the size of its units. With the diminution of face-to-face relations and the growth in the number of levels in the hierarchy, the problem of management of information has grown. Connected with this problem is the recognition of how crucial manpower planning is in organizations whose size makes them particularly susceptible to fluctuations in growth. The correct placement of personnel in the organization is considered to be critical. Information concerning the jobs to be done, the performance of employees and the manpower requirements of the company all has to be matched. Accurate and up-to-date information on people and jobs is therefore of major importance. Linked with this characteristic of large organizations, particularly those in the service sector, is the bureaucratic principle of systematicity and standardized application of rules. In addition to the requirements of a bureaucratic logic for successful information and employee management, such standardization of practices is also seen as a guarantee of fairness to employees. Psychological measurement has been a major contributor to bureaucratic forms of organization in its development of mass assessment methods which can be administered in ways which are economical of time.

The challenge of mass application of 'scientific' method came to psychology during the second world war. The War Office Selection Board was developed to 'cope with the massive problem of finding officer potential in the undifferentiated mass of humanity that passes through the recruiting offices' (Stewart and Stewart, 1979, p. 31). However, standardized testing was first applied very early in the century in France where Binet devised the first form of intelligence test in order to discriminate those children who were educationally backward from those who were 'normal'. His project was to administer the same test to all school-age children in Paris, such that the educational ability of each could be compared to the rest and an administrative decision made as a result. Newly developed statistical methods such as developing norms based on a normal distribution curve were crucial to these mass methods, as was the quantification of psychological attributes (see chapter 3, pp. 131–3, and Rose, 1979). The British Psychological Society's definition of a test reflects these administrative principles: 'a test is any standardised device from which an objective quantitative score is derived (British Psychological Society, 1966).

The 'fair' science of occupational assessment

The claim of objectivity made for psychological assessment is the basis on which its reputation in occupational psychology rests. That psychology is a science and that psychological assessment is therefore objective is a belief which continues to be fostered in organizations. The importance as far as organizational practices such as personnel selection is concerned is that the method is therefore 'fair'. Occupational psychologists have, for the most part, seen old-fashioned methods such as the interview as bastions of prejudice and the old-boy network. Moreover, as well as being inconsistent with progressive values, it seemed that such 'subjective' methods of assessment were unlikely to place people in the right jobs, particularly at a time when change was considered the passport to organizational success. That senior managers tended to appoint in their own image was therefore considered to be a danger. Testing has also been considered to be a much more reliable method for eliminating discrimination.

This in itself might not be enough to sell it to organizations though. Scientific psychological assessment is also cost effective:

> Proper validated, objective selection procedures make good business sense as well as helping to eliminate indirect sex discrimination; the costs of developing and using these procedures is offset by more effective use of personnel, both male and female, black and white. (Goodman and Novarra, 1977, p. 105)

I shall discuss below the question of the 'objectivity' of testing and its effects on occupational assessment. Here it is relevant to note that whereas testing has been associated more generally with unfairness, such as bias in intelligence tests, leading to minority group children being placed in special schools (Coard, 1971), and has been accused of treating people as objects by humanistic psychologists (O, Void, 1973), the advocacy of testing in occupational assessment – albeit based on dubious claims to scientificity – has been associated with improved assessment methods, in principle if not in practice.

Thus far, I have tried to place the practices of occupational assessment in the perspective of historical, economic and cultural changes which have affected the requirements of organizations. My brief review has aimed to show that psychology has not simply been imported wholesale to cater to these requirements. The history of the relation between psychology and organizations has been one of mutual effects as I shall demonstrate in detail (see pp. 38–42). Moreover psychology is not a unitary body of knowledge; there are differences between the values and emphases of psychometrics and humanistic psychology which themselves are expressions of changes in culture and applications to institutional requirements. The practical requirements of the personnel function, for example time economy, mean that some methods developed by psychology are more likely to be taken up than others. Frequently in the literature of occupational psychology assessment techniques are represented in terms of their cost benefits (Goodman and Novarra, 1977; Urwick Orr, undated). What is taken up is thus not necessarily related to its 'truth' value, nor even to its long-term efficacy. What is researched, reported, published and financed has a lot to do with applications rather than 'pure' research. Thus thousands of text books are produced whose market is practitioners, not psychologists. The psychology which is represented in these texts and in the work of consultants and in-house occupational psychologists has a common-sense, pragmatic and cost-conscious flavour to it and gets reproduced to a great extent independently of the pure discipline.

Tensions between the approaches of scientists and practitioners inevitably develop: whether psychology is working is being evaluated according to different criteria (see pp. 53–5). For example, in contrast to the technicalities bound up in the validity debate, Finkle, an employee of Standard Oil (Ohio), thinks that with regard to the Assessment Centres he runs, if his boss considers that he is doing a good job running the programmes, then they are valid (Stewart and Stewart, 1976). There are also consistencies between approaches. If there were not, the generic term 'psychology' would be untenable. I shall go on to look at two of these consistencies: the focus on the individual in organizational analysis and intervention, and psychology's claims to scientificity.

The individual and the job

So far I have focused on the production of psychological knowledges. Now I shall move inside the set of assumptions operating in occupational assessment in order to examine the theoretical and practical problems bound up with the concept of the individual as subject and object of occupational assessment. My overall object of analysis is the dualism between individual and job which reflects the wider individual–social dualism which we have discussed in the Introduction to section 1. A subtheme here will be to illustrate how recourse to 'science' and 'facts' has the effect of legitimizing the assessment methods (of both individual and job) which are crucial to organizational management.

This section of the chapter falls into two main parts, which reflect the dualism: the job and the individual. In the first part, the relation between job analysis, as an 'objective' technology for assessment, and job evaluation, which applies job analyses to questions of remuneration, exemplifies the murky area of application where particular knowledges are produced. In the second part, I discuss the problems for occupational assessment in assessing and predicting the attributes of the good worker (or manager). Again it can be seen how different knowledges are produced according to the problems addressed: assessing attributes of a VDU operator has little in common with the sophisticated and costly ways in which senior personnel in industry, the civil service and the armed forces are assessed. In the latter cases, where assessment is for a career rather than for a specific job, the prediction of potential becomes of vital interest. I look at two common methods for assessing potential: the use of personality tests, most commonly the 16PF, and the more recent idea of assessment centres which combine multiple methods of assessment.

Job analysis

> Job analysis enables the personnel psychologist to define the problem by specifying the critical worker requirements for success in a given job. (Anastasi, 1979, p. 27)

The meaning of the term 'job' has changed considerably over several centuries. The earliest definition given in the Oxford English Dictionary for a 'iobbe of worke' is 'a small definite piece of work especially in one's own calling'. It was only with the technology of the production line that 'job' could pick up the connotations of a fixed and routine set of activities to which a person was tied for a set amount of time in order to earn a livelihood. The rigidity of job definitions is expanding into an ever broadening sphere, partly through the requirements of large bureaucratic organizations. The social technology of job description and analysis is therefore a product of drastic changes in people's relation to work and its organization. Once the technology is in use, it produces its own effects on jobs and people's relation to work. Once a specification of a job is the standard according to which a worker is assessed, then it exerts constraints on that person's performance. The same job analysis is often used by an organization for selection, identification of training needs, appraisal of performance (for purposes of pay and promotion), comparison of jobs for the purpose of anti-discrimination legislation or preservation of the conditions of employment, and manpower planning. The job is not only prior to the job holder, but is defined according to the constraints, values, organizational hierarchy and budgeting of the organization. As the following example shows, the consequences are in the direction of increasing rigidity of work.

In my university department, three secretaries have been allocated. According to the financial resources of the college, these are specified as two grade-three posts and one grade two. (Grading is based on job descriptions, an equivalent way of accomplishing what job analysis does.) This means, however, that the responsibilities of the grade-two secretary must be circumscribed. The job could readily be developed in directions which would be more interesting for her and more appropriate to her previous experience and wishes, and the interests of the department. If she does these things, in principle we can make a claim that she is doing grade-three work (being careful not to imply that the other two are doing less – as if there was a fixed amount of work in a departmental office). However, in the present financial circumstances her chances of being regraded are minimal.[5] Does she therefore refuse to do more interesting (responsible) work on the grounds that she is not being paid for it? The logic of job descriptions and the way they are related to pay policies produces an increasingly rigid system where jobs are defined hierarchically in terms of increasing interest. For the majority who remain at the base of the pyramid, there is little room for development of any kind.

It is instructive to compare this with the virtual lack of job description characterizing the work of academic staff and to consider the absence of boundaries defining our activities and their unrelatedness to salary structures. It implies that administrative necessity is not the single reason for the technology of job evaluation.

The 'facts' about the job

In order for the job to produce what is required of it, it must be able to be specified in detail. Thus it must be independent of the individual who performs it, predetermined and static. For a job analysis to be seen as legitimate, it must appear objective. Here, notions of fact, objectivity and scientific measurement are put to work. Yet if the administration of jobs is to be relevant to organizational realities where job contents differ in status, the technology must also reflect values. It is around these requirements that the technologies of job analysis and job evaluation have been constructed. The demand for a non-individualized impersonal definition necessarily means that the job can only be specified in relation to the organization itself. Yet, paradoxically, the accurate specification of jobs can only be done through observing the job holder. Despite this, it is one of the most common claims of job analysts that the technique is 'completely independent of the person carrying out the job' (Urwick Orr, undated). In practice a 'benchmark' job is selected; that is a job which represents all jobs of a particular category. That this possibility exists at all demonstrates how jobs are fixed by technologies. Establishing benchmark jobs is extremely hazardous. It assumes, necessarily, that the job analysed is representative of the features of the job, rather than of the job holder. Job analysis has to assume that there is one best way to perform a job. Because job descriptions are very difficult to do (it is inevitable that workers will take for granted many features of their work), specialist job analysts are trained to help workers elicit 'the facts' about the job. These are ratified by the person's boss.

How does a job analyst collect job facts? It is impossible to elicit descriptions except in terms of some categories. This in itself is an indication of what psychology consistently fails to recognize: that facts about the job are a product of being organized into categories which themselves imply certain values. For example when features of a job are grouped under the heading 'responsibility' a whole set of social assumptions about what kinds of work are responsible (and to whom) are immediately brought into effect. Is it always desirable to take responsibility? Pym (1966), for example, found that managers assessed as below average in competence by their own bosses were the most favourably assessed by subordinates as 'giving responsibility'. The presentation of what are called 'facts' is always in terms of some specific practice and a set of power relations. Along with wider social meanings, these confer value on categories which are supposedly neutral. The job analysis exists in order to be used by bosses in the context of other functions such as appraisal and promotion. Thus value of responsibility is inseparable from its use as a category. By virtue of an outmoded (in the philosophy of science) concept of fact, psychologists none the less can claim that job analysis is objective and that values only enter the question when it is applied to job evaluation.

The Hay-MSL firm of consultants produced a highly popular job analysis system based on three factors (and no subfactors): problem-solving, know-how and accountability, which are claimed to be components of all jobs. The factors have been criticized on the grounds that they have a distinctly managerialist bias such that the features of typical blue-collar jobs are not elicited by them, thus rendering these largely invisible. This demonstrates that 'factors' are not value-neutral tools for organizing information.

The Profile method, constructed by Urwick Orr and Partners, a British team of job evaluation consultants, is part of a job evaluation system which was used, for example, in the British Steel Corporation to rationalize the pay systems in what had been many different companies. It has six major factors (each of which has subfactors, which are changed depending on the relevance to the kinds of jobs in the particular company). These are responsibility, knowledge, mental skills, social skills, physical skills and environmental conditions. Under the first might be: responsibility for company assets and physical resources; for generating profit; for supervising and controlling staff. It can be seen that to interpret job facts according to these categories is a matter of complex judgement. But more important, perhaps, is the prior question; where do these job factors come from? Urwick Orr (undated) represent their procedure as follows:

> Briefly we asked the question – how is work performed and what, therefore, is the range of possible job characteristics which can be demanded in a job?
> (1) The job holder brings to the work situation knowledge, physical and mental aptitudes.
> (2) The level at which the individual is asked to use his knowledge, aptitude and skills is structurally determined by:
> (a) the nature of the work
> (b) the way in which the organisation structures the job
> (c) the degree of responsibility which is assigned the job holder by the organisation
> (d) the environment in which the work is being carried out.

In a simple additive fashion which conceals the problem of the relationship, the six factors combine features which the worker must manifest, and also features which are given by the organization. If the worker takes more responsibility than that which 'is assigned by the organisation', how will that be described? If the worker is capable of doing so, but the job does not allow it, should this be counted in the same way as what she or he cannot do? The amount any of these factors enters into the job – what is called job size – is not taken into consideration in most job analyses. So, even within its own terms, it falls short. Ignoring the dimension of job size has the effect of giving more recognition to varied jobs than to repetitive ones, because in the former case some aspect of the job is more likely to appear under every category.

Jobs cannot be separated from the job holder. Neither can they be separated from each other. How is it possible to describe collective work? Do not boundaries between jobs, both vertically and horizontally in the hierarchy, remain fluid, depending on a multitude of changing circumstances? The job description must none the less assume a bounded and fixed character, although gross changes over time, for example with introduction of new technology, are catered for by a monitoring system.

Job evaluation

Both Hay-MSL and Urwick Orr have developed their job analysis systems as part of a job evaluation method. Job evaluation is 'a systematic process of establishing, for payment purposes, the relative importance of jobs within a specified group, based on a study of relative job content' (Urwick Orr, undated). Urwick Orr are careful not to claim that job evaluation is a science, though they do stress that it is based on 'job facts', and that it is often claimed to be an objective method. However, 'Consultants' claims of objectivity are usually exaggerated as all job evaluation is ultimately based on human judgements and assessments' (Incomes Data Services, 1979).

The non-analytical method of job evaluation simply consists of asking members of an assessment team (and that might range from a group of a few managers to a team representing trade unions as well as management) to compare one job against another until all comparisons have been made. In the Profile method, this produces what is called a 'felt-fair' ranking of jobs. The analytical method makes use of the subfactors given in job analysis. Quantitative ratings (on a 3- or 4-point scale) are made by judges of each factor with regard to each job. For example, they might be asked the following question (Urwick Orr, undated): 'How do you rate the importance of the job of a Grade 1 secretary with regard to responsibility for supervising and controlling staff?'

The Profile method uses both analytical and non-analytical techniques. Analytical methods, based as they are on detailed comparisons, render judgements which are more removed from taken-for-granted assumptions about the importance of whole jobs. However, this is precisely the weakness of the analytical method because when the points are added up, they are unlikely to match the non-analytical 'felt-fair' method in the relative importance attributed to each job. Moreover, they are much less likely than the non-analytical method to produce rankings which correspond to existing pay differentials. One could say that the analytical method is sufficiently objective (that is further removed from broad ideological judgements concerning the difference in importance between blue- and white-collar work for example) not to reflect so faithfully the *status quo* concerning the value of jobs (which has very little to do with fair evaluation but a lot to do with the values represented in the Hay-MSL three-factor system with its managerialist bias). In order to correct this discrepancy from organizational reality, the Profile method is obliged to weight the six factors differently so that they correspond to the present *status quo*. Urwick Orr (undated) describe the problem in the following terms:

> Some people have questioned whether it is necessary to weight any of the characteristics, ie, whether any characteristic should be given extra value in the total system. Applications show, however, that where no weightings are used, the results are often unacceptable in terms of the general value of jobs felt *by people within the organisation*.

This is achieved in the following way: 'Calculations (are) made to find weightings which give a *best* fit between the ''profiles'' and the ''felt fair'' rank order. These calculations, being long and tedious, are carried out by computer.'[6] The numerical value of the weightings indicates the importance of this step in the job evaluation procedure. One set derived (in an unknown company where the method was used) were as follows:

Responsibility	3
Knowledge	1
Mental skills	2
Physical skills	⅔
Social skills	½
Environmental conditions	⅓

With the part exception of social skills, the weightings result in higher value being given to the factors characteristic of middle-class jobs and reduced value to those factors characteristic of working-class jobs.

It is illuminating that the more thorough analytic methods elicit results which are so discrepant from what is 'felt fair' that they have to be transformed in such a way in order to be applied in practice in organizations (see chapter 4, p. 107, for a similar example in eleven-plus assessment). Clearly where the results of 'objective' methods do not fit the reality of organizations, it is not the status quo which is transformed as a result: 'Job Evaluation respects in practice the boundaries set by convention to which in theory it might offer serious challenge' (Baroness Wootton, quoted in Livy, 1975, p. 129). Job evaluation is an example of how the practical requirements of organizations, rather than psychological science, ultimately determine outcomes. This is not to say that technologies of measurement have no effects: psychometrics remains a useful tool for organizations. The method appears fair to employees because it appears to be based on fact and objectivity: 'No approach is scientific and allocation of scores, points or levels may be misleading. Employees may believe that the result has been mathematically proven and is therefore "right"' (Incomes Data Services, 1979). The Profile method is indeed successful in this regard, hence its popularity. For example, Urwick Orr (undated) claim that it has 'good acceptability' and that it is 'often accompanied by improvement in employee relations'. It is as if what people know about their jobs (and those of many others) is taken away from them in the form of a job analysis. It is compared, scored, weighted, computerized and given back as objective and factual. Moreover the processes whereby this is accomplished are ill understood and are credited with the authority of science. The effect of psychology is to furnish this legitimacy. It is a good example of knowledge producing power and that power, knowledge.

Attributes of the productive worker

> There are two very difficult technical questions . . . which selectors must be able to answer. First, has the selection requirement been

> set because of some demonstrably necessary feature of job performance? This is a matter of job analysis. . . . Second, does the selection instrument itself . . . have a demonstrably relevant and predictive relationship with the necessary elements of job performance? This is the time-honoured and perennial matter of validation.
>
> (Wallis, 1980)

I have shown how occupational assessment is dependent on the 'objective' description of job content in order to provide the criteria against which people can be assessed (the so-called 'criterion question'). I have argued that measurement practices in the sphere of jobs are subject to the same kinds of objections as in the sphere of individuals; that the job, like the individual, is not a given independent entity which can be measured in isolation. In the attempt to do so, job analysts have, paradoxically, had to measure the person as representative job holder. This unclarity as to the relation between individual and job indicates the second problem in this area: once the characteristics of the job have been specified (whether correctly or incorrectly, according to different perspectives), how does psychological measurement proceed to the specification of the required person? The answer is by no means self-evident. It would require an analysis of the relation of a worker to her/his work; precisely what psychology is incapable of doing by virtue of posing the two categories as fixed entities. Psychology presumes that its own task, then, is to describe these entities, which it does in terms of 'facts' which are pregiven and only require eliciting.

It is through the concept of validity that psychological assessment confronts the problem of how to assess the individual strictly according to stipulated criteria by which the measures are derived. According to the principles of psychological measurement, in order for a test to be valid, it must measure what it purports to measure.[7] In the context of occupational assessment, therefore: 'all legal and professional standards require the specification of the job content domain as a prerequisite to the development of a content valid test' (Kleiman and Faley, 1978).

When equal-opportunities legislation in employment was first introduced in the United States, the American Psychological Association (APA) was confident that psychological science could ensure the validity of occupational assessment and thus provide absolutely certain and objective standards against which selection decisions could be made and therefore against which discriminatory practices could be judged. In Britain, the Sex Discrimination Act 1975 and the Race Relations Act 1976 were seen as a new force which would provide an opportunity for psychologists to help develop fairer assessment practices (Pearn, 1976; Goodman and Novarra, 1977). Confidence in psychometrics was running high. In fact, legal cases in American courts have required standards of validity that even the most meticulous and objective of tests have not been able to demonstrate (Goodman and Novarra, 1977). The APA has had to reconsider its claims for psychological science and psychometricians in Britain have heeded the United States experience: 'for the first time, we must be prepared to defend our discriminatory procedures, not only on technical and pragmatic grounds, but on social and legal grounds too' (Wallis, 1980).

Problems of validity present themselves differently depending on the job criteria to which measures are trying to match the individual. For the same reason that behaviourism tried to avoid any notions concerning the individual which were not referring to behaviour and therefore not directly observable, psychometric theory – doubly bound by the requirements of the criterion and validity – attempted to remain in the limited and definable realm of job-specific behaviours. However, the problem of the relationship between job and individual is not solved by the dualism of the two concepts. Rather it is created by it.

The question of how to infer the desirable worker attributes from a job description or job analysis has been approached by McCormick in order to build 'a statistical bridge between job-related data and aptitude requirements' (McCormick, Jeanneret and Mecham, 1972). His 'worker-oriented' as opposed to 'job-oriented' approach attempts to describe jobs 'in terms of human qualities or attributes required' (ibid., p. 348). What is produced is not very different from a job specification (traditionally devised in terms of the kind of person required). Thus for example the job of a dough-mixer in the bakery-products industry 'demands finger dexterity, perceptual speed, computational accuracy and the ability to work effectively under confusing and distracting conditions' (Anastasi, 1979, p. 27).

Such specifications, for a manual worker, already show signs of getting into the murky area of general personality characteristics (rather than skills). This difficulty is much more pronounced when the assessment is for a professional or managerial job. Here personality measures are deemed to be necessary:

> There is no denying that when it comes to predicting potential most people are interested in personality tests. 'Let's have a test of motivation, drive and chief executive ability' they say, and their faces fall when they're told that it's not that simple.
>
> (Stewart and Stewart, 1979, p. 30)

A major reason why it is not that simple is that there is a contradiction between recognizing that 'personality' characteristics appear to affect job performance and the requirement that only job-related criteria be measured: 'They test only those personality dimensions that could be relevant to success at work. They don't probe too deeply into issues that shouldn't concern the employer' (ibid., p. 30). How could such limits be established? Is it not the person in entirety whose relation to the job (which includes a relation to the organization and the social relations in and outside work) determines performance?

Despite such intentions, I have never seen an exposition of how what is relevant to work performance can be isolated from what 'shouldn't concern the employer'. How, for example, do you establish whether someone is likely to be motivated to work in the particular circumstances of a new job? It would require a much more sophisticated (and social) theory of motivation than the one available to psychology to demonstrate the construct (or theoretical) validity of such a measure.

According to Cronbach and Meehl (1955), construct validity is necessary whenever a test is to be interpreted as a measure of some attribute or quality which is not 'operationally defined' (for example when intelligence is defined as what intelligence tests measure). 'Since predictive, concurrent and content validity are all essentially ad hoc, construct validity is the only validity from a scientific point of view' (Loevinger, 1957). Psychology's lack of theoretical sophistication has meant that almost no test where inferences need to be made about the relationship between job content and worker attributes would fulfil these criteria. However, it was not until the claims of science were challenged in the American courts that they were found to be wanting.

The different problem that manual and professional/managerial jobs pose for assessment is heightened by the fact that the latter are jobs which are seen as part of a career, often within a single organization. For example, the mandarin stream in the British civil service is specifically for people who are destined for top administrative posts in twenty years time. Such employees will not stay in any single job for more than a few years, thus job specification is an irrelevance. The problem is all the keener because of the cost of making a bad decision; in terms of salary, training and the difficulty of dismissal (a point which is raised by most literature on the subject of assessing potential). What can an employer afford not to know about a candidate in order to best predict potential for a career?

It is by measuring the individual 'as a whole' that psychology attempts to reconcile the pragmatic needs of employers with the 'criterion question' which represents psychology's obligation to the employee. In practice, there have been two rather different solutions to this problem. In private industry, measures of general personality such as the 16PF (16 Personality Factor) and the EPI (Eysenck Personality Inventory) have been popular. In large bureaucracies such as the armed forces, assessment centres are used. Basically these apply as many different methods as seem to have face validity (including methods as un(?)related to job performance as inviting wives (sic) to drinks and dinner).

I shall briefly describe the 16PF and a typical assessment centre in order to illustrate, through concrete detail, some of the problems of validity of these measures and to juxtapose how they work theoretically with how they work pragmatically.

The 16PF

This inventory claims to measure 'general personality' and is still much used for managerial selection because 'it works'. What is meant is that it succeeds in practice in selecting candidates who turn out to be successful managers. For my purposes here I have no interest in either supporting or refuting this claim; it is sufficient that the inventory has a long history of use. What I want to do is to cast some light on the assumptions about personality which underlie it and to indicate their history. Particularly, it is interesting to get down to the level of the test items themselves and ask what they may mean to the respondent and what relation this bears to a theory of personality (and hence to consider the construct validity of the test).

Cattell, the author of the 16PF, claims (and it remains no more than a claim) that 'the personality factors measured by the 16PF are not just unique to the test but instead rest within the context of a general theory of personality' (Cattell, Eber and Matsuoka, 1970, p. 1), the scales being 'directed to previously located natural personality structures related to the way personality actually develops' (ibid., p. 5). It is clear from these statements that Cattell is working with a personality theory based on an essentialist assumption about the individual. It also assumes that personality does not change either over time or according to situation. For example, Cattell asserts: 'the same client enters with the same personality into the clinic, job or school' (ibid., p. 10). These assumptions are built into the test through the way the items are posed and the instructions about answering.

I shall exemplify this by analysing what was in my mind as I tried to respond to the items on the 16PF (introspection is a rich source of information which, because of its claims to be a science, contemporary psychology rarely taps). Out of 105 items (on form C, which is described as being appropriate for people of average intelligence) I found that in 42 cases, I could not give an unambivalent response. By this I mean that I would have been distorting my understanding of my responses if I had forced an answer to comply with the instructions. These ambiguities fell into several categories. One problem of answering I can categorize as 'contradiction'. For example, in response to 'I could live happily alone far from anyone, like a hermit' (q. 2), I wanted to say 'yes' and 'no', both strongly. This is not at all inconsistent with my theoretical framework which recognizes contradictory constructions of subjectivities (see chapter 5). There were many questions where my answer would be 'it depends', and these were for several reasons. For example, 'if a good remark of mine is passed by I (a) let it go, (b) give people a chance to hear it again' (q. 12). My response depends on how confident I am in that group, whether I am with people who know me or who are in a position of authority and also what reading I have of why the remark was passed by (disagreement, avoidance, interest in something else, etc.). Another condition is when it depends on the social relation. For example, 'I get impatient and begin to fume and fret when people delay me unnecessarily' (q. 89). My response is a function of my relationship to a specific person and the purpose of the meeting which determines how I understand the lateness in terms of what they normally do, how it might be motivated, or if for that person time-keeping signifies differently (for example in a different culture). Finally, there are those questions where I disagree with the set of assumptions through which I reckon the question will be read. For example, 'I would rather be: (a) a bishop, (b) a colonel' (q. 26). First I cannot answer the question as a simple reality choice – women bishops are not allowed and women colonels number two or three. Most respondents read such an item through a value about pacificism and militarism and place themselves accordingly. However, it would be possible to reason that because the army/church is more oppressive than the church/army one could be a more effective change agent as a colonel/bishop than vice versa. Because the social differences in meanings people make of questions are left out of the account, the scores in either case would count the same way, but not mean the same thing in terms of personality.

Because of the statistical requirements that all items be filled in, and a satisfactory range of scores be derived, the respondent is strongly encouraged not to use the middle response and must answer all questions. Going over the test a second time, I did answer all the questions – with suitable distortions, overgeneralizations and simplifications. But in doing so I was representing myself within assumptions about personality which are inconsistent with my experience of myself. Cattell's 'natural' personality structures are not theorized. Rather, they are taken for granted in a way which reflects the period of the test's production in the 1930s. For example, the similarity between Cattell's premises and Burt's 'iron laws' of IQ are striking:

> By intelligence, the psychologist understands inborn, all-round intellectual ability. It is inherited or at least innate, not due to teaching or training . . . it is general, not specific, that is not limited to any particular kind of work, but enters into all one may do or say or think . . . fortunately it can be measured with accuracy and ease.
>
> (Burt, 1940)

Despite Burt having been discredited, such assumptions about both intelligence and personality are part and parcel of what is now taken-for-granted common sense. Without any construct validity, the claims of such a test to be measuring 'general personality' and the relation of that claim to occupational assessment make its use highly dubious. The fact that many practitioners go on using it because 'it works' does not alter these criticisms.

If the 16PF does not work in the way that personality theory claims, how then does it work? Although the test environment is in principle controlled, so that all variations in performance can be attributed to the specific variable which the test is supposedly measuring, no measure can control for the variability in meaning through which candidates will construe test items. It is only in the last few years, through attribution theory, that (social) psychologists have recognized that meaning is a major issue in understanding both action and identity. It is a theory now being applied to occupational assessment (Herriot and Rothwell, 1981). However, psychometrics was based on the belief that words were transparent, only designating the 'things' or 'facts' to which they referred. The 16PF even goes so far as to label some of its factors with neologisms in order to avoid the value implications of lay language (for example 'threctia', 'affectothymia', 'desurgency'). Even were there not also factors with value-loaded labels ('intelligence', 'submissiveness') this strategy cannot guarantee objectivity. Developments in the theory of signification (see section 3) have wholly undermined this view, insisting on the inextricability of value and language.

As I exemplified with my own responses, candidates can read test items according to their understanding of what is required for the job. The absence of face-to-face assessment (as in the selection interview) does not alter the fact that candidates will present themselves in a light which makes them acceptable to the organization (Silverman and Jones, 1976, ch. 2). Rather than theorizing this as a feature of social relations (that people spontaneously take up numerous positions depending on the values and practices within which they are inserted), personality inventories – set on measuring the 'essential' personality – consider such a factor as 'faking'.

Elliot (1976a) has shown experimentally that this is indeed the case with selectee managers' scores on the 16PF. He found that the scores of selectees (that is those who were seeking a job) differed from managers on training courses (those that already had one). He concluded that 'there was strong evidence of a response set in the selection situation which could justify the description of faking'. A follow-up study (Elliot, 1976b) found that psychologists' and personnel managers' ratings of individuals' profiles based on a 'faked' set of 16PF responses were more favourable than on an unfaked set. In fact, the 16PF avoids calling this 'faking'. In an attempt to recognize the complexity of people's relations to the test situation, Cattell calls the same phenomenon 'motivational distortion' (MD).

The term itself demonstrates the assumption of a true self which is distorted through 'artefacts' of context. The 16PF thus carries eight items which make up an MD scale (parallel to 'lie detector' items on other personality inventories). If the testee scores highly on MD, other scores are modified according to amounts specified in the user's manual. In principle, this corrects the score to an undistorted representation of the person. It must be assumed, for this correction to be applied, that MD always works in the same direction, an assumption which does not hold as soon as the social is not theorized as a unitary phenomenon where values are shared and homogeneous, but rather as a site of contradictory discourses within which members of social groups are positioned differently.

One high scorer on MD amongst my students went off the scale when the factor 'emotionally stable/affected by feelings' was corrected under the assumption that MD would be in the direction of emotionally stable ('higher ego strength' – the term itself suggests positive evaluation). In order to understand this phenomenon, we had to talk about how cultural values changed, both between social groups and over time. The revision of the 16PF so that it does not refer to obsolete social meanings tends to lag behind social change. And anyway, it can never be correct for all social groups. Its assumptions and standardization procedures tend to have reference to white, male, middle-class values (the reference for psychology's subject, see chapter 3, p. 130).

From this perspective, it can be seen that the kinds of applicants referred to in Elliot's experiment (he does not specify but it is likely that they were mostly white, middle-class, young men) were educated to be successful at putting themselves in the position of what the organization would require, and to have values consonant with the ones which resembled those of the sample on whom the norms of the 16PF were developed. It appears from his follow-up study that it is just such an approach which is a good predictor of managerial performance.

The experience which enables assessees to present themselves correctly (through a test as much as an interview) depends on familiarity with that culture. The child of an academic, unlike that of a factory worker, will have a taken-for-granted knowledge of the assumptions on which the undergraduate selection interview is based. Silverman and Jones (1976) demonstrate how these complex calculations work with regard to assessees' class background in selection interviews for posts in a large British bureaucracy.

Assessment centres

I have indicated that psychometric methods may end up tapping social factors without knowing it and that this probably explains the extent to which they work. If this is so it is likely that if the methods work in some situations, they will fail to work in others. For example, the assumption of stasis in personality theory may produce measures which work only in times and in organizations which are relatively stable. In 'times of change on all fronts' (Urwick Orr, undated), measurement of potential did not work sufficiently well when it resulted from methods which used such theories. In the Stewarts' introduction to the identification of potential, they exemplify the problem with a comment from a company: 'We're fed up with having mediocre people leave us, join the competition, and go streaking off making great successes of themselves when all we had predicted for them was middle management by the time they were forty' (1979, p. 28). The change they refer to, because it is a social change, could hardly have been predicted from the 16PF. It is during times of rapid change such as the 1960s and 1970s that the conditions of possibility existed for the development of new knowledges which produce a better fit with new exigencies.

In the expansion of this same period, assessment became a tool for generating information useful also to development: there was a shortage of experienced people to fill vacancies in the hierarchy. Although a method closely resembling assessment centres has been in use in Britain since the second world war, in American companies during this period they shifted their emphasis and were heralded as 'the first phase in an integrated programme of assessment and development' (McKinnon, 1975). In order to understand assessment centres and the contrast between them and psychometric tests, it is worth pointing out that the 'scientific' requirements of psychometrics did not penetrate personnel practices as thoroughly as this discussion might suggest. Irrespective of psychometricians' talk about the 'criterion question', common sense told personnel people that they and the managing director wanted to know as much as possible about the person they selected. This has always been the case when numbers and budgets do not forbid it. Assessment centres thus used a battery of eclectic methods which were more likely to have face validity than construct validity. Simulations of management or other job-relevant tasks, group discussions, cocktail parties, personality and intelligence tests, and track record are some of the methods from which data are derived. '*The* single criterion had certainly been junked' (Dunnette, 1976) in favour of multi, person-oriented methods.

The claim that all methods are strictly criterion-related is difficult to maintain unless it is recognized that there is no way of specifying what, concerning a candidate's 'attributes', is job-related and what is irrelevant. 'Attributes' are not distinguishable and isolable in this way. Any personality theory which deals in 'traits', 'attributes' or 'factors' as if they were isolable and directly relatable to job factors is not only misleading but finds itself in the kind of theoretical quick-step (the 'job' leads, then the 'individual') from which it impossible to escape.

Yet pragmatism has not cast aside scientificity completely. When the problem arises as to how to make a yes/no judgement based on the plethora of information garnered in an assessment centre, quantification has been the result and complex impressions have been calibrated by the use of five-point scales on job-relevant dimensions. For example, the American Telephone and Telegraph Company (AT & T) use twenty-five factors summing up their five-day assessment centre for senior managers.[8] As well as these scores, the final information typically would consist of a photograph and biographical details. Common sense tells us that these are highly important. Presumably the photograph serves to remind the assessor of the person whom they have observed for five days. With this reminder is called up all the non-quantifiable, non-scientific impressions about the 'whole' person-in-relations without which the assessor would be handicapped in making a decision. People who have experience on assessment centre panels say that it is at this point that assessors' 'subjective' preferences (and thus politics and values) become salient, however scrupulous they have been earlier in using psychometric techniques.

Psychology has been incoherent in the ways that it has approached relations between people in assessment situations. Psychometrics and social psychology have provided rather different ways of understanding the relations of assessment, but both are hidebound by the concept of individual. In addition, because of its adherence to positivist science, psychometrics has taken the assessee as its object. In this model, the assessor behaves like the scientist; that is s/he is a neutral instrument for gathering 'facts'. The scientist is positioned outside the phenomenon to be studied. In the highly political arena of occupational assessment, the inadequacies of such a model are glaringly obvious when even in laboratory experiments the 'experimenter effect' (Rosenthal, 1966) has produced problems for this view.

The relations of assessment

It is in the selection or appraisal interview that the relations of assessment are most difficult to ignore, and it is for this reason that social psychologists have been more visible in this area. However, because of the influence of the notion of objectivity and the belief in the possibility of gathering neutral facts, aspects of face-to-face assessments have been treated as contaminating variables which the assessor should be trained to wipe out. Thus, for example, the effects of liking in an interview have received much attention, but prove difficult to stamp out (Keenan, 1977). For similar reasons, interviews have been subjected to the standardization of protocols, context and interviewer style in an attempt to mirror as far as possible the scientific conditions of testing. At the same time it is recognized that the social skills of the interviewer are important if good information is to be elicited and therefore reliable judgements made. The interview must therefore not be depersonalized altogether. Thus for example interviewers are trained to emit a certain number of positive reinforcements and to balance negative with positive statements (Fletcher and Williams, 1976).

Similarly, work on performance appraisal has concentrated on training appraisers in the use of interpersonal skill techniques such as good interpersonal rapport, empathy and listening skills, in order to elicit information effectively.[9] Ann Oakley (1981) points out how the requirements of standardization and technique militate against the development of real rapport with interviewees. In discussing her relation to women she interviewed for research purposes, she exemplifies how this contradiction results from psychology's theorizing of face-to-face assessment relations.

Variations in rapport are seen as cognitive in origin and are supposed to be cancelled out by standardizing and formalizing methods. The effects of social differences (race, gender, class and age) are not perceived as integral to a theory of assessment according to the psychological knowledges used. Rather they are seen as confounding external variables which can be controlled out. Since it is through a commitment to making the interview fairer that much of this work has been done, it is particularly ironic that the differences which make the difference (social differences) cannot be catered for.

While psychologists' attempts to make interviewing fairer may not work in some respects, their theory of individuals, assessable independently of relations of assessment, works in the sense that it camouflages the power relations which are an integral part of information-getting in organizations. This contradication is particularly evident in the area of performance appraisal.

Power and performance appraisal

> Appraisal schemes are difficult to operate and fail to achieve their manifest purposes because of an inherent political naivety.
>
> (Pym, 1973, p. 231)

The assessor in performance appraisal is not the neutral information-gathering scientist. Rather s/he is the appraisee's boss, who has considerable power to affect things like promotion. Granted this state of affairs, the appraisee would be ill advised to give certain things away.

The technique of expressing feelings and listening is meant to convince the assessee that it is an honest, equal relationship. For example: 'Managers must gain insight both into themselves and into their subordinates and learn to express themselves both honestly and unambiguously' (Rowe, 1964, p. 21). However, as Pym, who quotes Rowe, remarks, 'it is precisely because they possess political insight that managers prefer to be vague and devious in their assessments' (ibid.). I concur with Pym's conclusions that honest, equal relations of assessment are not possible because of the bosses' responsibility and other effects of hierarchy. However, I see power as more intrinsic to social relations than Pym's use of the term 'political insight' implies. For theoretical purposes, the distinction is significant because I am arguing that the relations of assessment can never be understood in isolation from power relations which are specified by the social domain. (I do not just mean by position in the hierarchy, but by pervasive social differences as I have already mentioned.)

These points demonstrate what may be fairly obvious, that 'appraisal schemes legitimise the unequal distribution of power in organisations' (Pym, 1973, p. 231). Humanistic psychology has replied by advocating peer- and self-assessments but in doing so has fallen into the psychologistic trap of denying that hierarchical organizations produce a logic where decisions have to be made by bosses, who will not trust an employee's self-appraisal – quite rightly, under most circumstances. Self-appraisals are most accurate where the power relations which exist in real work settings are minimized (for example if an employee has another job and does not require references).

Making appraisals 'work': pragmatics versus theory

There is a contradiction, then, between psychology's model of the assessor as a neutral information-gatherer and bosses' and subordinates' experience of the politics of information. As a result there has been an 'almost universal failure of managements to maintain and use such schemes in accordance with the claims made for them' (Pym, 1973, p. 231). Pym recognizes that it is psychologists' adherence to an experimental model in training methods which is the cause of the mismatch between theory and practice:

> Psychologists still give too much weight to the more artificial situation of experimentation in which, for example, the effects of training may be examined. During experiments it is possible to contain those political elements which prove lethal to appraisals in practice.
> (ibid., p. 232)

However, Randell (1973), addressing the same problem, proposed a device for making performance appraisals work better, which is quite consistent with psychology's principle of neutrality and with managements' needs for information. Making performance appraisals work means eliciting maximum information from the appraisee despite the adverse consequences which can result from giving information which may be against her/his interests.

Randell distinguished four functions of appraisal: reward, potential, organization and performance. By suggesting that at least some of these should be conducted separately, he attempted to provide a solution to the earlier recognition that the 'functions of judge and counsellor . . . could not be combined in the average manager' (McGregor, 1960). It was hoped that, as a result, the performance review could work more successfully, based as it is on the principle that 'by encouraging an individual to decide for himself ways in which he could do his job better, the results of his self-analysis can be discussed and a course of action mutually agreed, then an improvement in work performance should occur' (Randell, 1973, p. 222).

This new knowledge produced by occupational psychology (the separation of the functions of performance appraisal into performance, reward, potential and organization reviews) is a direct result of the pragmatics of hierarchical organizations. Appraisees are meant to be convinced that what they say in a performance review will not count against them; for example when the organization is considering promotions.

The suppression of these power relations, which as Pym points out are obvious to everyone in practice, is produced in two ways through the belief in scientific psychology. First, by defining its object as the 'individual' and not the 'relation', psychological assessment cannot recognize power (which it would see in any case as a feature of the social and therefore as just a contaminating variable). Second, when relations of assessment cannot be ignored they are seen through the model of scientist/object, or assessor/assessee. The role of the assessor is seen, therefore, as neutral and external, and as one of fact-gathering. In regard to appraisal Randell (1973) echoes this belief when he says of information gathered – contrary to most of the evidence – 'data are neutral. How they are used is important, and their possible misuse is a source of anxiety'. By recourse to 'neutrality' he dismisses at a stroke the question of unequal power and management's need of information. He transforms the issue into use/abuse of what is in itself safe, and implies that most people can be trusted and that there's no real problem. Through such an argument people are encouraged to dismiss what used to be common sense; that by definition (because of their structural position), bosses could not be trusted with certain information. Now psychology produces an alternative view which has effects in practice through training in social skills: employees are confronted with positively reinforcing, caring, listening bosses who present themselves as trustworthy. The technique is explicitly one of eliciting information and no doubt it occasionally works. If it does not work often enough to make performance appraisals more effective, it is because the everyday relations of subordinates to their bosses (and vice versa) contradict what is being said and done in the name of scientific psychology.

Conclusions

The reason for going into detail about the claims and realities of job and individual assessment is not to demand that psychology should be more 'objective'. There are two points. First, I want to show how, despite its best efforts (and, it is worth pointing out, the honest intentions of many practitioners, operating within the belief in psychology's scientificity), occupational assessment cannot do what it sets out to do; that is to provide a method of assessment which is reliable and valid and which successfully predicts characteristics of the individual (or job) as if they were entities approachable in isolation from the social world. Second, I want to show that, nevertheless, it does work in the sense which I have discussed above; that is, it functions to represent to organizational practice an 'objective' description of that practice which provides it with a technical rationality and objectivity. It is able to do so because of the fundamental individualism which both share. The legacy of psychology as science is the belief that the individual can be understood through measurement:

> Psychology cannot attain the certainty and exactness of the physical sciences unless it rests on a foundation of experiment and measurement. A step in this direction could be made by applying a series of mental tests and measurements to a large number of individuals.
> (Cattell, 1980, p. 373, quoted in Rose, 1979, p. 49)

On this point, however, rests a more important one. While psychologists continue to convince themselves – and more particularly others – that their claims are plausible and their knowledges true, the way that psychological assessment works is not addressed. The differences that psychology finds are believed to be attributable to the essential individual, separate from the social domain. Issues of fairness which would be posed if psychology worked with a theory of social differences and how they construct subjectivity cannot even be thought in this framework. With such a theory, psychological knowledges would work to other ends.

In the meantime, it is worth emphasizing that there is not a psychometrics which continues to approach 'truth', uncontaminated by the pragmatics of the real world. It is true that academic psychometricians are usually the ones who are more concerned with 'fairness', in the sense of the validity of the measures used. But the methods and knowledges with and against which they are working at any historical period are a product of practices. Agreed, these practices are more diverse than just those of the organization or the laboratory. The power integral to organizational practices is productive of knowledges of a certain kind because these are needed to evaluate, predict and regulate employees.

One effect of that power of psychology is to privilege the individual as the focus of activities which are in fact specific characteristics of corporate organization. Thus the individual of psychology and the individualization in industry establish a system of mutual support. Existing social and power relations are left out in this approach. They remain as the already-given unchanging feature of reality. As I have already argued, it is precisely to the extent that occupational psychology does not challenge this assumption (indeed it reinforces it) that it 'works'.

The example of performance appraisal is a striking one to illustrate the way in which practitioners, through the discourse of scientific psychology, impose on the hierarchical relations in organizations a reading which sees people as involved in egalitarian and caring interpersonal relations where, in the service of 'neutral' data-gathering, the appraiser requires information which will not be abused. Even if in this case the knowledge produced is not powerful enough to have the desired effects, it illustrates how different this version is from the common-sense knowledge which is produced as a result of the power relations in organizations. The knowledge centred on testing, because it is closer to the practices of measurement, has been even more successful in modifying and legitimizing management practices: one need only consider the way in which the belief that an IQ score is a 'fact' about a person has entered into common sense. While the role of the psychologist may not be ultimately very powerful when faced with established organizational structures, none the less I hope I have shown that it is crucial in protecting profitability through helping to ensure what is euphemistically termed 'effective' work performance. When it is in the interests of the organization that the employee is happy, the practitioner can also pursue humanistic goals and even begin to influence unfair practices.

Those with humanistic sympathies have criticized the positivism of psychometrics, and have developed an account based on the importance of development, individual self-actualization, counselling and egalitarianism. However, while being sceptical of the claims of objectivity, this account has done nothing to remedy the effects of taking the individual as its object. It has tended to see undesirable practices in organizations as abuse, which can be remedied by good interpersonal relations and a new ethic.

To see power in this light, however, is to deny realities of organizational life which are produced by factors not within the immediate power of the individual to change. If power is seen simply as individual abuse of authority, it can be changed. Those who emphasize interpersonal relations tend to see any deeper conception of power as part of a determinist account emanating from Marxism or sociology which robs the individual agent of the possibility of changing things. From such a perspective, my emphasis on power in the relations of assessment (and indeed in all social relations) would be dismissed as pessimistic. I do not believe that this is the outcome of such an analysis. Foucault argues that the most pernicious and effective strategy of power is to camouflage its own workings. To deny the power of hierarchy, or of the technologies of assessment, is not to make them go away. The power relations in appraisal are all the more effective if the subordinate does not identify them as such. Similarly with job evaluation: the 'neutrality' of the methods helps organizations to retain differentials in pay of perhaps 500 per cent on the grounds that the jobs are 'worth' that objectively. (It is perhaps not surprising that to include the managing director's job in the method would place too great a strain on the idea of objectivity, so that this and other senior jobs are not included.) The effect of the technology of psychological assessment is to induce the willing co-operation and docility of individuals.

Many psychologists use and thus reproduce the discourse, believing in it either as 'truth', or as the nearest to fairness which can at present be achieved. (The science of psychology is still in its infancy, I was told time and again when I was an undergraduate.) Many others consider that it serves a legitimizing function and see this as either desirable, as a way to have influence, or as necessary, if they are to secure work. It is difficult to overcome a long training in seeing the world as if individuals were independent moral and rational agents responsible for the social domain. There is little incentive to overcome this if the only alternative seems to be determinism. A theoretical framework which recognizes the social construction of subjectivity in social relations and through discourses does not result in an inevitable lack of agency. On the contrary, it can make change more possible when it analyses the real relations and thus devises methods which do not conceal them. Moreover, such an analysis does not take away power from the people who have to live those relations, by presenting them in a form which is the property of experts and therefore mystifying, purged of all undesirable features as if the ideal could be made real by willing it so.

Notes

1 Professor Rodger was given the first chair in occupational psychology at London University (Birkbeck College) in 1961 and was seen as the 'founding father' of the subject in Britain.

2 Nomothetic methods are those which depend on quantification of an individual's responses, where scores thus derived are compared with those of others. They are standardized according to the assumption that the variable being measured follows a normal curve distribution. In this way any individual can be

compared to any other. Social differences are not visible with this treatment (see chapter 2, and chapter 3, p. 130).

3 The term 'organizational' as opposed to 'occupational' psychology does not only reflect a slightly different emphasis. It grew up in the United States and was imported both in the text books and through American companies and American 'experts'.

4 Lisl Klein (1976), a consultant with Esso (Fawley) in the late 1960s and early 1970s, describes how American consultancy teams were detailed to Fawley to prescribe and run management training based on interpersonal skills and encounter. In contrast her own approach was based on multidisciplinary and open socio-technical systems approaches which stress the importance of analysing structures at the same time as people. From this perspective, she indicates how the American approach failed to address the important issues of the time.

5 Several months later, after one secretary had left, it is worth noting that she has not been replaced (a 'frozen post') but the increased volume of work does not automatically entail an upgrading.

6 In fact, a multiple regression analysis is run which compared the scores of the analytical method with the overall 'felt-fair' job comparisons. It is a statistical method where one set of scores must be taken as the yardstick against which the other is measured, thus giving more weight to the yardstick set of scores. In the Profile method, therefore the less discriminating 'felt-fair' judgements are given more weight as the yardstick.

7 See Messick (1975) for a good critical discussion of the enormous complexities in psychometric 'validity'.

8 The 'predictors' AT & T rated their managers on were as follows: scholastic aptitudes; oral and written communication skill; human relations skills; personal impact; perception of threshold social cues; creativity; self-objectivity; social objectivity; behaviour flexibility; need approval of superiors; need approval of peers; inner work standards; need advancement; need security; goal flexibility; primacy of work; Bell system Value Orientation; realism of expectation; tolerance of uncertainty; ability to delay gratification; resistance to stress; range of interests; energy; organization and planning; decision-making. The cultural particularity of this set is only too obvious, and clearly relates to job culture, and not to features of 'natural personality'.

9 Maier's (1958) work on performance appraisal was an application of the Lewinian finding that a democratic leadership style was more successful than an authoritarian one (or a *laissez-faire* one) in getting a group to do what the person in authority wants of them (Lewin, Lippitt and White, 1939). He distinguished three types of performance appraisal interviews: 'tell and sell', 'tell and listen' and 'problem solving', where the role of the interviewer was characterized in turn as judge, judge and helper. With such labels, and given the increasingly egalitarian values of the 1960s, it is not surprising that it was the third type which in training (where Maier's categories are the most common system used) has been presented as the most desirable and effective. Under the category of 'gains', Maier characterizes the 'problem solving' approach as 'almost assured of improvement in some respects'. He defines the objective of this approach in terms which reflect changing values: whereas the first two types concern 'evaluation', the objective of the third is to 'stimulate growth and development'.

Maier's model illustrates the way that changing ideology – in this case towards democratic ideals – finds its way into psychological knowledge through what *works* as a means of administering and regulating individuals.

Social psychology and the politics of racism

Julian Henriques

Introduction

This chapter takes a comparatively progressive area of social science research, the social psychology of prejudice, and examines its political effects. In the Introduction to this section, we have argued that despite the progressive effects of radical psychology in the past, the theorizations that supported liberal social policies have lost their usefulness for a radical politics. We highlighted one feature of such theorizations to support our view, namely the premise of an individual–society dichotomy. Shared by all the various branches of psychology, this dualism and the concomitant individualism which is central to it allows even radical analyses to be pressed into the service of existing social relations, thereby reinforcing and perpetuating them.

In examining the concept of prejudice, I am concerned with establishing several related points. First is the already mentioned compatibility of social psychology's concept of racial prejudice with existing power relations and its implications for social psychology's reproduction of these social relations. A pertinent illustration of this is the manner in which the Scarman Report explained racism as the prejudiced behaviour of a few isolated individual police officers. I shall briefly examine Scarman's position to argue that this is an instance of the reductive effect of the individual–society couple whereby society is assumed to be basically unproblematic and social breakdown is ascribed to particular stray and abnormal individual actions; what might be called the 'rotten apple theory' of racism.

Second, I am concerned to link this aspect of social psychology's performance as part of the apparatus of social regulation with the way in which the concept of prejudice has itself been produced. The point here is to identify the historical context of that production, particularly in relation to the questions of social regulation. I do this by looking at the work of Gordon Allport and T. W. Adorno and the emergence of the social psychology of prejudice in the 1950s in the USA, outlining the political circumstances that conditioned that emergence.

Third, pursuing in greater detail the theoretical problems implicit in the above assertions, I shall pay particular attention to the social-psychological arguments themselves. The work of Allport and that of Henri Tajfel will provide the basis for demonstrating that social psychology's premise of the individual as a unitary rational subject leads it to regard the social as contingent. This is so although, ironically, it claims to distinguish itself from much of psychology, for example, behaviourism, precisely on the grounds that it takes its object to be the examination of the social components of our make-up. The conceptual poverty of social psychology's notion of prejudice is most starkly illustrated in Tajfel's retreat into cognitivism, that is, the reduction of prejudice and intergroup perceptions to effects occasioned by failures in the mechanism of cognition itself.

Finally I return to the issue of political effects to argue that the concept of racial prejudice leads a double life. Its theoretical face lays claim to the philanthropic aim of promoting radical harmony whilst its more practical profile insults blacks by shifting onto us responsibility for the racism we suffer. Both aspects draw on and effect a number of generally circulated common-sense assumptions, in particular the idea that 'we are all the same under the skin' and that there should be no real difference between races.

Prejudice: 'we all make mistakes'

In the Scarman Report, *The Brixton Disorders*, Lord Scarman's report on the uprisings which took place in a number of English cities in the summer of 1981, the use of the idea of racial prejudice is central to the analysis of the role of the police. Scarman cites the prejudice of the police as a cause of the community's attack on them. The community's reaction to police behaviour has 'plausibility', he says, because it 'is due, sadly, to the ill-considered, immature and *racially prejudiced* actions of some officers in their dealings on the streets with young black people' (Scarman 1981, para. 4.63; my italics). It is only 'some', that is to say a few individuals – the 'immature' and 'ill-considered' – who are racially prejudiced. Even when the Report is forced to recognize the existence of racial prejudice, it is careful to stress that it manifests itself only '*occasionally* in the behaviour of *a few* officers on the streets' (ibid., para. 4.63; my italics).

With this assertion the corollary point is made; that most of the time the great majority of police officers conform to the taken-for-granted norm of the humane, bias-free and objective 'British bobby'.

Thus prejudice is constituted as an individualized, exceptional phenomenon, automatically exonerating society as a whole. The terms used to describe it, and the implicit assumptions which make Scarman's claims at all intelligible, are understanding prejudice as an irrational response which originates in ignorance. Appropriately, Lord Scarman identifies this ignorance as the source of the problem among the lower ranks of the police: 'I am satisfied,' he says, 'that such bias (against black people) is not to be found amongst senior officers' (ibid., para. 4.63). Indeed, he reiterates this viewpoint so often that one might be forgiven the presumption that only if it were stated police policy would Lord Scarman consider prejudice as anything more than an accident.

Clearly, from such a point of view, society as a whole and social institutions, such as the police force and welfare agencies, cannot be irrational, founded on error and ignorance. It follows that anti-racist perspectives, especially those expressed by blacks, which describe prejudice as evidence of the deep-seated institutional and cultural foundations of racism, must be wrong. This challenge to understand racism as a fundamentally social rather than an individual phenomenon is firmly resisted by the Scarman Report:

> It was alleged by some of those who made representations to me that Britain is an institutionally racist society. If by that is meant that it is a society which knowingly, as a matter of policy, discriminates against black people, I reject the allegation. If, however, the suggestion being made is that practices may be adopted by public bodies as well as by private individuals which are unwittingly discriminatory against black people, then this is an allegation which deserves serious consideration, and where proved, swiftly remedied.
>
> (ibid., para. 2.22)

The two poles of the individual–society dualism are neatly summarized in that quotation. On the one side is the liberal wing of the establishment which admits the existence of prejudice as an individually caused phenomenon and is ready to introduce reforms to remedy anomalous, 'unwitting' failures, but which will adamantly stand by the existing social arrangements. On the other side stand the radical and black organizations which consider the responsibility to lie with the 'system'. The reformers are prepared delicately to remove the few rotten apples while the radicals plan to upset the whole apple-cart. Thus the terms of the theoretical and the political construction of the individual–society dichotomy are locked together in a perpetual mutually propelling antagonism. This criticism however is neither meant to imply that we should dismiss the Scarman

Report altogether – for it has had progressive effects in the public debate on policing (see Hall, 1982) – nor that radical critiques are off the mark when they point to the inscription of racist practices in social institutions of all kinds. Rather, I suggest that there are some observations that should be drawn from this apparent impasse.

The conservatism of the Report is typical of other attempts by the liberal establishment to reformulate policies to deal with the periodic crises in the regulation of the population. Their net effect is to leave power relations unchanged. In the case of racism, by directing attention to attitudes and to individuals it avoids questioning directly anything to do with the differences in power between whites and blacks. It is able to propose measures that seem feasible and reasonable from the point of view of the status quo while confirming what administrators regard as the mark of their political neutrality, namely that they do not impugn the legitimacy of the established social and power relations.

The key concept used in this case, that of prejudice, has functioned in much the same way before. *Colour Prejudice*, written thirty-six years ago by a colonial administrator of long standing, Sir Alan Burns, attempts to account for relations between English colonialists and their black colonial subjects in terms of the prejudiced attitudes that one group has towards the other (Burns, 1948). Two decades later the same argument was deployed by E. J. B. Rose and his associates in their monumental *Colour and Citizenship* to account for white British attitudes to black immigrant settlers in the UK (Rose *et al.*, 1969). The point I am outlining here is developed more fully in the Introduction to section 2. What I can signal at this point is the clear administrative and regulative utility of a concept such as prejudice. But it does not function in this manner independently from other knowledges and practices with which it is articulated. And that leads me to a second set of observations.

The familiarity and reasonableness of Scarman's assumptions and arguments is conditioned by the way in which they reach into the domain of common-sense understanding, and thus appear to rely on and confirm 'what we all know' (see Barker, 1981; Lawrence, 1982). There is the conviction that British culture is not essentially racist and has never been so, a conviction founded in a curious forgetfulness, as Hall (1982) has argued. Even the liberal view that there is no difference between black and white, that we are all the same under the skin, appeals to a widespread wishful magnanimity that borders on condescension. It is this view, captured in such common-sense slogans as 'One race the human race', which, in its refusal to acknowledge any reality to racial difference, has been drawn on by liberals and anti-racist radicals alike. It appears that both groups suffer from a similar desire to privilege the ideal of no difference between races above the practical strategies designed to achieve it. It is a case of putting the ideal cart before the real horse, with the result that nothing moves.

The social psychology of prejudice starts with this assumption of sameness and provides scientific legitimation of it. And it is clearly central to the administrative ideology of fairness as I have noted. After all the progressiveness of that view is confirmed and sanctioned when we remember that it has usually been asserted against the explicit racism of, for example, eugenicists and fascists in the 1920s and 1930s. But one of the effects, even if unintended, of the claim of no difference is to reinforce the explanations of prejudice that reduce it to individual aberration and irrational behaviour. (There are other political consequences that I will discuss in my conclusion.) Individualism is not only a theoretical doctrine; it is practised in a multitude of social encounters and indeed the everyday understanding of our own and other people's behaviour is premised upon it. So when the Scarman Report seeks an explanation of prejudice in individual errors and when the social psychology of prejudice searches for the factors that induce error in the cognitive process of the individual, they combine in an uneasy cohabitation with the conservative and simplistic common-sense view of social reality. As some of the arguments of Allport and Tajfel show, social psychology is not as comfortable in that relationship as compared to common-sense understanding which is comforted by it in its support of social regulation. However, whilst it remains trapped in the individual–society dualism with its implication of the individual as a rational unitary subject who is the locus of his or her judgements and capacities, social psychology cannot relinquish the relationship.

What the example of the Scarman Report demonstrates is the need for a new approach to the analysis of how and why social psychology in general and, in this instance, the notion of prejudice have the effects they do. This is preliminary to the establishment of a different perspective that could suggest a new and productive radical politics; different from, for example, the kind of tactics pursued by many anti-racist organizations, or implied in certain analyses of racism, for example, Sivanandan (1976, 1981). A new perspective should also suggest how it is possible to move beyond the range of approaches with which social psychologists have addressed the issues of race (see for example Jones, 1972; Bloom, 1971) and fascism (Billig, 1978).

Finally, I would insist that it is too easy and politically sterile simply to accuse Scarman of racism and social psychology of theoretical ineptitude. After all, the notion of prejudice continues to figure prominently in a lot of discussion on the left. What I have suggested, through my critique of the Scarman Report, is the need to challenge the assumptions at work in both the social sciences and most radical analyses. Part of this involves the recognition that the effects, for both theory and politics, of concepts like prejudice are specific and vary historically. More contentiously, it means that theory and politics, knowledge and power are locked in a mutually conditioning system of effects so that the analysis of one must directly engage with analysis of the other.

Prejudice, personality and attitudes

Prejudice became a central component of social psychology through a combination of pressing social problems and theoretical developments which occurred mainly in the United States in the 1950s. The social problems concerned the cold war and the fear of communism. The theoretical developments consisted of the production of attitude scales and other techniques of psychological measurement which were part of the construction of the new discipline of social psychology. As my outline will show, there was no simple relationship of cause and effect between internal theoretical development and the external political events; rather the emergence of the concept of prejudice as an object of scientific enquiry and as a political issue exemplifies the way knowledges on the one hand and practices and the powers associated with them on the other, are mutually productive.

The emergence of prejudice

There are two well-known early social-psychological works on racial prejudice, and both are American: *The Authoritarian Personality* (1950) by T. W. Adorno, E. Frenkel-Brunswick, D. Levinson and R. Sanford, and *The Nature of Prejudice* (1954) by Gordon W. Allport. The former is an account of original research into prejudice, the specific aim of which was to identify 'the potential fascist'. The latter is a review of theories of prejudice which particularly develops social–psychological explanations within a social-attitudes, or what Allport calls a phenomenological, paradigm. Adorno and his colleagues characterize their approach as follows:

> for theory as to the structure of personality, we have leaned most heavily upon Freud, while for a more or less systematic formulation of the more directly observable and measurable aspects of personality we have been guided primarily by academic psychology.
>
> (1950, p. 5)

Published only four years later, Allport's work represents a further shift towards 'academic psychology' reflected in his dependence on attitudes and perception, rather than personality, as the chief explanatory concepts.

To some extent both works express some of the problems of a shifting paradigm with the new confidence that social psychology was finding as a science. It is through analysing these problems that we can detect the effects of individual–society dualism, albeit in different guises in the two works. In particular, we shall see the effects of viewing causation as immediately stemming from the individual. These effects are apparent despite the authors' explicit insistence on 'long-range sociocultural etiology' (Allport, 1954, p. xii) and 'the total organisation of society' (Adorno *et al.*, 1950, p. 975). The shift towards a 'social attitudes' explanation also demonstrates the productivity of the new quantitative techniques; that is how our understanding today of racial prejudice has been produced through the dominance of those methods in formulating the approach to the problem. Despite some differences in their theoretical approaches (see below), Adorno *et al.* and Allport shared the belief that their work was vital for the defence of society against (in Allport's words) 'the threat to democratic values posed by twentieth century totalitarianism' (Allport, 1954, p. 477).

Two premises are common to both approaches: the belief in rationality as an ideal for democratic society and the emphasis on the individual as the site of the breakdown of this rationality and therefore as the object of research. The aim of Adorno *et al.* is thus:

> to develop and promote an understanding of social–psychological factors which have made it possible for the authoritarian type of man to threaten to replace the individualistic and democratic type prevalent in the past century and a half of our civilization.
>
> (Adorno *et al.*, 1950, p. x)

Allport's approach, too, clearly identifies the individual as the ground on which the battle for democracy is to be fought. The individual as the object of study needed strengthening as a bulwark against extremism:

> *Democracy*, we now realise, *places a heavy burden upon the personality, sometimes too great to bear*. The maturely democratic person must possess subtle virtues and capacities. It is easier to succumb to oversimplification and dogmatism.
>
> (Allport, 1954, p. 477; my italics)

The work on personality and prejudice was the key element in social psychology's task of achieving a better understanding of individuals so that those who could not see through communist or fascist propaganda unaided could be more adequately protected against the lures of such misinformation. It would thus further the development of democracy.

For Adorno *et al.*, the threat of totalitarianism came from the fascist right. The research originated in 1944 when the Jewish American Committee convened a conference on religious and racial prejudice which was followed by the establishment of a Department of Scientific Research. Several of the academics involved were European Jews who had escaped from Nazi Germany and the commitment of the Department was, of course, to understand anti-semitism:

> How could it be . . . that in a culture of law, order and reason there should have survived the irrational remnants of ancient racial and religious hatreds? How to explain the willingness of great masses of people to tolerate the mass extermination of their fellow citizens? What tissues in the life of our modern society remain cancerous, and despite our assumed enlightenment show the incongruous atavism of ancient peoples? And what within the individual organism responds to certain stimuli in our culture with attitudes and acts of destructive aggression? (Adorno *et al.*, 1950, p. v)

The association of irrationality with ancient peoples and the assumed necessity of historical development are characteristic of rationalist western culture (rationalism is dealt with at length in chapter 3). Irrationality was an incongruous anachronism, but the inevitable, because defining, counterpart of rationality: a term which captured the aspects of society which fell short of the rationalist ideal.

For Allport, in McCarthyite America of the 1950s, the threat of totalitarianism came rather from the communist left. One consequence was that he de-emphasized racial prejudice: 'When we speak of prejudice we are likely to think of "race prejudice". This is an unfortunate association of ideas, for throughout history human prejudice has had little to do with race' (Allport, 1954, p. xi). Nonetheless, the development of the concept of prejudice, inseparable from its take-up in practice, has been towards understanding and intervening in the 'problem of racial prejudice'.

The study of prejudice thus provided the comparatively new science of social psychology with a crucial role as a plate in the west's armour in the cold war. For Allport, social psychology's job became no less than to correct the mistakes of history:

> It was a *stuporous error* for the western world to believe that democratic ideology, stemming from Judeo-Christian ethic and reinforced by the political creeds of many nations, would of itself gradually overspread the world. Instead of this happening, *a frightful retrogression* set in. Mankind (has) revealed its weakness. . . .
> (ibid., p. 477; my italics)

Allport faces the task of promoting 'democratic ideology' with supreme confidence derived from taken-for-granted convictions that frame his approach. These, of course, are the rationalism privileged by much of the progressive thinking of his time and the individualism which has always been so peculiarly characteristic of the American ethos. Both these elements came together for Allport in the notion of science. It was science, after all, that was seen as the principal tool with which the American dream had been realized from the techniques of scientific management on the production line to those of objective assessment and IQ testing in schools and other institutions (see chapter 1). In the atomic age, Allport tells us, it was the scientists who were responsible for protecting society against subversion, a role that in previous epochs it had been safe to leave to the theologians and the moral philosophers. The taken-for-granted truths of rationalism, individualism and science formed the conceptual framework of his time: '*It is part of the democratic faith that the objective study of the irrational and immature elements in human behaviour will help us to counteract them*' (ibid., p. 477; my italics). With this coupling of 'objective study' and 'democratic faith' Allport makes a further assertion of the essential truth of the American way of life; it stands not only against immaturity and irrationality but also for freedom. It is entirely within this framework that the notion of prejudice achieved its position of dominance.

The authoritarian personality

Despite the shared common ideal of rationality that I have discussed above, the theoretical emphases of Adorno *et al.* and Allport dealt with irrationality in very different ways. Whereas Allport's emphasis on attitudes excluded irrationality from its main paradigm (though he cannot exclude it altogether), it was a central feature of the psychoanalytic theory of personality central to the approach of Adorno *et al.* In retrospect, *The Authoritarian Personality* can be seen as one of the final examples of the use of psychoanalytic theory within social psychology, and even then it was already manifesting the effects of the new quantitative methods (see p. 71). Thus the authors claim, first, that their study 'demonstrates that there is a close correlation between a number of deep-rooted personality traits and overt prejudice', and, second, that it 'has also succeeded in producing an instrument for measuring these traits' (Adorno *et al.*, 1950, p. vi). In order to understand what produces 'attitudes and acts of destructive aggression' (ibid.) it was not surprising that these researchers turned to psychoanalytic theory, coming as they did from a European theoretical tradition.

Adorno and his co-authors emphasized personality as the organization of needs (a concept which is problematic for psychoanalysis – see Introduction to section 3, pp. 210–11), and saw opinions, attitudes and values as dependent upon these (Adorno *et al.*, 1950, p. 5). They caution that personality is not to be hypostatized as an ultimate determinant but see it as accounting for relative permanence (ibid., p. 5). They stress that it is a potential rather than determining behaviour, so that, for example, 'personality structure may be such as to render the individual susceptible to anti-democratic propaganda' (ibid., p. 7). The other aspects which affect prejudiced behaviour are, of course, seen as being outside in the social world. Their formulation is identical to the dualism we have criticized in the Introduction to section 1:

> The soundest approach, it would seem, is to consider that in the determination of ideology, as in the determination of any behaviour, there is a situational factor and a personality factor and that a careful weighting of the role of each will yield the most accurate prediction. (ibid., p. 10)

It is the theoretical weaknesses of psychoanalytic theory itself which made it unlikely that *The Authoritarian Personality* could escape this dualism. Its most important manifestation is the tendency of psychoanalytic theory towards biological reductionism (see Introduction to section 3 for a further discussion of this point). So while psychoanalytic theory's ability to theorize irrationality was a great strength of this research, none the less it could be too easily reduced to a natural tendency based on instinctual drives. As this reduction fitted in with contemporary psychological theories in general, and in particular with psychology's explanations of prejudice, such as the frustration–aggression hypothesis (Dollard *et al.*, 1939), it was all too easy to subsume *The Authoritarian Personality* under the same rubric. So, for example, it was treated in Allport's review under the general heading of 'nature of man' theories, along with other psychodynamic explanations (Allport, 1954, p. 209). The researchers' emphasis on measurement and science had some responsibility, albeit indirect, for the way the research was taken up in American social psychology. It meant that their understanding of personality was weakly theorized and occupied a minor place in the book. Despite the range of their methods and the preservation of some clinical or 'depth' psychology methods, their theorization was not strong enough to mark a distance from the taken-for-granted notions of personality and attitudes which were dominant. This was exacerbated by the fact that the theoretical summary was extremely cursory because the business of science was seen to be the gathering of quantitative data. It is to this that the major part of their large volume was dedicated and to this that I shall now turn.

Adorno *et al.* recognized that academic psychology's methods could make '"depth psychological" phenomena more amenable to mass statistical treatment' (1950, p. 12). Using a conceptualization of personality as a series of levels, more or less accessible to indirect investigation, they developed a range of methods from questionnaires containing 'factual data' (what in modern jargon would be called biodata) and opinion-attitude scales to clinical techniques including depth interview and a projective test (TAT – the Thematic Apperception Test). However, the new 'scientific' measures which had come into use in social psychology – particularly the use of semantic differentials – were, to use their terms, oriented to the opinion and attitude levels of personality. It was on the use of these techniques to develop scales to measure fascism, anti-semitism and ethnocentrism that the take-up of *The Authoritarian Personality* hinged.

Despite their keenness to embrace the new quantitative methods of social psychology Adorno and his colleagues did not find their techniques adopted for wide-scale application as were, for example, the psychometric developments of the notion of intelligence (see chapter 1, p. 34, and Rose, 1979) or even the idea of social attitudes itself. This is in part because although they succeeded in devising an easily and quickly administered instrument to identify the authoritarian personality, and one which satisfied contemporary criteria of reliability and validity, they emphasized that the causes were complex and deeply rooted:

> It follows directly from our major findings that counter measures should take into account the whole structure of the prejudiced outlook . . . it is not difficult to see why measures to oppose social discrimination have not been more effective. *Rational arguments cannot be expected to have deep and lasting effects upon a phenomenon that is irrational in its essential nature.*
>
> (Adorno *et al.*, 1950, p. 973; my italics)

Similarly they point out that such measures 'are concerned with the treatment of symptoms rather than the disease itself' (ibid.). When it comes to treating the disease, they do not shy away from emphasizing 'the true enormity of the fundamental problem'. Nor do they advocate 'psychological means alone': 'the task is comparable to that of eliminating neurosis, or delinquency, or nationalism from the world. These are products of the total organisation of society and are to be changed only as that society is changed' (ibid., p. 975). The contrast between this understanding of the problem and that of Allport's, which, as we shall see, suggested that prejudice could be rationally corrected with the provision of accurate information, could not be starker. From the point of view of the regulation of dominant power relations Adorno was the pessimist, Allport the optimist. American instrumentality demanded both the posing of the problem and the tools for its solution to be sited in the individual so that the given social organization could be left untouched.

We shall see in the following part of this chapter how Allport's treatment of prejudice in terms of perceptual processes was more easily amenable to a translation into rational and individualistic intervention. It is Allport's emphasis which is the forerunner of the socio-cognitive accounts of prejudice which have had the most widespread take-up in contemporary Britain.

The nature of prejudice

The main impact on social psychology of Allport's study of prejudice has been felt through its use of a social-attitudes paradigm, though his approach to the issue was considerably broader than this. Social attitudes are the psychological subject's ideas and ways of thinking about the world; they are distinct from behaviours in the sense that they are regarded as the conceptual maps in the mind that determine behaviour. For instance, the behavioural manifestation of the social attitude known as prejudice is discrimination (see Ehrlich, 1973; Reeves, 1982). The study of attitudes is thus seen as a key to the understanding of behaviour. The concept of social attitudes is of particular interest here because it is seen as forming a bridge across the conceptual divide between the individual and society. Social attitudes constitute the polarity of these terms and at the same time lock them together in the way that empiricist notions of perception align subject and object (see Henriques, 1977). The investigation of the formation of attitudes and their corresponding effects on behaviour is supposed to provide insights into the information-processing mechanisms of the individual, so that we might understand how the individual processes inputs about the social world to produce specific, behavioural outputs.

The subsequent development of social psychology's emphasis on social attitudes and quantification (see for example Brown, 1965) has led to a reading of Allport that has privileged this component of his work. In terms of this emphasis, *The Nature of Prejudice* has been adopted as the foundation stone of much modern social psychology. The notion of prejudice superseded the need and instinct approach (McDougall, 1912) and, eventually the highly influential frustration–aggression hypothesis (Dollard *et al.*, 1939). What largely accounted for the growing dominance of Allport's prejudice approach was its amenability, along with the concept of social attitudes in general, to quantification and other statistical techniques. Thus the notion of prejudice was the product of a dominant line in social psychology, a line which included the construction of statistical techniques for the measurement of attitudes (Thurstone and Chave, 1929; Likert, 1932), the invention of the notion of 'social distance' between members of different groups (Bogardus, 1925) and work on the idea of stereotyped judgements (Katz and Braly, 1933; Bayton, 1941; see also Jones, 1972). And, of course, the developing notion of prejudice as something individual and quantifiable provided a site for intervention in and regulation of a commonly recognized social problem (see p. 83).

The significance of the increasing dominance of the social-attitudes paradigm, a trend marked by Allport's work, is that it consolidated individual–society dualism, in a new mode which reduced to information-processing mechanisms, rather than drives or instinct, as the underlying and determined cause of prejudice within the individual. The concepts of prejudice and stereotyping are part of the explanatory framework of social attitudes, their specific function being to account for the distortions which occur during the processing of incoming information. Prejudice, defined by Allport as 'thinking ill of others without sufficient warrant' (1954, p. 7), is based on the belief that distortion occurs when a person comes to a judgement prematurely (hence its etymology from the Latin *praejudicium*). The concept of stereotyping describes a different aspect of judgement: it produces inaccurate judgements through a tendency to attribute characteristics supposedly belonging to a group (for example black people) to every individual who is considered a member of that group. Scarman, for example, mentions one criticism of the police as being 'to stereotype all of the black community as criminals' (Scarman, 1981, p. 60). So, while stereotyping is one explanation of prejudice, it is supplemented by the idea of premature judgement being itself another process which causes prejudice. Both concepts refer to a human information-processing mechanism and contrast its specific products with the rationalist ideal of an undistorted judgement, the model for which is the objective view of the rational scientist (see p. 80).

A further dualism is now apparent in that the ideal of perfect information-processing is based on one of pure rationality. However, the relation between the two dualisms is not one of simple correspondence. Allport's eclecticism exemplifies the heterogeneity (and theoretical inconsistency) of social psychological explanations of prejudice. For example, as I shall demonstrate below, Allport's preferred explanation, the 'phenomenological approach', which stresses the information-processing capacities of the individual, has the effect of omitting questions about the content of people's judgements and why particular groups and characteristics are made the target of premature or over-generalized judgements. He is then obliged to resort to a companion explanation in order to deal with these questions, an explanation which relies on a quite different set of theoretical premises (see also p. 75 for Tajfel's account).

According to Allport there are two principal approaches to the study of prejudice: the stimulus-object approach and the phenomenological approach. The stimulus-object approach emphasizes 'earned reputation' (Allport, 1954, p. 211) or 'well-deserved reputation' (ibid., pp. 85–6) and 'looking for bona fide differences' (ibid.). The phenomenological approach maintains that the representation of the object is not direct but proceeds from a person's view of the world. While both of these approaches could arrive at a better understanding of the phenomenon within a different theory of the relation between the human subject and the social domain, within the limitations of individual–society dualism the combination of these two approaches expresses and legitimizes some of the central assumptions about racial prejudice that we find in common sense, and which I have illustrated using the Scarman Report.

Even within Allport's own terms, however, these two approaches are not sufficient because, as both are based on the assumption of rational cause, they do not explain the hostility which was seen to be characteristic of racially prejudiced attitudes. (This is an expression of a wider problem in attitude theory which differentiates between the cognitive and the feeling components of attitude, but does not theorize them within the same paradigm.) It is here that a dualism between rationality and irrationality is brought into play. In the following quotation, Allport's 'two essential ingredients' express this dualism: 'Why do human beings slip so easily into ethnic prejudice? They do so because the two essential ingredients that we have discussed – erroneous generalisation and hostility – are *natural and common capacities of the human mind*' (Allport, 1954, p. 17; my italics).

Despite his attempt to characterize them as equivalent 'capacities of the human mind', 'hostility' in fact is not successfully theorized within Allport's information-processing paradigm. When it is not reduced even more directly to biology through explaining hostility as natural aggression (as in the frustration–aggression hypothesis, for example), Allport's analysis of hostility relies on Adorno. However, his account does less justice to psychoanalysis than Adorno's original treatment, more easily reducing the theorization of personality to biology. Either way, then, hostility is something that Allport can only theorize in dualistic terms. The fact that Allport is forced to rely on other accounts of prejudice in addition to his social-attitude approach should, perhaps, be taken as indicative of the latter's lack of explanatory power. Nevertheless it was an early expression of what is the dominant paradigm today and so here, and in the following section, I shall be concerned with the second of Allport's 'ingredients' – erroneous generalization.

Because erroneous generalization starts from the individual side of the dualistic divide, as I have indicated, it requires its companion explanation starting from the society side: the stimulus object. The phenomenological view is thus based on a perceptual model which assumes that there is some relation between stimulus object and response beneath the effects of categorization, stereotyping or personality. The stimulus-object approach accordingly addresses that issue: 'there may be ethnic or national traits that *are* menacing, and that therefore invite real hostility' (Allport, 1954, p. 211). This explanation legitimizes (as well as being an expression of) the common-sense view that 'there are no real differences between blacks and whites' (the corollary of which is that only a few prejudiced people believe otherwise) and, in doing so, it rules out other ways of seeing racism. For example, within its framework, we cannot ask about the social and economic causes of differences between blacks and whites in racist societies such as Britain. We cannot ask in what conditions the hostility of whites towards blacks is produced (nor, therefore, what effect it has on blacks). Nor can we find out how negative generalizations made about blacks as a group are constituted. In my view the effect of the idea of prejudice as error is to suppress the recognition both of existing differences and of the racism which takes place in practice on a wide scale. It is not that social psychology has had this effect single-handedly. The take-up of certain assumptions about prejudice and not others (as I have exemplified in relation to Adorno's work) depends on the circulation between social psychology and common sense, each making the other more available and mutually reinforcing their chains.

An example of how the phenomenological model of prejudice shifts the question to one of 'earned reputation' or real cause is the transformation that was made in the frustration–aggression explanation of prejudice. Originally as put forward by Dollard, it derived from a psychoanalytic model and contained a key third term in the chain of explanation: frustration – aggression – displacement. I have already mentioned the weaknesses in the Freudian theorization of aggression. None the less, the concept of displacement fulfils the important function of recognizing and theorizing the way in which an object may have no logical relation to the response it triggers but rather be a displacement which occurs as a defence (see Introduction to section 3, pp. 224–5, for a fuller discussion of the defence mechanisms in psychoanalytic theory). The effect of dropping the third term from the explanation – a predictable effect given the dominance of biological accounts of behaviour antagonistic to psychoanalysis – is to put the responsibility for prejudiced responses back on the stimulus object.

The effect of this combination of approaches is itself twofold. First, the phenomenological approach locates prejudice in the perceptual processes. Second, and in apparent contradiction to the focus on the subject of prejudice (that is the prejudiced person) the object of studying is displaced onto the stimulus object. The black person becomes the cause of racism whereas the white person's prejudice is seen as a natural effect of the information-processing mechanisms. (This works as a subtle double exoneration of white racism, no doubt all the more effective because it is not conscious.) If it were not for this shift, Lord Scarman could not excuse the 'behaviour of a few officers in the streets' in the following terms: 'It may be only too easy for some officers, faced with what they must see as the inexorable rising tide of street crime, to lapse into an unthinking assumption that all young black people are potential criminals' (Scarman, 1981, p. 105).

Of course there is no explanation given for why they suspect young *black* people (as opposed to young people or indeed people) unless it is the covert belief that there is some truth in the matter. Such assumptions are further legitimated by the kind of ostensibly neutral statistical evidence with which the Metropolitan Police have shown black people to be involved in certain types of crime. So, despite its apparent focus on the prejudiced person, the social-psychological paradigm reflects, reproduces and legitimizes the common-sense racism which blames the victim. It will be argued, similarly, in chapter 5 that knowledges which are sexist succeed in putting blame on women (see also Hollway, 1981). As common sense has it, 'there's no smoke without fire'.

Cognition and error

In Britain in the 1970s the work of Henri Tajfel and his co-workers was influential in developing an account of the role of cognitive processes in intergroup differences. The Social Categorization Approach (SCA) addressed the issue of prejudice and discrimination that in the real world exists between groups that differ along religious, linguistic or racial lines. The SCA sought to demonstrate that the experimental investigation of the cognitive mechanisms of categorization in a laboratory setting could be generalized to such socially relevant areas (Tajfel, 1972, 1979) and it attracted researchers interested in making progressive use of social psychology. Some earlier approaches had stressed groups as the problem and therefore the correct object of study, and it was only in the 1950s that the individual had become the common object of study. Tajfel maintained that a focus on groups rather than individuals was more social and thus more progressive (Tajfel, 1978). Given this commitment it is an unfortunate irony that the SCA succeeds in evacuating the social content entirely from his explanation of the perception of intergroup differences. An account of how this happens is a further illustration of the unhappy effects of individual–society dualism.

Social cognition in groups

Tajfel's emphasis on categorization derives from the cognitive emphasis in experimental and social psychology which originated in the USA in the 1960s (for example Miller *et al.*, 1960; Neisser, 1966). The inadequacy of perceptual models' assumptions of correct objective representation led to the emphasis on cognition in order to focus on the idea of categories which organized the complex information coming in through the individual's information-processing system. In practice, as is evidenced by Allport's accounts, the earlier approach talked about categorization too. In many respects this shift from perception to cognition did not alter the assumption, underpinning the model of stimulus-processor representation, that correct (that is rational and objective) information-processing would produce a perfect representation. This similarity of limitations was increased by a shared adherence to the experimental method. In experimental psychology, content, meaning and value are usually treated as inconveniently complex variables that must be controlled in order not to affect the results. The methods used by Tajfel and his co-workers (for example Eiser and Stroebbe, 1972; Tajfel, 1974) to investigate psycho-social stimuli were an adoption and adaptation of the psychophysical methodologies on which the early experiments in perception of physical stimuli were based (for example Fechner, 1860).

What became known as SCA's 'minimal intergroup experiments' were designed to demonstrate that cognitive categorization processes had an autonomous role in the creation of psychological distinctiveness between groups (Tajfel *et al.*, 1971; Billig and Tajfel, 1973). To provide evidence for this hypothesis a series of laboratory experiments was devised which deliberately and systematically excluded all the variables which would normally be assumed to affect either hostility towards an out group or familiarity towards an in group. These included face-to-face interaction, previous hostility between groups and any instrumental link between individual response and self-interest. The experimental subjects were divided into groups on the flimsiest of criteria, such as a preference for one modern painter rather than another (Tajfel *et al.*, 1971) or their assumed cognitive styles (Tajfel and Brown, 1975), and eventually explicitly at random (Tajfel, 1978). They were then given the opportunity to make discriminations between members of their own group who were unknown to them and members of an equally anonymous other group by means of a series of matrices for distributing points. It was found that subjects invariably discriminated against members of the other group in favour of ingroup members. As there were no other variables in the laboratory relations between the groups, the conclusion drawn from these studies was that the discriminations were purely the product of the cognitive mechanisms of categorization within the individual.

The location of the origin of the subject's responses in the rational mechanisms of the mind is what would be expected from a social-cognitive approach working on the inside of the individual–society divide. Further the SCA specifies that these cognitive processes are in error. In the minimal intergroup studies this error was located in the discrepancy between the subject's perception of the groups and the scientist's perception of them. The comparison is made between the scientist's objective perception that there is 'no real difference' between group members and the subject's subjective perception that there are significant differences between the groups. The scientist's viewpoint, completely untheorized in the methodology of the experiment, produces the correct observations from which the subject's are considered incorrect divergences. This mistaken character of the subject's judgements is emphasized in the way the authors described the discriminations between groups as being 'gratuitous discriminations against the outgroup' which are 'irrelevant to ingroup-outgroup differentiations' for which 'on the face of it, there are *no reasons*' (Tajfel and Turner, 1976, p. 34; my italics).

The subjects whose cognitions see differences that do not really exist are, according to the SCA, making both unnecessary and irrational mistakes. Exactly the same would be said of the prejudiced person who thinks there is a difference between blacks and whites.

While such an explanation may appear to have some adequacy when apparently purely cognitive problems such as the properties of short-term memory are addressed, its shortcomings become more obvious when it tackles distinctly social issues (see Sinha and Walkerdine, 1978). The SCA, because it attempts an explanation of group relations rather than purely cognitive phenomena like short-term memory, steps outside the bastion of the individual psyche to claim a position on the social side of the individual–society dichotomy. To some extent this extension of cognitive explanation is camouflaged by the laboratory setting of the minimal intergroup experiments where the empiricist division between experimenter and subjects is unquestioned. It is not unreasonable to suppose that subjects, if they continued to co-operate with the rules of the experiment at all, were left with no option but to make 'gratuitous' discriminations. Positive and negative evaluations were required by the methodology. The power of the experimenter to make the rules governing subjects' behaviour resides partly in the more general authority relations (as was pointed out with Milgram's experiments on obedience – Milgram, 1977). In addition, it resides in the unrecognized power of formulating a procedure which limits the possibilities of response. For example, all meaningful criteria were purposely excluded and only one basis was provided for discriminating between groups. Furthermore, the rubric of the experiment required them to make judgement on individuals even when the criterion that had been provided was a group one. It is not surprising that they used it. This aspect of the experimenter's power is left out of the theorization (chapter 1 discussed a similar point with regard to the relations of assessment; see pp. 51–5).

The cognitivist conclusion is also determined by the theory which guides the experiments. For example, to address the more complex question of why subjects made consistently negative judgements against members of the other group would require more than the cognitive theory which Tajfel used. With conceptual tools such as 'resistance' and 'displacement' from psychoanalytic theory, it might be possible to understand the negative evaluation as an instance of displacement. The displacement might occur from the experimenter – the first object – to the other subject group – the new object – as a result of the difference in power and therefore the relative safety of criticizing the new object (see Henriques, 1977, for an account in these terms of the rivalries between Zimbabwean nationalist groups prior to independence). Though there may appear little need to theorize the relationship between experimenter and subjects in the setting of the minimal intergroup studies, similar relations involving power and social differences do appear relevant when the SCA attempts to explain relations between groups in the real world. Tajfel's way out is to conceive of cognitive processes as having their own 'autonomous function' in relation to the 'objective conflicts of interests' that normally affect group relations. He states:

> It must be remembered that I am not concerned here with hypotheses which would contradict the postulation of alternative causal processes. The aim is *not* to show that the 'objective' conflicts of interest between groups or the previously existing attitudes do not have certain well-known effects in intergroup behaviour; it is rather to show that *in addition* to these other causal processes, the establishment of psychological intergroup distinctiveness has its autonomous functions in intergroup behaviour. (Tajfel, 1974, p. 46)

It is clear from this formulation that the SCA has found no way round the principal dichotomies between the individual and society and between subjective and objective factors that affect group relations. For this reason its account of social phenomena, even in its own terms, remains severely limited.

Error

The idea of error continues to crop up in social psychology's attempts to explain racial prejudice without addressing either the socio-historical production of racism or the psychic mechanism through which it is reproduced in white people's feelings and their relations to black people. Error becomes a theoretical catch-all for what cannot be explained within individual–society dualism: the absence of 'correct' response.

Both prejudice and stereotyping in social-psychological theory make use of the same related assumptions in understanding error. The first is that individual errors can be contrasted with the correct perceptions and judgements of the scientist. The second assumption is that these errors are the result of the faulty workings of the cognitive mechanisms within the individual. Underlying both assumptions is the principle that completely accurate representations of the external world must be possible. The emphasis on rationality and the emphasis on error do not derive from the same theory. Rather they are competing accounts of the phenomenon of prejudice. It is surprising, therefore, that Allport, even with his avowedly eclectic approach, emphasized the irrational function of prejudice and notes his indebtedness to Freud (Allport, 1954, pp. 335–6). However, the 1950s and 1960s saw the demise of what little influence psychoanalysis had on academic psychology, with the dogmatic insistence on positivist science. In common sense now, 'irrational' refers more to behaviours or beliefs which cannot be explained according to the rationalist ideal, and which are at the same time negatively evaluated. It is this sense that is implied in Tajfel's description of discriminations for which 'on the face of it there are no reasons'. The theoretical function of the concept of the irrational is displaced onto error in the information-processing system.

For Freud error was motivated. The first phenomenon which he explained with his theory of the unconscious were the forgettings, misreadings and slips of the tongue that had previously been regarded as absence of correct response. For Freud they were not arbitrary, but were the interruption of the speech or actions of the conscious subject by the erupting of repressed wishes from the unconscious. It is most instructive that Crick's 'new' theory of dreaming should be at pains to deny precisely Freud's insight into the intelligibility of apparently meaningless phenomena by dismissing them as random electrical jolts (Crick and Mitchison, 1983). This is entirely in line with social psychology's discussion of error which has the effect of absolving responsibility for such responses as Freud's theory explicitly does not.

The notion of error is, however, well established for social psychology by its methodological role in the investigation of the rational processes of the individual. The concept of error has always been at the heart of experimental psychology's subject-matter of perception, cognition and memory so that from within the discipline it is very much taken for granted. In cognitive psychology's experimental investigation of human memory, for example, mistakes, errors and other performative malfunctions have been used as evidence of the conditions under which the mechanism cannot function correctly. Establishing the levels of tolerance of cognitive processes in this way provided a way of defining the working parameters or capacities of the mechanism investigated (see, for example, Neisser, 1966; Lindsay and Norman, 1977). In relation to prejudice one of the important consequences of the methodology of error and the cognitive paradigm in general has been its treatment of the content of cognitions. By and large in experimental psychology, content has been dealt with as an inconveniently complex variable that should be controlled in such a way as not to affect the experimental results. This is achieved by attempting to make content insignificant, for example in memory tests by using nonsense syllables, notionally, therefore, by using a quantitative rather than qualitative 'input'. Thus the methodology of error produces a very sharp split between process and content in which explanations are believed to reside exclusively in the former.

The relegation of content to a position outside cognitive explanation and on the other side of the individual–society divide cleared the ground for a vast proliferation of experimentation. When treated in this way information about 'the mechanisms of the mind' is forthcoming, for example, on the typical limits in capacity of short-term memory. I do not wish to suggest that such experimental results are the distortion of some real phenomenon. Rather, it should be said that the experimental practices I have been discussing produce knowledge of a specific kind. In turn these disallow, by the concepts through which they are fashioned, other ways of understanding the phenomena.

For psychology the belief in rationality and in perfect representation come together in the idea of scientific practice. The western idea of science could only spring from the long tradition of rationalism in the occidental world. (Chapter 3 provides a detailed consideration of the conditions of emergence of science and rationality – pp. 140–3.) In the earlier religious paradigms it was the idea of God that contained the possibility of perfect perception (for example in Leibniz's idea of the perfect monad). Now, as I have argued in the case of the minimal intergroup experiments, the scientist is considered capable of guaranteeing objectivity and therefore correct knowledge of facts in a way which is directly accessible through the scientific method (the guarantee against subjectivity and irrationality). In modern psychology, Kelly's construct theory is notable for making this explicit (Kelly, 1955). It posits that all individuals are capable of making and testing hypotheses – a model which is based on an exclusively rational idea of 'man the scientist'. Despite the discovery of the 'experimenter effect' (Rosenthal, 1966) the belief remains that psychologists can control irrelevant variables and arrive at the truth. The belief in rational individuals as the components of enlightened society was clearly demonstrated in Allport's and Adorno's comments on prejudice and totalitarianism. The belief is so widespread outside and inside psychology that it has not only impugned the Freudian attempt to theorize the non-rational subject but has denied it altogether in its own accounts (as in the above example of Crick and Mitchison's theory).

It is, of course, inherently problematic that social psychology's explanation of prejudice should depend on error. Since errors are by definition the exception rather than the rule, it is difficult to hold them accountable for such widespread phenomena as intergroup hostilities, attitudes and differences (of sex as well as race, see Hollway, 1982). Moreover the idea of science is premised on the ability to explain the reasons for things while error relies on the arbitrary nature of mistakes. However, I have shown that within the limitations of psychology's position in the individual–society dualism, it is not surprising (which of course makes it no less problematic). With content, meaning and value tied to the social domain and kept firmly outside the individual, psychology is left with theories of process alone. Denying, as it does, the processes associated with the unconscious (and thus the non-rational, non-unitary character of subjectivity), its processes can only be seen as those which bring outside information into the individual (perception, cognition, judgement and attitudes). Any failure of correct information-processing can thus only be accounted for by errors in that system. This notion of error not only removes the social from the rational individual, it also removes it from the correct view of science. Social processes and events, in the cognitivist perspective, are purely the emotional and non-cognitive source of error which induce mistakes in the rational processes of the individual. Not only are mistaken judgements in error, like that of thinking there is some real difference between blacks and whites, but also these very differences themselves come to be considered as aberrations in the objective view of science.

The logical consequence of the cognitivists' view is that the social world that social psychology would seek to explain is a contingent effect or illusion. This is either from the outside of the individual–society divide in the form of errors induced in the individual's attitudes, or from the inside as the produce of the judgements with which the individual constructs his or her world. Effectively we can say that with the individual so prone to error in line with the common-sense notion that 'we all make mistakes', the path is set for empiricist science to intervene with methodologies which can constrain the individual from the non-rational as, for example, Allport has social psychology protecting individuals against the lure of communist misinformation and society against subversion (see p. 66). In this way the erring individual can be coaxed nearer the truth of the rational unitary subject of science and accordingly, it is thought, progress can be made.

Prejudice in practice

So far I have traced the development of the notion of prejudice from Adorno's work, which recognized irrationality, and its effects, through Allport's emphasis on the notion of inaccurate judgement, to Tajfel's cognitivist explanation of it as error based on arbitrary mistakes. Each of these accounts considers prejudice as a counterpoint to correct rational behaviour, but each has different implications in practice. In what follows I shall examine how the explanation of prejudice as error has effects in contemporary political practices involving black people. These include the race relations industry, educational programmes, policing and government and other institutional formulations of the 'problem'. In each case the effects of the notion of prejudice hinge on the formulation of the nature of racial difference to which it contributes. Difference, as we shall see, has been variously considered as being due to unfamiliarity, ignorance and the exoticism of black people. Each of these explanations ties in with the 'no real difference' position on which the notion of prejudice is founded and evidences the extreme ambiguity of the way racial difference is regarded: as something that should be dispersed across housing estates, dissolved in mixed marriage or diluted in society's melting pot. The conditions of the production and effectively of knowledge, however, are too complex for us to read off political effects from the social psychology of racial prejudice.

It is clear from a comparison between the United States and the United Kingdom that despite a social psychology more or less in common, policies concerning race relations have been significantly different. For example, in *The Nature of Prejudice*, Allport reviews the findings of a number of American studies of the 1940s and 1950s that set out to test what has been called the contact hypothesis, according to which increased contact between racial groups reduced prejudice (Allport, 1954, ch. 16). He found that studies in specific settings, such as housing estates, professional exchanges and the army, produced considerable evidence in favour of the hypothesis. He also found that the degree of reduction in prejudice depended on other variables such as the relative status of the contacts and the level of prejudice in the first place. Another important variable was found to be the degree of common interest perceived between blacks and whites. This kind of evidence was used to support the beliefs about contact and integration already held by politicians at local, state and federal levels. For example, the policy of bussing children into schools to achieve a racial mix has been widely introduced and strongly contested, but adhered to over a long period.

In Britain, by contrast, the idea that familiarity could correct racial prejudice helped to legitimize a policy of doing nothing in the hope that blacks would eventually be assimilated. The theme of unfamiliarity as it is articulated in the contact hypothesis of American social psychology is closely paralleled in Britain in the 1960s, although with different policy developments. *Dark Strangers* was one of the early and influential books on race which set the tone for understanding the problem of prejudice as one of ignorance based on unfamiliarity (Patterson, 1963). The 'race relations industry', which grew up subsequently, perpetuated much of the kind of thinking that is contained in Patterson's book. A central position guiding its analysis is that blacks appear different because whites are unfamiliar with them. If they were familiar then apparent differences would disappear. This conviction appears from the opening lines of the study – described by the author as a 'sociological study of the *absorption* of a recent West Indian immigrant group in Brixton' (my italics) – in which she gives an account of her own 'colour shock': 'I was immediately overcome with a sense of strangeness, almost of shock . . . at least half of the exuberant infants playing outside the pre-fab nursery were *café noir* or *café au lait* in colouring' (Patterson, 1963, p. 3; italics in original). The colour terminology, and the effect of using French terms, are a vivid example of the exoticization of black people. It is significant that Patterson conveys this feeling in the context of talking about her own reaction to the unfamiliarity of black people. The feeling of difference and the reaction to it cannot successfully be cancelled out by a social psychology that rationalistically denies differences. The contradiction experienced by the social scientist and inscribed in social psychology's account concerning racial difference has been particularly paralysing for policy dealing with racism.

In Britain, the political effect of constituting the problem of prejudice as a lack of familiarity was a *laissez-faire* approach to the racism that black people had to face when we came as immigrant workers from the Caribbean and the Indian subcontinent. It was said to be the strangeness of blacks that caused prejudice leading to the mistrust and misunderstanding based on ignorance. Familiarity and consequently trust and understanding would only come with time, it was opined by the progressive liberals. Accordingly one of the solutions whose intelligibility is in part supplied by the notion is simply to take no action but wait for time to allow strangers to become familiars. The emphasis on the novelty and newness of the immigrants in newspaper editorials, parliament, the courts, police public relations statements, and in the ubiquitous common-sense voice of public opinion, made familiarization appear an automatic and natural process.

There is not the space here to consider in any detail the contrasting historical and political circumstances in the USA and Britain which led to different political strategies aimed at achieving familarity resulting from a more or less common understanding of racial prejudice. None the less, some broad differences can be indicated. The first is that between the history of slavery and twentieth-century European emigration to America and the history of British colonialism and black immigrant labour in Britain. Whatever the complex conditions of emergence, the practical political consequences were intervention in the USA and non-intervention in the UK. The violent urban crises of the 1960s must have contributed to the US administration's understanding of black/white difference as a problem which would not just go away if left alone. In Britain, the policy of ignoring the problem in the hope that it would go away could always be replaced by the notion of repatriation and the refusal to acknowledge that blacks belonged – the policy vociferously and violently advocated by the extreme right. It is significant in this regard that in the 1960s when the American government was compelled to address the issue of race, it did not draw on the idea of 'no real differences' that academic and liberal common-sense notions of prejudice asserted. Rather the *Report of the National Advisory Commission on Civil Disorders*, commissioned by President Johnson, is explicit in its discussion of institutional, white racism as one of the primary causes of black unrest (Kerner, 1968). As we saw at the beginning of this chapter, it was the charge of institutional racism that Lord Scarman was at pains to deny.

Thus what we are looking at is the way the different conditions in the USA produced different notions of the difference between blacks and whites. The differences could not be rendered superficial or denied, nor could American blacks be exoticized or removed. More recently in Britain, racism-awareness training has become in great demand, particularly in local government; this may reflect the greater similarity between conditions in American cities in the 1960s and in British cities in the 1980s. This approach, designed to change attitudes on race, was developed in the USA and is explicitly premised on the position that white racism, and not black people, is the problem (Katz, 1978). It is therefore not surprising that it draws nothing from the social psychology of racial prejudice (though it does use various humanistic and group-work approaches produced in a different tradition in psychology).

Education

In the field of education in Britain, the problem of 'unfamiliarity' has led, more recently, to active intervention, recalling the way in which the rationalism of the Enlightenment recommended learning as the cure for the ills of the poorer classes. In modern pedagogy this strategy has come to work hand in hand with the rationalism of science, seeing the provision of objective facts as the way to change attitudes and reduce prejudice. Rationality once again points the finger at ignorance as the problem: if we could all see the world as it really is, as objective facts, then we would have no grounds for prejudice. Also it incorporates the liberal position that white British people can learn to be less ethnocentric and less prone to stereotyping when they become familiar with other cultures. Currently such ideas are encapsulated under the label of 'multicultural' education. Social psychology's rationalism fits in with the rationalism of the kind of learning theory which underpins this approach. It is as if facts could be communicated without values. Thus, it is assumed that people will process them in an objective way and that their prejudices will be cancelled out since they were based, as we have seen, on the error of premature judgement.

The plethora of information packs, fact sheets, explanatory accounts of the reasons for immigation, descriptions of cultural habits – what Asians eat for breakfast – which have been produced by voluntary groups are all founded on the belief that once white people know all about blacks, the probems of prejudice will disappear. In the 1970s this public-education role was readily taken up by the newly established government-funded Community Relations Councils up and down the country, together with their central body, the Commission for Racial Equality. The development of the race-relations industry spawned a whole generation of race-relations experts – professionals whose job it was, especially if they themselves were black, to provide an understanding of blacks for whites. White remains the vantage point, the norm, from which black differences are measured and evaluated. To this end the ranks of countless sociology, psychology, anthropology, economics, geography and linguistic academics have made their contributions.

The notion of unfamiliarity and ignorance has the important effect of both paralleling and laying the way for the idea that blacks are themselves the problem. Multiculturalism thus expresses assumptions deriving from several areas: through it black people are exoticized for liberal whites to imitate 'ethnic' cooking, dress and music. While blacks remain the object in focus whites have no need to address themselves as the problem. It is in this way that social psychology has contributed to the production of blacks as the problem. Although this may appear inconsistent with social psychology's initial focus on white attitudes, I have tried to show that the logic of the dualism within which it operates makes this inevitable.

Information

Where the notion of prejudice is used to imply the need for the education of whites about blacks it might be thought that its effect was progressive or, at worst, neutral. The rationalism of the concept, however, makes it more dangerous. With the shift from looking at prejudiced individuals to looking at the objects of prejudice, the notion of prejudice in effect recommends that the problem of ignorance lies with black people as the unknown object rather than with the prejudiced individual as the unknowing subject. The rationalism of the concept of prejudice disguises the political implications of this move with notions of the objectivity of science and the rational need for neutral facts as the basis on which the problem can be solved. It does this by relying on and reinforcing the common-sense idea that 'facts allay fears', without the notion of prejudice itself ever providing any explanation of the fears such facts are supposed to abate.

The 'numbers game' played throughout the 1970s in Britain around figures on immigration from the Indian subcontinent is a testament to how the rationalism and individualism of the assumptions in the notion of prejudice channel discussion in such a way that neither liberals nor anti-racists are able to break from racism's agenda. The assumption, of course, that lies behind the whole immigration debate rests not on the supposed neutrality of scientific facts but on the political fact of racism that makes black people unwelcome in Britain. Thus the racist was bound to win the 'numbers game' just so long as it was played.

The assumptions contained in the notion of prejudice concerning information as the cure for ignorance makes it impossible to refuse demands for information given the implication that information should only help rational policy; in fact the more the better. In this respect the notion of prejudice surrounds and is surrounded by the same discourses that have informed the policies and practices on race of successive governments. Accordingly there is no good reason for refusing to answer Parliamentary Questions on the details of immigration figures or even the birth rates of black people born abroad, despite such information being requested by MPs like Enoch Powell or Harvey Proctor, whose views are well known. Similarly the Metropolitan Police have sheltered under the assumptions contained in the notion of prejudice. In 1982 they published for the first time a set of crime statistics that identified 'mugging' as a black crime. The consequent media attention given to the figures, together with their justification by the police on the grounds that the public had 'a need to know the facts', had the effect of branding the whole of the black community as criminal.

These two instances of the way in which the notion of prejudice can be used to serve racist ends are grounded, inevitably, in the concept's identification of black people as the problem, as I explained above. With the human object of prejudice as the subject for investigation, endeavours to measure our IQs, monitor birth rates and death rates, categorize migration and employment trends, and place the whole black community under the microscope to be dissected and quantified, have apparent scientific legitimacy. The fact that such requests for information on the black population have come from liberals and racists alike is not intended to suggest that such statistics are neutral scientific data which may be used or abused according to the intentions of those who gather the data. Rather it suggests the way in which the assumptions embedded in the notion of prejudice have their effects in practice. On the one hand stand the reformists who would like to use information on black people to argue for extra resources for housing, education or training, and so on. On the other are the racists for whom any black population figure is too large and evidence of the need for forced repatriation. Though the consequences of these two lines of argument may be different, their logic is the same – and is that of the notion of prejudice. As long as black people are seen as the problem then extra resources and repatriation are simply alternate faces of the same solution.

The manner in which the concept of prejudice identifies black people as the problem, bound up as it is with both scientific and common-sense notions of individualism and rationality, makes it impossible to use the concept to argue against its own racist effects. Such an argument has to come from outside the terms of the debate as set by the concept of prejudice. It has to challenge the neutrality of concepts and information gathered. It is only the rejection of the rationale of prejudice that can provide the basis for resistance. The task is therefore as political as it is theoretical. One such political campaign was that waged against the government's attempts to introduce a question on racial origin in the 1981 national census. The Haringey Black Women's Action Group and other organizations, such as the British Society for Social Responsibility in Science, helped to persuade black people not to return their test census forms on the ground of the government failure to demonstrate that it would make positive use of the information to the benefit of black people (see BSSRS, 1981). While such direct political interventions are of certain benefit when and where they can be mobilized, the individual participation required of the census making it a good issue to organize around, this type of challenge is very much the exception rather than the rule. This means that in most instances racist implications of the concept of prejudice are allowed full sway.

One example has been the blatantly racist proposals that came from the Select Committee on Race Relations and Immigration in its 1978 report (Select Committee, 1977–8). Here the Select Committee was able to draw on the rationality of the concept of prejudice both in its text and its surrounding assumptions and premises to justify the Committee's recommendations. One of these was for more money to be spent on the collection of information on immigration and on immigrants settled in Britain. Another was for the investigation of a system of 'internal immigration control' which it appears they thought should operate in the same manner as the pass-law system in apartheid South Africa. It is to these ends that the logic of the rationality of science and of the concept of prejudice in the British context has led.

Conclusions

My main contention in this chapter is that the social psychology of prejudice cannot have the progressive effects it may intend because of the limitations the dualism imposed on social psychological theorization. The nature of the 'individual' produced is premised on a rationalist idealization and the individual's social production is thus entirely externalized. This emphasis is not an ahistorical product of the science of social psychology. I have tried to show how theories of racial prejudice are productions, and how their take-up, inside and outside the discipline, depends on wider features of knowledges, power and practices. Thus the attempt of Adorno *et al.* to understand the production of a subjectivity which makes racist practices more likely suffered not only from the dualism within which the theory of personality remained trapped, but also from the rejection of approaches which did not approximate to dominant knowledges and practices and therefore to common sense. That the social psychology of racial prejudice is compatible with existing power relations is therefore hardly surprising: its production is bound up in those relations.

This does not mean, however, that I am arguing its inevitability. Rather, it implies that those who produce social-science knowledge (indeed any knowledge) should be aware of its specific historical conditions of production rather than assume that they are discoverers of immaculate truths. If knowledges were all consistent with the dominant power relations, it would be impossible to understand how they could have radical or reactionary effects. This being the case it can be said that the conditions in which the social psychology of racial prejudice was progressive have been superseded. The racist *status quo* is maintained to a large extent not only through coercive and blatantly racist practices, but through the liberal position which criticizes these as aberrations (precisely, as Lord Scarman criticizes the coercive racism of the police). I have thus argued that it is important to recognize the part played by social psychology's explanation of racism as residing within the information-processing mechanisms of individuals. Recognition of this – taken for granted within the assumptions of psychological theory – is one condition of producing a knowledge which challenges these assumptions about the nature of racism. It clearly rejects the reduction of prejudice to random error in the information-processing system.

It is just such a theorization and the development of the requisite analytic tools which is the project of this book. At this stage I can only indicate in what direction we can look for an understanding of racism which could provide a basis for an effective politics of intervention. We have characterized psychology's 'individual' as unitary and rational and, most important, reduced to biological or cognitive determinations as a result of individual–society dualism. What are the effects of these three features on the social psychology of racial prejudice and the production of the theories or politics of racism in general?

The premise of rational subjectivity (along with other conditions) has gradually produced a cognitivist account of prejudice. I have shown how Adorno's theory – partly because of its recognition of the non-rational character of prejudice – could propose no easy rational solutions. Any other theory of the departure by the individual from the scientist's standards of rational objectivity would require some concept of the non-rational, the subjective or the unconscious. Later in the book we shall advance two bases for understanding the non-unitary nature of subjectivity. One is the theorization of multiple positions which are available to people in discourses (see, particularly, chapters 4, 5 and 6) and the other is the recognition that subjectivity is not exclusively rational. People can have wishes and aspirations that pull in different directions. The norm of rationality promotes the suppression of contradiction. According to psychoanalytic theory repressed material is often dealt with by projection (a theory which Adorno *et al.* use in their account of prejudice). Systematic (unconscious) projection of denied characteristics onto another group results in the production of fantasized characteristics (see Sherwood, 1980, for a psychoanalytic account of British racism). If the power of knowledge production and associated practices is in the hands of one group – as it has been in the hands of whites – these attributions can contribute to the production of the other's subjectivity. Certainly blacks, like women, have been constructed as possessing the characteristics which are negatively valued in white western culture, for example emotionality, sexuality and hedonism. The valued norm remains white, blacks being evaluated according to their distance from it (see chapter 5 for a development of these arguments in relation to gender difference).

Without a theory of the production of social differences – between black and white or woman and man, for example – an account inevitably resorts to biology. We have already indicated that social theories which fall down on the other side of the dualism – which purport to explain social differences exclusively through historical and socioeconomic differences – are also reductive and caught in the vicious circle of the dualism. Of course the history of colonialism and white racism has been critical in producing race differences, but it cannot alone explain white racism or black subjectivity (see Fanon, 1968). The kind of theory of subjectivity which we are developing here will have some applications to this question.

Such a theory will have very different implications for practice because it will be able to recognize differences as a social or historical production (differences no less real for that). Unlike the position of the theory of racial prejudice today, there can therefore be a recognition of differences which do not reduce to biology. It is understandable that, given the history of biological theories of racial difference, a progressive position had no alternative but to deny difference (while it remained caught within dualism). But this idealism is now having serious political effects. To deny differences between blacks and whites means that the condition for successful intervention – the recognition of these differences and the analysis of their cause – cannot be achieved. Equally serious is that the awareness of differences, recognized in some and suppressed in others, lends plausibility to those theories which do base themselves on difference, but explain it in ways which have more pernicious, because determinist, implications.

Racism reproduces itself not only mechanically at an economic and social level but also through the power relations between white and black people and the subjectivities which these produce and reproduce in both. A non-dualistic theory of subjectivity can indicate strategies for change at this level to parallel and strengthen structural change.

Introduction to Section 2

Constructing the subject

The individual–society dichotomy both in social science and in politics has meant that radical critiques in the past have tended to look for answers to the problem of change in social theory, that is, in analyses that addressed 'society' rather than the individual. Thus political critiques of psychology's assumptions, highlighting its fundamental individualism, have dismissed its relevance to understanding change. That dismissal included the question of the place and importance of changing subjects in relation to the transformation of 'society'.

All of us to some extent took this path and only gradually recognized that retaining dualism reproduced an equivalent but opposite set of problems for social theory, namely that the latter, in its turn, remained blind to the process of subjective change. By and large, social theory, until the critique of positivism, took comfort in the supposed objectivity of its emphasis on social structure and global processes. However, it has not been atrophied by positivism to the same extent as psychology; the problems posed by the necessity of changing consciousness have generally been recognized.

For the above reason we find it useful to begin by summarizing recent debates on the left and in some social theory in order to outline how we arrive at our present theoretical position. In doing this, we make sense of present theoretical issues by showing their ancestry, and introduce readers to some of the concepts required to follow the alternative perspectives developed in chapters 3 and 4.

The line of argument in this section does not take us as far as a changed subject of psychology in the sense of beginning a new theorization of subjectivity; that task is the project of section 3. It does, however, explain our emphasis on two points: on 'meaning', or signification, and on practices and their effects. First we show how 'meaning' became an issue for radical social theory through the problem of how to change 'ideas'. Theories of ideology as false consciousness, theories of representation and theories of signification followed. None succeeded in theorizing the subject adequately. For different reasons, it has left almost as much of an empty space in social theory as in psychological theory.

However there is another set of criticisms of orthodox Marxist social theory which leads us to draw upon a range of recent radical perspectives in attempting to sketch more fruitful lines of approach to the problem of subjectivity. For example, Foucault (1982), along with writers who would nowadays be regarded as post-structuralists, claims to be addressing the question of the constitution of subjects directly. But the vital contribution in approaches such as Foucault's lies elsewhere: it is that they help deconstruct the monolithic, unitary character of power and the social domain which has characterized Marxist functionalist and structuralist social theory alike. This enables us to make links between a diverse and contradictory social domain and the multiple and contradictory subject.

First, though, we need to conceptualize knowledges – here psychology – as an integral part of the processes that constitute the social domain. In this view psychology is neither progressing towards scientific truth nor is it in conspiracy with the powers that be to oppress ordinary people. In order to move away from the taken-for-granted claim that they are motivated by the objective search for truth we emphasize the necessity of tracing historically the conditions of possibility of knowledges. The point of view we are developing starts out from the proposition that all knowledges are productive in the specific sense that they have definite effects on the objects one seeks to know. For the social sciences these effects are not separable from the practices of administration to which these sciences are tied. This means that in examining how and why psychology has come to be what it is, it is crucial to account for the effects inside it of historically specific circumstances that refer to social practices and to other discourses centred on the individual (for example, biology or philosophy).

In chapter 3 we illustrate our approach by tracing the historical conditions which permitted the emergence of psychology's subject: the individual. This reconstruction enables us to escape the assumption of the fact or naturalness of the individual and to see psychology as a body of knowledges with specific effects on our conceptualization of the individual. This also enables us to step outside this assumption in theorizing the subject.

The object of deconstruction as exemplified in chapter 4 is more specific; it takes for its target cognitive development as it is captured and formalized in Piagetian theory. The chapter illustrates the necessity of providing a historical context for the production of psychological theories, and shows how they are inseparable from their take-up in practice. One of the specific themes developed establishes that the insertion of Piaget's notion of child development into progressive pedagogical practice cannot be separated from the social and political conditions surrounding that practice.

Humanism

We approach the deconstruction of the central object of psychology, namely the individual subject, by way of the debate around humanism in Marxism. This will enable us to introduce a number of key concepts which have become the currency for the retheorization of subjectivity. Equally, it involves reviewing the issues which circumscribe both the debate and the attempts to provide a new perspective. The fact that the individual–society split, thought to be peculiar to psychology, reappears in various forms in other contemporary areas is consistent with our analysis of the fundamental assumptions of the social sciences. A clearer understanding of what was at stake in the polemics surrounding the humanism–anti-humanism debate should help establish what it is we are trying to move away from. They have a relatively long history. For instance, structuralism's anti-humanism contains reverberations running from the 'death of man' announced by Nietzsche to and through Lévi-Strauss's 'death of the subject'. The same rejection is echoed in Freud's decentring of the rational cogito on the one hand and, on the other, in Marx's critique of Feuerbach's foundation of the purpose of history in 'man'. Echoes of these polemics are still very much in the air today, for example in E. P. Thompson's (1978) attack on Althusser and in the issues raised by the peace movement regarding the strategy and grounds on which nuclear proliferation should be resisted. For example, are simple humanist defences of the sanctity of life enough, or should campaigning aim to attack militarism itself?

The central issue in these debates is the place of 'man' in social and political change, that is to say, it concerns the question of how initiatives and responsibility are to be divided up between the individual, the party and the class. The humanist position tends to see the individual as the agent of all social phenomena and productions, including knowledge. The specific notion of the individual contained in this outlook is one of a unitary, essentially non-contradictory and above all rational entity. It is the Cartesian subject in modern form; a notion of the subject which has been central to the whole of western philosophy founded on the principle of the cogito (see chapter 3 for details).

Cartesian subject

Taking a stance firmly on the social side of the dualist divide, both structuralism and Marxism have taken as their target this notion of the individual as agent of change. Althusser's anti-humanism combines these two positions in attacking as bourgeois any attribution of agency to the individual, and in privileging the structure of a social formation in the determination of the individual's behaviour and make-up.

Although the recent history of the anti-humanist position is most closely associated in the UK with the name of Althusser, it had its point of departure in a wider and earlier intellectual current which had started to question the roles of the Communist Party and of scientific socialism in the transformation of capitalist society. In France, the title of Merleau-Ponty's *Humanism and Terror* (1947 and 1969) aptly encapsulates the poles of what was at stake in the debate. Another key response was Sartre's contention that his existential philosophy, revaluing individual intentions, was consistent with both humanism and Marxism. The theoretical issues involved were taken up in Sartre's *Critique of Dialectical Reason* (1960) and in a number of debates about the place of Hegel's philosophy in Marxism. (Some of these issues had been fuelled by the 'rediscovery' of Hegel, through Hyppolite and Kojève, and the reappraisal of the 'early' Marx.) These debates all continued the search for a more complex Marxist philosophy and theory of society than had been provided in Lenin's and in Stalin's versions of dialectical materialism. In Germany it was the critique elaborated by the Frankfurt School that reopened questions of the place of 'man' in Marxist theory. The Italian Communist Parties, in contrast with their European counterparts, were developing some of the issues raised by Gramsci's concept of hegemony. (Even now, it is instructive for the kind of work developed in this volume to look at some of the passages in the *Prison Notebooks* where Gramsci discusses the way in which individuals are a mixture of 'subjectivities' locked in common-sense understandings and played out in social practices.) In Britain, finally, the humanist interest surfaced in a different form as part of a radical culturalism that gradually moved towards developing Marxist theories of culture, for example in the more recent work of Raymond Williams and the Centre for Contemporary Cultural Studies.

By and large, then, the humanist position asserted by the left stood for the defence of 'human freedom' and pleasures against the oppressive practices of the Soviet Gulags and the implied suppression of the individual in socialist strategies which advocated the subordination of individual needs to the goal of establishing the socialist state. To the extent that the latter position found support in mechanistic Marxism – that is to say, the view which explained all human misery, alienation and exploitation as effects of the capitalist mode of production – the defence and reconstruction of Marxism by Althusser meant a rejection both of humanism and of economism in Marxist theory. A number of ambiguities inscribed in the humanism–anti-humanism debate find their source in this theoretical conjuncture. The dilemmas he faced are not easily surmountable. For example, a successful defence of Marxism had to incorporate an explanation of human conduct which took account of subjectivity, whereas the old theory returned everything to class belonging (the argument referred to as class reductionism). On the other hand, such an explanation had to avoid the simple reintroduction of the humanist individual, the unitary rational subject as agent of all social phenomena and productions. A number of ambiguities inscribed in the humanism–anti-humanism debate find their source in this theoretical difficulty of escaping explanations which privilege either the subject or the structure.

Althusser's theory of ideology

In the main, Althusser's reworking of Marx and his anti-humanist position in his earlier work – *For Marx*, *Reading Capital* and *Lenin and Philosophy and Other Essays* – should be seen as an attempt to provide Marxism with the 'philosophy it deserves' without succumbing to the pitfalls of humanism, that is, without lending support to the liberal politics of bourgeois individualism and without undermining the Communist Party as the vanguard of the revolution. In addition, he also had to defend Marxism in the face of attacks in the form of the accusation of ideological dogmatism. We are familiar with this line of attack from orthodox social scientists like Daniel Bell (1961) and philosophers of science like Karl Popper (1957). In this context the theoretical strengths on which Althusser was able to draw were provided by structuralism, whose central theses were the critique of the notion of the individual as both the ultimate origin and the destination of history and the concomitant emphasis on social, linguistic and cultural structures as the determinant elements in the explanation of social phenomena.

There are a number of key theoretical problems implicated in the Althusserian enterprise and in structuralism. They have to do with a theory of history, with an account of causality and with the criteria of the scientificity of science. Clearly all these issues connect with an account of the process of production of knowledge. However, since we have chosen to focus on the questions directly relevant for rethinking the theorization of the subject, we shall orientate our discussion in that direction.

Is the subject constitutive or constituted? On the one hand Althusser poses it in terms of a process of constitution. Yet the same subject is banished from the scene in his theorization of science as a 'theoretical practice' without a subject. The dilemma is, as we have said, to advocate the reality and effectivity of the subject produced by and in ideological processes (through 'interpellation', as we shall explain below), yet at the same time to dissolve the individual subject of humanism and bourgeois individualism. In order to do this, two sets of problems had to be overcome. First, an account was needed which presented the individual not as a pregiven entity but as a constituted 'always-already social' being, a being locked in ideological practices. This was the way to explain the social constitution of people in a particular social formation. Second, Althusser had to find a formula which did not reintroduce the Cartesian subject through the back door (the same problem that we have referred to in the case of Mead and others, which in extreme form is the problem of the homunculus). The notion of a process without a subject seemed to satisfy the requirement that the status of historical materialism as a science be put beyond the reach of the accusation of Marxism as ideological, representing subjective interests. Yet an agency was necessary to effect social transformation. For Althusser that agency was class struggle, and its representative was the revolutionary party. In this way, historical materialism would be the scientific theory guiding the party in the class struggle. This appears neatly to sidestep the role of the individual, who is caught in the web of ideologies, but who can escape because the science of revolution provides the conceptual means for so doing. However, because Althusser did not account for the effectivity of class struggle and because the Party signally failed to deliver the revolution in 1968 when the conditions in France seemed promising, the whole question of agency and the subject became reproblematized in the late 1960s.

We should add that the events of 1968 did not provide the only conditions for this questioning. Earlier, work done by Lacan in psychoanalysis (utilized in Althusser's notion of interpellation), by Barthes in semiotics and by Foucault and Derrida in the history of both knowledge and the production of discourse (to cite only the more familiar figures) – all of this work has challenged the view of the subject outlined above. In addition, we want to stress that the changes were internal neither to theory nor to Marxist politics. For the liberation struggles of the time, class struggle was an unsuitable – in some ways an oppressive – principle. For feminism, for example, the Cartesian subject was patriarchal, premised on a specific form of rationality, something which Althusser did not begin to address. The new challenges, then, did not attempt simply to substitute the individual agent with some other equally originary and unitary agent such as class, or to sweep the issue under the carpet of scientific objectivity. It became more a question of thinking how different subjectivities could be constituted and how they would be differently located and locked into ideological practices. Althusser's response to these historical circumstances – though it still left his earlier antihumanism basically untouched – was to develop a more sophisticated understanding of the relation of ideology and the subject. Part of that understanding was to theorize the ideological as a level which, though determined 'in the last instance' by the economic, was in practice 'relatively autonomous'. Ideologies, in any case, were not 'ideas' but had real material existence in a variety of social apparatuses in which subjects 'lived' their specific positions. He argued that the primary 'ideological state apparatuses' in modern times are the family, the church and the school (different ones being differentially effective depending on the historical epoch). These Ideological State Apparatuses produced individuals as subjects in such a way that they participated in reproducing capitalism.

Althusser's formulation of the 'relative autonomy' of the ideological was a radical challenge to economism from within Marxist theory. What was the process by which people's ideas could be relatively autonomous from the forces and relations of production? Some notion of the subject – other than class struggle – is essential in this account. Althusser's answer was to make a distinction between the 'real' and 'imaginary' relations to the economy. In so doing he could break with the idea of ideology as a simple representation. If people were mere effects of the conditions in which they lived, their relation to the economy would be 'real'. The nub of Althusser's use of the 'imaginary' is that people act 'as if' the ideological were 'real' and by doing this, make it the reality they 'live'. This argument threatens to trap him back into the humanism he is determined to escape. In order to avoid this, he maintains that agency is an effect of the subject's self-delusion. To this extent his formulation (remaining anti-humanist) sidesteps the problem of the prior asocial individual (the Cartesian subject). But he is still left with a problem, and this becomes evident in his notion of 'interpellation'. Ideological State Apparatuses work by 'interpellating' subjects (rather as the social other 'interpellates' the 'I' in Meadian social psychology). The subject recognizes her/himself as such through a process of recognition whereby the authority of the institution and its representatives, for example the parents and teachers, 'hail' the individual. S/he recognizes her/himself through this relation, which is imaginary. In this view, the subject does not exist prior to its hailing or interpellation.

But in this formulation a logical problem is posed: what is the nature of the entity that must already exist in some prior form in order to recognize her/himself in the interpellation? It is the age-old problem of the homunculus again: the prior entity which rears its head (sacred or profane depending on the epoch) as long as the terms of the individual–society dualism are not transcended.

Furthermore, although Althusser challenged the classical view of ideology, he did not completely avoid the problem of representation because his notion of 'determination in the last instance' relates to an untheorized real: the economy appears as an independently constructed domain which has a constitutive effect on 'representations', including 'ideologies' and thus on subjects.

Clearly, we need to provide theoretical indications that go beyond Althusser. His own approach, though, has made that work possible; in particular, his use of Lacanian psychoanalysis to make the link between the 'relatively autonomous' domain of 'ideas' and language on the one hand, and the subject and the unconscious on the other. The approach for which we shall argue stresses the primacy of signification as opposed to representation, the main difference being that signification as the process of making sense does not represent anything, rather it is a production.

An extensive literature now exists which uses this concept in order to refer to the processes whereby meaning is produced at the same time as subjects are fabricated and positioned in social relations.

Representation

We shall outline our arguments and the recasting of the problem of the constitution of subjects by focusing on the theoretical concept of representation. We do this in order to draw out the connections that lead to the point of view that significations are produced and lived in everyday practices and social relations and that subjects are constituted and located as part of these same practices.

In psychology the idea of representation is used to conceptualize the relation between individual's information-processing procedures and external reality. Basically, the former is thought to represent the latter through the processes of perception and cognition. Thus thought would in some way be a representation of reality. In representation theory's more empiricist form, the relation is conceptualized in terms of a correspondence.

The same point of view in social theory, when applied to ideology, regards it as a particular representation of social reality. However, its theoretical attention is not fixed on the information-processing mechanisms which are thought to mediate between the two terms of the duality. Instead, it focuses on the distorting effects which ideology is supposed to have on these mechanisms. Therefore, it is not so much concerned with the objects or phenomena perceived as with the social factors which occasion 'distortion', such as class and ethnic category. This theory, then, explains any perception of social reality different from accepted, 'normal' description in terms of a distorted representation attributable to class or to subcultural belonging.

In orthodox Marxism, for example, it is the forces and relations of production constituting the capitalist mode of production which are thought to occasion ideological distortions. In particular, bourgeois ideology is seen as the system of ideas whereby the relations of production are represented in such a way that their oppressive nature is hidden. Classically, one could say that the relation of the ideological representation to the 'real' is the relation of appearance to essence or phenomenal form to real form. The determinant forces at work would be those locked in the economy, so that the source or cause of ideology refers to the economic position of class agents.

For example, where psychology would describe women's 'dependence' as a personality characteristic – innately determined and probably overlaid with learning from sex-role stereotypes – orthodox Marxist theory accounts for the behaviours attaching to 'dependence' in terms of women's dependent or subordinate position in the economy. In general, the economic level would determine subjective behaviour, including women's psychic make-up.

However, the details of the processes whereby these mechanisms of distortion or ideological positioning have their effects were lacking in representation theory. In the light of its failure to account for the political allegiances and developments in the 1960s, for instance the successful recruitment of part of the working-class by the right or the development of feminism, it became necessary to re-examine both orthodox Marxist theory and the notion of representation implicated in it.

We have already signalled the form of this rejection when we emphasized the term signification and its productive rather than reflective character. The argument is that the reality represented does not determine the representation or the means of representation. Instead, the process of signification itself gives shape to the reality it implicates.

It might be asked if this argument is merely inverting the language–thought couple so familiar in psychology. Is it asserting the primacy of language over thought in a kind of latter-day Whorfian hypothesis? If the argument were about language one might indeed infer that this was the case. However, the use of the term signification, and what Kristeva (1969, 1974) has called 'signifying practices', attempts to go beyond the language–thought dualism and the linguistic concept of language (see chapter 6, p. 281) by incorporating content in a way quite outside the scope of modern structural linguistics. That is, the argument is not that words determine but that those practices which constitute our everyday lives are produced and reproduced as an integral part of the production of signs and signifying systems.

This thesis is crucial to the position developed here because the issue of the real and representation, the posing of the relations of determination, is as critical for individual psychology as it is for social theory. In the language–thought couple, the issue is individualized (Chomsky reduces language to structural universals which in turn reduce to Language Acquisition Devices in the brain). Even Whorf's example of the eskimos' twenty-six words for snow fails to locate words as part of social practices in any convincing way. Furthermore, in the theories of ideology we have examined, the individual is an empty space.

The thesis we are proposing is not a simple inversion of the conventional relationship between language and social reality. It does privilege practice, but we want to justify this, bearing in mind that we regard theory as itself the product of certain specific practices of academic work. We shall do this, first, by examining some work which has developed the idea of the productivity of signification and, second, by extending signification to produce the notion of discursive (rather than signifying) practice, which includes the conception of social regulation. Third, we shall argue that it is not a case of 'discourse determinism' as some critics of Foucault would suggest. By this we mean that we have not thrown out the real, nor have we taken it to be in some sense determined by discourse, but have attempted radically to deconstruct the notion of causal determination itself.

Genealogy

The use of Foucault's approach to histories of the production of knowledge is an important feature of our theoretical enterprise. We use it in two ways which do not immediately come together. First, it permits the reconceptualization of psychology as a body of knowledge. This involves retracing its history from the recognition of the complexity and historicity of its production and development. Second, this alternative approach provides a starting point where the couple 'individual' and 'society' no longer constrains the questions posed because from the outset it is problematized: both are regarded as effects of a production to be specified, rather than as the pregiven objects of the human sciences. It is from this point of view that this new history feeds into the task of retheorizing the subject of psychology.

The lines of descent which Foucault is interested in tracing are those of concepts such as sexuality, madness and the individual. They are the concepts central both to the human sciences and in the administrative and regulatory practices which are formative of the relation between people and the apparatuses of administration. So, already, the discourse which is the object of analysis is not a discipline to be examined in terms of its internal rules of formation, but a set of specific discursive practices dispersed in a variety of social apparatuses which have sexuality, mental illness, etc. for their targets.

Furthermore, Foucault's history is not a history of ideas in the sense of starting out from some clear or accepted definition of, say, sexuality and describing its development. Indeed, the point of the new kind of history is to reconstitute the conceptual object from a point of view located in the present in such a way that the history produced is one which has calculated effects concerning present strategies for action (say about an object such as sexuality). This approach has many important theoretical implications for our project. Before drawing these out and developing the conceptual elements of our analytical method we shall use some concrete examples to establish the differences we have just claimed.

There have been a number of attempts to write genealogies of the human sciences, for example Donzelot's (1979), Rose (1979), Jones and Williamson (1979), to mention those studies close to the concerns of this book. Although there are recognized problems with all these exemplars, it is possible to pick out those insights which inform our own task. The first observation is that these kinds of studies start out from a perspective that already assumes that knowledges, for example psychology, are productions involving the participation of wider social practices. From such a point of view, one is already convinced that psychological discourse is inscribed in a network of practices which produce subjects in the multiple sites of their constitution such as the school, the family, the hospital, etc. Indeed, a genealogy is a history of the present precisely to the extent that it is structured by conclusions and considerations already established concerning present practices and institutions. This is not to say that the new history is a search for confirmation; rather one must start from a number of specific theoretical premises that direct the 'archaeological' investigation of the traces of the present. For instance, Rose contends that one must dissolve the demarcation between 'internal' and 'external' histories of psychological knowledge – always bearing in mind that one cannot read off the effects of the one on the other – thus immediately opening psychological discourses up for the effects of social practices in them; this enables one to seek in these practices the conditions of possibility of psychology.

Rose's analysis of mental measurement demonstrates the complex set of conditions and of mutual effects between educational practices and policies and psychological conceptual tools such as the notion of intelligence. The latter is seen as an integral part of this development of conceptual, technical and administrative apparatuses for training people, neither the product nor the originary conception. Importantly, what the analysis demonstrates is the extent to which mental measurement emerged and developed as part of the practices which administered individuals, securing their regulation and disciplining. These practices form a social technology; techniques for the mass measurement of individuals were part of that technology.

Similarly, chapter 4 argues that developmental psychology, in this case Piaget's work, must be understood in relation to the practices of administration indicated above and to a pedagogic discourse centred on the individual child. Departing from the usual histories which examine Piaget's theories and findings in terms of its internal coherence as a body of scientific work, the chapter starts out by searching for the conditions of possibility of such a theorization and describes its production by reference to an apparatus which includes existing discourses about children and their 'development', about biological processes and about rationality, as well as practices of education and training which have to do with establishing social relations and their imbrication in the materiality of specified, regulated forms of activity.

Chapter 4 demonstrates that the scientific object of developmental psychology, namely the developing child, is a product of a particular kind of discursive enterprise and not an independently pregiven object about which psychologists 'make discoveries'. It emphasizes that whilst there is a relation between the theoretical object of say, Piaget – the mind – and a specific materiality, the importance of a genealogy is to work out how and why that object is constructed in its specificity and how that specificity is anchored to social practices. That demonstration is part of understanding the way in which children have become the object of specific practices such as schooling and the function of developmental psychology in them. The emergence of the child both as an object of scientific enquiry and as the target in a number of what can be regarded as *normalizing practices* (e.g. schooling, child-rearing) is part of the production of the individual as the 'normal' subject-form. Indeed, the presupposition of the individual as a unitary entity, a thinking, feeling machine which is self-directed as far as thought processes are concerned, is basic to a child-centred pedagogy and to developmental psychology. It has become part of the common-sense taken-for-granted background for these practices. The science of psychology at once confirms this 'truth' whilst depending on it for its own intelligibility.

In the deconstruction of developmental psychology chapter 4 highlights other key conditions and parameters of its production: the growth of state intervention in education, psychiatry, social work, child-rearing, health, criminality and work; the concern about ensuring the health and capability of the population as a whole (a lesson learnt from the Boer War); and, later, in the atmosphere of fascism and the Russian Revolution, the widespread liberal assertion of the fundamental rationality of the human mind.

The interest in the means of classification of individuals became paramount. For example, Burt in Britain, Binet in France and Cattell in America achieved their fame mainly through developing new advances in statistical method to quantity and render scientific the categorization of individuals. Mass instruments such as the IQ test were above all practical, quick and cost-effective. Children were categorized and placed, their paths into more or less privileged positions in life dictated to them by a science which purported to know everything of importance based on the answers to a few questions and puzzles, by a science which presumed to decree that the key factor – be it 'intelligence' or 'personality' – would not change to any significant extent because it was determined by heredity. Such was the dominance of innatist assumptions about people (within the general dominance of biologistic discourses) that the early theories of intelligence and personality did not even have to be defended.

By the 1930s, positions were being voiced emanating from a more radical view of society stressing the necessity of social and economic change. Conditions in the recession were difficult to attribute to individual biology. In the United States, there was the particular, though widespread, question of the assimilation of thousands of immigrants. This makes sense of the preoccupation of social scientists with 'socialization': how were the people to be or become fitted to a different culture? Martin Richards comments that 'as that common identity was seen to emerge, it was not unnatural that social scientists should be impressed by the apparent effectiveness of schools and other institutions in moulding children to their new way of life' (1974b, p. 6). These conditions cast light on what Danziger in his introduction to the classic text on socialization simply refers to as 'the operation of a powerful undercurrent of ideas' (1971, p. 13) which emerged simultaneously in sociology, anthropology and psychology.

However, although this emphasis on the way the social world influences individuals had been progressive, challenging as it did, biological determinism, along with it went the implication of passive individuals moulded by social influence. It marked a very definite tilting of the balance in favour of society rather than the individual.

Theories of development and of schooling show the mark of these historically specific events and concerns. It is this complex interplay of conditions that chapter 4 explores to provide a different account of how pedagogy is as it is today. Clearly, it is far from an epistemological critique of theories' claims to be scientific or to describe the truth.

Interestingly, the questions which genealogical approaches pose are very different from those of traditional histories and most radical critiques. For example, it is no longer a question of whether specific data support a given theory or explanation, or simply of pointing to gaps and inadequacies. Instead, the questions have to do with why a specific notion of the subject as the individual entity should have become part of the home truths of psychology; why child development theory has taken the form it has; why the monitoring of this development has become the core of 'scientific pedagogy' and teachers' practice, encapsulated in terms like 'individualized learning', 'child-centred approach', etc.; what administrative strategies and requirements conditioned the emergence of specific psychological theories; what effects they had on each other; and how this whole network constructs the social domain with all its contradictions and differences as well as its regularities.

The field of research for these histories moves outside the internal calculations within the subdiscipline of psychometrics or developmental psychology to look for their conditions of possibility in other 'outside' practices and considerations. But they are not any possible conditions. They are the debates, the official reports, actual problems in schooling, real events such as the first world war, the level of crime and the state of the poor; a genealogy considers also the effects of all this on a variety of calculations, on developments in other disciplines such as biology. That is to say, these conditions are historically specific events and bodies of statements which have had demonstrable effectivity in the development of mental measurement or of the theorization of cognitive development.

One can retrace this complex by going back to the archival material and reconstructing a picture of development which seems possible and coherent. Note that internal histories have already covered over these historical traces by constructing an account which founds the coherence of the discipline in the rational calculations interior to it: its system of evidences – the data – its theoretical assumptions and underpinnings, its methodological protocols. Thus the claims of psychometric propositions and practices to rationality and truth are underwritten by their assumed scientific character and vice versa. It is for that reason that an initial task is to deconstruct its internal history as it is presented through the scientific articles and texts. The intention here is to show that the plausibility and rationality of any scientific specialism depends on a number of key assumptions and propositions established outside the specialism itself, both in contiguous specialisms and other disciplines and in wider, culturally shared beliefs. We might note that this is a conclusion supported by several studies in the 'hard sciences' beloved by positivists, and other sociologists of knowledge (see Venn, 1982, for a review).

What this kind of deconstruction asserts is that any given body of statements, whether in everyday conversation or a scientific paper, depends on a number of other bodies of statements, some of which carry deeply entrenched convictions and explanatory schemas fundamental to the dominant form of making sense of the world at any particular period in a culture. Deconstruction retraces the system of 'dependencies' of a discourse. At the same time, it also has a positive foundation, in that it reconstructs a history which accounts for how a discourse or practice emerged, for the conditions of its emergence and constitution (discursive, material and historical) and for how it comes to be what it is at the present. Foucault calls this kind of history a genealogy: a trace that reconstitutes the present from its traces in the past.

Clearly, different genealogies are possible, depending on the work to which a genealogy is put (and the erudition and judgement of the author, as Canguilhem, 1977, has argued). Nevertheless, not any genealogy is possible or warranted. Genealogy is constrained, like any other discourse, by its location in relation to other systems of statements, indeed, by its co-articulation with them; it is constrained by certain established historical evidences (for example, the theory of relativity did not emerge in the seventeenth century, and psychology at the turn of the twentieth century did not use concepts from nuclear physics). Genealogy is a history of the present in the sense that it finds its points of departure in problems relevant to current issues and finds its point of arrival and its usefulness in what it can bring to the analysis of the present.

There are problems with this kind of history which we shall briefly evoke later. For the moment, we want to highlight a number of other key features of our analytical framework in order to clarify the theoretical issues and make our own assumptions and point of view more explicit.

Discourse

The term 'discourse' features prominently in recent analyses of the production of knowledge. We have used it already, implicitly referring to its most general sense as any regulated system of statements. In an uncontentious way this can apply to everything that can be said and runs the risk of being too all-inclusive, too imprecise, to be of much use.

Discourse in this general sense has a long ancestry. Furthermore, a technique of analysing utterances that calls itself discourse analysis already exists in psycholinguistics. It is not by reference to these usages that we define discourse, but within modern semiotics and recent accounts of the production of knowledge. For instance, whilst the theoretical reference of psycholinguistics is to structural linguistics, with its emphasis on structural analysis and its relative neglect of content, discourse in the literature we are signalling here is centrally concerned with content. Indeed, part of its task is to uncover the intimate relation of structure and content, signifier and signified. Even there, however, the concept is not unproblematic. The accusation of 'discourse babble' that began to surface a few years ago when the term first erupted in public places does put the finger on an extravagant vagueness concerning the limits of application of the term. Is everything discourse? Are all practices and all subjects captured within the expansive nets of the discursive? Can we escape from it? Part of the difficulty in clarifying this recalcitrant concept is that the usage to which we allude is tied to a variety of theoretical work stretching from semiotics to the philosophical themes developed by Derrida and Deleuze and to the histories of knowledge that Foucault has attempted in examining the emergence and functioning of the human sciences. It also includes more specific analyses of discourse in its relation to the subject and to ideology, as in the work of Pêcheux (1975), Henry (1977) or Kristeva (1969 and 1974). We will consider discourse theory's theorization of the subject and power in section 3.

We can specify several other features of our approach to the analysis of the production of knowledge through the use of discourse theory. Our initial definition of discourse has highlighted the fact that it is regulated and systematic. An important proposition is related to this recognition: the rules are not confined to those internal to the discourse, but include rules of combination with other discourses, rules that establish differences from other categories of discourse (for example scientific as opposed to literary, etc.), the rules of production of the possible statements. The rules delimit the sayable. But (except for axiomatic systems such as chess) they do not imply a closure. The systematic character of a discourse includes its systematic articulation with other discourses. In practice, discourses delimit what can be said, whilst providing the spaces – the concepts, metaphors, models, analogies – for making new statements within any specific discourse. For example, concepts and developments in biology provided some of the key models and metaphors about the human organism and population which the discourses of mental measurement and of cognitive development, as in Piaget, utilized in the production of their propositions and findings. Furthermore, the latter had to be consistent with the models used. Equally, the further elaboration of genetics from the 1920s made possible a recasting of the explanations of differences in the performance of so-called cognitive tasks (see chapter 4).

The analysis which we propose regards every discourse as the result of a practice of production which is at once material, discursive and complex, always inscribed in relation to other practices of production of discourse. Every discourse is part of a discursive complex; it is locked in an intricate web of practices, bearing in mind that every practice is by definition both discursive and material. The problem is to decide which discourses and practices in a specific instance such as mental measurement constitute the complex, what effects the different parts of the complex have and for what reasons.

Discourse and genealogy: sciences and technologies of the social

The term 'sciences and technologies of the social' refer to this complex relation between the social sciences and the exigencies and constraints that are part of the administrative and regulative processes of the population. Foucault suggests that the social sciences are discourses and practices that positively help to construct the various apparatuses and institutions that together form 'society', or rather the 'social'. The social sciences, then, are actively imbricated in the practices and relations between people that constitute social existence. It is from that point of view that we regard the production of discourses and that of subjectivity and of sociality to be indissoluble. This is radically different from the approaches in sociological analyses. Indeed the term social is meant to mark a break from the sociological concept of 'society', which tends to regard it as an already given independently produced entity; sometimes it is attributed with volition or agency as in the expressions 'society effects', 'the impact of society on the individual' or 'society makes demands, has needs', etc. The concept of the social is used to problematize the complex of processes and relations which are glossed over in the term society. The former emphasizes that these processes are what analysis needs to specify. It stresses the constantly changing character of social relations and relations of power, that is to say, their mobility. And in dissolving the category of society as a unity, the concept of the social at the same time reopens the other term in the couplet individual–society.

Thus the rejection of the prime theoretical objects of the social sciences – namely, society and the individual – puts on the agenda two related questions, namely, what kind of knowledges do these sciences establish and what are the main principles of the different approaches we are proposing in order to produce these new objects: the subject and the social?

Several implications concerning the analysis of social-scientific discourse can be drawn out. First, there is a gap between the sciences and technologies so that there is both an interdependence and relative independence of their objects and concerns; for instance, between the practices we call schooling, learning theory and cognitive development: we can neither read off the take-up of concepts from what we know about the practice, nor disregard the effects on theory of practical, instrumental tasks arising from schooling.

Second, we need to pay attention to what these sciences positively construct in the domain of the social (their 'positivity', to use Foucault's term). There is a series of arguments connected with this point of view which we cannot develop in detail here. But we can summarize one salient aspect which informs our overall approach, namely that the sciences help to construct the norms that become the ideal behavioural goals valued in the practices of the social. Thus, the social sciences also have a *normative function* with respect to social relations. We should note that in constructing these norms, the sciences work upon principles and assumptions that are inscribed both in the discriplines themselves and in existing practices. For example, in the construction of tests for the eleven-plus exams, the fact that early tests showed a higher percentage of girls than boys succeeding was taken to be a practical problem for the distribution of places for grammar school entry; the mean on the girls' distribution was consequently changed so that fewer girls would be included in the upper quartiles, thus favouring boys in the selection process for grammar schools (see Walden and Walkerdine, 1981).

Third, technologies of the social bring into play a complex combination of several normative discourses. And since these discourses are not themselves devoid of contradictions, nor are they necessarily coherent among themselves, the relation of, say, psychology and pedagogy to practices of the social (for example, schooling) is complex, mobile and to some extent indeterminate.

Foucault's emphasis on specific technologies of the social recalls Althusser's notion of ideological state apparatuses. However, the latter places heavy emphasis on the role of the state and slides into a functionalist reading in which an ideological state apparatus functions for explicit goals determined by the state's interest in control and in domination.

The contrast with Foucault is in this monolithic state power. For Foucault, schooling, prisons, regulation of sexuality, and social work interventions in the family have been produced in specific historical circumstances, sharing some conditions of possibility and not others. They are not predestined, as in functionalism, to pull together. Nevertheless, demonstrable mutual effects exist between social scientific discourses and administrative practices regulating schools, families, hospitals, prisons and so forth. The point of genealogy is to retrace these mutual dependencies in concrete instances and thus to provide an account of the specific conditions of the emergence and production of a discourse such as developmental psychology. It is definitely not an internalist account.

Discourse and the real

Now, one main criticism levelled at the notion of discourse as it is used in recent accounts of the knowledge process concerns its relation to the 'real'. This criticism takes two forms. First, it argues that the analysis of conditions can only retrospectively attribute certain effects of material, social events on the discursive; second, it is claimed that in any case the explanation does not extend to these events themselves, that is, it cannot account for their occurrence.

For example the Centre for Contemporary Cultural Studies Education Group make the following criticism of the Foucauldian concept of genealogy:

> Foucault's histories suffer, however, from problems common to all abstracted or decontextualised studies of ideologies or policy statements. The micro-physics of power are supposed to work in the way described in the official manuals of method or the authoritative descriptions of 'the system'. Foucault retains a place in theory for relations or forces that exist outside the discourses he describes, but in his histories these are rarely elaborated.
>
> . . . In such work we stay *inside* discourses, unconcerned with their adequacy as knowledge and ignorant of the forms of resistance to them. We stay, in other words, in the fool's paradise of the powerful. It is impossible to explain, from this perspective, why regulative practices and their attendant knowledges collapse or are forced to innovate. A Foucauldian critique of post-war educational policy could certainly show us how certain professional knowledges and practices were implicated in a logic of domination. It could not tell us why the 1960s' policies fell apart or were transformed. This was not a product of discourse alone but of powerful social forces which the dominant knowledges failed to anticipate.
>
> (CCCS, 1981, p. 16)

There is in this argument the hint of extra-discursive phenomena, namely 'powerful social forces', that have a logic of their own, or at least are not encompassed within Foucault's theory. Whilst pointing out that those 'external' forces are themselves implicated in some discourse or other as soon as we speak of the details of their reality, we accept that the concept of genealogy may seem limited when we want to understand global changes. However, the latter task is not part of the aim of a genealogy, at least not directly or in the first place. One must locate its usefulness at other levels.

First, it enables one to examine the mechanisms of discursive practices at the micro-level of the detailed calculations which are part of the processes of production of the discourses and practices in question. Such an analysis tends to support the kind of history of knowledge which shows that the process of production of knowledge is uneven, full of inconsistencies, failures, new beginnings, changes in direction and unpredictable outcomes. Nevertheless it would be impossible to establish dependencies among discursive practices if regularities did not exist. The examination of conditions of possibility indicates what the limits are, what is sayable and what may happen. It therefore helps in the analysis of the more global level. The latter task does require other propositions, for example, about capitalism, in order to give shape to the task of genealogy. Foucault seems to acknowledge this when he says that he cannot see the difference between being a Marxist and being a historian!

Second, there is involved in this debate the wider issue of the relation between discourse and the 'real'.

One of the main criticisms of the term 'discourse' and of Foucault's histories of knowledge is that they slide into a relativist position (that is, when all truths are seen as *effects* of the discourses and thus when all discourses are equivalent with regard to their status as truth). This is of particular importance for our approach to psychology, confronting as we do some firmly entrenched beliefs about the nature of science and psychology's discovery of truths through the scientific method.

Because of this traditional history of science, the problem is currently posed in terms of the relations of determination between discourses and the real. The problem is demarcated by two main positions.

One claims that there are irreducible real processes (for example the economy or nature) that determine what may ultimately be asserted in discourse. The claim is often tempered with the proviso that other processes enter into the construction of specific statements, that the determination is not univocal or unmediated and so on. The other position – that of discourse determinism – privileges discourse in attributing to it the sole function of determining knowledge of objects as *its* objects; there can be no appeal to anything outside discourse since that outside can only be specified in some discourse that always already constructs it in a specific form.

The objection to the former position is that it appears to refer to something like the truth, and a truth that can somehow be verified independently of discourse, against which competing claims can be adjudicated. Furthermore it could imply the relative independence both of these primary processes and of discursive processes such that the former are put beyond the effects of discursive claims (and intentions) about them. There is a hint of this implication in claims such as 'the Earth moves in elliptical orbit around the sun' whatever one might say about it, or 'the economy ultimately determines intellectual production'.

The objection to the position which privileges discourse is that it is relativist in making the criteria of truth or rationality and adequacy internal to specific discourses; also it falls into idealism when it asserts that the real only exists insofar as there is a discourse which describes it. Thus intelligence would exist only insofar as psychology has constructed it as an object that it can measure and so on

Now, in discussing these conflicting claims, we need to avoid several blind alleys. For example, it seems reasonable at first to assert that the earth does move around the sun in spite of possible contrary views. But the question of how this claim – relying on the unspoken obviousness of what it asserts – can be established returns us to the problems of assessing particular scientific theories; it thus immediately reintroduces the problem of the relation between scientific claims and 'real' processes.

The other unfruitful approach, we think, is that of seeking an answer on the terrain of epistemology, especially when the range of issues above are reduced to the problem of finding the *general* guarantees, conditions and rules for reliable knowledge. The history of that approach from Descartes, through Kant, Hegel, Husserl or Popper points to the unlikelihood of arriving at some clearly unobjectionable solution. There are, nevertheless, attempts which have clarified the issues analytically, for instance Bhaskar (1978) and Benton (1977).

What we want to propose is not so much the definitive solution to everything; rather it is an attempt to re-pose the problem in such a way that a new avenue is opened up, one which does not thereby recycle the old arguments.

To start with, we want to point out that the problem of a search for guarantees concerning knowledge has always been inscribed in the struggle around the legitimacy and authority of the kinds of principles, interpretations, analyses and descriptions of the social and material world that provide the discursive bases for action. This was explicitly so for the authors we have just mentioned, even if the scientificity of the natural sciences has historically become a distinct and special case from the point of view of epistemology. The demarcation within knowledge between true and false, rational and irrational, and its resonance in the science–ideology couple, is locked into that struggle. In a sense then, the very manner in which the issue of truth and the associated question of the relation of discourse to the real have been posed, namely as epistemological questions (at least in classical philosophy), must be examined in the light of what is at stake in this strategy. One immediate effect of the epistemological approach is to remove the issue of truth from the public domain, that is from its direct involvement in politics.

Furthermore, it underwrites the claim of positivism to grant to the sciences alone, and their methodology, the ability to establish rational knowledge. It does this by providing the answer to the question of how one can accept a knowledge claim to be true, namely by asserting it to be so if it conforms to the norms of a science as defined by positivism, that is to say by scientific standards themselves.

Incidentally, the epistemologization of the issue of truth plays into the hands of the point of view that appeals to common sense as a criterion of rationality and reasonableness. This works in the following manner: contentious knowledge is left open but only as a problem for philosophical debate, leaving everything else to be referred to common sense, that is, what the dominant discourse in any specific field asserts to be true and to correspond to reality. The political implications of posing the question in an epistemological form should be clear from our analysis, namely it works for the strategies that enable the dominant claims about the real and existing power relations to appear rational and objective; it forces opposing views to establish their rationality and intelligibility according to norms that already favour that which they oppose. For example it is often the case that observational methods in psychology are called upon to justify their credentials according to the norms of statistical methodology, that is in terms of a form of validation taken from quantitative methods in order to support law-like generalizations.

If we accept that the process of production of knowledge is always open to the effect of politics, we do not have to abandon the question of the adequacy of claims to knowledge. For example, Althusser attempts to retain a demarcation between science and ideology and at the same time acknowledges that ideology must be accorded the status of knowledge. His dilemma arises from the recognition that the theorization of the relationship between knowledge and the real cannot be avoided.

There are several reasons for this. On the one hand, any answer to this problem implies a specific theorization of history: a view concerning the forces and agents that shape history. On the other, failure to address the relationship between knowledge and the real lays one open to two temptations. First, by default, we are likely to attach intentionality to the knower/actor and thus end up with a kind of voluntarism which retains the logocentric subject in a key location. (We have discussed this in relation to humanism. It can also be seen in a good deal of ethnomethodology.) Second, to escape this humanism, we may attribute determination to discourse itself, that is discourse would determine both its own history and that of subjects. So the answer to our initial problem has consequences for two crucial issues, the functioning of subjects in the production of knowledge and in making history, and the analysis of the functioning of discourse in the production of everyday social and material life.

In what we have said so far we have signalled the need for a displacement. Part of that shift involves the move that installs politics inside knowledge-producing activities. These activities themselves cannot be confined within the boundaries of scientific disciplines. For example, knowledge of human behaviour constantly goes outside psychology to knowledges inscribed in everyday practices in a variety of social institutions, say concerning schooling or child-rearing. We must therefore recognize that in speaking about knowledge one is referring to a wide domain which includes all beliefs and thought. Moreover, this wider understanding of knowledge inevitably locates knowledge-producing activities as part of the range of social practices that we have mentioned.

Consider the example of unemployment. We cannot claim that it is because the concept of unemployment exists that x million people are out of work: economic discourse does not create unemployment. Yet as soon as we use the term unemployment we have already classified those out of work, indeed we have already selected certain norms constructed within economic discourse which define who is to count as unemployed. Those not seeking work would not qualify. Interestingly, the dispute around what those norms are, that is who is to count as unemployed, is an eminently political issue. It is not a simple matter of a relation or correspondence to actual numbers out of work, the process of arriving at that number being itself already locked into the dispute. Indeed, some people could claim that there is no unemployment, that those with no work could find work if they really tried or that there is a surplus supply of labour on the grounds that the economy is by definition efficient at any point in time and would not require any excess. The 'reality' of people out of work would be classified in a very different way, with different effects on other discourses and for action. Thus we have on the one hand a discourse or variety of discourses concerning the economy's construction of unemployment as a concept and an object of theory using/modifying previously established norms. On the other hand, there are other activities such as industrial processes directly employing specific numbers of people, the activity of people seeking work or registering as unemployed, etc., and political and administrative discourses and strategies that make calculations, institute plans, gather statistics, etc., with regard to levels of employment. The material evidences of the former practice, although specific to the production of economic discourse, must utilize in regulated ways the kinds of material events that belong to the latter complex of practices. These are what are referred to as the real, but are in fact already caught in the processes of co-articulation of discourses whereby each set of activities condition the other.

Thus, more generally, sociological or psychological knowledge about schooling cannot be divorced from the practices and behaviours in educational institutions to which, in the end, it refers. Furthermore, discourses about schooling are also caught in this network of practices so that often a discussion or description of, say, learning in a primary school, or a particular child's learning strategies, would involve the co-ordination of statements from a number of discourses. In a sense, it is only analytically that one can attribute such statements to specific discourses.

Nevertheless, these discourses, for example, cognitive development, form specific systems of statements that are identifiable as disciplines and whose rules of formation can be described and understood. Their objects do not coincide with the range of activities and phenomena which they systematize as objects of specific discourses, though they bear relations to them. Thus the stages of development in Piagetian theory are not equivalent to the thinking processes that accompany human actions, though there is a specific relationship between the two domains of the theoretical and the material.

By extension we can describe the production of a discourse by reference to two sets of activities: on the one hand its development and transformation from an existing discourse or set of closely connected discourses and, on the other hand, the range of activities that are at once discursive and material (for example those we refer to as schooling) in relation to which that development occurs. There exists a system of mutual effects between the two set of activities, effects that do not refer to some pure stage of reality but to the previously established effects between them, thus to historically grounded and specific practices and phenomena. The reality we apprehend is always-already classified and distributed according to a system of discursive differences which are locked into differences in material effects.

Thus discourse does not start out as a system of statements and a set of questions about the 'real' anyway. It is caught in a materiality which is a historical product; its specific questions arise from there, where the instruments of its construction are to be found. Novelty is the result of two features. First, discourses are not non-contradictory, uniform processes (there isn't a single agreed definition of unemployment) but are complex systems of regulated differences that are intricated in ongoing struggles involving power and social relations (for example about what may count as unemployment and the politics around it). Second, a degree of indeterminacy and openness exists so that effects are not always predictable. This is probably related to the fact of struggle and resistance just mentioned, to the inadequacy of knowledges and to the complexity of the processes. (One may speculate that in a completely closed culture, the indeterminacy is already accounted for by appeal to unpredictable forces beyond human understanding yet completely enclosed in the existing order.)

The relation of knowledge to the 'real', then, is a question tied to the specificity of a given conjuncture of events and is not a general epistemological question concerning guarantees, rules and logical procedures, etc. It is always a historical question, involving the reconstruction of the effects inside a particular discourse of the traces of other discursive and material practices with which it is locked in a mutually constitutive relationship.

From that point of view, we can re-examine the problem of truth. Adequacy no longer refers to the 'facts', or to the internal rules alone of a specific discipline or discourse. Instead, it is implicated in a set of arguments that involve what counts as material evidence, what principles of intelligibility are at work, what calculations of effect and consequences are made and what other discourses and practices are thought to participate in the construction of the statements of the discourse. Indeed the question of adequacy is no longer formulated in terms of closeness to the truth but is part of a wider problem of what is to be done, that is to say part of a problem posed in terms of a regime of truth and the politics of truth.

It is within that framework that the new history we advocate is a specific reconstruction whose adequacy is arbitrated by a definite point of view located in the present.

There are also implications for the issue of a demarcation within knowledge between true and false, science and ideology and so forth. It is worth pointing out that that demarcation involves a divide within a discipline as well as implicating a demarcation in the wider domain of knowledge. Thus when psychoanalysis is described as unscientific, a separation is made within the domain of theory concerning the subject and its constitution, but also a divide is made in everyday talk which differentially evaluates explanations that utilize psychological concepts like, say, motivation and socialization, from those that refer to, say, the Oedipal stage and repression. All this has implications for action and for change. We could say that drawing a line of demarcation is always a redrawing, since there is already a system of inclusion and exclusion in all knowledge. One does not start with a problem of adequacy to the real or a problem of which theorization 'fits' objectively obtained data. Instead we are always dealing with already stated positions and continuing struggles about what makes sense and what is to be. The subject of discourse, author or speaker, is itself caught in this web of calculations. Truth is at once a material, discursive, political and subjective question.

The power–knowledge axis

Power–knowledge

This last part brings us to a key issue in our approach. It has to do with power and with change. In referring discourse to the wider network of the practices that constitute the social and the subject we bring to the forefront the relation of knowledge and power. Power is invested in discourse; equally, discursive practices produce, maintain or play out power relations. But power is not one-sided or monolithic, even when we can and do speak of dominance, subjugation or oppression. Power is always exercised in relation to a resistance, though a question is left about the equality of forces. It is our view that resistances, conflicts and what we have sometimes called contradictions are always-already inscribed in the processes we have been describing above. Change is an effect of the struggles that criss-cross them; it is related to the indeterminacy we highlighted and to the mobility of the relations. The position for which we argue does not essentialize either power or resistance. We do not make power the property of one group or another, inherent in the apparatuses, for example, of the state, and devised for its exercise. It is not sufficient for a class or group to occupy the seats of power in order to exercise it or to ensure dominance, as seems clear when we think of socialist governments in capitalist countries 'coming to power' through the electoral system. The 'system' we describe is riddled with sites of resistance and conflict. Contingent progress is possible in such sites, which can thus act as points of possible transformation. It is important to make the point that the above remarks are meant to contribute to a more incisive analysis of the microscopic processes of power, in contrast to the approach which tends to take it for granted that we already know how power is exercised and why it is successful. Thus, we want to emphasize that we do not essentialize discourse in relation to power; that is we do not make power an effect of discourse.

Furthermore, the talk of power and resistance does not imply that resistance is necessarily equal or successful or indeed that it is fundamentally subversive. One has to examine conditions and effects in every specific case. For example, concerning the greatly increased power of the social services and the discourse of social work in the processes of normalization, disciplining and production of the population, it is clear that the machinery of that power is now more effective and diverse in spite of resistances that we must presume to have existed and which continue in various forms. The concept of resistance itself, in the general sense in which it is used above, includes both conscious opposition and the mute automatic resistance of that which is in process of being shaped. Indeed the material to which we refer, namely particular individuals, is notably pliable: the success of a normalizing power also depends on the willing compliance of the subject who is the target of the technologies of normalization. *It is precisely this fact which largely remains to be explained.*

Power–knowledge–subject

The Althusserian attempt to deal with that question utilized the concept of interpellation but, as we saw, was unable to provide a satisfactory account either of this willing capture or of resistance to subjugation. Locked in this, change, whether historical or subjective, remains a problem for Althusserian and for structuralist theories. Foucault's advances, directing attention to the capillary complexities of the problem of power rather than to the global processes, have contributed to the re-opening of the question of the formation of subjects by directing attention to the minutiae of effects of power in the positioning of subjects in social relations. It could be argued that his focus on the positivity of the human sciences equally underplays change; it directs attention to effects of power in social action and transformation, but almost from the point of view of what the dominant power relations succeed in constructing. So, although one may speak of localized sites of resistances, the possibility of their co-ordination remains a theoretical problem.

One seems still to be caught between the two poles of the society–individual dualiam. On the one hand, there are the theories for which power is the possession of the dominant class, the ideological determined 'in the last instance' by the economic, so that power works for the dominant ideologies. On the other, we have the theories for which power is a matter of groups and individuals and institutional positions in which it is vested. It has been argued that Foucault's theoretical shifts in the problematic amount to a radical departure only at the cost of essentializing power, that is to say by referring the exercise of power and existing power relations to a fundamental *will* to power. Let us explore this a little to give an idea of how we attempt to move beyond these debates.

An example of the limitations of the orthodox Marxist position can be judged in Delphy's (1974) extension of the theory to patriarchal power, in such a way that power becomes the property of men as the dominant sex-class, whilst women are described as its victims, the objects of power. Thus the belonging of agents, as men and as members of a class, already determines their overall position with respect to the exercise of power.

For psychology, women's oppression and men's beliefs about women are theorized in terms of concepts of prejudice, of mistaken judgements based on incorrect information about women, of attitudes and of socialization into the roles of 'typical' men and women. We have exposed the shortcomings of this view in section 1. In the end, it only makes sense if one accepts certain basic presuppositions about the person concerning the rational, unitary, individualized subject. Chapter 3 demonstrates the historical and cultural specificity of such a notion. By contrast we have argued that power is not a property but a relationship. One can only examine its reality in its exercise. As Foucault explains, power does not act directly and immediately on people, rather 'it acts upon their actions':

> in itself the exercise of power is not violence; nor is it a consent which implicitly is not renewable. It is a total structure of actions brought to bear upon possible actions; it incites, it induces, it seduces, it makes easier or more difficult; in the extreme it constrains or forbids absolutely; it is nevertheless always a way of acting upon an acting subject or acting subjects.
>
> (Foucault, 1982, p. 789)

What is important in this statement is that power works through subjects' actions. The latter take place in practices that are discursive and material and that already delimit and condition action.

Furthermore, the subject itself is the effect of a production, caught in the mutually constitutive web of social practices, discourses and subjectivity; its reality is the tissue of social relations. Thus in the example we have just considered, the category 'woman' would itself be open to a questioning in terms of the different norms which circumscribe so-called women's 'roles' in different practices. The approach which expects multiple positionings corresponding to a multiplicity of subjectivities – as mothers, wives, consumers, workers of one kind or another, etc. – must refer to the specificities of the different practices in order to describe the different subject positions and the different power relations played out in them. It cannot simply speak of a specific subject's behaviour and attitudes or ascribe in advance the subject's position according to class or gender.

For example, Bennett, Coward and Heys (1981), in an analysis of taxation and welfare practices, demonstrate that there is no consistency across these practices fixing 'woman' as a subject position. Some welfare provisions, such as supplementary benefit, privilege 'mothers', while others, for example taxation, privilege males. They conclude that there is no general 'discrimination against women' in taxation and welfare practices. The relative power of 'woman' depends on particular practices which differently favour 'mothers', 'single women', 'married women' and so on. The welfare system is not a uniform ideological state apparatus but a complex network with equally complex histories.

However, this does not negate the fact of the differential treatment of women by these agencies. Indeed, the interesting question is whether the privileging of mothers – an act which seemingly accords more power to women – may not at the same time participate in the subjugation of women by reinforcing their role as mothers and tying them to that position. The experience of having more or less power in different social practices – that is the experience of contradictions in subjective positionings – can be tied to what is sometimes called 'contradictory subjectivity'. It is not a concept that fits into psychology's notion of the individual. Indeed, it is a key concept in the deconstruction of the psychological notion of the subject. It cannot be usefully worked on outside an approach which starts not from the unitary subject, or even a power–knowledge couple, but from a triad: power–knowledge–subject.

How we can begin to understand the formation of subjects within that complex is examined in detail in chapters 5 and 6. It should be clearer now that the argument for a new history of knowledge is one move in a complex stratagem which starts out with a series of refusals; principally, of the individual–society dualism in its various forms and of reductionist views of causality in the social domain. The aim is the construction of a problematic, signalled in our use of terms like 'signifying practice', 'nexus of subjectivities', 'regime of truth' and so on, which provides the elements for establishing the point of view that the politics of theory, personal politics and the politics of social change are inextricably entwined.

3

The subject of psychology

Couze Venn

For more than a hundred years now psychology has not ceased to calibrate the human subject. It has given itself the task of plotting the distribution of human characteristics, of charting people's 'abnormalities' and 'pathologies'; it has drawn up taxonomies of behaviour that seek to set the norms of human conduct. Its findings are inscribed in a multitude of practices in institutions of all kinds. But does psychology have the measure of the subject? And what do all these instruments regulate?

Canguilhem (1975), in his brief survey, gestures towards the same kind of interrogation of psychology when he remarks that

> behavioural psychology in the 19th and 20th centuries has thought it could achieve its autonomy by cutting itself off from philosophy, that is to say, from the kind of speculation which seeks an idea of the human being by looking beyond the biological and sociological accounts. . . . Thus, the question 'what is psychology?', to the extent that philosophy is debarred from searching for the answer, becomes 'what do psychologists expect to achieve in doing what they do?' In the name of what have they set themselves up as psychologists?
> (Canguilhem, 1975, p. 380)

I start with these questions because they immediately signal the gap which separates those who have come to vest their work as psychologists with the comforting authority of science, and those who want to pose the questions of what it is that psychology constructs, what its functioning in the social is, and in alliance with what practices it commands attention to its findings. On the one side stands the complacent group of those who imagine their task to be the objective, scholarly and neutral search for the psychic machinery of the human being. On the other are clustered those who anxiously wonder whether the cold instruments of their calibrations of human behaviour fashion the keys of our greater understanding or those for our less perceptible imprisonment.

However, as our Introduction to the book makes clear, our concern is not that of the status of psychology as 'bourgeois science' or as 'ideology', providing either the tools of liberation or the chains of oppressive power. As I shall explain below, the opposition between science and ideology is one which is problematized from the outset in the analysis that I propose.

I take this approach for two sets of reasons. On the one hand, addressing the question of the scientific credentials of psychology, or any other discipline, means that one has to take on board the epistemological debates that have raged for some time around the issue of the scientificity of science. It involves placing oneself on the terrain of epistemology and in the end accepting the grounds claimed by orthodox philosophy or by positivism for the ultimate guarantees of truth and rationality. Furthermore, the issue of scientificity is locked into a political question: that of the position for which some Marxists argue, namely that it is important to defend the scientific status of historical materialism against its detractors and the need to defend science itself in order to be able to ground Marxist analysis in its reassuring bedrock. From such an epistemological position, the critique of psychology becomes the interrogation of its '(mis)appropriation' by different agents and agencies, for example that of mental measurement by educationalists, social workers and so on.

On the other hand, if one starts out from a position that assumes science and ideology to form an opposition, it becomes difficult to examine the effects of the social on a scientific practice, except in terms of a distortion, even if this is thought to be inevitable. It would be difficult from such a start to write a history of psychology which focuses on its positivities, that is to say on what it positively constructs, under what specific conditions, in relation to what other disciplines, in response to what theoretical and practico-administrative problems and with what effects, both for the production of the discourse of psychology and for normalizing practices (in schools, hospitals, social services, etc.). So it will not be a question of cataloguing the 'errors' or 'complicities' of psychology, for the history of errors and horrors is but the other face of the narrative of successes which the history-of-ideas perspective has sustained for so long.

Instead I begin with the argument that the conceptual coherence that makes it possible for one to speak of psychology in the singular has to do with two crucial features: the notion of the subject which is at work in the various branches of psychology, and the positivist convictions that underlie psychology's findings. They form the bastions from which psychology spreads out and to which it retreats when attacked. They are the targets of my critique.

The subject of psychology, as the Introduction to section 1 has emphasized (see pp. 11–25), is the unitary, rational subject which begins to appear in western culture from the seventeenth century. It is the subject-of-science that classical epistemology takes to be the ideal representative of *homo rationalis*. I shall return later to the historically specific character of this notion. For the moment I would like to emphasize that it is the same notion of the subject that functions in the social scientific discourses and in the apparatuses of administration, namely the abstract legal subject of individual rights, of responsibilities and obligations; it is also the individual citizen who is the target of technologies of normalization, disciplining and punishment. Psychology on the one hand makes this subject its specific scientific object whilst the other sciences and technologies of the social assume such a subject to be the real object and target of their practices and the entity forming the basis of societal processes. In any case, it functions as a central concept – a 'relay concept' – which enables a degree of co-articulation at the level of social practices. For example, the family is a site of intervention for a number of practices that have as their concerns physical health, economic viability, social conformity within visible or invisible norms, child care, sexuality, and so forth. It is in the pursuit of practical goals attached to these concerns that discourses as diverse as psychology, medicine, law and sociology become inscribed in complex ways in the activities and the rules governing health visitors, psychologists, doctors, social workers in their interventions in the family. Clearly, there are often conflicts of interest and interpretation amongst the agents concerned, say between a social worker and a doctor. But it is a particular individual who is singled out as target, by reference to norms of conduct that establish degrees of deviation and the boundaries of acceptable behaviour; the measure of deviation points to the form of intervention. Practitioners of technologies of the social, for example social workers, may want to change a family, but they do so through intervention centred on members of the family considered as particular individuals; they do not aim to change the family form itself (except for radical social work which has to operate outside the existing institutional support and under constant threat). What makes possible any co-ordination amongst the variety of normative practices is the shared individualism of their notion of the subject. Even humanistic psychology (and derivative practices), which is subversive to the positivist principles dominant in most of psychology, partakes in this fundamental individualism. It is a position that blunts the edge of its criticism.

Second, whilst the positivist features of the social sciences have often been taken to task, the tendency has been to regard these as theoretical inadequacies. What it is useful to highlight in connection with the point of view I am developing is not only the instrumental rationality (see

Habermas, 1971) inscribed in positivism but the compatibility of such a rationality with the strategies of administration. It is not just a matter of the development of capitalist industrial social formations towards a rational society, as Habermas has argued. Nor is it simply the case that the sciences of the social and orthodox Marxism have been dazzled by the ideology of science that has bathed 'Science' in that immaculate light. For, if we accept the arguments for saying that the sciences of the social function as discourses that participate positively in the construction of the social, then instrumental rationality should indeed be central to their foundation.

In making this remark, I am not condemning the sciences of the social for being positivist or, for that matter, individualistic. Indeed, it is part of my argument about their functioning and of the conditions of their emergence that they should share precisely these features: it is part of their positivity, what enables them to have the effects they do.

The focus on the individual and the positivity of the discourses that address problems of social cohesion and social order have been starkly highlighted in the current plans of the present Conservative government in Britain radically to shift responsibility for care and health towards individuals and away from state provision. The aim is to promote family life and to 'increase individual responsibility and freedom of choice, by reducing to a minimum the extent to which decisions are taken for individuals by professionals' (Central Policy Review Staff, reprinted in the *Guardian*, 19 February 1983). The latter refer to doctors, teachers and a variety of social workers. Their role is explicitly tied to the growth of the social services and is described as 'embedded in state bureaucracies – sometimes with the statutory function of regulating people's behaviour' (ibid., p. 2). The change in the present system would be effected through more direct control of the professionals, including intervention in the disciplines and practices which participate in forming them – for example, in teacher training – as well as through modification of the more dispersed elements of the technologies of the social, in particular 'insurantial technology' (Donzelot, 1979) and through media manipulation. The interesting aspect of this new development is the explicit recognition by the radical right of the political effects, and the effects for the form of social relations, of the sciences of the social and the practices in which they are imbricated. This contrasts with the liberal position that assumes these sciences and practices to be neutral.

Psychology, as the science that speaks of the individual, plays a key part in the range of practices I have mentioned. Indeed that role is taken for granted in the radical right's calculations, for the latter include the need to 'identify characteristics of behaviour and attitude' which the government thinks desirable and to 'identify major influences on children', etc. (CPRS document, reprinted in the *Guardian*, 17 February 1983). So today's politics are making starkly visible the positivity of the social sciences, including psychology, and their insistent, if insidious, participation in shaping our lives: it is only their claims to neutrality and to the search for objective truths founded in the empiricist notion of science that have camouflaged that functioning. Let me turn, then, to the interrogation of that science of the subject.

My first task will be to establish the grounds for doing the kind of history of psychology which I am proposing. It includes the clarification of a number of concepts and the summary of the epistemological issues which have become part of the debate concerning the functioning and production of disciplinary discourses in a social formation.

My examination of psychology will focus on several themes, interconnected at the theoretical level. First, I shall clarify the theoretical point of view of a new history of the sciences of the social; second, I shall locate psychology within this wider domain, and, third, I shall deconstruct the object that psychology constructs, namely the human subject. I am particularly concerned to establish the historicity of the subject which psychology has taken for its pregiven object. I will highlight the essential individualism of that subject and demonstrate its centrality to the intelligibility of the social relations of modern capitalism.

The history of discourse

This chapter, then, is concerned with a different kind of history of discourse. The main features of this approach were outlined in the Introduction to section 2 where we introduced the concepts of 'genealogy' and the sciences of the social. The first premise of such a genealogy is the problematization of psychology as a category. Amongst other things, this means that I start by bracketing the disciplinary boundaries of psychology in order to examine how that category has been constructed in the first place: what objects have been thought to belong to it, what questions establish its domain of enquiry, what other knowledges and assumptions condition these questions, how are the practices that construct psychology located in relation to practices of the other sciences of the social and of social regulation.

I should start by pointing out the political relevance of the approach for which I am arguing. As I have explained above, its rejection of the history-of-ideas perspective has to do with the fact that from such a position it is difficult to examine the effects of power and of administrative strategies on scientific disciplines, since these are considered to be contingent anyway. The new conceptualization of the location of the 'social sciences' starts out instead with the explicit recognition that they are imbricated in the complex of practices that constitute what they call 'society'. So, the concepts discussed in the Introduction to this section concerning the point of view of the sciences and technologies of the social, and the investment of power relations in them, assert the centrality of social relations in the analysis of social scientific discourses; they do this in a manner which reconstructs their history by establishing that the conditions of their possibility included historically specific developments and problems belonging to the wider domain of the social.

It is worth making the point that it is not a matter of adding a social history to the empiricist account of scientific knowledge. Social history tends too often to be a descriptive story of social developments to put alongside political, economic, scientific histories in an attempt to provide a comprehensive picture and indicate connections; it neither problematizes the category of 'social', nor examines how the content of the category is constituted.

Perhaps it will help to summarize the main features of this approach. First, the approach rejects the demarcation between 'internal' and 'external' histories. Second, it claims that the rationality and intelligibility of the statements of a scientific discourse depend, in addition to the 'internal' arguments and the system of evidences, on culturally established norms of what is rational and plausible; indeed the 'internal' arguments often utilize or take for granted these norms: they are treated as common sense.

Third, it claims that the social sciences are directly conditioned by the practices, discourses and events that form what is usually referred to as the 'context': they have a constitutive effect and cannot be conceptualized either as contingent or as the independently existing objects of social theory.

Fourth, these form a complex network which does not uniquely determine any particular social-scientific discourse, yet constrains and regulates its production. A degree of relative autonomy and indeterminacy exists, though the effects are systematic: not anything is possible or sayable.

Fifth, the above suggests a more complex history of discourse than the tidy schemas assumed in empiricist accounts and the history-of-ideas view of the progress of Reason.

It follows that different histories become possible, depending on the questions one asks, and on the point of departure and the point of arrival. Starting from the question of how a particular discourse has come to be what it is today and to function in the way it does, one can retrace an account that would be relevant to the present whilst starting out from the past of a discourse. Genealogical histories are not complete (an impossible task anyway) but selective according to a clear pay-off for a present strategy for action. They construct a specific intelligibility guided by a definite point of view. As such they may appear distorting, a partial reading from a preconceived position. For example, Dale Spender's *Man-made Language* or Foucault's *Discipline and Punish* can be accused of twisting the arms of history. There is an issue about what is authentic history which I cannot pursue here. I shall simply recognize that this partiality exists, but justify the risks by arguing that the historical project of a genealogy is illuminating or confusing according to the trajectory of traces it constructs and its fruitfulness for further politically relevant exploration. Such illumination is not in any case independent of a respect for history. For example, a history of the atom that includes Democritus' notion of the 'atom' would be uninteresting because, as Bachelard has argued, the two concepts belong to two epistemologically incompatible periods of the history of physics. So, in assessing a genealogy, one utilizes both historical knowledge (other histories, genealogies, etc.) epistemological judgements (about what belongs to a conceptual category such as the atom) and political calculations (about the politics sustained by the analysis, about further politically relevant questions, etc.; see Venn, 1982, for detailed discussion).

A genealogy highlights those conditions and effects which make sense of the present state of knowledge without seeking guarantees in 'objective reality' (or the 'facts' or some other determining instance such as the economic system); it establishes the historical contingency of the present state of knowledge; it establishes its imbrication in the practices mentioned above, its articulation with them, and thus provides an analysis which specifies the effects of power on the kinds of claims to knowledge made in the discourse.

The analysis I am proposing proceeds through a deconstruction. This is possible on the assumption that the statements of any discourse – the text – are the strategic product of calculations inscribed in a number of other discourses and which have invisible effects on it. The example of unemployment figures discussed in the Introduction to this section illustrates the point. Deconstruction is at the same time concerned with a construction, namely that of a specific trajectory of the traces of discourses and of the calculations that condition a particular discourse and which deconstruction brings to the surface. Deconstruction utilizes an analytical apparatus which informs its task and guides the construction of the new history, namely concepts such as technologies of the social, practices of normalization, disciplining and so on, and a theoretical framework, for instance about the process of production of discourse as described in the Introduction to section 2.

The place of the subject in the discourses of the social

Several problems arise from this kind of history of the social. I'll leave out the issue of the place of the author (scientist, etc.) in the production of innovation. But the issue of change, and that of the principles which construct a certain coherence amongst the various practices, require some note of explanation.

For the positivist history of ideas, both issues are referred to the scientific process itself. Change is accounted for by appeal to the theoretical problems and to the outcome of crises in the puzzle-solving activity of a science, crises that appear in any scientific discipline. What drives the disciplines 'forward' would be the *internal* pressures towards more powerful concepts and for greater internal coherence and the solution of technical problems encountered in research, including applied research.

Correlatively, the coherence of the discourse is founded in the presumed rationality of science. Indeed, one need not pose the question of the rationality of the scientific discipline, since, by definition, science *is* the rational process of knowledge. Coherence is conceived of as an integral part of that rationality; it refers to the degree of fit between theory and evidence and the conceptual compatibility of the theories within the explanatory framework of the discipline; for example, modern physics cannot accept both the caloric and thermodynamic theories of heat. In challenging that view, one is faced with theorizing both issues in different terms.

I am leaving out of my critique any serious examination of broadly sociological accounts of the production of knowledge and radical critiques of science that explicitly reject some of the principles and suppositions I have been highlighting. The latter have constantly impugned positivism and have sought to establish the connections that bind the social sciences to capitalism (for example Young, 1977; Rose and Rose, 1976; Easlea, 1973 and 1980; or, from a different point of view, Feyerabend, 1975). The former occupy a broad terrain from the strident relativism of Barnes (1974) and Bloor (1976) to the 'culturalist' approaches of, say, Knorr (1977), Manier (1978), Collins (1981), Kleiner (1979) and a host of others. Now, whilst they are all concerned to demonstrate the effects of the rest of a culture on its scientific practices, they neither radically deconstruct the subject or agent of these practices nor examine the sciences from the point of view of their productivity or positivity for the social. My approach, by contrast, borrows from the kind of work done by Foucault, Canguilhem, Pêcheux and Derrida, to mention the better-known names; it is concerned with a different questioning of knowledges, namely with their functioning, the conditions of their emergence, their intelligibility in relation to a culture, their 'regime of truth' and their location as part of the complex web of processes that constitute us.

The beginnings of a psychology

To return to psychology, I will focus on establishing the conditions of possibility and the main conceptual instruments which produce a science of the individual in the second half of the nineteenth century. I have already summarized the main elements of such a task in my outline of the structural components of this chapter. I have emphasized the key functioning of the unitary subject in psychological discourse as well as in the human sciences. What I want to stress is the fact that psychology, when it emerges as a science, understands itself as primarily a science of *mind* and its behavioural manifestations. My aim in what follows is to discuss the reasons for the manner of this emergence and the means of its realization.

What I have said above, to the extent that it locates psychology as a science of the social with implications for the instrumental interest in social regulation centred on the individual, already indicates the reasons for choosing the concept of the unitary subject as the prime target for deconstruction and for the related analysis of the psychological instruments for measuring the 'individual's' behaviour.

Canguilhem (1975) highlighted a basic underlying principle informing the sciences of the social when he claimed that the new psychology that emerged from the middle of the nineteenth century was informed by the principle of the 'utility of the human being'. It is not punishment or exclusion which motivates these discourses, but the disciplining and the amplification of the powers of the human body, the attempts to maximize its utility and produce its willing docility.

The subject, then, becomes this amazing instrument: it is at the same time the object of a science, the target of social technologies which plan its regulation, and the elusive persona not quite captured within the complex matrix of these practices, whose voice, in other forums continues to protest and survive. It is significant that this voice of resistance and secret desires becomes the object of a competing 'science of mind', as Freud described his psychoanalytic theory; it is interesting that psychology generally spurns psychoanalysis, in spite of its unsystematic and opportunist borrowings from the latter (see the discussion of Adorno and Allport in chapter 2, pp. 68–75).

I want to argue that from the time when a science of mind becomes possible as a result of the materialization and the naturalization of reason implicated in the Darwinian theory of evolution, psychology begins to occupy the key position linking biological discourse to all the discourses that speak of the individual. Underlying that location is a displacement, developed in biology, that founds behaviour on the twin principles of the organism as an organized system and of the individual as a specific exemplar sharing the general characteristics of a population but particularized at the level of individual variation. The description of the most general form of organismic processes is the province of biology whilst the culturally specific manifestations of social behaviour are the objects of the then emergent sociology. As far as causality is concerned, psychology occupies a place between the two poles of the biological and the social, sometimes relying in the last instance on biology, as in most empiricist and positivist psychology, sometimes seeking support from the social, as in humanistic psychology. Behaviourism, ostensibly not concerned with causes, in the end must found the assumed universality of the processes it describes in biological or organismic origin. The basic concern of many of these approaches is not so much with the universal processes as with the systematic study of individual variations, especially those that are thought disfunctional to the good order of society. (One must except Piagetian developmental theory and language development from this, but significantly these have functioned as the radical pole of psychological discourse.) Measures of the norms of behaviour, for example in mental measurement, are but part of the process of establishing degrees of deviation. It is from that kind of start, and the overall framework of the sciences of the social, that one can make sense of psychology's focus on deviation, on patholodgy and on error.

Let us establish the trajectory that leads to the emergence of psychology as such a discourse. Psychology as a science of mind finds one condition of possibility in the displacement of the site of sensation and of motor activity to the brain. But in the context of the notion of rationality anchored to a cogito and to the experience of a cognate subject, its first project is one of accounting for the errors that the senses induce in the mind. That science is at first a psychophysics, for example with Descartes and Malebranche, or with Hume, who all proposed accounts of the functioning of mind which conceptualized mind in the same terms as other physical entities, an approach consistent with mechanical philosophy. Mind would be subject to laws in the same way as the material world; these laws would express the quantitative measurement of the kinds of regularities which obtain for bodily activities: motions and regulated associations of ideas. Canguilhem has described this attempt as a 'physics of the external senses' (1975, p. 37). Meanwhile, values, emotions and so on continued to be the object of the 'moral sciences'.

For a long time, however, psychology was concerned with two projects: that of the natural history of the self (in the works of Locke, Condillac and the Utilitarians) and that of a wisdom founded in the intuitions and self-reflections of the 'I'. Kant partly synthesizes the two poles of the experiential and the transcendental subject in a phenomenology of mind. It is worth pointing out that this phenomenology is the basis for Hegel's idealist solution to the problem of knowledge in his privileging of Absolute Spirit as the teleological and transcendental principle which would be the foundation of the temporary states of human consciousness. It is also a condition of possibility for Marx's materialist solution via the transformation of the Hegelian dialectic, that is by founding consciousness in the here and now of the material state of society. It is not until Piaget, though, that this philosophical problematic is transformed into a science of cognition (see Venn and Walkerdine, 1978).

The development that made possible the emergence of psychology as we know it is the new natural history of species which biology inaugurates. The Darwinian naturalization of reason, which is a key component of the theory of evolution by natural selection, is central to this emergence. Before enlarging on this claim I must point out that earlier it is Maine de Biran (*Mêmoire sur la dêcomposition de la pensêe*) who first signals the importance of the biological model for a psychology, as opposed to the earlier physicalist model; he proposed that the human subject should be regarded as a living organism served by the faculty of intelligence and not the other way round, as the more mentalist or rationalist accounts assumed.

However, when we examine the history of the discourse of mental processes in the period when Darwin first formulated the sketch of natural selection (1837–9), we find that its focus was on pathologies, that is to say on the abnormal functions of the mind. This is so in the writing of, for example, J. Abercrombie (1838), T. Mayo (1838) and D. Stewart (1829). Darwin himself, discussing mental processes in relation to variations in instincts and the possibility of development in reasoning and linguistic capacities, focuses on abnormal, out-of-the-ordinary behaviour (in the Notebooks, 1837–9).

Interestingly, Freud also starts his investigations towards a 'science of mind' by considering pathologies, though he argued that both pathologies and 'normal' behaviour should refer to *similar underlying processes* (Sulloway, 1980, p. 12).

In a way, in their studies of madness, the 'Alienists' Pinel and Royer-Collard, around the end of the eighteenth century, also share this point of view of pathology, that is of seeing 'alienation' as an illness or as error, with a specific symptomatology and, like other illnesses, open to the possibility of a cure.

Quite crucially, this view is entirely consistent with the principle of classification of organisms which was founded on the notion of the fixity of types and which, consequently, understood deviations in terms of monstruosity and error. It is not until the theorization of variation in characteristics as *normal* – a feature of Darwin's theory – that measures of variation become part of the study of normal types, so that error becomes amenable to the same kind of explanation as 'normal behaviour'. I shall draw out this argument more fully when considering the effects of the theory of evolution on the study of mental processes.

Psychopathology and deviation from the norm

The focus on psychopathology which characterized the beginnings of psychology echoes the approaches in the new medical and clinical gaze that emerged from the eighteenth century (Foucault, 1966 and 1973). And one could add that the studies of Galton, later, and all the work which was concerned with the simple-minded, share that point of view. I am arguing that such a focus is an index of two very important features of the psychological gaze (and that of much of the social sciences). First, the 'normal' subject is regarded as unproblematic, that is, it is what can be taken for granted and, indeed, can be construed as the *model* that fixes the norms. Ideally, the model is the male European rational individual: both *homo rationalis* and *homo economicus*. Psychology has often been criticized for the tendency to take the behaviour of males (say, in cognitive development) or the middle-class (say, in language development) to be the measure of the 'normal'. The poor, the 'criminal', the mad, the non-European and women are, almost by definition, abnormal, deviant. Their behaviour is quantified as a measure of the degree of deviation from the norm. Yet, it is an unexamined norm, shrouded in the mysterious clarity of common sense and translated into 'facts' through quantification. We know from the arguments of Gramsci, Althusser or Pêcheux that common sense is the ideal ground of the ideologically dominant values and forms of behaviour (see Introduction to section 2). Thus the norms which psychology constructs and fixes are those consistent with the dominant form of sociality, that is to say that reproduce the social, intersubjective relations and relations of power as they are played out in social institutions of all kinds, from the family to the shop floor.

It is significant that the bulk of sociological studies operate with a similar implicit or unconscious assumption about what is normal. Thus most studies focus on deviance, on the working class, on suicide, on crime and delinquency and on subcultures of one kind or another; comparatively little effort is spent on the investigation of 'middle-class' behaviour. More specifically, most of these studies seem to work with the taken for granted assumption that the established dominant forms and norms of sociality are unproblematic, requiring no change.

But psychology's functioning is not simply that of providing the 'instruments of reproduction'. My initial discussion of the sciences of the social has emphasized their positivity. This means that one needs to conceptualize a *dynamic exchange* between the domain of existing practices and the discursive practices that construct psychological knowledge in such a way that whilst 'ideological', common-sense concepts (of, say, the child, the individual, the mother, etc.) are at work in the latter practices, the product of that work within psychology is a modification of these concepts. Thus the take-up of psychological knowledge in everyday action in the apparatuses of the social would bring an element of novelty, although the transformations would continue to be in tune with the 'deep-structure' of the social relations inscribed in them. For example, mental measurement, itself a response to existing problems of needing to establish the 'scientific' bases of differentiation and of differential performances and training in schools, the army, etc., did provide new accounts and measures of cognitive processes that acted as the instruments of change in the practices of normalization in schooling and training. Yet these changes had little effect on the overall distribution of opportunities or the classification of success measured by class or gender. A clear example of the working of common-sense beliefs in mental measurement is the disbelief which greeted the results of initial eleven-plus tests showing a greater percentage of girls than boys scoring in the upper half of the scale (see Introduction to this section).

By and large it can be argued that psychology is concerned with the calibration of error, that is to say, with the scaling of deviation as a means of quantifying the degree of error and thus as indicators of the degree of correction required to return to the norm. Typically, the normal curve, that symbolic instrument of the psychologist, is primarily useful as the index of deviations. Psychological explanation attempts to account for the deviations; it does not address the question of the normality of the norm. For example, IQ tests notoriously by-pass the question of what normal intelligence is by the exasperating device of defining intelligence as that which is measured by IQ tests. Indeed, psychological discourse refers that 'normality', in the end , to biology or to the essentially human. This is, of course, entirely in agreement with the claim that psychology, along with the other sciences of the social, takes for granted the specific conceptualization of the individual as the unitary, pregiven rational (and male) subject. It is the main reason why in this chapter I deconstruct that concept to show its historically produced character.

The other key feature of the focus on pathology or error is related to psychology's functioning as part of the apparatus of the normalization and disciplining of the population. For, from the point of view of administration, it is deviation which is problematic. The position is explicitly stated in the debates that attended the emergence of a new concept of police in the eighteenth century. Pasquino (1980) has pointed out that during that period society itself became the agency against which crime was defined. It is the period when a new notion of 'man' is born, announced in the birth of the human sciences which take 'him' as their object and target.

As Foucault (1976) has argued, the trajectory of the strategies of administration from the emergence of capitalism in the seventeenth century was increasingly that of the more efficient disciplining and amplification of the capacities of the population. Furthermore, the poor in the eighteenth century and the first half of the nineteenth century, potentially the 'dangerous classes', presented a special set of problems. These had to do with the inculcation of good habits and work discipline suitable for the factory form of production, with the development of standards of hygiene that would improve the health of the population in the slums, with the improvement in the skills required by the new industrial processes and with the development of consent to the new forms of administrative and legal authority (see Jones and Williamson, 1979). The target for the appropriate practices is the population as a whole and particular groups of individuals that could be singled out for one reason or another.

Foucault has used the concepts of a bio-politics of the population and an anatomo-politics of the body to refer to the range of the strategies and practices of power in constituting individuals, singly and in their ensemble, according to norms of behaviour beneficial to the economic mode of production and to the well-being of the state (1977 and 1979a).[1] Anatomo-politics refers to the disciplines which centre on the body as a machine and govern 'its training, the amplification of its aptitudes, the extortion of its forces, the parallel growth of its usefulness and docility, its integration into efficient and economic systems of control' (1979a, p. 183) whilst bio-politics refers to the regulative systems that aim to control the mechanisms supporting biological processes and the disciplines that orchestrate the 'organisation of power over life' (ibid., p. 183).

We can utilize that point of view to understand one level of the normalization of the subject, namely the mechanisms which apprentice the body itself to the norms of social statistics (see Hacking, 1981). By these norms I refer to the notion of statistics as 'an inquiry directed at the conditions of life in a country, in order to establish the quantum of happiness of the inhabitants' (Sinclair, 1791–9, quoted in Hacking, 1981). It is allied to the Benthamite social programme of 'the greatest happiness of the greatest number', a programme which required that the Administration count

> men and women and to measure not so much their happiness as their unhappiness: their morality, their criminality, their prostitution, their divorces, their hygiene, their rate of conviction in the courts. . . . [But the] bureaucracy of statistics imposes not just by creating administrative rulings but by determining classifications within which people must think of themselves and of the actions that are open to them. (Hacking, 1981, p. 25)

It is to these mechanisms which normalize the subject that those of psychology and psychiatry and the whole apparatus of education add. It is for all these reasons that the discourse of psychology takes its cue from the techniques and concepts of the biology which emerged with Darwin. One could argue that modern capitalist society was founded on a number of new principles: society as the ultimate bedrock of the values expressed in notions of the social good; the utilitarian understanding of the maximization of the happiness of the greatest number; the health of the social body; national prosperity and the sacralization of the state. Such a foundation is both a condition and a product of the new forms of production and administration and of the new processes of subjection/subjectification. These processes constitute the modern subject, although psychology does not recognize that constitution, in much the same way as positivist sociology takes 'society' to be a pregiven entity independent of its own discourse.

Birth of the individual subject

I now want to deal with two related tasks. To start with I need to unpack the concept of the subject which psychology takes to be its pregiven object. Subsequently, I shall establish in greater detail the discursive conditions that made possible the birth of psychology.

The subject that I have been describing as the unitary, non-contradictory subject in fact combines a double subjectivity: on the one hand, the subject of science and reason born with modern science (and the new social order that replaces feudalism) and, on the other, the abstract legal subject, the subject of general rights and of possessive individualism. The first is ideally represented in Descartes's dictum: 'I think, therefore I am'; the second refers to the new conception of the individual which, in theory, equalizes and generalizes the subject with respect to law, to contractual obligations and to property. It must be said, though, that not all members of the community stand in that relation with respect to the law and to rights. Thus, for a considerable time, women, children and the propertyless were excluded. It is important to make the point that this was mainly done on the basis of the supposed ability to make rational judgement, demonstrating a clear relationship between the two notions of the individual subject. Locke, for example, excludes the propertyless from political participation using the argument that only those who have property are able to make rational calculations about wealth, or could be held to be responsible or moral. Blacks and women were excluded on the claim that they were naturally less endowed with reason than (white) men.

The close connection between these two aspects of the subject makes it necessary to bring both aspects to light in deconstructing it. The importance from the point of view of a history of psychology's object, is that the critique of the assumptions about mental processes highlights their connection with notions of the individual which are more clearly founded in administration and in economic calculations; it shows these notions to be historically specific constructs. But psychology as a science of the social *interiorizes that connection*: it produces the identity between the 'normal' subject of individualism and that of rationality, and locates that identity inside the subject. Thus it naturalizes that notion of rationality and of normality.

Now, the notion of the cogito, that is the mind guaranteeing its own basic rationality – even if in the end underwritten by divine creation – itself has its conditions of possibility in a number of developments that announce the end of feudalism. I shall signal those that are significant for what I want to say by pointing to a number of displacements.

To start with, the decentring of the Earth from the centre of the cosmos which the Copernican revolution announced. The episode is part of a wholesale transformation whereby the fundamental principles which function to make sense of the world, that is which underpin the matrix of intelligibility of the physical and social world, gradually become reconstituted. The transformation refers not only to scientific evidences and arguments but to epistemological, ontological and ideological principles. For instance, one could point to the work of Galileo as the symbolic turning point in the transformation of the basis of western rationality precisely because it summarizes the redefinition of the scientific intelligibility that marks modern science, namely by 'elaborating a conceptual system in which *rational* necessity took the place of physical causality' (Clavelin, 1974, p. 383).

The other principles of this new framework of intelligibility are one of order founded in mathematics (what Foucault, 1966, has discussed using the term 'Mathesis'), and the theses contained in mechanical philosophy. Together they effect a difference within and in opposition to the previously dominant Aristotelian–Thomist doctrines (Easlea, 1980) and the teachings of the Church and its norms of conduct and rationality. They open up a conceptual space in which new concepts of the body, of nature and of the process of production of knowledge emerge. I should mention that an ideology of science emerges from the seventeenth century, initially with Bacon, that sees all science and all reason as masculine, powerful, productive, belonging to *this* world and providing the most secure basis for action in the world (Easlea, 1980; Dickson, 1979).

But another displacement was also taking place in this long struggle, perhaps more important than the themes I have mentioned: it is the shift which locates Reason and the Subject-of-Reason at the core of that new '*ratio*', as its ultimate guarantee. Gradually, rationality and logic come to be regarded as primary: the basic elements of the logocentric subject. The shift is absolutely crucial, for it ensures (in alliance with the other themes) the insecure unity of a new explanatory structure for both the social and the natural world. That structure replaces the previous schema based on 'signature' and on representation, that is to say on the idea of a *signus dei* imprinted in the world, knowledge of which was also knowledge of God (Aquinas). The world became no longer transparent; those authorized to read its language could no longer speak its truth. Language itself and its authoritative texts – scriptures or theological and philosophical works – could no longer be trusted to reveal the secret of the order of things.

And it is precisely with the practice of doubt that Descartes starts the search for a new certainty and a new Reason. It is a scepticism which has one main aim: to proceed to the systematic exclusion of all those ideas, sentiments, feelings, desires and values which could be thought to belong to an old decaying order, or to be competing to replace it, and to the exclusion of everything which threatens the purity of a Reason that alone becomes the source of knowledge and of truth.

So it is with Descartes that the theme of Reason and a Subject-of-Reason most clearly emerges, a theme of the ultimate foundation of rationality and of true knowledge that has come to haunt the search for certainties beyond the guarantees previously inscribed in the conceptual and ontological configuration of feudalism. Whilst Descartes is obviously not alone in the manner in which this new Reason is founded, the form of the argument in the *Meditation* (1641) and in the propositions developed in the *Discourse* (1637) together co-ordinate the key concepts of the modern philosophical logos in their clearest initial form.

It should be pointed out that Descartes has no doubt about the claim that mathematics is the foundation of the order of the world and that the principles of mechanical philosophy provide a sufficient explanatory basis (i.e. motion as the only natural power, the index of measurement and location; the reduction of phenomena to combinations of simple material entities in some state of motion; and the search for mechanical, measurable causes alone, denying occult and essential properties). These are principally developed in opposition to the accounts supported by Aristotelians and by the 'natural magicians' (say, Paracelsus) and their politically subversive stand for social change and against property. Descartes, for instance, is opposed to social change, holding that 'present institutions are practically always more tolerable than would be a change in them'. The political stakes stand out more sharply when we add that Hobbes, a little later, in *Leviathan* (1651), and Locke in *Essay Concerning Human Understanding* (1690), in spite of the radicalism of certain of their positions, argue in the same breath for mechanism, for individualism and for the emergent capitalist social relations and state. Additionally, the Cartesian view of bodies as machines, and the new anatomy that such a model suggests, sets the scene for a good deal of new useful work (e.g. Harvey on blood circulation); it supports the model of the human body as an automaton which has continued to dominate medical practice. When the mind is finally reduced to the same material status as the rest of the body, that is after Darwin, it becomes integrated within the same model, with the difference that it is conceived as the logical machine and information processor (see Introduction to section 1).

Thus the birth of the modern subject is tied to the co-articulation of the three themes – Mathesis, mechanism, modern reason and the subject-of-reason – upon which pivots the conceptual framework for an understanding of the world. But there is more than that. For the point is the substitution of 'man' for God at the heart of *this* world, a substitution which makes sense when one considers that man was already God's privileged creation (in *his* image) endowed with reason, and indeed is the only entity or agent who could have filled the place left empty by the evacuation of the divine from matter. One could say that the emergence of the subject-of-knowledge/science/Reason, *in that form* – that is to say as the unitary and singular (and masculine) origin of true knowledge – was overdetermined. It is perhaps possible that another subjectivity, a collective subjectivity, and a different conception of the world could have emerged, but it is a battle that was lost, though it continued to be fought. I say this in the light of the struggle between mechanical philosophy, with its emphasis on the discrete and the singular, and a point of view asserting a fundamental symbiotic relationship amongst all things, including human beings; that point of view is politically egalitarian and anti-capitalist, although it remains attached to religion and patriarchy. But it does not split off the 'cognitive' from the 'affective', it does not regard nature as barren, to be conquered and put to use; it privileges the community and the whole over the individual. The writings of Paracelsus, Porta (1650), Andreae (1619), Campanella (1622) and Crollius (1624) provide a range of examples expressing that alternative point of view.

Indeed, it is against this background of a struggle in which a specific rationality becomes dominant that one must understand that which becomes dominant and that against which it asserts its dominance: the forces that must be domesticated, brought under control in the new order, the forces which continue to besiege a reason that knows itself to be vulnerable and prone to error.

Madness

Foucault's examination of the normalization of reason in *Histoire de la folie*, 1972, (translated as Madness and Civilization) casts a theoretically stimulating light on this. His initial concern is to plot the history of the transformation in western European culture in which, beginning in the sixteenth century, the theme of madness increasingly comes to be a central source of anxiety. The question is what brought about this dramatic change. Foucault reconstructs how the image of madness earlier had invoked that of the vagrant and the sinner. The attitude towards it in literature and philosophy is that of satire, that is to say of pointing to the tragic element of insanity. But others, such as Breughel, Bosch and Dürer in the fifteenth century depict a more disturbing critical picture. It is this difference which grows in the sixteenth century, accentuating the critical image that had always sensed madness to be part of the critical conscience of man. Its conceptualization shifts from being thought of as one of the bad sides of the human soul – along with idolatry, luxury, anger and so on – to become one of the most feared pathologies, the gap through which the whole of reason threatens to topple into irrationality. Symbolically, the change proceeds from the ship of the mad – *stultifera navis* – to the psychiatric hospital in the seventeenth century with its technology of control and disciplining. Madness becomes something that must be tamed or silenced, an unpredictable and diffuse threat that must be tracked down and forced to the conformity of the norms of the rational.

The old Christian theme that the world is madness in the eyes of God is given a new lease of life which fundamentally denies to the mind of 'man' the power to discover the truths of the world. Our reason is limited and we only grasp the surface appearance of things. Foucault explains that

> that contradiction between appearance and truth is already present at the heart of appearance: for if there were some coherence in appearance it would at least make allusion to truth and be its empty form. It is in things themselves that one must discover this reversal.
> (Foucault, 1972, p. 42)

This appearance of things upside down is not, however, a clue to truth, which would be its right way up, but is 'that implication of the opposites which denies us, for ever perhaps, the unique and straight path to truth' (ibid., p. 42).

The Platonism of the sixteenth century is a Platonism of irony and criticism; but measured in terms of the truth of essences and of God every human order seems nothing but madness. At the same time, it is only by reference to Reason that madness can be specified. Madness becomes almost a form of reason, a form that reason can know as its dark side, and against which it measures its rationality. Erasmus and Montaigne and a host of other authors concur on this intimacy between reason and unreason, the thin dividing line which is maintained at the cost of constant vigilance. Foucault has noted the view commonly held in the eighteenth century that novels and the theatre could make one mad probably because unreason and its signs (hidden desires, passions, deviant behaviours) are played out there, defying the orderly safety of objective reason for the reckless temptation of a subversive imagination.

But it is also Christian thought which provides the means of escape from the darkness of madness or the violence of irrationality. For the sovereignty of 'Divine Reason' can contain the forces of disruption, insanity can be tied to such a 'Reason' and thus become accountable.

> Madness becomes a form relative to reason, or rather madness and reason enter into a perpetually reversible relation which provides every madness with its reason, that sits in judgment upon and masters it, every reason its madness in which it finds its derisory

> truth. Each is the measure of the other, and in this movement of reciprocal reference, they impugn each other, yet each founds the other. (Foucault, 1972, p. 41)

Second, 'madness becomes one of the very forms of reason' (ibid., p. 44); it can only have meaning on the terrain of reason, as one of its secret parameters. The recognition of the immanence of madness to reason, explored by Montaigne and Pascal, becomes almost one of the stratagems of reason in distancing itself from madness, a hazardous stratagem which so many, from Descartes to Althusser, have lived out. Foucault proposes that the

> truth of madness now coincides with the victory of reason . . . for the truth of madness is to be the inside of reason, to be one of its figures, a force and seemingly a momentary need in order for reason better to provide itself with the guarantee of its difference. (ibid., p. 47)

Towards the end of the sixteenth century, this new theme of madness comes to occupy an important place in literature and the theatre; Don Quixote, Hamlet and King Lear are just the best-known examples from an extensive exploration of madness. It becomes the means by which old values and beliefs and old forms are questioned and new ways confusedly explored.

One should correlate this fact with all the other signs of the loss of faith in the rationality of the old order: the belief in the decay of the cosmos presaging the second coming, peasant rebellions that are seen by the authorities as the work of irrational or demonic forces – there is the fear of the mob or what is later called the *dangerous classes* (expressed, for example, by Bacon, Hobbes and Descartes), a mob sometimes clearly demented, as in the case of Ranters and Ravers, and which continued for a long time (Lefebvre, 1973) – the fear of witchcraft, and the appearance of deviant religious movements such as Hermeticism. And relate it then to the forces which work towards establishing a new 'rational' order: mechanical philosophy, protestantism, an increasingly confident merchant capitalism and the 'new science' of Bacon and of the experimental philosopher-artists.

Within such a context it is Reason, and not some other faculty, and a Reason divinely founded in the unitary subject, which is invested with the burden of guaranteeing the new rationality and a new order of truth: Pure Reason with Descartes, for whom experience could not generate ideas, but reason with Locke also, as *reflection* on experience as the source of truth. Nor is it surprising that madness, along with occult forces, women, the poor, the criminal, should be exiled. Foucault says: 'If *man* can be mad, *thought* as the exercise of the sovereignty of a subject who takes it upon himself to perceive the truth, cannot be insane' (1972, p. 58). Reason can no longer afford to be unreasonable nor madness rational, as in the Renaissance. A new *ratio* is born, but

> it is fitting that the history of a *ratio* such as that of the Western world should disappear in the progress of a 'rationalism'; it includes for an equally large, if a more secret, part that movement whereby Unreason has become embedded in our soil, doubtless to disappear in it, yet, to take root in it. (ibid., p. 58)

In their study of the Enlightenment, Horkheimer and Adorno (1979) make several points which bear a similarity to what I have been arguing. They regard the principal programme of the Enlightenment to have been the desocialization of nature in alliance with the disenchantment of the world (1979, p. 3). They also point out that the concept of knowledge which emerges with Bacon is one in which knowledge is equated with power. Habermas (1971) has suggested that it is a form of knowledge in which technical and practical interest is dominant. Such an interest seeks dominion: 'what men want to learn from nature is how to use it in order wholly to dominate it and other men' (Horkheimer and Adorno, 1979, p. 4). It is a view echoed by Luther for whom 'knowledge that tendeth but to satisfaction is but as a courtesan, which is for pleasure, and not for fruit or generation'.

The disenchantment of the world which took the form of the rejection of magic and of the Aristotelian–Thomist cosmology, which was also the Christian cosmology of the presence and of the magic of God in his works, is part of the project by which 'the many mythic figures are brought to a common denominator and reduced to the human subject' (ibid., pp. 6, 7). The centrality of the subject in the explanatory structure and the philosophical logos of the new order can be judged from this. The birth of 'man' is synchronic with the birth of Bacon's *una scientia universalis* and Leibniz' *mathesis universalis* and, I would add, with a *lingua universalis*. The concept of a subject constitutive of knowledge functions as a relay making possible the discursive substitution of the sovereignty of God over the world by that of 'man'. Those excluded in this privileging of *homo rationalis* are denied access to the discourse of power and the ability to speak in their own name, though they do not cease to be caught in the play of power, and indeed do not cease to resist. How can one be surprised that such a system of exclusion should require a whole series of apparatuses of normalization and discipline both for the positive production of a specific 'normal' subjectivity and the policing of the systems of exclusion?

It is worth highlighting here the fact that the hospital of the seventeenth century contained the poor, the insane, the sick, the vagrant, petty criminals, in a mass that only gradually became differentiated in terms of distinct technologies of intervention and distinct discourses: of psychiatry, of criminality, of prisons (Foucault, 1973, 1975; Pasquino, 1980). The scientific discourses and the practices of differentiation and formation are coextensive, the one relaying the other.

Generally then, the first form of exclusion is the 'great confinement' which Foucault describes (1972, ch. 1, part 11, pp. 56–91). Unfortunately, I cannot go into the details of this history. I refer to it in order to add to my general thesis that the modern form of rationality emerges in definite circumstances with definite conditions of possibility and is actively constructed as part of the constitution of a specific form of sociality and of intelligibility. The question of its construction is not simply an epistemological question, nor one of the specificity of 'modern science' *alone*. It should be clearer now why the examination of the modern ratio, and with it the norms of truth and rationality, involves a deconstruction of the subject placed at its centre, of the process of production of knowledge and the apparatuses of the social in which they are intricated in a mutually constitutive relation.

The rational, ahistorical being of psychology

Thus we witness a double birth: that of a new 'rationality' and of 'modern man'. The history of the one cannot be separated from that of the other. It is not without consequence for psychology. First of all, psychology ignores the historically specific character of what it takes to be its pregiven object; the subject of psychology is the 'rational man' with no past, or rather whose past has receded to a mysterious point of origin. It appears on the scene in the guise of the naturally normal 'man', behaving according to norms that in the end are underwritten by biology. But all is not well with that subject. I have already pointed to the focus on pathology, especially of mental processes, attending the beginning of psychology. It seems that psychology can only theorize this ahistorical entity by conceptualizing anything that attaches it to a definite society and epoch as potentially inimical to its rationality and normality. (The next chapter will demonstrate the deep-rooted character of this view in its discussion of cognitive development.)

So the *philosophical* exclusion of feelings and desires from reason, though not mind, has meant that psychology has found it difficult to deal with the effectivity of the domain of the social on the subject's knowledge processes and behaviour, referring them to something *outside* the individual that gets inside: the socialization angle criticized in the Introduction to section 1.

The cleavage between psychoanalysis and psychology is another crucial consequence. One could say that it is the domain of 'unreason' (and of ideology) that Freud begins to explore in focusing on the unconscious, and that therefore what is asserted in psychoanalytic theory is inimical to psychology's project. It follows that the subject of psychology that I have outlined earlier is the 'individual subject' minus everything that pins down its identity and its lived experience of social relations. It is a partial subjectivity: that which fits in with the subject-of-science of the positivist ideology of science; also, it is a subjectivity which is consistent with the rationalizing subject of capitalist economic exchange. Within the conceptual terrain of the concept of nature of mechanical philosophy the Cartesian subject is a being reduced to the abstract laws of the calculating machine and the accounting rules of the administration of bodies and commodities. This reduction is entirely compatible with the techniques of disciplining and training which seek to maximize the capacities and productivity of the body. Thus Foucault's notion of an 'anatomo-politics' of the body finds an unintended support in the view of the human subject as a profit-maximizing organism embodied in Thorndike's Law of Effect. Such, indeed, is the subject psychology takes for granted.

Mind as the object of a science: the naturalization of mind

I want at this point to return to the question of the conditions of possibility of a science of mind and in particular to the developments to which I have already referred in speaking about the naturalization of mind. Given that reason, before the theory of evolution, is placed outside the realm of human cognition it is not possible to conceive of a science that would take the processes of mind to be its object: with Descartes it is a divine attribute, the essentially human, it is that *a priori* faculty whereby we are able to know anything at all. Later, for Kant, the subject is placed beyond such a science: it is the *transcendental* condition for knowing. Hegel, rejecting Kant's solution, thought that consciousness could be the affair of self-reflection, that is to say the prime object of a *philosophy*; the science of logic would uncover the principles informing such a philosophy, but it is not equivalent to a science of mind. Clearly, a lot is said about minds and rationality. A lot is inferred from the sciences, since the latter are claimed to be the ideal product of rational thought. But the idea that mental processes could be directly studied and measured required other assumptions.

It could be argued that the observation and treatment of madness provided certain clues. However, as I have argued, in the earlier clinical work madness was conceptualized in terms of 'alienation', i.e. as error, as an unnatural event. Indeed, it was Freud who first clearly formulated the principle that psychopathology and normal behaviour referred to the same underlying processes. Darwin, in his early working out of the implications of the transmutation of species, made full use of the contemporary works which examined mental pathologies. However, these relied on medical observations, or common-sense notions and projections based on what was known about the inheritance of characteristics from the domestication and breeding of animals. Mind as such remained a separate object, the province of philosophical reflections.

So we come to the problem of the conditions that enabled that displacement from philosophy to natural science. First of all, I should stress the importance of the historical transformations from the end of the eighteenth century – in particular the emergent ascendency of an industrial 'class' fighting out the power struggle with both the aristocracy and landed gentry and the working classes. Three forces are at work in shaping the sites, both politico-economic and theoretical, of struggle and change. (The form of the struggle and what was at stake from the point of view of political economy is probably best displayed in Ricardo, building upon A. Smith, when they discussed class struggle amongst the land-owners, manufacturers, traders and the labouring classes during the agrarian and industrial revolutions of the eighteenth and nineteenth centuries.) First, the rising economic power based in manufacturing and commerce whose ideological discourse is, at its most developed boundaries, progressive for the time. In England one such discourse is utilitarianism in its various forms, including, more obviously, the later versions cobbled together by J. S. Mill, who advocated a radical liberal politics, limited suffrage for women and others, mass education, etc. Another powerful force includes the workers and peasants, disunited politically, but who as a consequence of mechanization, urban growth and mass poverty, pursued strategies of resistance that included revolutions, for example, in France and North America, the physical destruction of machines (Luddites), 'rioting', forming solidarity groups for struggle (combinations, early unionization, nonconformist churches – Wesleyans, for example, included members of the Tolpuddle Martyrs) and the emergence of radical discourses demanding greater equality and freedoms.

Finally, the old established ruling class, its economic domination based on agriculture gradually eroding, responded by the rationalization of agricultural production and the support of conservative policies and values: a return to the mythical happiness of agricultural communities.

Romanticism, for example that of Wordsworth (as in *The Excursion*), is a complex expression of the contradictions inscribed in these positions: the celebration of Nature, the rejection of industrialism and the defence of ideals of a *communitas*, of justice, liberty and human dignity. How is this complex of positions relevant to the problem of the birth of a new discourse concerning the subject and a science of mind? The point which stands out is the fact that it expresses the dissolution and the inadequacy of the frame of intelligibility and explanatory grid (the concept of *episteme* – Foucault, 1971 – attempts to capture what is meant here) that had so far made sense of the social world and informed its strategies for the administration of the social. It is concerned with the fashioning of the main principles which guided action and positions in the development of the new politics and the new norms of social relations. It centrally involved a new notion of the subject.

It is for this reason that in examining the theoretical frame of signification I want to highlight the doctrine of the 'uniqueness of man', and its association with the Great Chain of Being scheme (see Bonnet, 1769). The latter, basically, depicted all living things in terms of a sequence of connections, hierarchically organized, so that mammals were placed at the top of the chain and the human species appeared as the most complex developed being in the chain. But it is not an evolutionary schema, for there is no change in the species; the *fixity of places* is what characterizes the chain, fixity determined from the beginning as part of 'creation'. The classification of species, with Linnaeus for instance, also asserts the fixity of types and defining characteristics. The doctrine of the 'uniqueness of man' is completely consistent with this scientific classification. It agrees with the scriptures' story of creation but, equally crucial, it ascribes to 'man' a special place with respect to the divine order. It is only 'man' that would have reason, language and morality.

Moreover the whole conceptual framework supports the view of the fixity of places in social relations. This is the sense in which the doctrine was used in political thought and in common-sense representation. The verse of Alexander encapsulates the conservative ideal:

> The rich man in his castle,
> The poor man at his gate,
> God made them, high or lowly,
> And order'd their estate.

It was written in 1848 at a time when the old order had virtually disappeared, but at the end of a period of intense struggle which witnessed the Chartist movement of the 1830s and 1840s, the Poor Law Act which criminalized the poor, the 'Hungry Forties', and so on.

Darwin

It is with that historical context in mind that I want to re-examine the displacement in the notion of the subject that takes place with Darwin's theory of evolution and the naturalization of reason and the mind which is part of the intelligibility of the theory. The key point on which to focus is that the naturalization of mind and evolutionary theory before the middle of the nineteenth century was subversive to the hegemony of the time. In the name of the supposedly divinely ordained 'naturalness' of the inequalities of power, property and rights, this claimed the existing social relations to be not only natural but normative and rational. Darwin's early draft of transmutation (1837–9) in the *Notebooks* shows that he was aware of the implications. Indeed he ranged over the issues concerning rationality, morality, aesthetics and social behaviours of one kind or another because any convincing account of evolution that included the human species had to explain how reason, language and ethical and aesthetic values developed gradually from their form in other animals and developed according to the same processes that accounted for physical changes. Darwin started out from an explicitly materialist basis (see Venn, 1982), in direct opposition to the view of the 'uniqueness of man' with its implied unchanging nature of human beings and human societies and the implication that the human was outside materialist, scientific understanding.

Furthermore, the proposition that mind and its capabilities and faculties were emenable to scientific explanations of the same kind as physiological changes clearly brought with it the idea that these capabilities could be investigated using appropriate *scientific* methodologies.

Concomitantly, the specific theoretical conditions of possibility of a science of mind via biology and natural history meant that the conceptualizations of mental processes and characteristics (and of changes in them) borrowed from these sciences. In particular, the emergent science retains the idea of a population, the concept of the norm and of the relation between the individual exemplar and the population of which it is a member. Jacob (1970) summarizes this nicely; writing about the conceptual transformation brought about by biology, he says that from around the 1850s knowledge of living objects became secondary to knowledge of the *type* to which they belong. Objects are thought to reflect the type, whilst the population is regarded as a collection of slightly different objects of the same type. Knowledge of the population can thus be drawn from a census of the distribution of the characteristics of its *individual members*. The average type becomes an abstraction: '*only individuals acquire a reality, with their peculiarities, their differences, their variations*' (p. 191, emphasis added).

I used the term displacement above rather than transformation, because in spite of the radical shifts, the individuality of the 'individual' as a thinking, acting, feeling machine but principally as a thinking, calculating, machine does not change. What is different is the foundation of these characteristics. Whereas previously they were attributed, in the final origin, to divine creation and will, or to forms of development or becoming, themselves ultimately founded in some spiritual destiny, religion now ceased to provide the principles of the guarantees. Instead it is nature itself that becomes the origin and foundation; all explanations have to find their basis in natural processes. Additionally, they are the processes *as described by science*, so that the question of how we know that the natural processes are as we think them to be is answered by an appeal to scientific authority. Henceforth, nature and science mutually underwrite each other's claims. Concerning the mind and the rational processes of the subject, we are referred on the one hand to science in the positivist sense as the measure and norm, the arbiter of cognition, and, on the other hand, to natural origin and development to account for its present state.

So the human subject is biologized; indeed, it has not ceased to find a handy last refuge in the soil of biology since that time. Individualism has become the normal because it is now thought to accord to the *natural state* of existence.

The techniques for studying the individual: questions of the normal type, measures of variation, of dispersion, abnormalities and so forth have come to appear as the most important questions and the most appropriate scientific methodology. Furthermore, mental processes such as those of memory and perception are theorized within the mechanical perspective of a psychophysics, thus minimizing the need to take into account the effects of the social dimension inside these processes.

The science of population that develops continues a trajectory from W. Petty, *Population Arithmetic* (1672), which was primarily concerned with establishing more accurate measures of the wealth and health of the population at a time when the redefinition of the nation-state in legal terms and the emergence of capitalism implied more definite boundaries of citizenship and precise calculations of the wealth of nations. It becomes part of a new science of life which associates it with the science of wealth. It becomes part of the rational calculation of a governmentality (Foucault, 1979b), ensuring the security as well as the 'happiness' of the population and the state (Pasquino, 1980). Indeed, for psychometrics, an unbroken line connects Galton, Pearson, Cattell and other major figures in the development of the methodology of mental measurement and statistical analysis; that they all subscribed to eugenics supports the view that their work is locked into a science of the population.

Utility and rational planning

I would like to make two other connections that will add to the explanatory structure for the notion of sciences of the social and thus further help to locate psychology within that framework. I have already mentioned the functioning of the natural sciences and the ideology of science that has emerged since the seventeenth century in the formulation of the social and natural order. From Comte's positive science of society (1831–3), the idea that society was amenable to a scientific study whose rules would be those of the natural sciences steadily gained recognition. Interestingly, given that the period is that of the confrontation between the intelligibility of the old order vested in religion and the search for a different site of conceptual coherence, Comte explicitly impugns the 'theological state' of social theory. Darwin took great comfort from the Comtian project of a science of society; he envisaged such a rational form of investigation to be in support of the materialism, including the naturalization of mind, which he advocated. Both moved in the direction of establishing a new understanding of society, one implication of which (not clearly developed in Darwin's early texts) was the possibility of a *rational planning* of society. Social Darwinism, later, fully drew out these implications (see Jones, 1980).

The other connection relates to the principle of utility. What I have said above implicitly locates such a principle at work in the discourses of the social that I have mentioned. That principle is very fundamental in the arguments that Darwin deploys to account for the survival of variations and varieties, that is to say in terms of their comparative advantage and, more explicitly, in the arguments about characteristics surviving that are to the greater *benefit and pleasure* of the species. (I have established this in detail elsewhere – Venn, 1982). In line with the central tenets of utilitarianism, the goal of maximizing pleasure and utility is extended to account for both physical changes and the fixity of characteristics and instincts as well as to the development of moral values, to rationality, taste and patterns of behaviour. The proposition that what is beneficial or useful is also pleasurable and good becomes almost a natural law applying to all life and human action.

Thus a nexus of concepts and principles emerged during that period which provides the foundation for the sciences of the social and which circumscribes and is at work inside them. It includes the naturalization of all human characteristics, guaranteed in biology and natural law as described by the sciences and the acceptance of positivist rules for regulating the discourses concerning society and the individual; it also includes the principle of utility whereby norms of behaviour and action beneficial to the existing dominant social relations and forms of material production become *normative* on the assumption that they work for the greater good of the whole community. An older principle remains central: that of the individual as the basic unit and the target for the apparatuses of correction or training. It is all of these that condition the production of psychology.

I will illustrate these interconnections through a brief analysis of the first issue of *Mind* (1878), the quarterly review of 'psychology and philosophy' until 1920, which admirably demonstrates the extent to which the above considerations were present in the calculations of those involved in working out the conceptual framework for a psychology.

The project of the journal is discussed by the editor (G. C. Robertson) who, arguing for a new departure in philosophy consonant with the contemporary developments in biology, says:

> The real and natural beginning is a rigorous investigation of the phenomena of mind. If all Philosophy must be essentially Philosophy of Mind . . . the question as to the innermost nature of mental action must surely be taken first. . . . *Psychology then is the only true point of departure in philosophy.* (my italics)

Thus psychology as a science of mind is considered to be the rational and objective foundation for philosophy.

This is an interesting reversal of the place of philosophy with respect to the psychology of emotions. He goes on to rehearse arguments about 'our constitution', utilizing several biological metaphors of bodily organs, and its connection to the constitution of knowledge.

The contents of that issue reflect the range of interconnected positions, and the authors who have contributed to the development of the conceptual framework that has naturalized reason: H. Spencer, 'The comparative psychology of man', H. Sidgwick, 'The theory of evolution in its application to practice', S. H. Hodgson, 'Philosophy and science', H. Bain, 'The early life of James Mill', James Sully, 'Physiological psychology in Germany'. This lends compact support to my claim that biology, psychology and the philosophy of science emerge as the main discourses that condition and provide the main concepts for the new discourse of mind. It contains a clear materialist and empiricist commitment which regards mental activity as subject to laws and regularities that owe more to biological processes than to cultural constitution.

Furthermore, the whole orientation is suffused with the individualism which is a nodal point or relay point at the intersection of political philosophy, of the 'moral sciences' and of epistemology during the whole of the period I am examining.

So the manner and circumstance of the emergence of psychology already privileged certain rules of formation of its discourse. To a large extent and in spite of the diversity of practices that now constitute the system of differences within the 'psychological complex' (Rose, 1979), psychological theorizations have remained attached to the presuppositions and methodological rules that I have described.

On several occasions I have indicated what this has meant for the way different psychologies have constructed their object, namely the subject. I have also stressed the instrumental calculations of the sciences of the social that have taken the individual to be the prime target for practices of normalization in the diverse sites of intervention such as the family, the school, and so on. It is clear from the arguments I have presented that the instrumentality of the discourses of the social, including psychology, and the specific rationality of the western Logos from the seventeenth century have mutually conditioning effects.

The case of language

Now, it could be argued that this only applies to cases such as mental measurement or personality grids for which the practical implications are present from the beginning. I will briefly show that the effects of the social are formative of psychological science even in the less visibly normalizing discourses such as psycholinguistics and language development and cognitive development. The problem of language from the birth of modern rationality has been inseparable from the discussions about the latter. Most of the authors concerned with the construction of the norms of that rationality and the norms that order the social formation from the seventeenth century have thought language crucially important.

Hacking (1975) has argued that the interest in, and the point of view from which most philosophers have approached, the problem of language has centred on 'the nature of the mind'. From that point of view, Moore, Wittgenstein or Chomsky are not attempting anything different – at the level of the general project – from Hobbes, Hume, Locke or Mill. That is to say, they are concerned with the relation between 'the way in which we conceive the world and . . . something dimly reminiscent of the Cartesian "ego", the knowing self' (Hacking, 1975, p. 11).

The relation between mind and language is still central in psychological work today, and whilst psychologists do not examine language simply as part of finding an answer about mental processes, deep-seated assumptions about mind and about language continue to have crucial effects on theories of language development. These assumptions gesture towards a conceptual homogeneity in the discourses I have discussed, that is to say the network of key principles that make possible the alliances and affinities which are part of the conceptual solidarity, that one could refer to as a 'hegemonic complex'.

In their critique of the accounts of language in psycholinguistics, in social psychology and in classical theories of language, Pêcheux (1975) and Henry (1977) have made two important points. They argue that the notion of the unity of language together with that of the unitary subject covers over the question of struggle, that is the play of power and resistance (they use the concept of class struggle). At the same time, and related to the above, the individual–social dichotomy and its functioning in linguistics, philosophy or psychology presents the problem in terms of a *socialization process*, reinforcing the individualism of the unitary rational subject. Thus differences in behaviour are reduced to individual differences, measured as deviations from norms; that is to say they are seen as the result or the index of personality differences, of variations in cognitive abilities, rates of development or, in gross cases, of pathologies. One effect for politics is that of *eliding the antagonistic processes* at the heart of both the regulation of a society and the production of discourses. Instead of antagonism, classical theories of language – and psychology in its turn – have tended to conceptualize inconsistencies and 'contradictions' in terms of a langue–parole division, in which logic and speech are the privileged elements. Pêcheux (1975) has argued that the linguistic conception of language, including its apparently opposite statement in the logico-mathematical formalism of Chomsky, Lévi-Strauss or Piaget, is inscribed in the philosophical problematic of modern empiricism. Even attempts to overcome the dichotomy, when they remain within that same problematic, only propose combinations of the logical and the representational which produce either concrete realism (logic being viewed as essentially a property of objects, that is, inscribed in the way objects are constructed, for example in J. J. Katz) or an idealist rationalism: thought is conceived as adding to reality and recreating it. What this epistemology elides is the historicity of the production of knowledge and of the individual subject:

> Empiricist as well as realist theories of knowledge seem to have an interest in forgetting the existence of scientific disciplines as historically constituted, preferring a universal theory of ideas, whether the latter takes the realist form of a universal and a priori network of concepts or the empiricist form of an administrative procedure applicable to the universe conceived as an ensemble of facts, objects, events or acts. (Pêcheux, 1975, p. 68)

The homologous problem in psychology is expressed in the cognitive–affective couple and the problems concerning language and context. In either case, problems of value, and problems that could be discussed using concepts of, for example, subjective positionality and of power in accounting for success or failure in cognitive or linguistic performance (as they are in section 3 below), are instead reduced to a problem of the 'influence' of the social environment on the unitary individual, an 'influence' that can be mitigated in 'gross' cases by taking appropriate corrective action.

By contrast, the theory of signification that this book outlines interiorizes differences within the social process of signification, accounting for them by reference to differences of power and gender and different canalizations of desire. Such an approach places social relations at the centre of the stage. It opens onto the whole of a culture and the specificities of that culture at particular historical moments. I have demonstrated that for the logocentric subject of psychology the social and the cultural is a contingent embarrassment, which needs to be watchfully disciplined.

Towards the fabrication of the subject

In order to concretize the differences I shall very briefly outline the main components of the new problematic and indicate the consequences for the problem of the constitution of the subject.

My analysis points to three main areas. To start with, the need for a materialist theory of knowledge which regards knowledge as a specific kind of production with definite relations to the social and material world. It would reject the autonomy of science, the science–ideology divide and accounts of the production of knowledge which leave out cultural effects on the internal system of statements of scientific discourses. Much work has already been done in this area and, although there are clear differences among various materialist theorizations, one can find sufficient grounds for asserting that scientific statements are the result of two things. First, a labour of production which is constrained by the material processes that are the general real objects of scientific investigations – for example geological or biological processes and properties of materials. Second, however, in their production we can claim a difference between the real object and the object of knowledge; specifically, the latter can be regarded as a construction which depends on the apparatus of construction available (the techniques, the physical means of production, etc.), on current theorizations (not independent of the apparatus of production), on the cultural system of intelligibility (what at any point in time is considered rational and plausible, for example the naturalness of mind) and on the historical and cultural circumstances: on the historically specific ways in which the questions thought to be important are posed, the problems prioritized by specific agencies, etc.

In addition, social scientific discourse constructs objects that are more clearly cultural in the sense that the intelligibility and rationality of their descriptions and the rules of formation of statements about them are part of a process of signification which is at the same time intricated in the process of constitution of sociality. This is not a position reducible to the 'social construction of reality' thesis or to the thesis about the intersubjective character of meaningful social action and of understanding. The latter positions, even when they recognize the social character of the 'individual subject' do not problematize the subject in the way in which I have done in this chapter. In particular they cannot escape resorting to a subject-form which has the same conceptual function with respect to knowledge and to action as that of the unitary subject of modern rationality. This dependence is implicit in the philosophical position guiding these approaches, for instance in the notion of the transcendental ego of Husserl's phenomenology. The individual subject is even more clearly the central figure who acts, understands, negotiates, plays roles in the discourse of phenomenological sociology (see Hindess, 1979b, for an interesting critique). It is not possible for these positions to begin an examination of the subject which regards it as a constituted figure; specifically, which regards its process of constitution to be part of the process of production of discourse (including scientific knowledges) and of the whole complex of social relations.

The new problematic includes a theory of discourse which recognizes the investment of power and desire in the discursive process, its imbrication in a complex of practices that are always already historical and social, its circumscription within the materiality of these practices and its relative openness. The implications of such a theory are developed in section 3.

In rejecting the category of the unitary, individual and rational subject and problematizing the notion of the 'subjective', the theoretical departure that I am signalling seeks to recover the domain that positivist psychology had abandoned to that other science of mind, namely psychoanalysis. Although I am not claiming that psychoanalysis should be taken on board uncritically, this domain of the unconscious, of invisible desires and feelings is central to any account of subjectivity. The constructive aspect of that recovery is the attempt to conceptualize the constitutive relationship between the so-called 'cognitive' and 'affective' dimensions of behaviour by decentring them from the subject and locating their construction in the domain of the social. The subject itself is also theorized as constituted in these processes, hence the concept of the 'radical interiority' of subjectivity to such processes (see Derrida, 1972; also Adlam *et al.*, 1977). Considered alongside the theory of discourse to which I have referred above, the implication is that the processes of signification and subjectification form one intricate machinery. Any discourse which aims to speak of the subject must at the same time speak of the social, and it must do so *not* in terms of a complementarity but on the basis of the fabrication of subjects in and for signifying material practices.

However, the subject is not altogether caught in the web of discourse. There is the fact that biological constraints set certain limits to its constitution. (I use biology here not in the way meant by say sociobiologists but gesturing towards what D. Riley (1978a) has called a 'socialized biology'; see the Introduction to section 1 and our discussion of that concept there.) There is also the fact that discourse itself is not an autonomous or originary domain of practices, but is historically and materially constituted in the sense that its production is always-already conditioned by existing discursive practices and what is materially and socially at stake in them.

One may well ask what the implications of the deconstruction of psychology's subject are for politics and for psychological discursive practices. The question is discussed in several places in this book. But a problem remains since, if psychology, from its emergence, is in alliance and in articulation with the sciences of the social, can one imagine a different science of the subject? From my arguments it follows that such a different discourse would itself fully emerge only in quite different conditions. One of these conditions is precisely the critique of what now exists from definite political and theoretical positions and the beginning of the construction of a different subject, that is to say a different politics and different social relations. One of my principal aims has been to justify such a new approach, and to demonstrate that the new theorization of subjectivity cannot occupy the theoretical space of existing psychology but is part of a wider project. The fact that I am at all able to do the critique I have done and indicate the premise of a new theorization of the subject is itself a sign of resistance inside the discourses that speak of the subject and of the fraught reconstruction of social relations in day-to-day politics. Psychology, fortunately, does not have the measure of the subject.

Note

1 The idea is based on a number of prior propositions which claim that biology and new systems of representation and of economic production became, from the eighteenth century, the parameters that governed material and social life. These parameters refer to the 'quasi-transcendental' concepts of Life, Language and Labour (Foucault, 1972, p. 262). They replace 'transcendental' signifiers such as Mathematics or Representation, which established the configuration of the previous form of intelligibility. Thus the new sciences of the social that develop as part of the new form of sociality centre on establishing the laws of life, of language and of the production of wealth. All regulation gravitates around the processes relevant from that point of view. The discourses that articulate the new knowledge are those of medicine, of political economy, of governmentality.

Developmental psychology and the child-centred pedagogy: the insertion of Piaget into early education[1]

Valerie Walkerdine

Introduction

The British primary school is taken to be a paradigm of practice for a considerable proportion of the western world. Here, children are to be enabled to develop at their own pace, to work individually, to be free and to grow up into rational adults. Such at least is the ambition of the pedagogy. In her book *Children's Minds* (1978) Margaret Donaldson begins by painting for us a picture of such a school, with children full of wonderment at the joy of learning. What, she asks, goes wrong? Why, in this model, do so many children apparently fail to learn and why does such a promising start end in failure for so many of them? The dream of the pedagogy which will set children free, which will serve as the motor of liberation, is not a new one: it is present in the early progressive movement of the 1920s and 1930s and is a familiar feature of the progressivism central to radical approaches to education in the 1970s. Is it a pipe-dream, this dream of the pedagogy to aid the liberation of children and thus promote some transformation in the social domain? Is it that the conditions for such a pedagogy are not possible? Why do so many children fail and what part does developmental psychology play in all this?

In this chapter I shall argue that one of the major problems with the notion of developmental psychology as implicated in a pedagogy of liberation is in the way the terms of the argument are posed. Margaret Donaldson's answer lies in a *more effective psychology* which can be more accurate in telling us how children 'really learn' and therefore how to produce better, lasting learning. This seems an unproblematic enough goal. But is it as simple as it looks? What I aim to demonstrate is that the very lynchpin of developmental psychology, the 'developing child', is an object premised on the location of certain capacities within 'the child' and therefore within the domain of psychology. Other features are thereby externalized as aspects of a social domain which influence or affect the pattern of development and, consequently, the conditions of educability. It is axiomatic to developmental psychology that there exist a set of empirically demonstrable foundations for its claims to truth about the psychological development of children. In chapter 3 (pp. 119–52) we examined how psychology's claims to truth are premised on the constitution of the individual as an object of science in certain historically specific conditions of possibility. In the light of that analysis I will examine the conditions which make possible and produce our modern form of primary schooling which I have referred to as the 'child-centred pedagogy'. My aim, then, is to demonstrate the problem in assuming that the way out of dilemmas about the possibility of both a liberatory pedagogy and a 'social' developmental psychology is in the limit-conditions of the project of a developmental psychology itself. Because of the way that the object of a developmental psychology is formulated, it is impossible to produce the radical theory which would fulfil the hopes of many within the discipline.[2]

However as we have already stated (Introduction to section 2, pp. 100 ff.), psychological knowledges have a positive effectivity in that they are implicated in the production of forms of sociality, and the apparatuses and practices of administration and normalization. My task, therefore, is twofold: it is to demonstrate that developmental psychology is premised on a set of claims to truth which are historically specific, and which are not the only or necessary way to understand children. In addition I seek to establish that those practices, such as particular pedagogies and forms of schooling, are not mere applications of a scientific apparatus, but should be understood as centrally and strategically implicated in the possibility of a developmental psychology itself.

These are shock tactics, and they are intended to go beyond epistemological critiques. For example, epistemological critiques of Piaget (such as that written by two authors of this volume, Venn and Walkerdine, 1978) certainly examine the claims to truth upon which Piaget's enterprise is founded. However, they rely on treating the claims as valid or invalid in a way which fails to locate them in a historically specific regime of truth. Locating the work of Piaget within the constitution of the developmental psychology/child-centred pedagogy couple allows me to examine the very formation of the objects upon which Piaget's enterprise was founded and the practices in which his work was utilized.

Particular disciplines, regimes of truth, bodies of knowledge, make possible both *what can be said* and *what can be done*: both the object of science and the object of pedagogic practices. Pedagogic practices then are totally saturated with the notion of a normalized sequence of child development, so that those practices help produce children as the objects of their gaze. The apparatuses and mechanisms of schooling which do this range from the architecture of the school and the seating arrangements of the classroom to the curriculum materials and techniques of assessment. Now clearly the claims to truth about child development are many and varied, so we should not expect the apparatuses to be all of one piece and without contradictions. However, if we examine particular apparatuses, it is possible to display the intimate connection between the practices and the set of assumptions about learning and teaching premised on child development.

The child-centred pedagogy in operation

> I hear and I forget
> I see and I remember
> I do and I understand

The above quotation forms the frontispiece to the first teachers' guide to the Nuffield Mathematics project, *I Do and I Understand*. This was the first and most influential curriculum intervention into primary school mathematics in the 1960s. This quotation juxtaposes hearing and forgetting on the one hand and doing and understanding on the other. The polarization of passive remembering and active learning produced the most important theoretical tenet in the recent history of the primary school:

> children, *developing at their own individual rates, learn through their active response to the experiences that come to them*; through constructive play, experiment and discussion children *become aware of relationships and develop mental structures* which are mathematical in form and are in fact the only sound basis of mathematical techniques. *The aim of Primary teaching*, it is argued, *is the laying of this foundation of mathematical thinking about the numerical and spatial aspects of the objects and activities which children of this age encounter.*
> (Mathematical Association, 1955, pp. v, vi)

The central statements from the above quotation are those which I have italicized. To a developmental psychologist or a teacher of young children such statements will appear obvious, being the common sense of modern pedagogic practices and developmental psychological principles. They have become so taken for granted that it is difficult to see precisely what could be questionable about them. That children did not learn by 'hearing

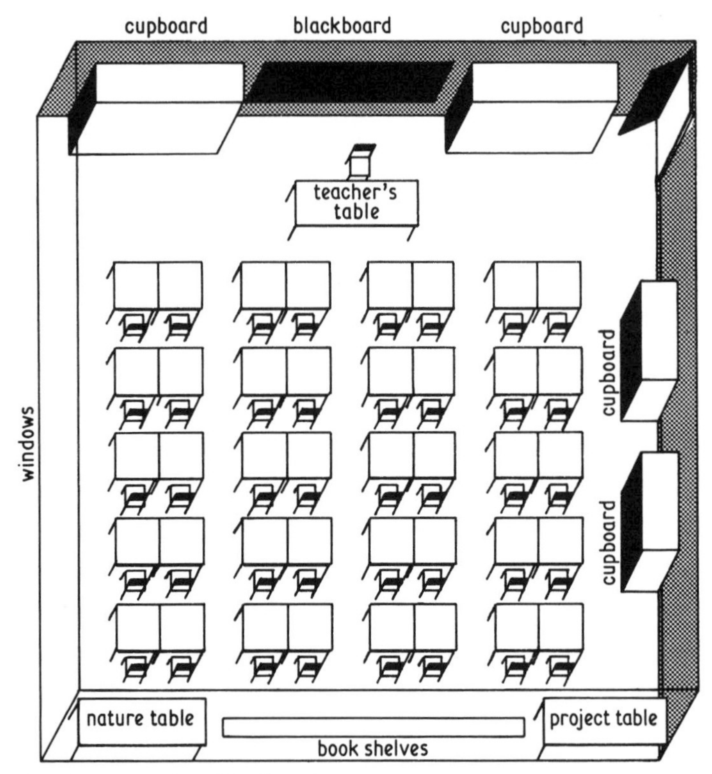

Figure 4.1 A conventional junior classroom

Source of Figures 4.1 and 4.2 Reproduced from The Nuffield Foundation (1967) Nuffield Mathematics Project, *I do, and I understand*, London, W. & R. Chambers and John Murray, pp. 30 and 31.

and forgetting' but rather by doing, itself leading to understanding, became embodied not only in assumptions about children but the conditions of their learning. Thus *I Do and I Understand* sets out two classroom plans, the old and the new: (see Figures 4.1 and 4.2). Notice that in Figure 4.2 the classroom has 'been rearranged to make better provision for active learning'. What does 'active learning' mean in this instance? It requires a rearrangement of the desks from rows (listening to the teacher talking) to groups (thereby severely limiting the possibility for instruction of the whole class). The teacher is no longer in front of a class. There are no sets of textbooks. The 'nature table' has disappeared in favour of 'science'. There is even room for spontaneity: 'the sudden unpredictable interest that requires space'.

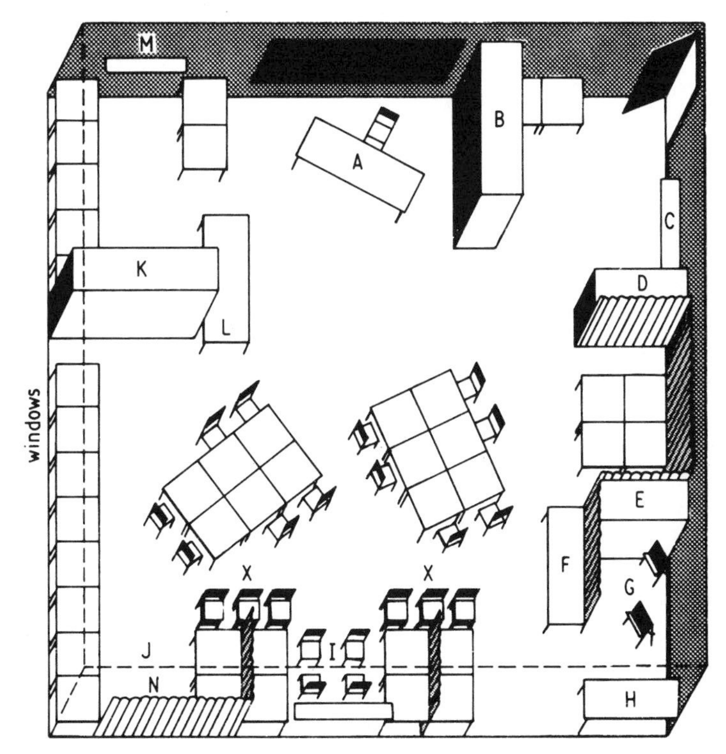

A Teacher's table

B Lockers containing equipment for mathematics, possibly made from old, tall cupboard

C Books on mathematics

D Cupboard containing equipment for muthematics and science, possibly those items that need to be locked away at night

E Cupboard containing materials for art and craft work

F Table for display

G Painting easels

H Woodwork bench

I Area reserved for reading

J Uncommitted area for the sudden unpredictable interest that requires space

K Lockers, similar to B, containing general scientific materials

L Table for display

M Scientific books

N Corrugated cardboard depth 5 feet

X Chairs stacked out of the way

Figure 4.2 The same classroom rearranged to make better provision for active learning

What is it which produced such a radical reorganization of the pedagogical space? This reorganization clearly cannot be understood outside the terms which make it possible: doing, activity, development, experiences, individual concepts, mental structures, to name some of the terms which are significant. If the pedagogic space and the terms of the discourse are so intertwined, it becomes important to understand how it happens that learning and teaching come to be expressed in the terms of individual cognitive development.

Let us take this a stage further by examining another apparatus of the pedagogy, this time in the form of a record card, of the type commonly filled in by nursery school teachers (see figure 4.3). As can be observed from the card, certain features of an individual child's 'development' are recorded on the card, ranging from language development, physical and motor development, hearing, emotional/social, 'responses to the learning situation' and 'medical'. What does this tell us? Why are these categories chosen as salient to record? It will be noted that, for example, every category requires an observation of behaviour which is stated as a developmental accomplishment: a capacity, itself produced through 'activity and experience'. There are no facts, no knowledge stated outside the terms of a developmental accomplishment.

Figure 4.3 Nursery Record Card

NURSERY RECORD CARD

Language, speech and communication

1. Is his speech free from:
   (a) defective articulation e.g. 'dat' for 'that'
   (b) grammatical errors e.g. 'me want'
   (c) baby words e.g. 'gee-gee'?
   (d) Does he need treatment?
2. Is his speech fluent with clear enunciation?
3. Can he understand and convey the meaning of a simple verbal message?
4. Can he describe his experiences coherently?
5. Does he describe vividly?
6. Does he use gestures instead of words?
7. Can he phrase relevant questions?
8. Can he give explanations of how and why things happen?
9. Does he listen and respond to a simple command?
10. Does he use the book corner with interest?
11. Has he a good vocabulary?

Perception – motor

1. Is he reasonably co-ordinated?

Figure 4.3—continued

2. Can he understand and use simple tools and construction toys?
3. Can he use:
   - scissors
   - do up buttons
   - hold a paintbrush well
   - hop
   - pedal
   - catch
   - throw
   - kick
   - follow a line on the ground
   - climb confidently
   - use his body with confidence
   - hold a pencil well?
4. Is he left- or right-handed, left- or right-footed?

Emotional/Social

1. Can he cope with new situations?
2. Can he build satisfactory relationships with:
   - one child
   - a small group of children
   - one adult?
3. Is he accepted by, and does he accept most of his peer group?
4. Is he friendly and at ease with other adults?
5. Is his play:
   - isolated
   - parallel
   - associative
   - co-operative
   - group?

Response to learning situation

1. Is he keen to learn?
2. Is his concentration sufficient for the task?
3. Does he show persistence in the face of difficulties?
4. Can he avoid being distracted from his work?
5. Can he choose between options?
6. Does he choose a balanced programme of activities, over a period of time?
7. Does he listen with interest to stories, music etc.?
8. Can he create experiences through the use of imagination, both verbally and in play?

Medical

1. Is his hearing satisfactory?

Figure 4.3—continued

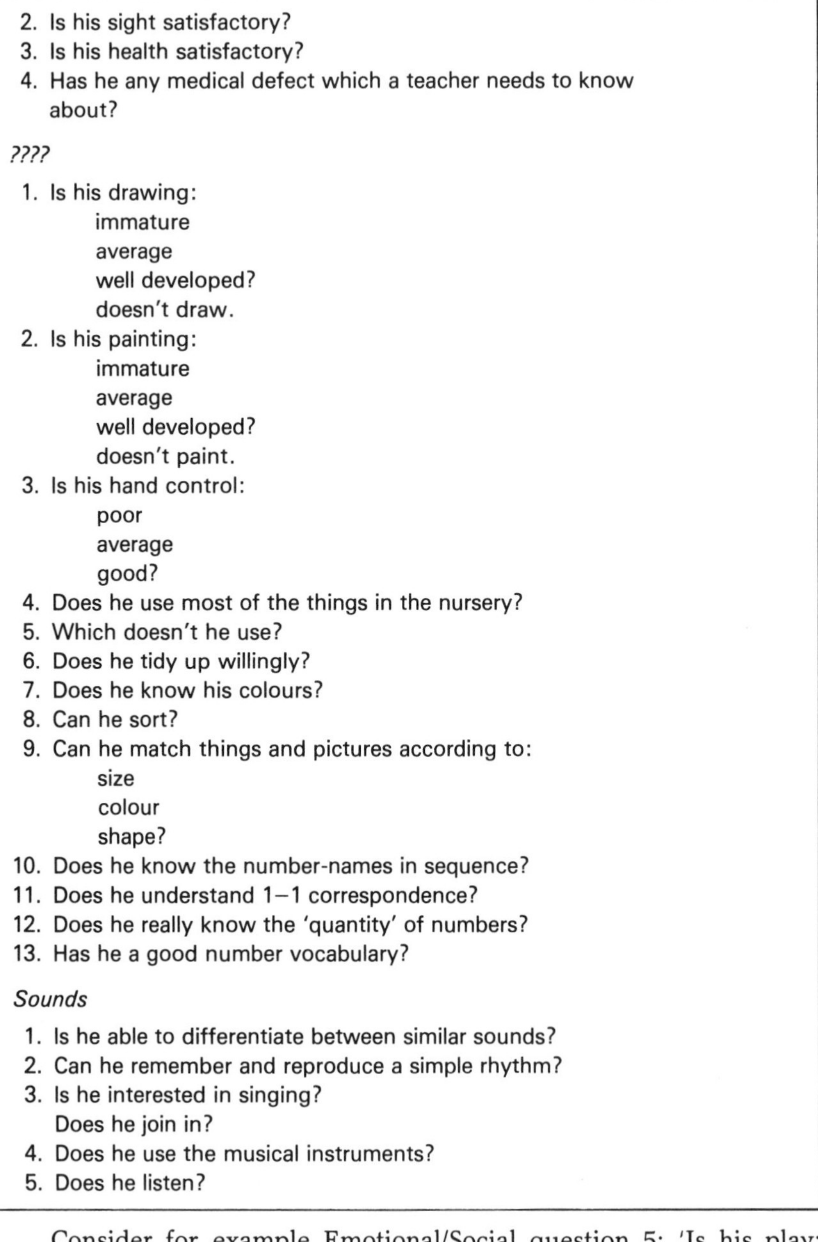

2. Is his sight satisfactory?
3. Is his health satisfactory?
4. Has he any medical defect which a teacher needs to know about?

????

1. Is his drawing:
   immature
   average
   well developed?
   doesn't draw.
2. Is his painting:
   immature
   average
   well developed?
   doesn't paint.
3. Is his hand control:
   poor
   average
   good?
4. Does he use most of the things in the nursery?
5. Which doesn't he use?
6. Does he tidy up willingly?
7. Does he know his colours?
8. Can he sort?
9. Can he match things and pictures according to:
   size
   colour
   shape?
10. Does he know the number-names in sequence?
11. Does he understand 1–1 correspondence?
12. Does he really know the 'quantity' of numbers?
13. Has he a good number vocabulary?

Sounds

1. Is he able to differentiate between similar sounds?
2. Can he remember and reproduce a simple rhythm?
3. Is he interested in singing?
   Does he join in?
4. Does he use the musical instruments?
5. Does he listen?

Consider for example Emotional/Social question 5: 'Is his play: isolated, parallel, associative, co-operative, group?' Let us deconstruct the assumptions which are contained in the formulation of the question. Here are listed five types of play. First of all then, we can assume that a category, play, can both be differentiated from other aspects of classroom behaviour and performance and is pedagogically important; that is play is something which is expected as a classroom activity – it is part of the pedagogy. Second, the list exists as a framework of classification of *types* of play. This in turn assumes that each teacher is (1) familiar with the terms, (2) recognizes the types of play when s/he sees them and (3) can discriminate good and normal from abnormal play. The teacher, therefore, must both recognize play as a significant category and have been *trained* to recognize and classify it along the lines set out in the record card. A whole apparatus of teacher-training is thereby implicated. To produce the effectivity and possibility of the classification, therefore, there must exist a related pedagogy in the colleges of education which both presents opportunities for guided observation of play and offers explanations of the system of classification in terms of statements of the form: 'there are several types of play.'

To illustrate this point, consider the following extract from a college of education student's lecture notes. The title is 'Emotional development' (similar to the record card), the subheading, unsurprisingly:

OBSERVATION OF PLAY

(1) This shows the child's real desires, etc., and feelings and his wish to experiment;
(2) Through play he can be independent – because he is someone else.
(3) He can also begin to feel what others feel, and so mature.
(4) Children construct fantasy world but cannot differentiate between real and unreal. They show in night terrors that they need an understanding of reality.
(5) Much aggression – need to hit out against frustration but some trying out of feeling.

In the same student's notes the following advice is offered to teachers:

(1) Under emotional stress – interruption of [the child's] intellectual development may occur.
(2) A young child may use an unreal object, e.g. teddy bear to convey her feelings – e.g. We must stop playing – Teddy wants to go to the toilet.
(3) A child learns to love by being loved.
(4) Acceptance of expression of feeling.
(5) Need adult for emotional stability.
(6) Teachers need to know children as individuals and developing their self concept.

In a student essay on emotional development the paragraph reproduced below contained the only tick (✓) and comment in the whole essay:

> ✓ A teacher then can do much at all these stages of development. It is important for him to provide an emotionally stable environment, particularly in an area where the children's home life may be far ✓ from stable. Here they need a free atmosphere in which they can work out their emotions in many media.

What can we learn from these notes and the extract? First, that the observation of play is singled out as an activity for the teacher to engage in. Second, that there is a specific link between play and the letting out of aggression. Third, that freedom to express feelings and the importance of an *individual* environment are stressed. This is reiterated in the essay in which the 'free atmosphere' mentioned by the student is singled out by the tutor as 'most important'. In numerous ways, therefore, various concepts and aspects of practice are singled out as crucial features of the pedagogy and, consequently, of what it means to be a good teacher.

It is possible to disentangle a complex web of related practices and apparatuses which together produce the possibility and effectivity of the child-centred pedagogy. Central to these is a system for the classification, observation monitoring, promotion and facilitation of the development of a variety of aspects of individual psychological capacities. In apparatuses and practices such as these it is axiomatic that there must exist a set of observational and empirically verifiable facts of child development. Central to the practice therefore is the *production* of development as pedagogy. By this I mean that development is produced as an object of classification, of schooling, within these practices themselves, made possible by the apparatuses which (among many others) I have singled out: record cards, teacher-training, classroom layout and so forth. Others would include teaching notes, work-cards, school and classroom organization, architecture. It is in this sense that developmental psychology and the child-centred pedagogy form a couple: the apparatuses of the pedagogy are no mere application but a site of production in their own right.

At this point I would like to anticipate a criticism which has been levelled at the kind of presentation I have set out. It has been put to me that many teachers are not child-centred, so that my presentation does not reflect the 'reality' of many classrooms. While I agree that classrooms are many and varied, the criticism misses my point, which is that the parameters of the practice are given by the common sense of child development which is everywhere, in apparatuses from teacher-training, to work-cards, to classroom layout. The apparatuses themselves provide a norm, a standard of good and possible pedagogy. We would find no classroom which stood outside the orbit of some constellation of discursive and administrative apparatuses.

What then is assumed in the pedagogy? How is this system of classification arrived at and why is the observation, monitoring and facilitation of an actual sequence of development the central focus of pedagogic practice? In order to answer these questions, my intention is to explicate those historical conditions of possibility which produce the present, that is the existence and hegemony of these practices. This necessitates prising apart the taken-for-grantedness which makes it difficult to imagine how it could be otherwise or how the 'scientific truth' about children could be deconstructed. As we argued in the Introduction to section 2, the use of the term 'conditions of possibility' allows for an analysis of the complex interplay of conditions which produce the possibility of a science and pedagogy of child development (see pp. 102–3). I aim to show how these pedagogic practices form part of those apparatuses which Foucault (1977) describes in terms of administrative apparatuses for providing techniques of social regulation, of which the sciences of the social form a central condition. By examining the power–knowledge relations which are made possible by the regimes of truth of developmental psychology it will be possible to demonstrate the conditions which have produced the classification and monitoring of development as a science and as a scientifically validated pedagogy. In this way I hope to demonstrate the inseparability of scientific truths and the conditions of their emergence, development and transformation as conditions of practical necessity, in which regimes of truth created by psychology are internally related to shifts and transformations in pedagogic practice.

Thus in order to understand the place of Piaget, we can examine how his work is constituted and made possible historically, that is in relation to existing discourses, practices and conditions. It is in this sense that it is possible to go beyond both epistemological and empirical critiques. Claims both to theoretical and empirical validity do not stand outside the discourses and practices for producing what counts as scientific evidence. Such practices are historically constituted in relation to existing conditions and practices. Epistemology does not stand outside such historical conditions. As we argued in the Introduction to section 2, the relations between the 'real material' object and the practices of its production are complex: there is never a moment of 'reality' which is comprehensible or possible outside a framework of discursive practices which render it possible and transformable. It is in this sense that we were critical of a position which tended to understand the 'real' and 'material' as somehow, potentially at least, separable from the discursive.

My argument is that the understanding of the 'real' of child development is not a matter of uncovering a set of empirical facts or epistemological truths which stand outside, or prior to, the conditions of their production. In this sense developmental (as other) psychology is productive: its positive effects lie in its production of practices of science and pedagogy. It is not a distortion of a real object 'the developing child' which could be better understood in terms of a radical developmental psychology, for the very reason that it is developmental psychology itself which produces the particular form of naturalized development of capacities as its object. The practices of production can, therefore, be understood as productive of subject-positions themselves (see Introduction to section 2, especially pp. 116–18).

This chapter will set out to examine the historical conditions which produced the possibility of the developmental psychology/child-centred pedagogy couple and ensured its sedimentation in the set of taken-for-granted practices that exist today. It will end with a tentative examination of how subject-positions are produced within existing practices, suggesting a way forward for the analysis of the production of subjectivity.

Science, psychology and the possibility of a 'scientific' pedagogy

In order to understand the conditions which make possible the modern developmental psychology/pedagogy couple we have to examine several issues: first, the school as an apparatus of regulation and classification and second the relation of that to specific forms of regulation and classification founded in *science*. Later we shall see how progressivism was at once made possible by specific sciences but was the result of a 'precarious congruence' (Donald, 1979, p. 17) in which regulation, classification and liberation coexisted as simultaneous promises. This unlikely coexistence was allowable because the true nature of the child to be liberated was guaranteed by the techniques of classification themselves. I will begin by sketching out the conditions for schooling as an apparatus of regulation and then examine the relation of schooling to the rise of scientific administration, which produces the possibility of a transformation from regulation by overt coercion to regulation by covert normalization, based on apparatuses and techniques for the classification and therefore regulation of the normal. The production of scientific norms has two roots in relation to pedagogy: mental measurement and child development.

The previous chapter referred to the rise of science from the seventeenth century, together with the development of the administrative apparatuses which permitted normalization and regulation and the production of the normal subject. The belief in science and the concomitant struggle to find forms of legitimation and guarantee in science rather than religion forms a significant backdrop to the genesis not only of modern forms of rationality, but for the idea of rationality as natural and therefore to the search for a pedagogy which could produce the desired forms of individuality by means of natural development. While I could refer to a whole ensemble of scientific apparatuses which relate to the possibility of human sciences the reader can be referred both to the previous chapter and to other work in the field (see Venn, 1982; also Easlea, 1973). For the present argument it is important that the struggle in favour of scientific legitimacy over religion was adopted by forward and progressive thinkers: it was modernism and has continued to be so.

The claims for a science of the rational were from the first intimately bound up with the possibilities of a scientifically validated and rational pedagogy. In *Discipline and Punish* (1977) Foucault documents the emergence of techniques of administration which were founded in the sciences. This body of apparatuses was made possible by changes associated with the rise of capitalist manufacture in which forms of power emerged wherein scientific knowledges allowed for the possibility of certain techniques of producing knowledge and in knowing about human beings, of classifying, normalizing and regulating. These techniques of social regulation were taken up in many ways. But it is not the case that they were produced by some monolithic superpower for the domination of the emergent working class. On the contrary, while the effect might well have been to produce 'docile bodies', it was often liberals and radicals who proposed the new forms of scientific administration and pushed for them as preferable to the forces of religion. This tendency was certainly one which characterized the work of Marx among others. His belief in the science of history and the scientific basis of historical materialism has to be understood as part of and not separate from such movements. If so subversive a figure as Marx opted for the legitimation of science it is easy to understand how scientific forms of knowledge and administration were privileged. The point here is to understand how it came to be the case that certain tendencies often inaugurated by individuals and groups outside public education and administration introduced ideas and practices which came to dominate public education. The particular moments of struggle in the public take-up of forms of education are very important because they reveal the way in which science envisaged as a tool of liberation was by its naturalization the very basis of the production of normalization.

Compulsory schooling was established in England around 1880. In order to understand how compulsory schooling became a site for political struggle it is important to understand the form of the arguments used for it. Jones and Williamson (1979) argue that all popular texts of that time note two problems in particular for which schooling (at first popular and later compulsory) was offered as a solution. These were crime and pauperism,[3] understood in terms of principles and habits of the population. It was this understanding of bad habits as the cause of crime and pauperism which led to the possibility of seeing popular education as the answer to the nation's ills, that is by the inculcation of good habits, notably of reading, in order, especially, to read the Bible. In this way, the problems of poverty, of pauperism and of poor relief were presented as moral issues concerning the habits and life of the poor. The argument went that if the poor were dependent on poor relief then they would not be independent of spirit (good moral fibre, etc.). Jones and Williamson suggest that: 'the deterioration in moral character was related to a deterioration in the religious character of the populaton and the *political threat which this posed*' (p. 67; my italics).

What was proposed as a form of popular pedagogy was the monitorial school, based, like Bentham's dream of a panopticon (described in Foucault, 1977), on a model of constant surveillance. Moral regulation of the habits of the population would be produced by constant monitoring and ceaseless activity. However, one of the conditions which clearly permitted a shift to a pedagogy of normalization is a set of scientific practices which transpose habits to a medico-behavioural model which can then be normalized. To understand all the conditions for the introduction of monitorialism and its transposition to a pedagogy based on covert normative regulation requires an exposition beyond the scope of this chapter. We would need to examine who supported monitorialism, and what were the terms and conditions in which it was opposed and therefore transformed. It certainly never commanded universal support.[4]

However, one of the conditions for the transformation appears to have been monitorialism's relative failure as a regulatory device. Some teachers were 'unutterably shocked by the cynical readiness of certain children to recite the Lord's Prayer for a half-penny' (Jones and Williamson, 1979, p. 88). At the same time there were significant new discourses and practices of population-management being produced. These related particularly to the science of topography in which areas or districts of cities were surveyed in terms of housing conditions, amount of crime and family histories in order to attempt to account for those conditions which produced crime and pauperism. The term 'class' first emerges in the demographic sense in this discourse, particularly in the isolation of the 'dangerous classes' as the object of study. What we have here is the change in the object of study and therefore the consequent discussion and operation of the mode of instruction. The identification of the dangerous classes as units in themselves is therefore of paramount importance. A central feature of the production of scientific forms of regulation of the population was the development of population statistics. It is these which provided the basis of classifications of the normal in the many domains relating to the social regulation of the population, scientific rationalism: regulation according to the nature of the individual was covert, liberal, forward looking and sought greater effectivity through the promotion not of habits, but of understanding.

'Rational powers of mind' were put forward by some as the solution to a social problem which coercion had failed to remedy. As time progressed the anti-coercion lobby was thus to turn a moral into a scientific imperative. The importance of the scientific discourses in providing a rationale in support of a practical solution is testified to in Hamilton's assertion that:

> above all the fate of the monitorial system was sealed by the argument that the civilising goals of elementary education would be realised more successfully if pupils could be taught not merely to memorise their 'lessons' but also to understand them. As James Kay-Shuttleworth (a Manchester physician and philanthropist) pointed out, a 'little knowledge' (of the kind provided by the monitorial system) was indeed a dangerous thing. To him the issue was very simple. The 'disturbances of social order' that marked the parliamentary and economic upheavals of the 1830s were, in part, the responsibility of a people only partially instructed.
>
> (Hamilton, 1981, p. 2)

The form of pedagogy advocated by people like Kay-Shuttleworth was one in which understanding could be promoted by class instruction and a curriculum based on the study of natural phenomena. Such methods had been pioneered earlier by people like Robert Owen, following the tenets of, among others, Rousseau.[5]

Robert Owen, a Scottish philanthropist who provided schools for the children of the workers in his New Lanark mills, was an important figure in the development of forms of pedagogy which were seen as left-wing and progressive. Like other radicals particularly in Scotland, he was a supporter of the French Revolution. While Robert Owen had at first admired the monitorial system he later denounced it as 'this mockery of learning' which could render a child 'irrational for life' (Owen, 1813).

> No longer were children, in Owen's mind, to be treated as the recipients of those values that the middle and upper classes thought were necessary for them if they were to know their place in society. It was a decisive break with the old philanthropic attitude to the education of the poor, the tradition in which Bell and Lancaster (the monitorialists) were firmly rooted and its importance in the history of British education cannot be overestimated. . . . Owen's educational principles could almost be summed up as Rousseauism applied to working-class children. He was the first to demonstrate that what was later called elementary education could be based upon affection, imagination and the full realization of the potentialities of the child. (Stewart, 1972, p. 35)

Affection, imagination and the realization of potential: all attributes understood as being in opposition to monitorialism. Here was no 'constant surveillance' but *love* (though love, as we shall see later, medicalized, hygienized: platonic not passionate). Here, too, ceaseless activity was made unnecessary through techniques which would claim to be based on the amplification of the natural and therefore the development of the normal. Both children as objects of schooling and the form and content of the pedagogy itself were to be naturalized. In Robert Owen's schools teaching took the form of 'object lessons' based on the study of natural phenomena. This represents a considerable break with the study of Biblical texts, and also relates to contemporaneous shifts from classics to sciences in the education of the upper classes.

Owen, among others, was suggesting that the introduction of such techniques in the education of the poor would produce better citizens:

> The importance accorded to these objects in the Rational schools sprang from the Owenite insistence that the knowledge of the natural world was one of the means by which the mind could be freed from the pre-conceptions of existing society. Objects were fragments of the world of nature, and children's appreciation of them came through the senses, whereas books and teachers were a source of pre-conceptions. (Stewart, 1972, p. 47)[6]

The form of the pedagogy was also subject to transformation. The proposed replacement for the schoolroom of the monitorial system was the classroom: the site of simultaneous instruction of children of the same age. This division of children into classes is consonant with the emerging practice of dividing the population into classes.[7] Simultaneous instruction was designed to render it suitable to the individual: hence grouping by age and the necessity of fitting the lesson to the age, through the mechanism of love. Hamilton (1981) suggests that the popularity of the new system was partly due to its resolution of certain contradictions, by being all things to all parties:

> Its 'equalised classification', for instance, resonated with new ideas about the social structure of society: its oral methods signalled a rejection of book-based learning: its 'familiar' (or 'conversational') style met utilitarian (or rationalist) calls for 'understanding' as well as 'memorisation': and, above all, its 'interrogative' discipline satisfied those whose concern was to ensure the 'perpetual employment' of the children of the labouring classes. (Hamilton, 1981, p. 6)

It is important to point out that there was no easy and simple flow from the one form of pedagogy to the other. There were struggles and political battles which took place in conjunction with other conditions. However, for our purposes, it is important that the transformation in the form of pedagogic regulation was simultaneously a discursive transformation and a transformation of apparatuses and practices: a new regime of truth included a field of administration. And it is in relation to the new form of scientifically produced regulation that psychology first enters the pedagogic stage.

Scientific psychology and the study and education of children

At the beginning of the twentieth century there were two parallel developments which related to the scientific classification of children: the first was child study, the second mental measurement.[8] As twin aspects of scientific classification they emerge always intertwined, proceeding as they do from the development of the whole panoply of apparatuses of sciences of the social, of population classification and so on. As part of the study of the population, children, as we have seen, were singled out as a class, to be classified in their own right. Characteristics, including those specific to children, were charted with a view to establishing what environmental conditions might produce physical illness, immoral and criminal behaviour. This survey work included histories of family 'pathologies'. It is important that at this moment developments in evolutionary biology, particularly the work of Darwin, were advancing in ways which were absolutely related. Consider, for example, the now well-known concept of the 'survival of the fittest'. It corresponds precisely to the relation between suitable 'stock' and environmental conditions. Indeed, Social Darwinism[9] utilized these concepts with direct reference to forms of social control and engineering, and it is not coincidental that eugenics was offered as a solution to the problems of the poor and 'degenerate' by a considerable number of those associated with the rise of psychology, population statistics and scientific education, such as Galton, Spearman, Cattell, Terman and Montessori (see Kamin, 1974; Rose, 1979). The shift of emphasis in control of the population from habits to degeneracy carries with it a central and strategic production of the *norm(al)*:

> a double movement which consists in both a *moralisation* and a *medicalisation*. For if this explanation retains the traditional links between these dangers and threats, the character of those subjects who continue to wilfully stand outside the social order, it nonetheless transfers the conception of character which is implicated from an ethical to a scientific domain: feeble-mindedness as a category of science, of psychology, becomes inextricably linked to a threat to civilised existence. And this explanation is doubled through its linkage with heredity which provides simultaneously the elements of a solution – and this is precisely the eugenic move.
>
> (Rose, 1979, p. 13)

Although the point of Rose's discussion is specifically feeble-mindedness as a form of degeneracy, the point at issue here is the conversion of a moral problem into a scientific one which is part of that very movement towards science and away from religion which I outlined earlier. Having established the individual as the proper object of the scientific gaze (itself an aspect of modern and forward-looking thinking at that time) the new psychology linked and implicated the twin poles of heredity and environment from the very beginning. As was pointed out in the previous chapter, once certain forms of social problem were located as an object of science, methods of detection and cure were also implicated. This is where the techniques of population statistics become centrally important, for they provide the tools for establishing the scientific basis of the normal (see Hacking, 1981), that is in respect of the normal curve of characteristics within the population. The movement which produces the possibility of the individual as an object of science defined in terms of the twin poles of heredity and environment produces simultaneously the need for the development of scientific and empirical apparatuses and techniques of detection and some form of institutional provision which help produce and normalize such individuals.[10]

Certain fundamental issues and concerns provide some of the conditions of possibility for the emergence of Piaget's theory and empirical work in the form that it took. These are the issue of heredity and environment, the 'naturalness' of the development of rationality and the concern for a solution to the problems of the social order in a science of the individual. There is one more very important aspect. This is the development of the idea of 'the child' as an object both of science in its own right and of apparatuses of normalization. These provided the possibility for a science and a pedagogy based on a model of naturally occurring development which could be observed, normalized and regulated. Thus, as it were, they permitted the idea that degeneracy could be nipped in the bud, by regulating the development of children in order to ensure their fitness as adults.

The 'child study movement' is taken, not surprisingly, to have begun with Darwin. As part of his work he made a study of his own son: 'A biographical sketch of an infant' (1840, 1887). The very terms of this study, of studying and observing human children in the same terms as other 'species', are crucially important, for in this act is the basis of the idea of 'natural child development'. Now clearly, no one doubts that children change as they grow older. The point, however, is that this isolation of patterns of growth from patterns of development of mental functioning was now taken for granted within the emergent developmental psychology. Following on from Darwin's study there were a number of other studies of scientists' children, for example William Preyer's *The Mind of the Child* (1881), Granville Stanley Hall's *The Contents of Children's Minds on Entering School* (1883). It is perhaps worth indicating the proximity of such titles to modern ones, such as Margaret Donaldson's *Children's Minds* (1978). The terms of the discourse have shifted little. Such works as these led to a whole movement of child study. Child Study Societies were formed and the practice of observing children became very widespread. Children's bodies were weighed and measured. The effects of fatigue were studied, as were children's interests, imaginings, religious ideas, fetishes, attitudes to weather, to adults, drawings, dolls, lies, ideas and, most importantly for us, their stages of growth. (All this a full twenty years before Piaget began to study children.) What is important is that children as a category were being singled out for scientific study for the first time and the discourses which produced children as the objects of that study were drawn from biology and topography, and everyday-life common sense.

Certain concerns become, at this particular time, medicalized and moralized. Among these is that of the child as an object of scientific enquiry. Clearly, the documentation of just how this comes about is a large task and beyond the scope of this chapter. However, it is important to point out that it is a multiplicity of conditions which enables the child development/pedagogy couple to take off as it does. Let us therefore summarize certain important details. The rise of science and its harnessing for the development of the industrial revolution and the rise of capitalist manufacture are centrally implicated. Certain important social issues, from the middle of the nineteenth century on, become objects of science. As well as, and related to, the scientization of the child, we can add the development of what has been termed 'insurantial technology' and the development of welfare practices, and the increasing embourgeoisement of the family. This latter is accompanied by the shift from traditional patterns of extended family with the development of a mobile and urbanized workforce and the consequent medicalization of the family as a site for intervention and normalization (see for example Donzelot, 1980).

The naturalization of the mind as an object of science goes together with that of the family, child-rearing and the child. It is not, therefore, surprising that child development, and particularly in our case the naturalization of reason, should become the object of scientific study. That is, a science in which the object of study is the naturally occurring development of first and foremost the *mind*, then, in addition, as a *developmental* psychology, the development of the minds of children, and the concomitant naturalization and biologization of knowledge as capacity. If knowledge becomes naturalized then, as we shall see, facts (as social phenomena) can become of secondary status to concepts, so that content is subsumed in process. Knowledge as a social category is thereby marginalized in favour of knowledge, as both individual production and competence, hence the *reading* of children's responses to questions testing scientific and mathematical knowledge as evidence for the development of appropriate mental capacities. The discursive slip produces both the object of classification, the scientific techniques for its production and the pedagogic techniques for its normalization and regulation.

It must by now be apparent that those twin techniques of mental measurement and child development were not formulated in the opposition in which they have been placed both pedagogically and psychologically, in the liberal and radical discourses and pedagogies of the 1960s and 1970s. Here, individualism and progressivism were posed as the liberatory alternative to reactionary forms of classification based on intelligence testing. In this sense, child development was not understood as a system of classification, an elision made possible by its interdiscursive relation to the humanistic moment of individual liberation.[11]

While it is indeed the case that theories such as Piaget's were set up in opposition to a view of inherited or pregiven intelligence, the general project within which his work is sited and the terms of its construction do not fall outside those already described. These psychological movements were always associated with techniques for classification such as the development of tests and with administrative apparatuses such as forms of schooling. Binet, in whose Paris laboratory the young Piaget worked, was one of the first to begin to devise such tests. It is commonly asserted (for example by Gruber and Voneche, 1977) that Piaget was more interested in the reasoning behind the responses which the children gave to the test items than in their normative performance on them. There is in this explanation a kind of embarrassment that such a liberal/radical figure as Piaget could ever have soiled his hands with such reactionary instruments as intelligence tests. There was no reactionary embarrassment that Piaget began in Binet's laboratory, nor is it unusual or incongruous that he took as his task the examination of the reasoning which lay behind test responses. As should be clear by now, Piaget did not invent such a notion, the scientific enterprise into which he was inserted already existed. He simply developed in one direction work in a tradition which was already firmly rooted in the scientific community.

Other allied exponents of a scientific pedagogy, such as Maria Montessori, clearly supported the cause of eugenics as a possible solution. She popularized the work of Itard and Seguin in France which had begun with the attempts to train the Wild Boy of Aveyron. The domestication of the savage, the animal, the teachability of humanness, was something which Montessori applied first to the training of idiots and then to the education of the poor children of the Italian city slums: 'the child who has not the force to develop and he who is not yet developed are in some ways alike' (Montessori, 1912, pp. 44–5). This slippage from degeneracy and idiocy to child development in Montessori's discourse indicates the proximity of the two positions and the force of the methods of training children. Montessori's methods depended on the use of pieces of apparatus, such as geometrical shapes, cylinders, and so on. She placed these before an individual child, making certain formations and patterns. 'If the child replies by seizing upon the game and repeating it with avidity, this is a case of pure self-expression: *the child has revealed himself as in need of that particular exercise'* (C. A. Claremont, English interpreter of Montessori, quoted in Selleck, 1972, p. 29; my italics).

It is important to note the production of conditions for scientific evidence: the child's interest expressed in repetition of the game is taken as evidence of an underlying need, linked, therefore, to a biologized developmental progression. There is, of course, nothing essential in the perception of the child's interest as evidence of a need.

We should also note Montessori's insistance on individual liberty:

> The fundamental principle of scientific pedagogy must be, indeed, the *liberty of the pupil*: – such liberty as shall permit a development of individual, spontaneous manifestations of the child's nature. If a new and scientific pedagogy is to arise from the *study of the individual*, such study must occupy itself with the observation of *free* children. (Montessori, 1912, p. 28; my italics)

For the pedagogy to work children had to be free from adult intervention: that is in their natural state, as individual beings, uncontaminated by culture.

The concern with the future of the 'human stock' also has to be situated in relation to certain political developments which took place in the early 1900s around imperialism and national efficiency. While the Labour Party was struggling and gaining strength, after its inaugural conference in 1893, the Conservative government, elected in 1895 for a term of ten years, was giving its attention to the development of imperialism. The concern with degeneracy finds expression in the necessity of building an 'imperial race' and the consequent concern for national efficiency, that is the building of an efficient workforce suitable to the development of the empire: 'An Empire such as ours requires as its first condition an imperial race, a race vigorous and industrious and intrepid . . . in the rookeries and slums which still survive, an imperial race cannot be reared' (Lord Rosebery, leader of the Liberal Imperialists, quoted in Simon, 1965, p. 169).

In this discourse, then, the fitness of the race and the efficiency of the workforce combine to ensure Britain's domination of her empire. In this context the link between scientific racism, degeneracy and the empire becomes clear, as does the concern about eugenics. However, it is important to note that I am not arguing that the political concerns of the time caused in any simple sense certain developments in the science of the individual. Rather, each should be taken as mutually implicated, making and remaking the other possible, intertwining to produce a discursive and political nexus. The rational, the savage, the animal, the human, the degenerate, the normal, all become features of the modern scientific normalization and regulation of children.[12]

The emergence of Piaget's genetic epistemology

In sketching out developments in psychology and education I have outlined some of the conditions which laid the foundations for Piaget's enterprise. Here I want to mention the beginning of Piaget's work and show how it fits into and builds upon the limits and conditions already set. After this I shall go on to discuss the consequent developments, concentrating particularly on the periods of the two world wars.

Many features of an approach to the study of children which stresses the development of naturally occurring stages, culminating in the attainment of scientific rationality, have already been discussed. Piaget's first paper concerning the topics which were to become his life's work was written when he was a student in Switzerland and it displays the elements we would expect. Entitled 'Biology and war' (1918), it sketched out his position on evolution and the development of the psyche in terms of discursive concerns which clearly lock into those already articulated above. He examines Darwinian and Lamarkian evolutionary biology and states that they both come to the conclusion that war is an inevitable consequence of the struggle for survival. Piaget rejects such a view, arguing that:

> as far as intellectuality is concerned, understanding things does permit real assimilation (as common-sense already indicates). As far as ethics is concerned, only love, *caritas*, permits the full development of the self. As far as society is concerned, only co-operation and peace contribute to the good of social groups.
>
> (Translated by Gruber and Voneche, 1977, p. 41)

Although Piaget places himself in opposition to the view that war is biologically necessary, he counters that view with elements which we have already come across: naturalized rationality and platonic love (*caritas*). Passion is counterposed to *caritas* and reason as the force of destruction, linking with the naturalized aggressivity of some forms of psychoanalytic discourse (see p. 183). In his prose-poem, 'Mission of the idea' (1915) the 'search for rational truth' is counterposed to passion.

In 1918 Piaget wrote a Rousseauesque novel about the searches for self of a young man, Sebastian. The book appears autobiographical and relates to Piaget's own struggles as a young man. For this reason I shall reproduce here the synopsis of extracts from the novel set out by the translators Gruber and Voneche:

> The ego of Sebastian, the hero and only character of the book, is entirely absorbed in working out a few fundamental preoccupations: the relations between science and faith, the value of science as a theory of knowledge, the relations between science and morality and, finally, social salvation. . . . Sebastian, who had previously

> been satisfied with a vague biological philosophy consisting of a universal sympathy for all life, experiences his own crisis of identity at the moment when the occidental world is collapsing in the tragedy of the First World War. He is conscious of the connection between this individual crisis and that of the world in which he lives: this gives a certain dramatic force to the first part of the novel. 'Intelligence was thought to be the power that could lead humanity: we see it reduced to serving passions'. Sebastian wants to remain, in the words of Romain Rolland, 'above the battle'. But there is nothing firm to which he can attach himself. His need for logic tears him away from the churches and directs him toward philosophy. 'For he always had faith that the power of reason was capable of breaking out of the circle of experience'. But the philosophers disappoint him, too, one after the other. These metaphysical disappointments bring Sebastian back to science in which he has an 'unshakeable faith'. This gives rise to a first formulation of the idea of a circle of sciences, which assures knowledge its own foundations without external recourse. (Gruber and Voneche, 1977, p. 42)

The 'circle of science' first mentioned in this novel is later developed in other works, for example, in *Insights and Illusions of Philosophy*, published in English in 1972. It is instructive to examine those sciences which fall within his circle (see Figure 4.4).[13] Because mathematics follows psychology one is led to assume that mathematics can occur naturally on the basis of natural and sound psychological principles.

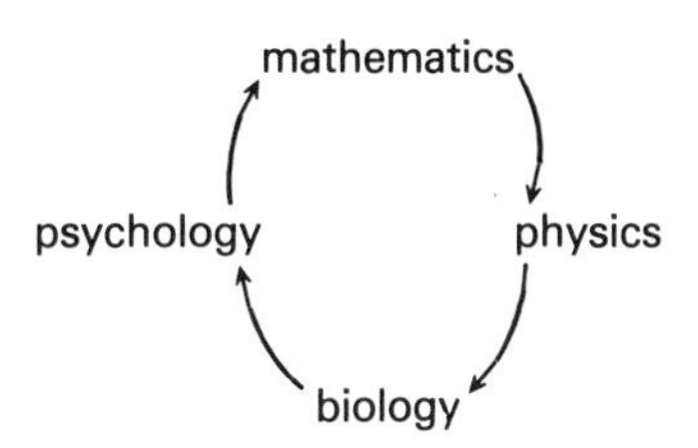

Figure 4.4 Piaget's circle of science

Although it could be argued that this early novel is unrepresentative of Piaget's work, it is pertinent here because it not only outlines the discursive conditions, the concerns, the theories, the modes of argument available at the time, it also shows the terms in which, and the theories in relation to which, Piaget's discourse and enterprise were formulated. Piaget began his career as a biologist and therefore it is consistent for him to express his concerns by reference both to contemporary biological discourses and to the political debates about war into which those discourses were inserted. These concerns emerge and re-emerge in Piaget's later work in a variety of different ways. His interest in the view that ontogeny recapitulates phylogeny meshes with other current discourses about play.

When later in Paris Piaget came into contact with both the work of Binet and psychoanalysis, he asserted the importance of the power of reason, the concern about 'what makes us human'. Using arguments recruited from psychoanalysis he suggested that the best course for mankind was to channel children's development away from the dominance of the emotions towards that rationality which alone would be the guarantor of progress. It is perhaps here that his search began for an analysis of spontaneous development which would chart the 'naturally occurring' progress of childhood towards scientific rationality. In a paper delivered in 1920 ('Psychoanalysis and its relations with child psychology') Piaget demonstrates his use of psychoanalytic concepts linked to a science of emergent rationality. He uses the term 'pre-logical thought' and suggests the move from childhood sexuality towards adult rationality which leaves the 'animal passions' behind:[14] 'the love of beautiful bodies elevates itself to the love of beautiful souls and from there to the very idea of beauty' (Piaget, 1920, p. 57). It is the 'idea of beauty', the rational dream, towards which Piaget's work gestures. He concludes:

> Now autistic thought, creator of personal symbols, remains essential in each of us throughout his life. Its role changes with age. In the child autism is everything. Later, reason develops at its expense, but – and this is the real problem – does it ever extricate itself entirely? Apparently not. There remains therefore an extremely instructive psychological task to be undertaken in order to determine in each individual the relations between the state of his intelligence and the state of his autistic or unconscious life. And certainly psychoanalysis is full of insights in this regard. (ibid., p. 59)

Although Piaget recognizes the interplay of reason and emotion, in this piece he understands it as the influence of emotion on reason, which can never be properly outgrown. It is because he sees the cogito, *homo rationalis*, as the desired goal that he asserts the naturalness of the progression from emotion to reason. Indeed Piaget's early work is clearly situated in relation to the psychoanalytic edifice. The empirical apparatus of logico-mathematical structures only appears later, although the concept of stages is already apparent.

The above characterization of Piaget's early work is not meant to be in any sense a study of his enterprise as a whole. Rather, it is meant to demonstrate the necessity of understanding his work in terms of a set of conditions which made it possible within a particular body of scientific discourses and regulatory practices. It is these regimes of truth and these administrative apparatuses which help to explain how Piaget's work came to be taken up in a particular way within early education. His work is not applied to education, neither does it cause transformation in practice. Rather, its positioning within an ensemble of discursive practices is precisely what ensures its form and its take-up in a particular manner, in helping to legitimate and redirect forms of classification of stages of development as regulatory and normalizing pedagogic devices. The development and transformation of the pedagogic apparatuses which produced the form of child-centred pedagogy we recognize today will be the focus of the next part of this chapter, in which I shall concentrate on the conditions of possibility which surrounded the take-up and sedimentation of those practices we now take to be common sense.

Scientific experiments in pedagogy

1912 saw the English translation of *The Montessori Method*, while already in 1911 the then Chief Inspector of Schools, Edmond Holmes, had published a book sharply critical of what was by then traditional class teaching. This book was based on a discussion of a country school in which children were offered 'free and joyful learning':

> The importance of freedom was announced, and the child was said to be 'by nature a child of God rather than a child of wrath', who would be put on the path of self-realisation, of which its higher stages is the life of love. (Selleck, 1972, p. 25)

Several points may be drawn from Holmes's approach: they are the references to the country, freedom, individuality, nature and love. In certain of the terms we can ascertain continuities from the class-based pedagogy which some had hoped would form the rational education only a few years earlier. Certainly, love and nature were already present, but the stress on individual freedom is a new departure. It is at this point that the first ideas of an individualized pedagogy emerged. Empirical work, including that of Piaget's natural normalized stages of development towards scientific rationality, provided a set of apparatuses making possible the monitoring of individual development and therefore the naturalization of pedagogy itself. Indeed, what followed was a series of experiments in pedagogy which were also taken to be psychological experiments. That is, the observation and monitoring of child development became a pedagogy in its own right because those understandings taken to underlie the acquisition of knowledge were presumed to be based on a 'natural' foundation. The new notion of an individualized pedagogy depended absolutely on the possibility of the observation and classification of normal development and the idea of spontaneous learning. It was the science of developmental psychology which provided the tools and in which the work of Piaget is particularly implicated. As I mentioned earlier his personal role in the movement towards naturalization of mathematical and scientific knowledges as individual capacities, developing in a quasi-spontaneous fashion given the correct environment, was a central part of that movement which permitted the curriculum to be understood as spontaneous and permitted the teaching of facts to disappear in favour of the monitoring of the learning of concepts. Recognizing such a movement is absolutely crucial to understanding how the present pedagogic common-sense 'facts' themselves have become concepts, structures – stripped of their content and located in individuals. It is the work of developmental psychology which made that move possible by providing scientific legitimation of a process of knowledge as development.

Hamilton observes that this new view of pedagogy 'took shape as a reaction against the claimed mechanisation of simultaneous instruction, just as the work of Stow and Kay-Shuttleworth represented a reaction against the arbitrary nature of pre-nineteenth century individualized instruction' (1981, p. 11). It is in this sense then that the term 'class teaching' began to take on the pejorative and reactionary connotations which it has in British primary schools today.

What was the nature of the scientific experiments of the time? In what senses did the classroom become a laboratory? And why did the particular form of individualized pedagogy win the day with such force?

Class-teaching could take on pejorative connotations because, although it stressed understanding, it was an understanding which was based on 'facts'. It was the advances in mental measurement and child development which permitted the possibility of a pedagogy of the individual in which understanding as a goal was transformed into a normalized and regulated stage-wise progression. Teaching a class, therefore, whilst representing a break with monitorialism, was outmoded in view of the possibility of going beyond class to individual regulation. Class-teaching, then, came to stand for the old order – modernism and progress lay with the individual. Indeed, those 'reactionary' teachers who dared to retain class-teaching were, so to speak, flying in the face of scientific evidence. Such evidence was, therefore, crucial in legitimating the new practices. Such developments paved the way for the production of the classroom as a 'laboratory' for the study and monitoring of child development.

I will briefly outline the parameters and conditions of some of the many experimental pedagogies which were put into operation in the first three decades of the twentieth century. I shall consider the discursive constitution of such experiments and then review some of the conditions which permitted their transformation from small (and mostly private) forms of schooling to the discourses in power, the present pedagogic regime of state primary schooling.

In 1913, an American called Homer Lane founded a school called the 'Little Commonwealth' as a reformatory for 'juvenile delinquents'. It is important that in the years leading up to the first world war the problem of juvenile crime became the prime focus of attention. It is at this time that the term 'delinquent' first entered common parlance, and it is itself another indication of the psychologization of particular social problems associated with crime and poverty, as we shall see later. Thus it is not surprising that the first educational experiments utilizing the new psychology should be about the reform of young criminals. Indeed, Lane went to great lengths to put forward the results of his experiment as proof of the efficacy in this case of the application of Freud to education. He took the worst offenders from the juvenile courts to a country house where he allowed them complete freedom. He would offer no intervention but allowed the children to govern and regulate each other. He took the success of this exercise as evidence in support of education which opposed coercion with natural self-government. What is important for us is his stress on the natural. Like A. S. Neill at Summerhill[15] several years later, he believed that leaving children alone without the intervention of adults proved that forms of democratic self-government which emerged were the result of natural phenomena, in this case the natural state of the psyche. The naturalness of the result accorded both with the founding conditions of the psychology and with the Romanticism of many in the liberal and left traditions. The use of the country as a natural environment is important, but it is equally important to remember that this natural countryside, holder of all that is good and beautiful, is the country of the 'country house' of the aristocracy or the idealized rurality of natural life (swains and shepherdesses) and not the poverty-stricken farmland of peasants and farmworkers.

Several other developments happened around the same period. As we have seen, Maria Montessori's work gained considerable public acclaim and following. Additionally there began to appear several books which established individualized pedagogies as the way forward, for example Caldwell Cook's *The Play Way* appeared in 1915: 'It argued that play was the "natural means of study in youth" and terms others reformers had made familiar were called on parade again: interest, activity, joy, learning – not teaching, self-government' (Selleck, 1972, p. 41). In the 1920s perhaps the most famous experiment was Susan Isaacs' Malting House School in Cambridge, set up explicitly as a scientific experiment. Here the pedagogy was legitimated in several ways. Susan Isaacs was no mere popularizer: she was a trained analyst with a considerable academic reputation. The result of her observations, written up in the form of academic books (for example, *Intellectual Growth in Young Children*, 1930 and *Social Development in Young Children*, 1933) had considerable impact in legitimating the science–pedagogy couple. For example, the first words of *Social Development* were: 'This book is addressed to the scientific public and in particular to serious students of psychology and education. It is not intended as a popular exposition, whether of the psychological facts or of the relevant educational theory' (1933, p. 3). Indeed, Susan Isaacs came to head the newly formed Department of Child Development at the London Institute of Education, a position which is highly significant both in its legitimation of child development with psychology and of the position of the Institute of Education in relation to an apparatus of teacher-training.[16] The central features of Isaacs' method lay in the focus on certain basic problems and patterns of development. The function of the pedagogy, therefore, was to classify, observe and monitor the developmental sequences. Monitoring was crucial in order to ensure the normalization of development. In this regard, it is important that Isaacs followed Melanie Klein's approach to child analysis, which stressed play as the form of fantasy appropriate to the study of children (as opposed to dream analysis in adults). Second, aggression is a central feature of Klein's psychoanalytic discourse; its expression and rechannelling were understood as vital to the prevention of problems in adolescence associated with abnormality (in the form of deviance, crime: in short, juvenile delinquency). In these respects, then, certain pedagogic devices were announced: play becomes a crucial site for observation and normalization and is introduced as a pedagogic device.[17]

In intellectual terms activity, experience and playing were placed together: the child's spontaneous creation of scientific rationality grew out of play-like (because spontaneous) exploration of objects. It is the work of Piaget more than any other which provides the grounds for such a move. It should be noted that Susan Isaacs does not offer wholehearted support for Piaget or for other pedagogical experiments. However, what is important for our purposes is that the differences become lost because the practical legacy exists as the legitimation of regulatory practices. All that is required then is for the child to be provided with the conditions for spontaneous activity. It is observation, monitoring and above all normalizing of the sequence and effects of development which become the central pedagogic device. In these practices, early childhood was a crucial site for intervention in order to produce, in a medicalized sense, prevention of problems associated with adolescence and adulthood. These involved making sure that the individual developed away from passion, emotionality and aggression, towards love (*caritas*), rationality and sanity. The production of the democratic citizen was naturalized, as in A. S. Neill's terms – leaving children alone could produce a spontaneous form of parliamentary democracy.

The questions we have to ask ourselves next are why these issues assumed an importance at that particular historical moment and how they got taken up in ways which moved them from being marginal, private experiments to becoming the basis of state primary schooling. I shall indicate how certain political conditions were understood in the terms offered by psychology, so that psychological discourses provided not simply the legitimation but the factual basis for understanding these problems at all. This will disclose a complex interplay in which political events are understood and the practical interventions proposed in a way which both centrally implicates psychology and helps to sediment it within the apparatuses of regulation. What, then, was happening? What were the issues, events and concerns?

The theory of play is significant in the medicalization of certain problems connected with poverty, especially in respect of child health. Monitoring of child health was inaugurated by the Liberal government of 1910. Concern with 'appalling physical conditions' and extreme poverty was what fuelled the work of those, like Margaret MacMillan, who advocated a nursery movement and the development of physical education.[18] Supporters of the child-health and nursery movement argued that 'Millions of children are robbed of their earliest days of happiness, underfed, badly housed and without medical oversight, sometimes till death is in sight' (Dr Kerr, assistant to Margaret MacMillan, quoted in Simon, 1974). The theme of play, of open spaces in contrast to the overcrowded conditions of city slums, was a major feature of the movement. The new nurseries had gardens and much of the education took place out of doors in the 'fresh air', so that if the children could not be in the country they could at least be outside.[19]

In relation to the theme of play, the claim of *freedom* became increasingly vociferous. This was tied to the idea of individual, naturalized freedom from coercion, important in its discursive association with the rise of Germany and fascism in the period of the two world wars. The natural, the unfettered and the free were terms which came into increasing focus with the onset of war. It is significant that these were put forward at a time when the enemy, Germany, was being attributed with certain national characteristics which were laid at the door of her education system. That which made Germany great, the working capacity and regimentation of the people, became at one moment an object of envy (in the moment of the 'imperial race') and at the next an object of opposition. Thus any kind of new expression in education which could have made the war worth fighting and which contributed to building a new generation which in A. S. Neill's terms would be 'free from hate and fear' was considered a first priority. In 1918 the post-war Liberal government introduced an Education Act which established a national system of education. As part of this package nurseries were to be nationally organized. Post-war reconstruction depended heavily on notions drawn from the new psychology and education: regimentation, a term associated with the characteristics of the enemy (as militarism, Prussianism) became the enemy. If regimentation was the cause of German aggression did this not sound remarkably similar to the old discourse of education, now itself cast as regimentation, and thereby countered with individualized learning according to individual child development, at once free and natural? Individualism, then, was the key term in opposition to regimentation. The natural individual was the hope for the future:

> It is not difficult to understand the appeal of a word such as 'freedom' at that time. *The Times Educational Supplement* claimed that the Germans were the first to realize 'the possibilities of large-scale organisation, penetrating into every corner of life, securing ready submission from the individual to the orders of the expert controller'. And why this ready submission? Partly because their system of education 'created by Germans of an earlier day for loftier ends, has served as a willing tool in the monstrous achievement'.
>
> According to MacMunn, the older school discipline 'has found its *reductio ad absurdum* in the grotesque tragedy of German subserviency'. Against this could be put what he and the progressives offered. Nunn, the apostle of individualism, thought that the German belief in the State could be attributed partly to the education system which has been used as 'an instrument to engrain these notions in the soul of a whole people'. The war-time enemy was the enemy of freedom: thus Edward O'Neill could show the errors of the old educational way, with a telling comparision: they represented 'the real militarism of education'. 'It is for freedom that we are fighting this war,' said William Temple in 1916, making the point explicit, 'it is for freedom that those who care for education are struggling at home. . . . In the name of those who have died for the freedom of Europe, let us go forward to claim for this land of ours that spread of true education which shall be the chief guarantee of the freedom for our children for ever.' (Selleck, 1972, p. 87)

The centrality of scientific discoveries in producing and legitimating possible positions is attested by a statement made by a prominent exponent of nursery education of the time, Lillian de Lissa:

> Science has discovered that the development of mentality and of spirituality is part of nature's plan for the human being and, consequently, that they develop as naturally as do bones and muscles. It has been discovered that they are governed by their own natural laws, which, when uninterfered with and unhampered, bring the development to far higher planes than when they are thwarted by human interference. (de Lissa, 1918, p. 36)

Note here the importance of the use of the term 'discovery': that is the factual basis accorded to the evidence of scientific enquiry. It is the status accorded to scientific discoveries which allows the statements to be read as unproblematic statements of fact, not the product of theoretical or other speculation.

Given the cuts in government spending, the Geddes Axe of 1922 and the depression of the 1930s how was it possible that the child-centred pedagogy was able to come into its own? Indeed, a simple economic analysis would predict its downfall at such a moment – a downfall which did not occur. In fact the practices can be said to have been established, at least as the basis of state provision, in the two volumes of the Hadow Report published in the 1930s.

In order to understand this phenomenon one would need to examine the struggles in some detail.[20] However, it is important for the purposes of this chapter to remark on the effectivity of the relation of the various scientific discourses as explanations for current 'social problems'. There was, for example, the emergence of a scientific discourse which constituted the object of adolescence. This can be understood in relation to various conjunctural issues and events. There was considerable disquiet about the increase in juvenile crime, with the concomitant introduction of the discourse of 'juvenile delinquency' as an explanation for this (cf. p. 179 and Lane's 'Little Commonwealth'). Second, as Brian Simon reports:

> Referring to the 'Workers' Control' resolution of the 1926 Labour Party Conference, Percy asks future historians not to 'underrate the reality' in the England of the twenties of a 'revolutionary frame of mind'. If upheavals on the continent were not paralleled, there was an admiration for the Russian Revolution among 'many Englishmen', and it was 'against all reasonable expectation in the middle twenties that England should escape'. (Simon, 1974, p. 123)

A skimping and saving in education therefore might be the downfall of 'British democracy'. The kind of education and the changes needed were thus dictated by the concern with adolescence. This brought about continued pressure for the raising of the school-leaving age and the dividing of schooling into separate types along age lines. The tripartite system was supported by notions about stages of development and by apparatuses of selection linked to the discourse of mental measurement. The kind of pedagogic strategy was conditioned by a third discursive intervention in the form of Kleinian psychoanalysis in relation to the association of infantile aggression and problems associated with adolescence. Thus the education of young children according to free and individual principles was an imperative not only for promoting healthy development, but also for solving problems associated with both juvenile crime and political extremism. It is hardly surprising to find the discourses of child development and mental measurement sharing a platform.

The Hadow Consultative Committee was first set up under Conservative government but took off in the months of the short-lived Labour Government. The first report published in 1928 dealt with the education of adolescents. It is important in that it proposed secondary education for all from the age of eleven. The case for the proposed change rested on the 'discovery' of the psychological basis of adolescence as a distinct period:

> There is a tide which begin to rise in the veins of youth at the age of eleven or twelve. It is called by the name of adolescence. If that tide can be taken at the flood . . . we think it will 'move on to fortune'. We, therefore, propose that all children should be transferred, at the age of eleven or twelve.
> (Report of the Consultative Committee of the Board of Education on the Education of the Adolescent, 1926, Introduction)

In essence the report introduced the tripartite system of secondary education, controlled by the eleven-plus examination, with streaming at the upper end of the junior school, according to arguments based on the concept of capacity:

> In the first place there is the argument of the psychologist. Educational organisation is likely to be effective in proportion as it is based on the actual facts of development of children and young persons. By the time the age of 11 or 12 has been reached children have given some indication of differences in interests and abilities sufficient to make it possible and desirable to cater for them by means of schools of varying types, but which have nevertheless a broad common foundation. (ibid.)

Mental measurement and child development work together to produce and legitimate different forms of school provision for different ages and groups of children. What is particularly important for practice in the convergence of the two discourses is their differential effect on primary and secondary school practice. It was a stage model of development which allowed adolescence to be singled out as a separate period in the first place (different from childhood and adulthood). This stage model was used as a justification for a break at eleven which, given considerations about the provision of higher education, preparation of the workforce and so on (see Simon, 1974; CCCS, 1981) meant that selection had also to be introduced and of course it was a 'happy accident' that psychology had the tools to hand. It is often a mystery to students and teachers why nursery and infant education is so much more child-centred and progressive than junior, with secondary as the most 'reactionary' of all. Infant education is often held up as the model of good practice towards which teachers of older children should aspire. It is however not usually recognized that there are specific historical reasons why the practices at different phases in the education system should have different emphases. The introduction of eleven-plus selection with its emphasis on capacity profoundly touched the junior and secondary schools in ways which left the earlier ages unaffected. The discourses of mental measurement and development were not understood as being in opposition until the attacks on selection and streaming of the 1960s:[21] the Plowden era. At this and only this point was the difference marked, the discourse split, the discontinuity produced.

The second and third Hadow reports (*The Primary School*, 1931; *Infant and Nursery Schools*, 1933) take up the simultaneity of the two discourses. Both reports basically legitimate, in the form of state recommendation, everything I have spoken about in terms of the child-centred pedagogy. Individual freedom 'is essential: and freedom only becomes dangerous when there is nothing to absorb the child's restless activity and provide an outlet for his experimental spirit.' Innate tendencies relate to biologized natural development. Pedagogy becomes the observation and recording of naturalized development. Physical, emotional and mental development are presented side by side in the same terms: the facts of child development.

Of teachers it is argued that

> the first essential for a teacher of young children is that she should have the right temperament. A teacher of young children should not only have a real love and respect for young children, but should be a person of imagination, understanding, sympathy and balance.
> (Consultative Committee of the Board of Education, 1933, p. 153)

However, love is not in and of itself enough for teachers (as for mothers – see Donzelot, 1980, p. 31); they have to be trained:

> such work as this will demand wide and thorough theoretical knowledge and also the ability to apply this knowledge in actual experience with particular children. Child Study – the study of children's mental and physical development – should form the basis of her training. Her studies in psychology should be connected directly with descriptions and observations of actual behaviour of children. The young teacher in training should study the stages in development of children up to the age of seven with due regard to every aspect of growth.
> (Consultative Committee of the Board of Education, 1933, p. 153)

It is scientific training which ensures correct normalized loving.[22] The apparatuses for the production of the pedagogy in terms of forms of training are now introduced as a possibility and therefore a large-scale project.

The positive reception of Hadow was helped by the rise of totalitarianism and the impending second world war. The threat of totalitarianism fanned the flames which made the greater take-up of pedagogy appear as a psychic necessity. For example, Whitehead, in his famous work *The Aims of Education* (1929) states:

> Today we deal with herded town populations, reared in a scientific age. I have no doubt that unless we can meet the new age with new methods, to sustain our populations, the life of the spirit, sooner or later, amid some savage outbreak of defeated longings, *the fate of Russia will be the fate of England.* Historians will write as her epitaph that her fall issued from the spiritual blindness of her governing classes, from their dull materialism and from the Pharisaic attachment to petty formulae of statesmanship.
>
> (Whitehead, 1929, p. 65; my italics)

Denise Riley describes the threat of 'aggression' in children as it surfaces in the practices of war-time nurseries:

> Embryonic maternal deprivation theorising then blended with popularised Kleinian ideas produced in the 1944 British Medical Journal Leader a prophecy of doom. Entitled 'War in the Nursery' it described how 'in the years from two to five the battle between love and primitive impulses is at its height. . . . Winnicot, Buhler, Isaacs, Bowlby and others all note the turbulent characteristics of the age. Destructive impulses let loose in war may serve to fan the flame of *aggression natural to the nursery age.* . . . If the nerves of staff strained to breaking point cannot hold out, delinquency may ensue: the age of Resistance may thus be prolonged to adolescence or adult life in the form of bitterness, irresponsibility or delinquency'. The war in the nursery was the infantile psychic parallel of the War in Europe. By implication, state-provided childcare determined by wartime conditions would reinforce the pre-given psychic war.
>
> (Riley, 1978b, p. 95; my italics)

Margaret Lowenfeld, in her work on play, expressed a political imperative for play which linked directly with the concern signalled in the 1944 BMJ article mentioned by Riley:

> The forces of destruction, aggression and hostile emotion which form so powerful an element for good or evil in human character, can display themselves fully in the play of childhood, and become through this expression integrated into the controlled and conscious personality. Forces unrealised in childhood remain as an inner drive for ever seeking outlet, and lead men to express them not any longer in play, since this is regarded as an activity in childhood, but in industrial competition, anarchy and war.
>
> (Lowenfeld, 1935, pp. 324–5)

In a textbook produced for nursery teachers in 1939, Lillian de Lissa spelled out the imperatives in the form of a pedagogy:

> not only is play the surest index of a child's character it is also an indication of the normality of his development and of his mental and emotional health. Every nursery teacher should continuously watch her children at play and make some record of it. She should also make as comprehensive a study as she can of play itself, for this will enable her to interpret and evaluate her observations, and give some insight into each child and the kind of help and guidance he needs. It will help her to understand when and how to come forward and when to leave him alone. It will also guide her in her choice of the materials and playthings most helpful for each particular phase of growth. (de Lissa, 1939, p. 191)

In a photograph accompanying the text, the teacher-as-scientist is shown, observing, monitoring, recording, classifying: the child-centred pedagogy legitimated. The teacher is depicted with the notebook, her gaze taking in the children's play – the powerful fiction of the continous and total gaze of (dispassionate) observation: the teacher as all-knowing, all-seeing, 'knowing her children as individuals'.[23]

The accomplishment of the present

> Sometimes you can intervene and it's the wrong time. . . . I think it's something you get to know with practice . . . and nobody's ever going to be completely right. . . . I think observation's very important, to be aware, to watch a child. Be totally aware of what is happening. . . . It's a practice that comes from working with children. It's having a knowledge of how children develop; it's knowing the children as individuals. It's so many factors altogether. It's not just intuition. It might be with some people, but I think it's a lot more than just that.

The above quotation comes from a nursery-school teacher in 1981. The continuous and total gaze I noted in the pre-war discourse is present in this teacher's remarks, especially in her emphasis on observation as the basis of 'knowing the children as individuals'. The possibility of this knowledge is founded in her training in the 'knowledge of how children develop'. The pedagogy and the facts of child development are inextricably intertwined. Although there are some important post-war shifts and transformations which bring us to the common-sense practices of the present I shall not include these in this chapter.[24] It is, however, pertinent to note how the features of post-war constructivism (see e.g. Riley, 1978b; CCCS, 1982), the 1944 Education Act and the setting up of state-funded apparatuses helped ensure the dissemination and sedimentation of the new pedagogy. Importantly also, Piaget's work which developed the empirical apparatuses and refined the tools of classification concerning the stages of development was not published until after the Hadow report. It is, therefore, significant that transformations in the pedagogy, particularly in relation to mathematics and sciences, should take place after the second world war. It is in this sense, then, that the apparatus of concepts and discoveries produced some noteworthy transformations in the pedagogy of observation. The consequent shifts in mathematics education were significant in this respect (Corran and Walkerdine, 1981). There are, of course, many other specific transformations. For example the 1960s and 1970s provide the basis for an important study in their own right, particularly in terms of the relationship of child-centredness, progressivism and liberatory politics.[25] The relation of the attacks on progressivism and libertarianism to the stringencies of the 1980s is an important issue for enquiry.[26]

For the moment, let us return to the nursery record card set out on pp. 158–60. I hope that I have demonstrated the relationship between the sets of categories on the card and the production of the common sense of 'pedagogy as the observation and monitoring of normal development' as exemplified in the above quotation from a nursery school teacher. In the record card are produced both what is to be observed and monitored and the techniques of that monitoring and observation. Centrally implicated are a set of similar and surrounding apparatuses and practices, an edifice of teacher-training, of in-service education, of the monitoring and normalization of teachers themselves (advice and inspection) an apparatus of educational research, textbooks and so forth. Having shown how this common sense and these practices were historically located, produced and transformed, how are we to understand them? My argument has been that the object, the developing child, is a production which has to be understood in relation to its historical formation and conjunctural effectivity. In understanding its claims to be true and its evidences, therefore, I am arguing that there is a complex but strategic between the theoretical formulations of a particular object of study and their particular conditions of possibility. That there is no simple pre-existent 'real object' which developmental psychology has distorted is what I have attempted to demonstrate by analysing the productivity of its practices of classification.

Moreover, I have sited the psychology–pedagogy couple within a set of administrative apparatuses of regulation through normalization. In this sense, then, I have argued that such practices produce children as subjects. Concepts linked to, and to some extent derived from, Piaget's work play a central part in that process of production. In this respect, the issue of purity and distortion is central. It has often been asserted that the transformation and utilization of Piaget's work within education constitutes a distortion of an object which it is possible to free from those practices. In addition, Piaget's liberal/radical political position is taken as an indication of the usefulness of his work to the possibility of a radical pedagogy. The point, however, which I have attempted to make in my historical sketch of the conditions of possibility and emergence of the child-centred pedagogy is that in order to understand the relation of Piaget's work to educational practice it is necessary to chart the particular conditions which made such work possible, with a particular kind of theoretical object related in a specific way to educational practices. My concern is to chart the effectivity of Piaget's work, that is how it is implicated in the child-centred pedagogy. In this task Piaget's radical intentions and the rectitude of his object do not matter. What matters is that the way the work is taken up within educational practices could not be otherwise and this selective take-up is, itself, inserted into a particular pedagogy as a central component. This pedagogy is not Piagetian: what is being charted is the incorporation of a set of apparatuses related to, and in some respects derived from, Piaget's work alongside a whole network of other practices and discourses. Additionally, the radical potential and contribution of Piaget's work cannot be considered outside a historical context. I want to make a distinction between the radical intentions of the author, in this case Piaget, and the, radical or otherwise, effects of his work at any particular moment. If we first consider his intentions, we can see that these cannot be understood outside the conditions of possibility of his work. It appears clear that in some sense at least Piaget pitted his work in radical opposition to a Social Darwinian position, which seemed to indicate the biological inevitability of war, envisaging instead a peaceful world peopled by rational human beings. It is in that sense that his search for the grounds and evidence for a naturalized approach to the development of a scientific rationality can be understood.

The terms of that search link us into the second issue: the effects of his work. These have to be considered in relation to specific sets of historical conditions and their effects at one historical moment. In the sense that Piaget's work was inserted into radical critiques of the *status quo* at any one moment, we can assert that it has had radical effects. But the effects are not cut and dried and cannot be understood in terms of a simple radical–reactionary polarity. In the 1960s and 1970s Piaget's work was part of the legitimation and production of practices aimed at liberating children. We can argue that there were indeed positive and important effects in such practices but the way in which the liberation of children was formulated around an object of naturalized development also had consequences in possible political positions and practices which do not stand as timeless truths, nor are they necessarily adequate for the present conjuncture.[27] Particularly important is the repositioning of developmental psychology as progressive in reaction and contradistinction to the concept of innate intelligence, relating to mental measurement. Inasmuch, therefore, as it was implicated in pedagogic discourses and practices which sought to challenge what was considered reactionary, then we can understand the radical effectivity of the utilization of Piaget's work. However, what were radical effects at one moment in history are not necessarily adequate for all time and for all purposes. It is precisely the impossibility of setting the 'individual' free which is being contested in this volume.

It is perhaps the supreme irony that the concern for individual freedom and the hope of a naturalized rationality that could save mankind should have provided the conditions for the production of a set of apparatuses which would aid in the production of the normalized child. It is the empirical apparatus of stages of development which of all Piaget's work has been most utilized in education. It is precisely this, and its insertion into a framework of biologized capacities, which ensures that the child is produced as an object of the scientific and pedagogical gaze by means of the very mechanisms which were intended to produce its liberation.

In this sense then we can understand why Piaget's work appears in educational practices in such an apparently pragmatic way. If, for example, Piaget had not provided such an extensive and coherent set of empirical evidence and monitoring procedures one might speculate about his insertion into educational practices. It is those procedures which form part of the day-to-day running of classrooms, providing the taken-for-granted forms of a pedagogy which teachers frequently do not associate with the name of Piaget, who appears as a dimly remembered figure from college days.[28]

Finally, since there neither is, nor ever has been, a Piagetian pedagogy, the relation of Piaget's work to pedagogy should be considered neither as application nor as distortion. It is the conditions which made possible the development of both his work and the child-centred pedagogy, and their mutual interrelation, which I have attempted to spell out in this brief historical sketch. In the next part of this chapter I shall examine the effectivity of the present pedagogy in its work to produce children as subjects.

Classroom practice and the acquisition of concepts

Apparatuses of classification are central to the possibility and effectivity of practices of a particular form and content. In relation to the parameters of these practices it is possible to specify the production of the schemes and forms of teaching and learning and the process of acquisition of knowledge. The system of regulation and normalization produces what counts as 'good pedagogy'. It produces, therefore, what counts as a 'good teacher'.

A normative positioning in the power–knowledge axis is a subject position through which and in relation to which an identity as teacher is made possible (see e.g. Walkerdine, 1981a). The discursive practices and positionings also, therefore, provide the teacher's method and the possibility of her reading of the children's actions. Since the parameters of the pedagogy also limit what is and is not allowed, what does and does not count as performance of a particular kind and the classification of that performance, regulative devices and normative positions are thereby produced for children as pupils.

The irony of the productivity of the discursive practices is that developmental psychology, in providing the apparatuses for the production of truth about learning, in an important sense produces what it means to learn. What I am saying is that we can, as it were, deconstruct the relations of the discourses and the practices which constitute the pedagogy to examine how children and teachers are subjectively produced, but more than that, we can actually analyse the activities and sequences which comprise learning itself. In section 3 we will examine in more detail what it means to say that subjectivity is produced in and by discursive practices, but in the concluding pages of this chapter let me offer a small example.

The example comes from the practice of an infant teacher engaged in teaching mathematics to a group of 6 to 7 year olds (top infants). She has been doing some work on place value (the nearest equivalent in old mathematics is 'tens and units'). Her view is that children discover number relationships by physically grouping and carrying out operations on concrete objects. She wants the children to discover aspects of grouping in tens from activities with objects which require that grouping. Her view is consonant with that expressed in the most popular textbook for teachers, Williams and Shuard's *Primary Mathematics Today* (1974). Williams and Shuard entitle their introduction to place value as 'The emergence of the place-value concept'. Such a teminology immediately locates place value as arising out of and in relation to the properties of the mind of the child – something which 'emerges' spontaneously. By implication, therefore, it is not taught and cannot be located within anything to do with the system of representation or notation or existing practices of discourses. This reading is further supported by the authors themselves:

> From the variety of forms in which children *experience* our number system – the cubes and rods, recordings of sums of money and measuring, graphs, the abacus and symbols for numerals – *there develops a capacity* to read and write numbers with a confident recognition of their meaning.
>
> (Williams and Shuard, 1974, p. 163; my italics)

As part of her various practices the teacher in this example asks the children to bundle together groups of ten matchsticks, putting elastic bands around them. The children then work in pairs, each child putting out a number of bundles of ten and a number of single matchsticks in separate piles. These are to be put together, counted and an addition sum 'recorded' on paper. The teacher maximizes the importance of the operations with the objects and minimizes the importance of the written work by treating it as 'recording', which is to be understood as subsequent to, and consequent upon, the mastery of relevant concepts, which takes place through discovery based on action. In the sequence which I have taken for analysis, one pair of children, Michael and Tony, does not engage in the task which the teacher has set up. Michael, in particular, wrote down the sum first never bothering to count the matchsticks. He worked out the answer by adding the columns starting with the tens – a procedure which he had not been taught. Indeed, such procedures were antithetical to the teacher's practice, smacking as they did of rote-learning rather than proper conceptualization or real discovery. We know Michael's rationale because he conveniently explained it to his partner and to the teacher. His explanation to Tony is reproduced below:

M. Shall I tell you how I do it?
T. How?
M. Well, look you see when you get to a sum like this, right, look, you write the two numbers down, don't you – they're the tens and they're the ones. You put three tens down and I put two tens. We didn't put any ones down any of us, did we?
T. No.
M. So, we've got this sum thirty and twenty, haven't we? And altogether I add up this and that's three and two and that's what?
T. Five.
M. Three, that's five so you write down five and there's no there [*sic*] so you put five and that's how you make it. It's easy, innit, see?

(During this explanation Michael points to the sum on paper as an example.)

Now, several things are important. First, Michael's technique succeeded for some time – until he had more than ten in the ones column and did not know what to do. Second, the teacher would not have known about this unless she had seen my videotape. On doing so, she became very upset, saying, 'I'll have to take him back. He obviously hasn't got it. I'll have to take him back and give him more experience. . . . He shouldn't really be trying to do that yet.' So we have the failure of Michael's procedure understood in certain terms which have consequences for practice. The teacher understood his failure to get the correct answer as caused by conceptual failure, the remedy for which was to give him more concrete experience – he had gone too far too fast. Thus the remedy was more practice. His failure was also understood as *her* failure – that she had 'pushed' him – the worst sin of the child-centred pedagogy; she had not allowed him to go 'at his own pace'.

In this way we can note the complex interplay of relations between the objects and techniques of the discursive practice, the provision of teaching of a particular kind, the reading of the child's performance and the construction of the teacher's identity. I have shown this videotaped sequence to several groups of primary teachers. Although I had been at pains to select this teacher because she was well-known to be extremely competent, the teachers watching the videotape always tended to find fault with her, saying that she was not progressive enough: they never challenged the pedagogy itself. My reading of this response on the part of the teachers was that they actually recognized only too well teaching which was consonant with their own practice and actually felt threatened. So when I next showed the videotape to a group of teachers, I asked them to imagine that *they* were the class teacher in question and to tell me at the end of the tape how they would feel if Michael was in their class. Every time that I have used this method with a group of teachers the same thing has happened. The first things which were blurted out were: 'I'd feel I'd failed,' 'I'd feel guilty.' Then the teachers would go on to say what Michael's teacher had said: too far too fast, etc. The normative production of 'good teaching' means that the teacher must experience herself as inadequate, feel guilty, anxious and insecure. If the child has failed, by implication the teacher's gaze has not been total enough, she has not provided enough experience, has committed the 'sin' of 'pushing' the child. After all, within the parameters of the discursive practice, all children would and could develop correctly if only the teacher were good enough.

But, given a different discursive framework, it is quite possible to identify Michael's failure as *success*. Certainly a different set of assumptions about mathematics as knowledge would implicate a whole other further set of practices, producing different norms and readings of learning. Even given these practices, however, it is possible to argue that place-value is not produced through action but is an example of what Kline (1953) has called 'notation-directed change': that is one produced through changes in mathematical notation. Hence learning would not be about the internalization of action but the recognition of the relation between the written signifiers and their combination on paper, since place-value is about that system of signification and not about action. In this sense we would read Michael's methods as very sophisticated and we would argue that he was but one small step from success, a step which could have been remedied by his starting by adding the ones column instead of the tens! In this very important sense, then, neither children's nor teachers' actions stand outside their insertion within a particular framework of practice, which provides both a reading and a 'solution'. To bring this point home let me elaborate it a little further. Let us consider an 'arithmetic fact' such as 2 + 2 = 4. In one sense we can say that it appears to be a timeless mathematical truth. However, it depends not only on a binary system of notation, but, as I have argued elsewhere, relates to the system of signification which is mathematical discourse (see Walkerdine, 1982b; also Rotman, n.d.). In a sense of 2 + 2 = 4 as a statement incorporated into the discursive practices which make up primary school mathematics teaching, it is not timeless either. If we consider the shift from 'hearing and forgetting' to 'doing and understanding', what the statement 2 + 2 = 4 means changes radically as do the practices for its production.

For example, it becomes viewed as the outcome of an understanding produced on the basis of internalized action leading to the development of number concept. The mathematical statement is therefore not a number fact, but the articulation of an underlying conceptual apparatus. The writing of the statement itself is minimized as 'recording', seen as the icing on the cake of real understanding: it is secondary and relatively insignificant. The practices for producing it, therefore, also shift dramatically. Since it is the product of individual cognitive development it requires, for its production, a whole set of apparatuses to facilitate individual learning.

The mastery of 2 + 2 = 4 is at worst taken as evidence of parroting and therefore not proper learning, or at best as an indication of the child's having reached the requisite conceptual level: it is therefore an indication of a mental capacity. In this sense then what it means changes drastically at every possible practical level.

This brings me up against the most important point of trying to set out what kind of position I am advocating in relation to developmental psychology. I have shown that it is important not to dismiss developmental psychology as biased and thereby avoid engaging with its positivity in producing practices and therefore processes of learning. I hope that I have also identified the necessity of deconstructing the taken-for-granted basis of developmental psychology itself. That is I have deconstructed the power–knowledge relations central to the production of the object of developmental psychology. Let me make it quite clear, however, that I am not saying that historical deconstruction is in any sense enough. Laying bare the historical constitution of psychology's objects of study is the first step, but it is only the first. We still have to explain the constitution of children as learners; in this case we are interested in how children come to 'know'. How can we approach these issues in a way which does not reduce to that very psychology of which I have been critical? We certainly do not want to replace a unitary subject with capacities with the kind of socially determined subject, such as we have criticized in the Introduction to section 1. In section 3 we hope to make some of these issues clearer, looking at what it means to argue for a deconstruction of the unitary subject and a relation of absolute interiority between subject and discursive practices. I am not advocating disposing of all we know about children. Rather, my point is that developmental psychology's object is constituted in such a way as to reduce all problems to 'the child's acquisition of . . .', 'the development of . . .'. It is precisely such formulations which I have sought to deconstruct.

As we shall see in section 3, theorizing subjectivity is not coterminous with a theory of the individual. Because its boundaries and limit-conditions are differently placed, it means that we may need to question the very assumptions it is so difficult not to take for granted.

Conclusion: changing the present?

Throughout this chapter I have stressed that the production of the truth of developmental psychology is specific to a particular set of educational practices whose object is the developing child. I have argued that such psychology and such practices are normalizing in that they constitute a mode of observation and surveillance and production of children. Given this, it is difficult to conceive of these practices as being the basis of any kind of pedagogy which could potentially 'liberate' children. Indeed the notion of liberation which underpins such political calculations assumes precisely that 'natural' child development which has been the focus of criticism in this chapter. However, the role of educational practice within some notion of radical transformation remains an important and unresolved question. In order to address it I will begin by reiterating some important conclusions. There is no psychology which exists outside the framework of a particular set of historical conditions of possibility, and, in the case of developmental psychology, those conditions which make possible this body of discourse and practice also produce the possibility of the child-centred pedagogy. The fixing and sedimentation of those discourses and practices is assured by the administrative apparatuses which produce particular forms of organization and of sociality. Thus, empirical critiques within developmental psychology which argue about ages and stages or even about the importance of context will never be able to get outside the limits of the transcendental unitary subject.

Neither the child nor the individual can be liberated by a radical stripping away of the layers of the social. Such a model assumes a psychological subject laid bare to be re-formed in the new order. This was the aim of the liberatory pedagogy – to lay bare the psychological bones. But if social practices are central to the very formation of subjectivity the laying-bare is an impossibility. In this analysis there is no pre-existent subject to liberate.

It is important to point out that the processes of normalization are not the product of some repressive superpower hell-bent on keeping people in their place. That is, disciplinary power does not function through overt repression but through the covert reproduction of ourselves. Thus, liberals, radicals, feminists alike will advocate the child-centred pedagogy and will teach and learn within its orbit. Education is therefore more contradictory than suggested by those theories of 'reproduction' which assume a determinate or linear relation between the economy and schooling, which underplay it as a site of productivity in its own right.

In attempting to explain the production of the developmental psychology/child-centred pedagogy couple I have argued that psychology's status as science with particular practices for producing evidences and claims to truth is crucial in understanding the historical construction of the present form of schooling. This is in marked contrast to some other treatments of education in which ideology is taken to be the central component. For example, Sharp and Green (1975) in their study of progressive primary schooling use a model of false consciousness to explain the production of teacher identity. Because they understand child-centredness as ideology they have no way of understanding the centrality of its claims to truth and therefore its effectivity in producing practices. For instance:

> There is no direct logical relationship between the child centred vocabulary and the teacher's actions in all their complexity. The vocabulary does not immediately inform or motivate all their actions. Rather the teachers' actions are directly informed in an *ad hoc* manner by routines, habits and motivations, many of which in the immediacy of the classroom work will either be unconscious or only minimally reflexive. (Sharp and Green, 1975, p. 175)

They are forced into the above position because they do not have the theoretical apparatus to examine the complex relationship between teachers' statements and practices as set out in this chapter.

Using a different model of ideology, the Centre for Contemporary Cultural Studies Education Group (CCCS, 1982) in their historical analysis of the rise and demise of social democratic education place their faith almost exclusively in culture, representations and ideology. Notwithstanding the problems with this position discussed in the Introduction to section 2, it is crucial to point out that they simply fail to mention science. That scientific knowledges cannot be reduced to ideologies or cultural representations is supported by the power–knowledge position exemplified by Foucault, which the CCCS group reject because it cannot explain change. I would argue that by leaving out science they are attributing no importance in understanding change to the modern form of sociality founded in science's claims and guarantees to truth. A failure to deconstruct those claims is grave for it places us back in the circularity of the material–ideological debate analysed in the Introduction to section 2. While statements from the human sciences do not cause change in educational practices, they are centrally implicated not only because of the forms of legitimation they offer and, therefore, the grounding in fact; but because they also offer the terms in which the scientific pedagogies are to operate. These terms, as we have seen, cannot be understood without access to the debates within, and the production of the science of, psychology.[28]

Change cannot be understood simply in terms of transformations in the representation of the same object, the same problem. Rather, transformations in the production of knowledges shift what the object is taken to be. Certainly there are continuities which are often minimized in the discursive shifts, but the very productive nature of those shifts assures us that they are not shifts in the representation of an underlying object. If we were talking about shifts in representation we would have to operate as though psychological statements were ideological: an ideology that essentially distorts real relations. But psychology operates with a system of practices for producing evidences; it has claims to truth and to the production of fact. It is its very status as a science which is so important in understanding the history which I have signalled. In so far as it constitutes individuals, in this case children, as objects of its gaze it produces them as subjects. In so far as it creates a regime of truth premised upon a psychological individual then it prohibits other formulations which do not repeat individual–society dualism.

Notes

1 This chapter would not have been possible without the considerable help and support which I received from the co-authors of the book. In addition I would like to thank the following people for invaluable comments following readings of various draft versions: James Donald, Keith Hoskin and Bill Schwarz. Previous versions of this chapter have been presented to the Social and Political Sciences Committee, University of Cambridge, 1980, and the British Psychological Society Developmental Section Conference, 1982. The members of the Department of the Sociology of Education, Institute of Education, have been an important source of support and stability which helped to provide the conditions of possibility for production of this work. I am especially grateful for pertinent discussions with Basil Bernstein.

2 The 'social developmental psychology' of Richards (1974b) is an example of such a hope. In addition, work in the tradition of 'social cognition', 'cognition and context', critiques of Piaget and so forth is often understood as providing the potential for a radical theory of child development.

3 The term pauperism is used rather than poverty because of the way in which, as Jones and Williamson make clear, poverty was taken to be the result of the habits of the poor themselves.

4 See for example, R. Johnson, 'Really useful knowledge', in Clarke, Critcher and Johnson (1977), pp. 77–9.

5 Many would site the beginnings of the idea of a 'Natural' education in Rousseau's *Émile*, published in 1762. Several things are important for our purposes: firstly, Rousseau produced the first comprehensive attempt to describe a system of education according to nature. The key idea of the book was the possibility of preserving the original perfect mature nature of the child by means of the careful control of his education and environment 'based upon an analysis of the different natural stages through which he passed from birth to maturity' (Stewart, 1972, p. 15). His assertion of the child as naturally good was posed in opposition to the 'original sin' of religion. It is not surprising then that 'In England, it was among those concerned with problems of science, industry, public health, education and philosophical speculation that the ideas of Rousseau found their most receptive audience. The philosophical societies, the majority of whose members stood outside the social, religious and political establishment, were the focus of the new critical and scientific spirit' (ibid., p. 18). Already, therefore, in the eighteenth century forces of 'progress' were on the side of science which was also on the side of 'nature'.

6 It is also important that the movement which normalized and biologized Reason excluded the female from the normal. Women thus became, by definition, unreason, abnormal. This can be witnessed in relation to struggles in relation to sexuality (Bland, 1981), domesticity (Hall, 1984) as well as education. The relation of psychology to women's education is explored in Walkerdine (1981b). A revised version of this paper will appear in Walkerdine, Walden and Hayward (forthcoming).

7 'The new domain was defined at the point of intersection of two new ways of making statements about the population which were themselves formed during the early nineteenth century, as the result of the constitution of town police forces and town health boards, on the one hand, and as a result of the reform of prison administrations and those of Poor Law institutions on the other. These two new ways of making statements about the population formed a topographical analysis and a historical analysis respectively: and by their intersection defined a new field of objects of analysis, that is to say, the classes of the population. A class was accordingly defined by a web of topographical connections, which also characterised conditions whereby children were trained up as members of a class, and it was this that formed the moral topography of the class' (Jones and Williamson, 1979, p. 96).

8 The emergence of techniques of mental measurement is described in detail by Rose (1979).

9 See Greta Jones (1980) for more detail.

10 One aspect of this documented by Rose (1979) is the beginning of educational apparatuses which distinguished between those of normal and 'subnormal' intelligence and educated accordingly.

11 Such elision is present in many of the liberal and radical pedagogies from free-school movements to the stress on individual discovery in, for example, Barnes, Britton and Rosen (1971). The focus on 'the child' as a person, an individual in its own right, an autonomous agent was what allowed it to be counterposed to the grinding norms of the oppressive pedagogic classificatory

machines of selection and grading. I am at pains, therefore, to establish that the child-centred pedagogy and developmental psychology rely equally on systems of classification and regulation – though, because, as we shall see, it was, being linked to 'freedom', more covert than overt. It was not 'sorting and grading'. This stress on 'developing potential' has led many primary school teachers to understand their pedagogy as, at the very least, liberal. This helps to explain the significant lack of radicalism on the part of primary school teachers compared with those in secondary education. It is additionally important to note Basil Bernstein's (1971) use of the concept *invisible pedagogy* to designate a similar relation.

12 Although there is no space in this chapter it is important also to position psychoanalysis within the framework outlined above. Psychoanalysis merits considerable attention in its own right. Although it is now considered external to scientific psychology Graham Richards (1982) has argued that there is very little to choose between the terms of the psychological discourse of James, one of psychology's 'founding fathers', and Freud, although the latter came to be seen as antithetical to psychology. This means at least that the concerns, debates, discursive conditions which surrounded the founding of psychology are also relevant to Freud. This is particularly important in respect of the biologization of 'drives'. An understanding of the animal, irrational forces is not antithetical to a science of natural rationality, especially if a relation is seen between the latter and the former. Rationality then can be attained not through coercion, but through freedom which permits outlets for 'natural' passions, such that they are dispersed, dispelled and rechannelled. For our purposes those developments in child psychoanalysis associated with Melanie Klein will be particularly important, especially in relation to early infant 'aggression' and later antisocial behaviour, infancy being understood as the causal point of problems which, in fact, only become obvious in adolescence. Such discourses have had profound effects, not only in early education (the point of intervention and possible prevention) but also in psychoanalytically validated social work (the point of cure). Psychoanalysis both built upon the rationality and the freedom implied in the earlier discourse, but transformed it in terms of scientifically given 'drives', not forces for good, but forces for potential evil founded in science, for which the 'cure' was free and individualized pedagogy.

Donzelot (1980) points out that the insertion of psychoanalysis into the practices surrounding the normalization of the family means that techniques which had previously been concerned with the poor, now become generalized and applied to *all* children and families. I think this is significant for education, too. For it is also the case that what in the nineteenth century was a concern for the poor and the education of the masses, becomes in the twentieth century based on scientific statements which are taken to be *facts* about *all* children.

13 See Venn and Walkerdine (1978) for a more detailed treatment of the circle of science.

14 In this respect *passion* signifies unhygienic 'love', the danger of women's bodies represented by their abnormality within medical discourse. Bland (1981) examines how women's bodies were considered dirty, unhygienic. This is further explored in relation to psychoanalytic discourses and women's sexuality in the Introduction to section 3.

15 A. S. Neill stated that he had been influenced by Lane's debt to Freud, but himself later was far more swayed by Reich.

16 It is highly relevant that, until very recently, there were two departments at the Institute of Education: Psychology and Child Development. The former was formed out of the developments in mental measurement, while the latter related to child study, psychoanalysis, genetic epistemology and so forth. The developments and relations of the two departments in relation to the production of modern forms of teacher education are very relevant indeed.

17 Play is also legitimated on other grounds from other coterminous discourses, of course, not unrelated for example, to Piaget's use of play, animal studies and so forth.

18 In relation to this the normalization of *mothering* through science meant that the nanny of the upper-class home became the middle-class mother at home (who could be kept there by the earnings of her husband) whose job it was to regulate development. Since working-class mothers were by definition abnormal their children would stand a better chance in state nurseries.

19 I am grateful to Basil Bernstein for pointing out to me the predominance of horticultural metaphors associated with growth, not *agricultural* metaphors associated with farming. This tendency can be related both to the urbanization of the gentry but also to the development of an urbanized workforce which lived in towns with a promise of *gardens*.

20 In producing a historical analysis of this as of any other period it would be important to go beyond the secondary sources I have quoted to the source material itself, to examine who supported and opposed what educational and psychological moves and in what terms. In others words, it would examine the complex interplay of conditions of possibility in a way which centrally implicated forms of political, psychological and educational argument and struggle as well as the matter of the individuals and groups who were so positioned in those struggles. In this way it should be possible to produce a history which would reduce neither to a simple causality nor to that rather myopic interpretation of Foucault, presented by CCCS (1982), but rather in Donald's (1979) terms a 'conjunctural analysis of the balance of social forces'.

21 It is important in this respect to understand the recent singling out and vilification of Cyril Burt as a perpetrator of reaction. It is clear that while Cyril Burt did, indeed, provide evidence for the Hadow Committee his views were not expressly opposed by exponents of child development. It is also important that while the Plowden Report is similar to Hadow in many respects it does not contain any reference to mental measurement.

22 Note the professionalization of love both in relation to teaching, but also in the 'caring profession' of nursing, social work, etc., jobs for which women are naturally endowed with training to *amplify* their *capacities*.

23 This goes together with the dream very dear to the hearts of many teachers of young children. It is, that in 'helping their children to develop' they are engaging in a humane act, it is not oppressive or harmful, but helpful, loving, beautiful: the 'mother made conscious' (Steedman, forthcoming). Such sentiments work powerfully in relation to the identity and desires of teachers to perpetuate the pedagogy (Walkerdine, 1981a).

24 For some discussion of these issues, particularly in terms of the progressivism

of the 1960s and 1970s see Walkerdine (forthcoming); see also Walkerdine, Walden and Hayward (forthcoming).

25 In this respect the series of Penguin Education Specials, the Children's Rights Workshop, the Little Red Schoolbook and so on form important texts. In relation to the radical/liberal face and the study of contradictions the demise of Risinghill and Tyndale Schools provide important sources (see for example Berg, 1969, and Ellis *et al.*, 1976).

26 In this regard it is instructive to consider the position, for example, of Neville Bennett's *Teaching Styles and Pupil Progress* (1976). The importance of this work lies in its status as scientific evidence for or against the efficacy of progressivism. Its position is, therefore, central in providing legitimation for a particular set of practices, economic stringencies, etc. We need to consider, for example, the funding of the study, the criticisms of it – i.e. internal, usually on the grounds of method and the interpretation of statistical data. As with other examples of shift in practice we have seen scientific legitimation through fact is central to providing grounds for change – in this case increase in class size was important. It is also significant that Neville Bennett subsequently obtained a chair in Educational Research at Lancaster University. In other words, the conjunctural fit of a piece of work like this is important to understand – its antecedents, what produced it as apparently necessary, its theoretical and methodological tools, its evidences, its consequences, its placing within political, economic, administrative and pedagogic apparatuses.

27 For example in the 'Tyndale affair' the teachers supported, as a matter of principle, a non-oppressive non-authoritarian form of pedagogy based on pupil choice and therefore liberation. It was working-class parents who opposed this most vociferously. This put the teachers in a double-bind: that is the working-class parents were, in political terms, their allies, yet they 'did not understand'. This produced a retreat on the part of the teachers to a discourse of professionalism and placed them in a contradiction which was untenable and had the effect both of the teachers seeing themselves as 'critics' and of engineering their own demise. (See also Walkerdine, 1983.)

28 It is interesting in this respect to note that such is the taken-for-grantedness of the pedagogy that it can and has produced opposition on the part of teachers to efforts by developmental psychologists to intervene in relation to the changing theories and evidences within the discipline. For example, Jerome Bruner speaking of the Oxford Pre-school project, stated: 'There seemed to have developed a nursery ideology of extra-ordinary dogmatism. It rested on a strikingly narrow interpretation of the . . . "development idea", that children must be allowed to develop in congruence with their own needs and modes of thought. In its most exaggerated form this ideology translated itself into ideas about how nursery play should be organised. In general terms it should be unstructured, spontaneous and undirected' (Bruner, 1980, p. 203). Here then is no simple *application* of developmental psychology to education, but a complex relationship which can be understood with recourse to the kind of historical explanation I have undertaken. It is significant that Bruner uses the term *ideology* to differentiate the teachers' position from the current state of developmental psychological *science*. In making this distinction the status of the teachers' knowledge is questioned and the relationship between the two elided.

29 The kind of analysis undertaken here elides the problem of the competing claims to truth *within* a discourse, since there are claims, evidences and counterclaims. This is certainly important but cannot be understood outside the issue of the limit-conditions of the discipline itself. Also, importantly for this analysis, it is not always *all* of one theory which is taken up, as in the example of Piaget's stages of development. The stages were, as it were, prised apart from other aspects of the theoretical edifice and rearticulated with other, sometimes theoretically quite distinct, approaches. This process is very important in so far as it helps to explain how and in what circumstances particular pieces of work are taken up and utilized. So a particular pedagogy may be adopted because it satisfies a variety of people holding different interests and positions. For example the individualized child-centred pedagogy satisfied those concerned with juvenile crime, with psychoanalysis, with freedom, with 'keeping the masses in their place' and more, all at the same time and in different and contradictory ways. Thus the discourses informing the practice are not all of one piece, without seams or ruptures, but we can say that they get taken up in this popular way precisely because there are many discourses and interests which appear to be solved by the introduction of the new practice.

Introduction to Section 3
Theorizing subjectivity

Thus far we have achieved two things. In section 1 we exemplified the theoretical weaknesses and political disadvantages of psychology's construction of the individual within individual–society dualism. In section 2 we demonstrated the positivity of psychology in constructing the human subject both as the object of its study and as a site for social administration and regulation. In this section, we intend to develop further analytic tools which are required in order to theorize subjectivity, and to exemplify what this development means in practice through analyses of social relations between adults (chapter 5) and between adults and infants (chapter 6).

Our work in the previous sections did not simply demonstrate pervasive characteristics of contemporary psychology. It gave us many of the elements which form a part of an alternative approach. For example, in section 1 our critique of psychology's assumptions about the unitary, rational character of the individual implied that it was necessary to theorize subjectivity as multiple, not purely rational, and as potentially contradictory. In section 2 we showed that the unitary rational subject is itself a historical product, and, through the example of mathematics, we argued that particular forms of rationality are produced through and depend on particular technologies and practices[1]. There we stressed the way discursive practices provide subject *positions*. It will be remembered (Introduction to section 2, pp. 116 ff.) that the post-structuralists' deconstruction of the subject-as-agent allowed an understanding of the subject as a position within a particular discourse. This meant that the subject was no longer coterminous with the individual. Rather, the power–knowledge relations which produced a subject-position implied that there was no necessary coherence to the multiple sites in which subject-positions were produced, and that these positions might themselves be contradictory.

In this process, then, the unitary subject was deconstructed. As Hirst and Woolley put it: 'The concept of "person" is intelligible only with reference to a definite substratum of categories, practices and activities which together give the agent its complex and differentiated form' (1982, p. 120).

Now in displacing the individual as a simple agent the post-structuralists achieved a massive and important step. However, we are left with a number of unresolved problems. First, in this view the subject is composed of, or exists as, a set of multiple and contradictory positionings or subjectivities. But how are such fragments held together? Are we to assume, as some applications of post-structuralism have implied, that the individual subject is simply the sum total of all positions in discourses since birth? If this is the case, what accounts for the continuity of the subject, and the subjective experience of identity? What accounts for the predictability of people's actions, as they repeatedly position themselves within particular discourses? Can peoples' wishes and desires be encompassed in an account of discursive relations?

By leaving these questions unanswered, this position implicitly invokes the rationalism, or the assumption of a pregiven subject, which we have criticized in relation to psychology, leaving a figure in the background which opts for particular subject positions (see Introduction to section 1). Alternatively we are left with the kind of discourse determinism, criticized in the Introduction to section 2, which implies that people are mechanically positioned in discourses, a view which leaves no room for explicating either the possibilities for change or individuals' resistances to change, and which disregards the question of motivation altogether.

We suggest, then, that although we have argued for the deconstruction of the unitary subject, the post-structuralist displacement of the unitary subject, and the revelation of its constituted and not constitutive character, is not enough to explain the possibility of subjectivity. That is, the work at the level of discursive constitution of subjects elides the specificity of the construction of actual subjectivities in the domain of discursive practices.

Our purpose in this section is to address this site. We do this through developing certain ideas from psychoanalytic theory, and the work of the French psychoanalyst Jacques Lacan in particular. Here we are following certain developments in feminism, in media and cultural studies, and in attempts to formulate materialist theories of ideology. (See, for example, articles published in the journals *m/f* and *Screen*, and Coward and Ellis, 1977, and Hall, Hobson, Lowe and Willis, 1980.) However, our adoption of psychoanalytic concepts is both critical and selective, and we introduce some major shifts in emphasis, here and in the chapters which follow, which go beyond what is available in current analyses. In principle these emphases allow us to link our analysis of subjectivity with the account of subject positions produced through power–knowledge relations to which we have pointed so far, though the links are not ones of simple determination. For instance, chapter 5 analyses the production and effectivity of gender difference and gendered subjectivity in heterosexual couple relations. It uses some aspects of psychoanalytic theory to account for what we call the 'investment' or, very loosely, the emotional commitment, involved in taking up positions in discourses which confer power and are supportive of our sense of our continuity, confirming ourselves as masculine and feminine in accordance with frames of reference which are themselves socially produced. Chapter 6 on the other hand tackles the question of the emergence of subjectivity with the beginnings of language and the child's insertion into discursive relations. Although these chapters use psychoanalytic concepts and the idea of power–knowledge relations with different emphases, the two together demonstrate continuities in and correspondences between the principles governing subjectivity as it is expressed in the relations of adults and infants. By the end of these chapters we have not only illustrated the motivational dynamics through which individuals are positioned in discourses, but we have also opened the possibility that those processes which position us are also those which produce the desires for which we strive.

The remainder of this introduction explains the psychoanalytic concepts which are used, beginning with a brief discussion of psychoanalysis and its political implications in general. We then present a fuller account of Lacan's views. Finally, by using examples, we elaborate the shifts in emphasis which we are proposing.

Psychoanalysis and left politics[2]

We turn to psychoanalysis for a view of ourselves which is in many ways in direct opposition to that presented by traditional psychology, theorizing what is occluded by that discipline. First, in contrast to the rational subject of psychology, psychoanalysis gives space to our fundamental irrationality: the extent to which will or agency is constantly subverted to desire, and the extent to which we behave and experience ourselves in ways which are often contradictory. Second, the assumption of a unitary subject is immediately undercut in psychoanalysis by its focus on unconscious processes, which are on the whole excluded in psychology. Third, where psychology divides cognition from affect, in psychoanalysis these processes are intertwined in complex ways. Fourth, it provides an account of the continuity of the subject, of the past implicated in the present and a view of development which is in direct contrast to the oversimplified social or biological determinisms which we have criticized in the Introduction to section 1. For instance, although psychoanalysis stresses that particular life events have effects on the psychic development of individuals, particularly in the early years through the family constellation, these effects and their implications are neither entirely predictable nor reproducible, nor are they controlled from within. In short, psychoanalysis profoundly challenges any attempt to separate the individual and the social, and to think about this individual in terms of its consciousness of self or a unitary capacity for rational action.

An analysis of how and why the discourses and practices of psychoanalysis and psychology have diverged so strikingly cannot, unfortunately, be attempted here (but see Ingleby, 1980a and b). However, the uptake of psychoanalysis within our project is not unproblematic. The theory and practice of psychoanalysis is frequently dismissed on the left as bourgeois, highly culturally specific, and therefore 'invalid' for general application, and as anti-feminist. For example, in Freud's account the position of the father in the family is privileged, and his explanation of characteristics of female psychology rests heavily on the concept of 'penis envy'. Psychological differences between men and women thus easily reduce to biological differences, with the implication that women's subordination is inevitable. (See Introduction to section 1 for a discussion of this position.) Moreover, those post-structuralists which we have cited extensively in previous chapters, Foucault and Donzelot, have directly implicated psychoanalytic discourses in the production of particular sites for intervention and social regulation; for instance, in the prescription of sexual norms (Foucault, 1979), and in the management of child-care and what constitutes the role and responsibilities of parents within the family (Donzelot, 1979).

The historical specificity of psychoanalysis, the exclusivity of its practice, and some of its anti-feminist implications are indisputable. Nor are we challenging, here, the particular effects which Foucault and Donzelot have demonstrated. But it is first necessary to point to the implications of a too simple and rapid dismissal of psychoanalysis, implications which themselves suggest that psychoanalytic theory may be particularly apposite at the present time. Donzelot, for instance, has dismissed psychoanalysis as 'normative' and simultaneously rejected it as an account of the formation and motivation of individuals. But as we have noted above, he has not put in its place any explanation of either how individuals are positioned in discourses, or their effectivity at the level of the individual subject. In consequence he is left with an account of agency which is rationalistic, and a view of change which is extremely voluntaristic. As Adams (1982) has pointed out in her critique of his account, the effectivity of norms implicitly assumes that individuals are free to choose to accept their own normalization, to take on board at will whatever normative images are presented to them, such as those of 'proper parents', in this case. This implies that they are equally free to stand outside the norms and to reject them. This assumption, of course, makes nonsense of the claimed effectivity of normalizing apparatuses.

This voluntarism accords with much of the traditional left's approach to change and we have criticized it explicitly with respect to the liberatory politics of the 1960s and early 1970s (see the Introduction, p. 3). Furthermore, we have argued that the political crises of the present time make it imperative that we develop a clearer understanding of what militates against change, what accounts for reaction and for resistance. This has been recognized particularly within feminism. The task of working out what, exactly, a personal politics might consist of has forced women to recognize limitations in what can be achieved through consciousness-raising. This has proved to be particularly so in the area of sexuality, where as Adams has pointed out, the intransigence of desires defies any simple rationalistic manipulation.

Given this political conjucture, psychoanalysis is increasingly being recognized as less of a theoretical edifice to be rejected than an account of subjective processes and their production which we cannot afford to ignore. First, psychoanalysis provides the clearest available theorization of the psychic processes which contribute to our resistance to change, and why we repeat courses of action which are apparently detrimental to us, though its explanation of how change comes about outside the confines of the analytic situation is admittedly weak. Second, because of the particular ways in which psychoanalysis links sexuality with the unconscious, it is directly implicated in any attempt to understand the forms and possibilities of change in personal life.

But our acceptance and appropriation of psychoanalysis need not be uncritical, and there is considerable scope for selection. Not only did Freud himself continually develop or modify his account, but psychoanalysis has now produced a wide range of therapeutic and theoretical emphases. Within this diversification it is possible to state some priorities.

First, if the attempt to appropriate psychoanalysis is to have politically progressive implications, it must obviously utilize the potentially subversive aspects of the theory. There is a marked tendency for these to be suppressed in favour of therapeutic techniques which in effect focus on fostering the individual's adjustment to his or her environment. This is witnessed particularly in the remarkable rapidity with which psychoanalysis was appropriated in the United States between the two world wars, to which Freud (1914a) himself apparently responded uneasily by claiming that if the Americans really understood psychoanalysis, they would not accept it so easily! (See for example, Turkle, 1979.) Second, such an approach must also recognize explicitly the historical specificity of the psychic phenomena and reading of unconscious life which psychoanalysis produces. This is recognized in most feminist appropriations of psychoanalysis, which likewise point to the fact that Freud himself asserted that it was not the aim of psychoanalysis to produce conformity to societal norms, and which stress that psychoanalysis is not a prescription for, but a description of, psychic life under existing patriarchal capitalist social relations (Mitchell 1974). But granted that we may not be able to afford to ignore these descriptions, we need to take this further. Unless its appropriation enables us to envisage the possibility that things can be otherwise, and to move towards a theorization of the possibilities of change, psychoanalysis will lock us into a closed circle. Furthermore, psychoanalytic theory has largely been developed through material produced within the exclusivity of the analytic situation and the particular power relations which operate between analyst and analysand. Any appropriation of psychoanalysis must, of course, assume that there is some correspondence between the phenomena which this situation produces and the motivations, conflicts and repetitions which occur in day-to-day situations. But ultimately we will need to work at a level which is not the privileged property of analysts, but which is accessible to us all.

A first step in this process is to examine how far psychoanalytic traditions acknowledge or theorize links between the psychic life of individuals and the social–cultural domain.[3] There have been a number of psychoanalytic schools or applications which have acknowledged the importance of this question, pointing out, for example, how the particular conditions of Viennese society and the clientele with whom Freud was working influenced both the presenting pathologies and the analytic material. Recognition of this inspired early anthropological studies which claimed to challenge Freud's explanation of the universality of the Oedipus complex, for instance, in the famous Freud(Jones)–Malinowski debate (cited in Hirst and Woolley, 1982), and the well-known studies of Margaret Mead. However, though Margaret Mead's work, in particular, has contributed to challenging certain assumptions about inevitable differences between psychic structures in men and women, and the form of those structures, essentially her analysis of social relations and psychic functioning rests on an argument of covariation. As Hirst and Woolley (1982) have pointed out in their recent discussion of the Freud(Jones)–Malinowski debate, the terms of anthropology or sociology and psychoanalysis are not commensurate, such that the two types of explanation by-pass each other. (See Introduction to section 1 for a similar argument concerning attempts to mesh sociological and psychological concepts in accounts of socialization.)

However, there are psychoanalytic traditions which have aimed to theorize how social processes interpenetrate the workings of the psyche. These include the social psychoanalytic accounts which developed in the United States between the wars, such as the work of Horney, Fromm, Erikson, and the school known as ego psychology, of which Harry Stack Sullivan is generally taken as the founding figure. Introducing the concept of 'self' and diffusing the centrality of sexuality, this work was heavily influenced by sociology and G. H. Mead. Indeed it flourished in reaction to the same social issues raised by a massively increasing immigrant population and the expansion in American capitalism, as Mead's own work shows (see Roberts, 1977). Unsurprisingly, as Holland (1977) points out, in addition to suppressing some of the more unpalatable aspects of psychoanalysis, it reproduces or shares some of the problems with Mead's work which we raised in the Introduction to section 1. That is, it assumes a conformity between the individual and the values and social regulatory systems of the society, taken as necessary for both social order and a harmonious existence. This is made explicit in Erikson's work, which is based on the idea that under ideal circumstances child-rearing practices produce the personality characteristics which the smooth running of the particular society requires. Though based on a liberal ethic, within this account contradiction, conflict and inability to act in accordance with social norms are no longer part of the cost of entering culture (Freud, 1930), but evidence of socialization failures and a target for intervention. Though all these criticisms do not apply to Horney, who was one of the first to stress that women's psychological characteristics were related to their subordinate position in society, her account was premised on rescuing the essentially feminine, a biologism which is, as Mitchell (1974) has argued, as handicapping as Freud's own theorization.

Though the pitfall of essentialism also applies, the suppression of potentially subversive aspects of Freud's theory is not a criticism which can be made of the work of Wilhelm Reich, which represents a third major attempt to place psychoanalytic concepts in a social context, and in this case within a Marxist account of social relations. Indeed in Reich's work we see one of the first attempts to theorize the relationship between the forms of human subjectivity and their relation to the productive process. Since he was trying to understand crucial problems thrown up for Marxism within the particular conjuncture of his time, such as the nature and role of the family under capitalism, the growth of fascism in Germany, the rise of Stalinism, and so on, we cannot but be struck by parallels between Reich's project and our own contemporary concerns. However, though the historical importance of the work is considerable, it wandered into inevitable stumbling blocks. These we can now recognize as being due to the particular aspects of Freud's theory which he took as a starting point.

Reich based his work on Freud's theory of the instincts and, in particular, on the thermodynamic model which he used to conceptualize the regulation of instinctual energies in the psychic apparatus. Although Freud repeatedly referred to this model, or more precisely, to the problem of the management of energy, in his own work he also shifted between this emphasis and one in which movements in psychic life do not result from instinctual forces themselves, but from the mental representatives to which they become attached through particular life experiences, thus displacing the emphasis away from energy *per se*. As we shall see, it is this emphasis which is developed in Lacan's work. In Reich's account, however, there is no problem of representation, and the issue of signification or meaning is by-passed. For Reich, what is unconscious is purely instinctual, and the sole economic principle of psychic life was the movement of libidinal sexual energy. The ego was regarded as a superstructure imposed upon this semantic base, as a set of resistances to the discharge of libidinal energy built up in the conflict between natural instinctual forces and the repressive forces of social life. Under capitalism these instinctual forces are necessarily repressed, and the ego resistances were thought to solidify into a 'character armour', the repressed and repressive character structure of the majority of the population. Reichian therapy aimed to break through this armour, to loosen it, and hence allow the sexual instincts to be released and satisfied. In a socialist society sexual mores would be such as to allow the natural expression of these fundamental and essential forces.

Reich's work eventually lost contact with its original roots in Marxism, giving way to the essentialist techniques of vegetherapy and orgone therapy, concerned with the regulation of life energy. Such a conclusion may strike us as bizarre. But even if it was not an inescapable outcome of his theory, the implications are at least recognizable.

It is just this position which we have criticized with respect to liberation movements in general and the sexual liberation movement in particular (see Introduction, p. 4). Though of course the influence within these movements was as much due to Marcuse as to Reich, the tradition prompted an oversimplified notion of the relation between social 'oppression' and individual 'repression'. As we have discussed, the power of these movements was that they promised a better, freer, unrepressed psyche, loosed from the shackles of capitalism. But as we have tried to show throughout the book, a 'repressed psyche' is not a simple product of capitalism, or patriarchy. If, as we have argued, psychic states are produced in relation to social practices, there is no simple source of oppression which, through its removal, would produce the 'individual laid bare'.

This essentialism is, we suggest, a direct consequence of the simple application of Freud's instinct theory and energy model. It is also an implication which follows from many of the relatively recent accounts which have given far more space to the mother–infant relationship – the first 'object relation' – and the role of the mother than did Freud. This is an important omission in Freud's theory which, as we have noted, privileges the position of the father. However, many of the approaches aimed at redressing this imbalance, such as Object Relations theory and the work of Winnicott in particular, entail particular normative tendencies. First, as Mitchell and Rose (1982) point out, the father has become marginalized in these accounts, such that the issue of sexuality is diffused, and they contribute little to our understanding of the production of gender. Second, the theorization of the mother's role has focused not only on her providing the first experience of satisfaction through feeding, which provides the foundation for the first object relation, but on the idea that she is responsible for meeting the baby's needs. This emphasis is particularly evident in the work of Winnicott (1956). Wanting an environmentalist account of pathology, Winnicott proposes a biologically based model through which he argues that mothers go through a period of adaptation called 'primary maternal preoccupation' which puts them in a particularly receptive state after birth. This enables them to read and meet the baby's needs accurately. Failures in this process, through the mother's 'illness', for example, will have deleterious consequences for the baby's psychic development.

This account has had unfortunate and unforeseen consequences, since it is now relatively easy to place the source of all pathology onto the mother for failing to meet the baby's needs. More than any other psychoanalytic account, Winnicott's emphasis has contributed to the normalization and regulation of motherhood, through social work and medical practice, in the arguments used against providing nursery provision, and so on. (See Riley, 1978a.)[4] This implication is a direct consequence of the fact that, although clearly very different from Reich's account, it retains the same simple relation between biologically based predispositions and an environmental process which may more or less facilitate their expression.

Now it is certainly true that Freud remained preoccupied with relations between biological, or, more accurately, neurological processes and the workings of the psyche. Yet his own theorizing continually subverted any simple reductionism (see Mitchell in Mitchell and Rose, 1982). Moreover there are other possibilities within Freud's account which allow us to break free from these dualistic implications and at the same time specify links between the social domain and the psychic life of individuals. These include, as noted above, an emphasis on the role of ideational representatives in the unconscious which, though deriving their energy from biological need-states and their satisfaction in the first instance, ultimately govern the workings of the psyche. Second and inextricably related to this, it is possible to read Freud's theory not as simply a theory of mechanism, but as a theory of meaning, such that the symbolic material of dreams, free associations and what is produced in the analytic situation implicates the role of signification in the functioning of the unconscious. It is through a focus on signification that it is possible to link the psyche to the social domain. As we shall see, it is this emphasis that is developed principally by Lacan, contributing to the particular merits of his approach.

Lacan: the deconstructed subject, signification and desire

Of all psychoanalytic accounts, Lacan's approach is generally recognized as extremely controversial, alternatively renegade and revolutionary, or heretic, mystical and mad. He has continually attacked the orthodoxy and sanctity of analytic practice, and mounted a perennial challenge to other theoretical developments and therapeutic endeavours (Lacan, 1953). For example, not only does he challenge the American tradition for its conformist tendencies, but also the Kleinians and Object Relations theorists, as well as others who emphasize the infancy period, for harking back to a myth of missed experience in babyhood. Of other developments he targets those stemming from Freud's own work, particularly those proposed by Anna Freud (1968), for their preoccupation with mechanism and the centrality of the ego. Not only does he point to the individual behind the notion of bolstering the ego as the rational monitor of consciousness, but he forcibly argues that the notion of rational self-determination is an illusion, a chimera produced through the social conditions of bourgeois society. More than any other psychoanalyst Lacan aims to deconstruct the notion of the unitary subject as a myth, to put in its place an account of subjectivity which is fundamentally decentred from consciousness. This position is well brought out by Mitchell in her discussion of the implications of Lacanian analysis for the notion of sexual identity.

> Lacan takes the . . . perspective [that]: the analysand's unconscious reveals a fragmented subject of shifting and uncertain sexual identity. To be human is to be subjected to a law which decentres and divides: sexuality is created in a division, the subject is split: but an ideological world conceals this from the conscious subject who is supposed to feel whole and certain of a sexual identity. Psychoanalysis should aim at a deconstruction of this concealment and at a reconstruction of the subject's construction in all its splits.
>
> (Juliet Mitchell in Mitchell and Rose, 1982, p. 26)

An admittedly far from straightforward endeavour therapeutically, Lacan's project appears to relate precisely with our own concern to deconstruct the unitary subject, and to reveal its precarious congruence in bourgeois identity. But more than this, what is particularly crucial for our purposes is the use which Lacan makes of semiotics, the science of signs and meanings. This is because such a departure both provides a bridge between social and psychic domains and, as we will show, suggests ways in which we may theorize how this fragmented subject is produced and positioned within discursive relations. For Lacan, not only is the subject split, but its very production depends on the use of language. As is discussed at length in chapter 6, in Lacan's account, over the course of the individual's development, it is the entry into language which is the precondition for becoming conscious or aware of oneself as a distinct entity within the terms set by pre-existing social relations and cultural laws. Moreover he argues that this process simultaneously founds the unconscious. Since language is by definition a social system, it is through this emphasis that Lacan is able to assert that the social enters into the formation of the unconscious. This is what is meant by what is now a well-known slogan, 'the unconscious is structured like a language'.

Now in arguing that the workings of language provide a key to unconscious mental processes, Lacan stresses that he is remaining consistent with Freud's theory, and that the emphasis is implicit in the psychoanalytic method itself. 'The Talking Cure', as psychoanalysis was dubbed in the 1890s, is, after all, a verbal transaction which relies on using the patient's own words, memories, dreams and fantasies which must be spoken of in order to recover repressed ideas. Lacan is, however, stressing the importance of Freud's early texts, and *The Interpretation of Dreams* (1900) in particular, where Freud is perhaps at his most expansive on the relation between symbolic processes and the working of the unconscious. In addition, here Freud introduced a distinction which is equally important to Lacan's theory, which distinguishes his account from those we have touched on so far. This is the distinction between needs and wishes or desires.

For Freud 'need' derives from a state of internal tension, and it can be satisfied through specific action which procures the adequate object, for example 'food' which satisfies hunger. Needs can thus in principle be fulfilled. Wishes and desires on the other hand are based on needs that have once known satisfaction, to which, as it were, they hark back. They are thus indissolubly bound to memory traces. In so far as they are fulfillable, for Freud this is through the hallucinatory reproduction of the perceptions which have become signs of this satisfaction. Wishes or desires are thus relations which are mediated in fantasy. Moreover, because the search for an object in the 'real world' which would provide satisfaction is entirely governed by this relationship with signs, wishes and desires involve an inevitable distancing or disjunction from the original experiences of satisfaction. Later the notion of ideational representatives was given central importance by Freud in his structural theory of the mind, the Ego and the Id, and the introduction of the tripartite division in the psyche between the unconscious, preconscious and conscious systems. In this account the unconscious is the site of repressed ideas, and the preconscious consists of memories not currently present in consciousness but to which it has ready access. What is crucial in this theoretical development is that the unconscious is not the seat of drives or instincts, but of ideational representatives, signs or memories. These can, in principle, become attached to words, and thereby find psychical expression. Thus in this model, language again assumes a fundamental importance

However, Freud himself did not fully develop the theoretical implications of his distinction between needs and wishes or desires (see Laplanche and Pontalis, 1973, p. 482). Lacan, on the other hand, raised the workings of desire to a central position within his account, and went considerably further in theorizing the functioning of the unconscious in terms of language. Where Freud lacked a theory of signs and thus resorted to ideas like 'memory traces' Lacan looked to linguistic theory. He drew particularly on de Saussure's (1974) account of the linguistic sign, and on Jakobson's theory of the linguistic code (Jakobson and Halle, 1956). This stresses processes of selection and combination as fundamental to the organization of meaning in language, whether at the level of the choice of words, or their arrangement in a structured string. However Lacan has modified the classical Saussurean account of the signifier/signified relationship in crucial respects. The classical account privileges denotative meaning, or something in the world to which to refer, such that the real becomes the determinant of meaning. Lacan argues, in contrast, that denotative meaning in the strict sense could only exist (that is, there could only be fixed *a priori* signifiers) if speaking subjects were themselves the source of language. This directly contradicts his emphasis, which is that subjects are themselves produced through symbolic relations. To get round this problem, Lacan inverts the usual signifier/signified relation. (For a fuller elaboration of these issues, see Lemaire, 1977.) Unfortunately this solution is only a partial one since, as we have pointed out in discussing Althusser's appropriation of Lacan, and the issue of representation (see pp. 98–100), this inversion does not itself solve the problem of the real; Lacan's account is thus poorly equipped to deal with the material. We will return to this problem later.

Developing these theoretical arguments, Lacan regards the unconscious as consisting of chains of signifiers, or relationships between them; he uses Jakobson's notions of metaphor and metonymy to refer to these relationships. 'Metaphor' applies to synchronic relationships, relationships or substitutions based on similarity, or to vertical aspects of the linguistic code. 'Metonymy' on the other hand, applies to the diachronic aspects, relations of contiguity, or the successive, linearly progressive, relationships between signs. (For examples and discussion, again see Lemaire, 1977.) Lacan regards these concepts as homologous with Freud's notions of condensation and displacement, respectively, which are demonstrated particularly in the imagery and workings of dreams.

But Lacan does not simply provide a more sophisticated version of Freud's own theory. There is a further crucial difference in emphasis which has important implications for his view of development, discussed in chapter 6, and for the centrality he gives to the working of desire, and its nature. To put this difference at its simplest, Freud's central concept in the psychosexual development of the child, the Oedipus Complex, rapidly reduces to biological differences between men and women, seen in terms of having or not having a penis. In contrast, Lacan's account privileges not the biological difference *per se* but the sign of difference, the phallus. This stands as the 'signifier of signifieds', or the ultimate difference which fixes meaning in language, which is itself regulated through the systems of power through which the society is ordered. Here Lacan follows Lévi-Strauss's structural analysis of the incest taboo and the laws of kinship and exchange which, according to this account, underlie all human societies. From this position, the resolution of the Oedipus Complex, in which the child resolves problems associated with desire for the mother or father by identifying with the same-sexed parent, is the point at which the child becomes a subject according the cultural laws which preordain it and, to a certain extent, constrain its destiny. Hence gender difference enters into the production of subjectivity in Lacan's account. Moreover, given his emphasis on the centrality of language, he argues that the resolution of the Oedipus Complex and the production of the gendered subject co-occur with and are dependent on mastery of the use of language. This marks the child's entry into what Lacan calls the order of symbolic relations.

The resolution of the Oedipus Complex and the acquisition of language, of course, occurs after a relatively long period of development. Though Lacan's account of the mother–infant relationship is nowhere near as full as that provided by the Object Relations theorists, he expands Freud's own account considerably through the addition of what he calls the 'mirror stage'. This is discussed in detail in chapter 6. In brief, this period of development marks a first step in a disjunctive process, a splitting or distancing which is fundamental to human consciousness and which lays the foundations of desire. Like Freud, Lacan regards the mother as providing the infant with his or her first experience of satisfaction. But the infant must come to terms with the loss of satisfaction, or the absence of its source, the mother. In Lacan's account, the child uses his or her first words to establish, in fantasy, control over the loss of the object which gave satisfaction. As words displace the original object, we see the first step in the process of repression which forms the unconscious; entry into language inaugurates the production of subjectivity. In addition, Lacan emphasizes that this process introduces an inevitable distancing, or gap, between the infant and the object longed for, and in consequence any satisfaction that the infant obtains subsequently will always and irrevocably contain this loss within it. This brings into being the dimension of desire which is itself rapidly displaced or transformed through the impact of the Oedipal triangle and the Law of the Father as the child takes up a position as a gendered subject. While the origins of the infant's longing is in the relationship with the mother, now the mother is refused the child through the cultural prohibition on the 'child's desire to be what the mother desires'.

Lacan asserts the exclusivity of this desire to be the object of the mother's desire and, as is shown in chapter 5, it is a phenomenon recognizable in adult sexual relationships, particularly in jealousy. But he does not simply give more space to desire than Freud. Because he stresses the fundamental loss or gap involved in its production, desire here is inevitably unfulfillable, to be governed by or subordinated to fantasy. Moreover, because the disjunction is brought about retrospectively through the entry into language (see chapter 6), desire itself permeates the workings of language, which in consequence is ultimately related to the original loss, the search for satisfaction. The argument that in the process of entry into language metaphoric connections, though always idiosyncratic, relate back to this source, enables Lacan to account for the continuity of the subject. Yet, because of the disjunctions brought about by language, it is a subject which is fundamentally decentred from itself. Furthermore, since the desire which inhabits significations is regulated through Oedipal relations it not only always contains a loss, but also contains a reference to the Other, or a third term. Again, the implications of this view are well brought out by Mitchell and Rose:

> Subjects in language persist in their belief that somewhere there is a point of certainty, of knowledge and of truth. When the subject addresses its demand outside itself to another, this Other becomes the fantasised place of just such a knowledge or certainty. Lacan calls this the Other – the site of language to which the speaking subject necessarily refers. The Other appears to hold the 'truth' of the subject and the power to make good its loss. But this is the ultimate fantasy. (Mitchell and Rose, 1982, p. 32)

Some problems with Lacan's account

Compared to many psychoanalytic approaches, the subversive implications of Lacan's position are evident. However, it is not without problems for our purposes. First, Lacan's theory has attracted a good deal of interest within feminism because the emphasis on the production of gendered subjectivity via signification implies that it is possible to escape the subordination of women inherent in Freud's recourse to biological difference. However, in privileging the phallus as the sign of difference as opposed to the penis, Lacan's analysis does not in fact escape being any less determinate than Freud's. This is because he relies heavily on Lévi-Strauss's universalist analysis, such that the terms of the debate are already fixed around the Law of the Father. This means that the theory does not provide what we argued for previously: an account not only of subjectivity 'as it is' under existing social relations, but one which would enable us to envisage that things could be otherwise. (For a fuller discussion of Lacan's phallocentricism and its implications, see Rose in Mitchell and Rose, 1982.) Second, the way Lacan conceives of signification or, more particularly, language also contributes to the limited usefulness of the account. The use of semiotic connections to understand the signifying relations from the conscious to the unconscious has certainly produced some interesting analyses, particularly in work on film and literature, demonstrating the fruitfulness of using Lacan's ideas in investigating non-analytic material. (See, for example, articles in the journals *Screen* and *Screen Education*.) However, quite how far the workings of the unconscious can be understood through rules of language has been questioned (see Thom, 1981), particularly if these are those provided by structural linguistics. As in all structuralist accounts, here there is an inbuilt tendency for the specificity of content and process to be subordinated to a universalist mode of explanation, a problem which applies equally to the work of Lévi-Strauss. As Hall (1980) has argued, one of the implications of using a structuralist paradigm is that Lacan's theory tends to collapse into an account of a universal, albeit contradictory, subject who is not situated historically, who is tied and bound by pre-existing language, and is incapable of change because of it. This, of course, is precisely the position which we wish to avoid.

Despite these problems, both the deconstruction of the unitary subject in Lacan's account and the focus on signification remain exciting. We suggest that it is possible to rework his account in such a way as to produce a more historically specific reading; one which is consonant with our emphasis on the importance of understanding the unconscious as central to approaching subjective change. By implication, such an account provides the possibility of an approach which is both less universalistic and less pessimistic than Lacan's.

What we are proposing is to replace Lacan's emphasis on a universal and timeless symbolic order with an emphasis on discursive relations, viewed in their historical specificity. That is, using the concept of 'positioning' within discursive practices, introduced in section 2, in so far as we can link this to an account of psychosexual development, we can still specify relations of signification consonant with an analysis of signification in the unconscious. Now, however, this is understood not in terms of the signifier/signified relations of Saussurian linguistics (even if inverted to privilege representation rather than denotation), but rather as discursive relations produced through positioning within discursive practices.

In this way we are avoiding Lacan's failure to deal with the material, as discussed in the Introduction to section 2 (p. 98) where representation is dealt with at length. We are also providing, in principle, an account of motivational dynamics through which people are positioned in discourses, which is not addressed in the post-structuralist work. Though we do not claim to provide a complete account of how subjectivity is produced and regulated through discursive relations, we will show how the view of ourselves which this analysis opens profoundly challenges both traditional psychology and psychoanalysis, and clarifies the kinds of issues which we will need to address.

Both of the chapters which follow exemplify our attempts to mark this shift. However it is important at this stage to be rather more specific about what we mean. As an example, we will examine in a very limited way those discourses and practices in which female sexuality is understood and regulated. We will firstly illustrate how the discursive categories and norms which produce subject-positions according to the post-structuralist account may provide the specific content of desire and, by implication, the workings of the unconscious. We will also outline the kinds of questions which such a supposition would need to address, and the kind of account of development which it may presuppose. We will begin by looking again at the problems raised by Donzelot's work, mentioned previously.

The discursive production of desire

Consider, for example, Adams's conclusion to her critique of Donzelot's analysis of the normative functions of psychoanalysis:

> That relational space, for example, of desire is discursively produced and can function as a space of intervention is easily understood. *But must not the actual desire for a child or the lack of desire for a child itself be explained?* This is not to say that one is seeking an explanation of individual cases: rather, the contrast is with the simple having of a child, or having a child as a source of support in old age. Of course, the question of the conditions of desire is a meaningless one for psycho-analysis. But it is an important one for Foucault and for Donzelot for whom a social and historical explanation is required. (Adams, 1982, p. 14; our italics)

It is that relation – the conditions of desire, seen in relation to the exigencies of norms and positions of social practices – that we will try to address, beginning with women's desires to bear children. In his critique of the traditional left position that motherhood is an 'oppressive' condition, Rose points to the coercive or conspiratorial nature of such an account, in so far as it fails to explain the fact that, in an important sense, women may actually want this condition.

> Perhaps, rather than regarding the 'maternal instinct' as an ideological and oppressive myth, it would be more useful to investigate it in terms of the functioning of social regulation in advanced liberal democracies through the register of desires and the instrumentalisation of pleasures. (Rose, 1982, p. 86)

Rose implies in this that social regulation can function, not only in a sense through overt oppression, but rather through defining the parameters and content of choice, fixing how we come to want what we want. In chapter 6, Cathy Urwin refers to a study which explores women's expectations and feelings about being mothers. What was striking about this study was that there was no doubt that the women interviewed saw mothering as a positive choice and tried to be 'good mothers', enjoying many of the results. How did they come to have such desires, and what does it mean to be a 'good mother'?

Urwin (1982b) has argued that 'good mothering' cannot be understood outside the discursive practices which construct its parameters and norms. These include, for example, the child-care books, the hospital visits, the routine check-ups, the normalizing techniques which define satisfactory maternal health or development, and so on. Thus desires to have children, to be a mother, or for oneself in relation to one's children, imply particular positioning within these discursive frameworks. Yet the effectivity of the regulatory practices depend, in this case, on the fact that the mothers already desire to be good mothers. This, then, directs attention towards the relation between their motivation and the discursive practices which position them.

There are at least three issues here. The first is to understand the content of the desires, that is why *these particular desires* for a child, to be a mother, to be fulfilled in motherhood. For in our attempts to transform, it is important not to operate on a level of *denial* of desire, but rather to understand desires as produced and therefore, potentially at least, as changeable. The second is to understand how the psychic operates in relation to those desires, such that there is no simple relationship between, say, images of mothering perpetuated through discourses, as the mother–child relationship is presented in child-care books or glossy magazines, for example, or which is implicit in regulating the decisions made by social workers and the complex workings of the unconscious. This is not to say that they are unrelated, but a major lesson from psychoanalysis is that there is no simple relation between the workings of fantasy and 'external reality'. Fantasies based on idealized memories of one's own mother, for instance, bear no simple relation to the actual management of the care one received in babyhood. The third point is, how are these desires produced over the course of development, whether in childhood or in adulthood, and under what conditions are they accessed? This question is not one that can be answered in rationalist terms. It is neither a question of free choice, nor of false consciousness. For example, women can recognize child-rearing as restricting and oppressive and yet still want to bear children.

But if the relations involved are not simple ones, this does not mean that we need not, or cannot, explore the interconnections. For example, we can examine the particular conditions in which individual women actually choose or wish to become pregnant. For instance, Urwin has pointed to a possible increasing investment in the rewards of family life which have accompanied the recent reduction of employment opportunities, and to the paradoxical fact that an acceptance of lack of paid work amongst the women in her sample brought with it a new desire to have children and to be fulfilled in that role. Secondly, referring back to what Rose discusses in terms of the 'register of desires' and 'instrumentalization of pleasures', and following the post-structuralist emphasis, we can explore the historical location, production and specificity of the discourses for understanding desires. In this sense we can go further than a simple assertion of the importance of situating the development of psychoanalysis in a historical context. Moreover, although this will not lead us to an analysis of the working of the psyche as such, we can at least speculate about how particular discourses set parameters through which desire is produced, regulated and channelled.

Let us consider female sexuality in this light, examining those discursive practices in and through which women's pleasure is prescribed and produced. We will mention briefly discussions which relate to historical material which is covered in much more detail elsewhere (for example, Bland, 1981; Hall, 1984; Mort, 1980). The point is to suggest how the historical conditions which produce the modern forms of female sexuality can be related to the fixing and content of desire.

In his *History of Sexuality* (1979a) Foucault has argued that in many of the ninteenth-century discourses and practices centring round sexuality and the position of women in relation to the domestic, sex was not 'repressed'. Rather, he has pointed to a proliferation of medical discourses which produced sexuality as an object for new interventions. Indeed the very production of discourses producing sexuality as 'repressed' ensured that much, but not everything, could be spoken of quite freely. Bland (1981) notes that at the same moment various splittings or differentiations were produced in relation to women. These clearly relate to other and more ancient discourses and positionings for women. But what was important at this time was their relation to medicalization and therefore their basis in 'fact'. Women's sexuality became the object of hygienization, of the splitting of cleanliness and pleasure. Sexual pleasure in women became seen as perverse. Good and therefore clean women were not passionate. Passion was animal, destructive, dangerous, so that a passionate woman was not, therefore, a good woman. The good woman did not experience sexual pleasure but obtained her fulfilment in terms of her reproductive capacity and through the raising of her children. Sexuality for women was in their wombs. To quote from Bland,

> When Foucault writes of the nineteenth-century feminine body 'analysed . . . as being thoroughly saturated with sexuality' it is more a suffusion of her body with the wild workings of her reproductive system rather than with wild sexual desire. If, for man, sexual desire was the beast within, whose demands could be curbed by the training and exercise of will, and the avoidance of *objects* of desire, for woman there was no escape.
>
> (Bland, 1981, pp. 58–9)

Given this equation between women's reproductive capacities and their sexuality, their bodies became, in Foucault's sense, hystericized. At the same time, science understood women as the holder of the womb, the guardian of the moral order, the future of the race, and as outside the rational (Le Doeuff, 1974; Walkerdine, 1982a).

Several things followed from this conjuncture. Firstly, the notion of mothering produced and approved by scientific discourses was definitely not passionate loving of children, but calculating observation and monitoring. The mother who was 'made conscious' in the child-centred pedagogy (see chapter 4) was a sanitized, hygienic mother. In this role, as science informed their practice, women were allowed rationality, but not desire. As attention was focused on their bodily functions, by definition 'abnormal' through reference to a male norm, women were produced as weak, potentially dirty, prone to fainting, incapacitated by menstruation, to be kept in check, monitored and observed; they could not display sexual arousal and passion.

Now in relation to the above practices it is not unreasonable to posit a medicalized syndrome of hysteria. Hysteria becomes a 'reality' in relation to the social practices of the time. In addition, it is possible to speculate on the content of desires which these practices produced. For example, it is possible to imagine desires and fantasy directed in two ways. On the one hand, we have women, as it were, living for and through their children, and therefore developing particular and important psychic relations to them: the all powerful, all-seeing mother. On the other hand, given what is denied them, we have women's self-effacement, depression, 'lack of strong ego boundaries' and over-arching desires to be good mothers, to search for self-understanding in reflections obtained through service to others. All of these positions can be understood in relation to these practices which confine and define available options. It is also perfectly plausible that fantasies and dreams involving the possession by women of a penis, as in Freud's penis-envy theory, should occur (though his claims were admittedly based on rather limited analytic material). Now, however, they become comprehensible in terms of practices which prohibited 'good' women from engaging in activities other than the rearing of children. The possession of the penis/phallus thus represents and relates to desires to be positioned like a man.

Further to this conflation of reproduction and sexuality it comes as no surprise that, with the development of modern forms of contraception, the 'liberalization' of women's sexual practices should stress vaginal and not clitoral pleasures and sexuality. The dominance of penetration in this respect as the correct form of pleasure for the mature woman and the debate on the vaginal orgasm has only been eroded by recent feminist sexual politics. Clitoral pleasure was not spoken. Though clitoral masturbation may have been accepted as common in young children, it was not associated with the practices of adult heterosexual sex. Children's sexuality may be in the terms of Freud's early writings, 'polymorphous and perverse'. But what has been, and is, prescribed and proscribed for adult women is a different matter altogether. What we have seen instead is that women's desires and pleasures have been channelled into romance. At the same time, women's pleasure is still associated with nymphomania, and their unwillingness or lack of desire for penetration with frigidity. Both of these are understood as clinical 'abnormalities' which can be remedied.

The content of desires, then, is neither timeless nor arbitrary, but has a historical specificity. We are suggesting that its production can be understood in terms of the emergence of particular discursive practices. Similarly, particular anxieties, phobias, depressions and so forth become comprehensible when seen in relation to practices which produce particular norms and positions for women. Here, of course, it is not a simple question of determination through labelling. Women may, indeed, be oversexed or frigid under particular discursive conditions. Here there is a materiality which is both accounted for and treated.

However, as Adams argued in her critique of Donzelot, and as we have stressed above, pointing to positioning produced through discourses is only a partial answer. As Adams points out, the relation between the workings of the unconscious of any particular woman with respect to positions in any particular practice is not one of simple recognition and acceptance. That is, we need to understand the motivational basis through which such an uptake is produced. Here, desire is not an energizing process onto which specific content is grafted. Rather, in order to take our account further we need some way of explicating how discursive relations enter into the very production of desire in the first place.

This has important implications for how development may be understood. Walkerdine (1984) has begun to develop such a viewpoint in an analysis of children's literature, which goes beyond a simple revealing of bias or stereotyped images. Focusing on the production of romance, she has argued that social practices and cultural forms (such as books, comics and films) which surround it do not just concentrate on the strategies for getting and keeping a man, thus emphasizing the importance of heterosexual relations as McRobbie (1978) has suggested. Rather, through looking at comics for young children, she has argued that this emphasis is preceded by practices and forms which prepare young girls for a romantic resolution to the problem given centrality in Lacan's developmental account, separation from the mother and the transfer of desire to the father. This is effected in these practices through the specific positioning of girls within discursive positions, notably those involving 'caring', 'helpfulness' and 'selflessness'. It is argued that such cultural practices, forms and positions are not simply overlaid upon a pre-existent desire but actually help to produce the fixing and channelling of desires by virtue of their production of power–knowledge relations.

It is precisely the formation of power–knowledge relations through the positioning of subjects within discursive practices, itself simultaneously producing relations of desire, which we now recognize as central and which we are concerned to explore. Both of the final chapters of this book begin to analyse co-relations of power and desire with respect to infants on the one hand and adult heterosexual couples on the other. In each case the notion of discourse is developed or modified such that it differs in some respect from that which we have worked with so far. In the case of infants, a modification is necessary to deal with the fact that, by definition, infants are not yet speaking. Furthermore the chapter includes under the notion of 'discourses' which contribute to defining appropriate action on the part of parents not only bodies of knowledge produced by professionals, where links to regulatory apparatuses are obvious, but also received wisdom, culturally based beliefs, folklore and so forth, all which have historically contributed to defining the nature of development. In the case of heterosexual relationships, we are concerned with implicit or explicit sets of assumptions which enter into the practice and regulation of interpersonal relations and the production of positionings. Again, these assumptions can be situated historically and imply the workings of power–knowledge relations, though they may not be linked to the particular sites of instrumentality which Foucault has identified.

A view which sees power and desire as simultaneously produced, whether in infants or adults, implies the active engagement of the subject in a way which differs dramatically from previous attempts to link psychic and cultural domains. Apart from the inability of previous approaches to transcend the terms of the dualism, this difference of emphasis has important political implications. As we have argued in section 1, roles and stereotypes are social impositions on the presumed pre-existent subject. One implication of that position is that change is possible through the production and reinforcement of *positive images* for women. The voluntarism of this approach relates closely to that described in chapter 1. But we believe that the intransigence of desires, recognized for instance in general in consciousness-raising, relates precisely to the resistance to change which is involved in the production, fixing and channelling of power–desire relations. The investment of the subject is such that it is not changed by images or choices in any rational or voluntaristic sense. (See also Deleuze and Guattari 1977a and b; Venn, 1982). It is precisely this resistance which we need to understand. At the same time, just as the subject is non-unitary, our account also allows for our desires to be contradictory.

Chapter 5, for example, while drawing on Lacan's account, also adapts Melanie Klein's psychoanalytic account of the mechanisms of defence, or ways in which we defend ourselves against unconscious threats, to show how this may operate in interpersonal relationships in accordance with discourses which position men and women differentially. Two features of defence mechanisms are drawn on in this analysis. First, they do not only occur within the individual subject, but operate as relations. For instance, mechanisms such as 'splitting', in which characteristics of the object are firmly divided into good and bad, for example, with implications for the subject's relation to them, or 'projection', in which feelings or desires denied by the subject are attributed to another person, do not observe the boundaries drawn by the concept of the individual. Second, defence mechanisms operate such that feelings which were caused by one event can be displaced onto another, less threatening event. But psychoanalysis generally stresses the arbitrary nature of the objects (events, things or people), which are the vehicles for the expression of feelings. Here, in contrast, the chapter both stresses their specific content and its historicity and the role of signification generally. Second, it uses the notion of mechanisms of defence to clarify the workings (within couple relationships) of power–desire relations which are themselves produced through gender differentiated discourses. This is not a simple question of one member of the couple dominating the other as the 'more powerful'. For instance, the chapter illustrates how a man and a woman in a heterosexual couple might *both* produce and reproduce positionings in which each invests power in the other by virtue of gender-differentiated readings of positionings. Thus it is possible to understand a woman's emotionality as weak within a 'feminine' discourse and 'strong' within the man's experience of emotionality, as 'power over' him. That such readings help to produce 'split' positions which are resistant to transformation is examined in the chapter. For example, a woman may be persistent in her demands for power, understanding herself as weak, while at the same time these are understood as overpowering and annihilating demands by the man.

The chapter raises several points which we will touch on here. First, it may well be possible for us to read our actions through alternative discourses. For instance, it might be possible for the woman described above to 'recognize her power'. But this intellectual engagement has itself been historically produced as the masculine province of 'reason' (rational argument), which is set in opposition to emotionality, the sign of weakness which is the prerogative of the female. Here we need to understand how these divisions may themselves be perpetuated through the ways in which they position us within relationships.

Second, in this analysis we are neither totally powerful nor powerless, but fragmentary and positioned and repositioned from one moment to the next. This has important implications for an analysis of contradiction. For instance, a woman academic is in contradictory relations of power and powerlessness by virtue of her positioning as both woman and academic. From this it is possible to argue that such simultaneous positionings of power and powerlessness produce anxiety states resulting from distress at such contradiction, and the consequent desire for wholeness, unitariness – a coherent identity. Such anxiety states can clearly be manifest in a variety of ways, from the denial of contradiction to a variety of mechanisms for apparently achieving conscious 'closure' or coherence. But while we may be positioned in a non-unitary way, the normative practices which fix us produce for us a model of a whole mature 'individual' with an 'identity'. Much is therefore invested in our recognizing ourselves as unitary, whole, non-contradictory, mature, rational. In consequence those normative applications of psychoanalysis which we have discussed help to produce and sediment that unitariness.

It is clear from our arguments so far that the examination of the unconscious is an essential precondition for understanding our resistances as well as the possibilities for change. Psychoanalysis supports the view we have developed of subjectivity as produced through contradiction and conflict, a subjectivity whose machinery is not entirely accessible because of the subterfuges of the unconscious. But we do not consider the subject incapable of change as if it were produced and positioned in an originary moment and held constant in the vice of refractory desires. So we need to move beyond what psychoanalysis offers, whilst positively utilizing its lessons. In particular there remains the task of outlining the disposition of power–desire–knowledge complex, wherein subjectivity is intricated. Chapter 6 elaborates the problems involved in such an enterprise; it attempts to rework Lacan's analysis of the positioning of subjectivity in the structure of language and discusses concretely, with reference to mother–child interaction and 'language development', the historical specificity of the content of unconscious processes and their relation to the complex we just mentioned. It is demonstrated how the infant's separation from the mother and its production as a subject can be seen in terms of successive moments of transformation and its insertion into discursive practices. These are culturally and historically specific, but also changeable and to some extent idiosyncratic. Such practices are always already locked in power–knowledge relations, and the production of desire is inextricably intertwined in them.

From the point of view of a politics of change, a theory which combines these sets of relations between power, knowledge and desire within the same theoretical framework would combine two often unfortunately separate struggles: the changing of subjects and the changing of circumstances. As Deleuze and Guattari (1977a) has argued, the struggles for 'bread, peace, freedom' and that against the 'microscopic fascism installed at the heart of the machinery of desire' (1977a, p. 2), whilst they require different strategies of resistance, are bound up with each other in the wider objective of radical transformation.

Notes

1 Walkerdine and Corran (1979) and Walden (Eynard) and Walkerdine (1981) have worked out in detail an approach to children's learning of mathematics in the school setting based on these notions. Here mathematics is viewed as a discursive practice, and children's learning is conceptualized in terms of their positioning within this practice. This work is referred to in chapter 6, where it is contrasted with usual approaches to relations between cognition, language and social development in psychology.

2 Our discussion of psychoanalytic theory must necessarily be slight, and Lacan's work is particularly complex. Juliet Mitchell's *Psychoanalysis and Feminism* (1974) remains the most accessible introduction to psychoanalysis within the context of feminism. For a very readable introduction to Lacan's work and its political implications, see Sherry Turkle's *Psychoanalytic Politics* (1979). For more technical discussion of his theory, see Anika Lemaire's *Jacques Lacan* (1977), and in the context of feminism, Juliet Mitchell and Jacqueline Rose's *Feminine Sexuality* (1982).

3 We cannot discuss all attempts to link psychoanalysis with an account of social processes. But see Mitchell (1974) and Turkle (1979).

4 For a fuller account of Object Relations theory and Winnicott's work applied within a feminist analysis, see Chodorow (1978). For a critique, see Sayers (1982). Some of these problems also apply to the account of feminist therapy presented by Eichenbaum and Orbach (1982). Notwithstanding the considerable importance of this venture, we suggest that it is constrained by an over-simple environmentalism, which in this case focuses on apparent inadequacies in mothering of daughters. Though the mother–daughter relationship is undoubtedly important, a focus on 'unmet needs' may not be the most useful axis through which to approach the issues.

5

Gender difference and the production of subjectivity

Wendy Hollway

Introduction

In this chapter I attempt to analyse the construction of subjectivity in a specific area: heterosexual relations. My framework depends on three conceptual positions which we have developed: the non-rational, non-unitary character of subjectivity; its social and historical production through signification; power relations and the re-production of systematic difference.

I have introduced the term re-production (with a hyphen) since the term reproduction is less than ideal owing to the limitations in its theorization. The dangers are ones for which Althusser has been criticized for failing to avoid. First, the concept stresses maintenance rather than change, and second Althusser's notion of economic determination 'in the last instance' avoids recognition of the effectivity of sites such as heterosexual relations – the one I use in this chapter – to re-produce gender difference. My use of the hyphen is intended to signify that every practice is a production (what we have called its 'positivity'). Hence recurrent day-to-day practices and the meanings through which they acquire their effectivity may contribute to the maintenance of gender difference (reproduction without the hyphen) or to its modification (the production of modified meanings of gender leading to changed practices). I am interested in theorizing the practices and meanings which re-produce gendered subjectivity (what psychologists would call gender identity). My approach to subjectivity is through the meanings and incorporated values which attach to a person's practices and provide the powers through which he or she can position him- or herself in relation to others.

Given the pervasive character of gender difference it is more than likely that all practices signify differently depending on the gender of their subject and object. However, I consider that heterosexual relations are the primary site where gender difference is re-produced.[1] This claim will be substantiated in the detail of the analysis which follows.

The chapter is organized into five parts. In the first I illustrate what I mean by gender difference as it impinges on subjectivity. I show how femininity and masculinity cannot be taken as fixed features located exclusively in women and men. In a descriptive manner, this begins to demonstrate how subjectivity is a non-unitary and non-rational product of – in this case and among other things – gender difference. The next three parts are all oriented to an analysis of the relation between gender difference and gendered subjectivity, a relation of mutual re-production. In the second part I explore gender differentiation in discourses by taking the example of women's and men's different positions in discourses concerning sexuality. In the third part I focus on individual women's and men's subjectivity, that is the product of their history of positioning in discourses, and the way this constructs their investments in taking up gender-differentiated positions in heterosexual relations (thereby re-producing the discourses). In the fourth part I consider the multiple meanings, deriving from discourses which produce the practices of heterosexual sex. I demonstrate their connection, expressed or suppressed, with 'desire for the Other' and how this relates to the take-up of gender-differentiated positions with an investment in exercising power. In the fifth part, I consider the recurrent splitting between women and men of gender-specified characteristics.

One way of seeing the different elements of this account is as follows. Gender-differentiated meanings (and thus the positions differentially available in discourse) account for the content of gender difference. The concept of splitting provides an account of how these positions are constantly taken up. Power difference (imaginary as well as real, intimately linked in the psyche with the early desire for the Other) is both the cause and effect of the system of gender difference and provides the motor for its continuous re-production. (See chapter 6 for a detailed analysis of these developments in infancy.) The concepts of splitting and desire draw on psychoanalysis (albeit on different theorizations within it). Splitting (in the Kleinian sense) is consistent not only with our stress on the non-unitary and non-rational nature of subjectivity, but also with our emphasis on relations (see Introduction to section 3, pp. 205 and 224). Desire and 'desire for the Other' draw on a Lacanian analysis which theorizes their relation to signification (see Introduction to section 3, pp. 211–18).

The analysis in this chapter is not just a reworking of important theoretical developments. Rather it uses these to illuminate people's accounts. The material comes from dialogues and discussions conducted in the course of my PhD research (Hollway, 1982). Participants talked about relationships, sexuality and gender. I talked to them singly and in groups, and without using a structured format of questions. They were not chosen to represent a range of social differences. Rather, it was my intention to make detailed readings of their accounts, recognizing their specific social location and its effectivity in the re-production of gender difference in discourse and subjectivity through power and signification.

Living the recent history of gender difference

First I would like to illustrate the theme of gender difference, and the inseparability of subjectivity from the social domain by summarizing the contradictions of my own gender. What does it mean to be a woman in my class and culture? I have grown up in the 1950s and 1960s in a western industrial society, in a middle-class home where education and the career possibilities it conferred were – in certain important respects – as available to me as they were to boys. Educational and job opportunity, unisex and permissiveness, were ideas which were, at least in principle, gender-blind. I went through university with as much money in my pocket as the men students (though I couldn't get such well-paid holiday jobs). The pill meant that I could have sexual relationships without becoming a mother.

Being as good as men

Early modern feminism (Greer, 1971; Firestone, 1972) was telling women like me that we were equal to men because we were the same as them. Certainly this fitted in with my pre-feminist assumptions that men represented all that was interesting, admirable, powerful and desirable. I was attracted to men, partly because I aspired to being like them.

I was keen to develop so-called masculine skills. For example, I learned to service my car, how to build houses and wire up electrical circuits. I disdained helping hands over gates and in general determined to walk, swim, run, drive – as far and as fast as my men companions.

Why was this a problem? Surely equality was desirable? To compete with men like this necessitated a negative definition of myself as woman, and it reproduced the signifier 'woman' unchanged. Women were a group I put myself outside of. When I made generalizations about women (almost always derogatory), I did not include myself in the group I was talking about.[2]

Difference as otherness

As my own recollections demonstrate, the difference between women and men was not just a neutral difference. It is based on the principle of 'otherness' (de Beauvoir, 1972). In many practices, to be like men I had to be not like women.[3] This is the crucial feature of gender differences. It also means that equality, in that earlier meaning of the term, produces contradictions, rather than simply offering additional and complementary possibilities. It is also more likely to produce reaction.

One of the participants in my research who changed sex to become a woman when she was in her twenties described how she felt at a very early age about being a boy:

> *Sheila:* Yes it mostly wasn't a question of what I wanted to be, it was more a question of what one didn't want to be, what one didn't want to do. Because one was constantly faced with the things one was being told to do, one was taught to do, and that one was rejecting.

Whereas for boys and men the alternative gender-differentiated positions are clear-cut and appear mutually exclusive,[4] for girls and women it is easier to move among them. At a theoretical level it is quite easy to see why: 'man' and 'person' have been synonymous in western, patriarchal thought, as is evidenced by the use of the terms 'man', 'mankind' and 'he/him' as universals. As women we can strive to be 'people' and 'women'. Logically there is no contradiction. However, because 'person' actually consists of all the attributes which are meant to be characteristic of men, there is an underlying contradiction.[5] I think I managed this contradiction by being (or trying to be) as good as men in the public world, and even competitive in my relationships with men. At the same time, by virtue of maintaining a heterosexual relationship, I preserved my feminine identity. Ever since I had grown up I had been in a couple relationship with a man, and however well I succeeded at doing things, they were always there – men who knew more than me, men whom I could learn from – to guarantee my femininity. Those qualities of men which 'guaranteed my femininity' demonstrate well that the differences which confer gender were not neutral in value. My position in relation to men demonstrates the non-unitary nature of my gendered subjectivity. I aspired to similarity in some spheres because of the value attached. At the same time I preserved my difference.

Gender difference in three discourses concerning sexuality

Foucault's use of the term discourse is historical and this is crucial to the analytical power of the concept. For my purposes the emphasis must be shifted in order to understand how at a specific moment several coexisting and potentially contradictory discourses concerning sexuality make available different positions and different powers for men and women. Thus the references to the histories of these discourses will be only in passing (but see Foucault, 1979a; Bland and Hollway, unpubl.; Heath,

1982). Given my objective of theorizing subjectivity as it is re-produced in discourses, it is personal genealogies which are a necessary part of the analysis. (See Introduction to section 3, p. 204 and for our discussion of the limitations of positions which see subjectivities merely as the sum total of positions occupied in discourses by a person.)

In order to make a reading of the accounts I gathered concerning sexuality, I delineated three discourses: the male sexual drive discourse; the have/hold discourse; and the permissive discourse. I arrived at these three through a combination of my own knowledge and what was suggested by the data (an approach which Glaser and Straus, 1967, call 'grounded theory'). Clearly my own assumptions and those of research participants share a largely common historical production; they will also be recognizable to most readers. Some assumptions are more widespread than others (indeed, some would say that the discourse of male sexual drive was universal and that this supports a claim that it is based on the biological 'fact' of male sexuality). It would be relatively easy to identify more discourses, with different boundaries. For my purposes however, what is more important is the use I make of these three in my analysis of the effects of gender difference in positioning subjects.

The male sexual drive discourse

This needs little introduction because it is so familiar – so hegemonic, or dominant – in the production of meanings concerning sexuality. A man friend of mine captured it succinctly: 'I want to fuck. I *need* to fuck. I've always needed and wanted to fuck. From my teenage years, I've always longed after fucking.' Its key tenet is that men's sexuality is directly produced by a biological drive, the function of which is to ensure reproduction of the species. The discourse is everywhere in common-sense assumptions and is reproduced and legitimized by experts, including psychologists. For example Anthony Storr asserts that

> Male sexuality *because of the primitive necessity* of pursuit and penetration, does contain an important element of aggressiveness; an element which is both recognised and responded to by the female who yields and submits.
>
> (quoted in *The Observer*, 24 May 1981; my italics)

A more recent example of the discourse being made respectable by experts through recourse to scientific explanations is Glenn Wilson's (1979) use of sociobiology to attack feminist accounts of sex differences which are based on social theories of women's oppression. The effect and intention of his argument is to represent women's position as biologically determined and therefore unchangeable. Elsewhere I have tried to show how psychology is particularly vulnerable to such biologism because of its own history and theoretical starting points (Hollway, forthcoming).

The have/hold discourse

This has as its focus not sexuality directly, but the Christian ideals associated with monogamy, partnership and family life. The split between wife and mistress, virgin and whore, Mary and Eve, indicates how this and the male sexual drive discourse coexist in constructing men's sexual practices. In some aspects the discourses are consistent; for example both share assumptions about sexuality being linked to reproductivity, and also that sex is heterosexual. Yet the two recommend different and contradictory standards of conduct for men.

This contradiction is resolved for men by visiting it upon women. Either women are divided into two types (as above), or more recently a woman is expected to be both things. In effect we end up with a double standard (the widespread recognition and criticism of which has not wholly changed the practices): men's sexuality is understood through the male sexual drive discourse: they are expected to be sexually incontinent and out of control – 'it's only natural'.

The following letter from a man in *Spare Rib* (a British feminist magazine) demonstrates how these discourses can coexist in the beliefs of one person:

> As a mature male, I am in total support of the new 'women against violence against women' campaign, with the proviso that the supporters should realise that the majority of men are decent, of reasonably high principles and respect women as equal partners, and only a small proportion are grossly anti-social. But man being the animal he is, do you think that the answer to rape is well-ordered government-run brothels to cater for the large section of single, sexually-frustrated men in our society? (*Spare Rib*, 104, March 1981)

The picture is more complicated for women. Underneath the insistence on our asexuality within this discourse is the belief that our sexuality is rabid and dangerous and must be controlled. This is far more explicit in Mediterranean cultures where women are traditionally seen as being in one of two categories: 'fallen' or 'not yet fallen' (Du Boulay, 1974). The implication is that women's sexuality is inevitable and dangerous. (It is not defined as a lack, as in post-Victorian northern Europe). The only way to preserve the family honour is thus the total subservience of women to male control. Here men project onto women a rabid and ever-present sexuality, which leads to irrational jealousy (Moi, 1982). Later I shall approach the question in terms of men's 'desire for the Other' and the reasons for their projections, rather than falling into the assumption that this has something to do with women's sexuality.

According to the have/hold discourse, women's sexuality is seen as a lack, the possibility avoided by the stress on their relationship with husband and children. For example, Eustace Chesser, a liberal sexual reformer in the 1950s, argued that the sex act for women was only a prelude to satisfaction of the 'maternal instinct' and 'finding joy in family life' (quoted in Campbell, 1980).

Gender-differentiated positions

Before going on to comment on the permissive discourse, I will indicate the main implication of the coexistence of these two discourses for gender difference. It is not that women's sexuality is not constructed in the male sexual drive discourse. Rather woman is seen as its object. The position for a woman in this set of meanings is as the object that precipitates men's natural sexual urges:

> *Will:* Well certainly in adolescence I felt that there was a very impersonal sexuality. But it wasn't anything particularly that women did. It was my need – as it were – that did it to me. That meant that any woman would be doing it to me – in a sense – even if she hadn't noticed my existence. And that's what I mean by feeling *quite enslaved* to an abstract impersonal sexuality.

However, in the practices of courtship and sexual activity, women are not just the hapless victims of this male sexual drive. Angela McRobbie in her work on adolescent working-class girls concludes that 'their goal is to attract and keep a man' (McRobbie, 1978). Commonly accepted practices of femininity take it for granted that there is status and power attached to being attractive to men. In order to attract them, women can take up the object position in the male sexual drive discourse. Women are often seen as 'trapping' men by their powers of sexual attraction. But sex can also derive its meaning from the have/hold discourse. For example:

> *Dot:* The one time I did fuck with Charles, it felt really good, like there was an awful lot that was important going on. But I didn't have an orgasm . . . maybe the tension was too great or something. I don't know, I was very *turned on*. It was the idea of fucking with him rather than with someone else. The image I get makes me physically shudder with excitement. That reinforces my hunch that it's what's invested in the *idea*. I was in love with him. It's not fucking itself, it's something to do with the rights it gave me to see myself as having a relationship with him. I didn't have any of course.

Despite positioning herself in the permissive discourse (see below) by saying 'of course' she didn't have any rights to a relationship, Dot's reading of this one-off sexual encounter, and even her physical sexual response, were constructed through the set of meanings associated with the have/hold discourse. In another epoch, 'keeping a man' would have meant marriage. Here it is expressed as wanting a relationship. It entails positioning the woman as subject of the have/hold discourse. Although nothing was said on that matter between Dot and Charles, those meanings were an inalienable feature of her feelings. We don't know whether Charles positioned Dot through the have/hold discourse. When this is the case, in complementary fashion, the man is positioned as object of this discourse. This constructs the meanings, and affects the practices, of some men. For example Jim avoided casual sexual encounters because of what it might mean about commitment. Not specified, but a basic assumption in the following extract, is that a relationship was what the woman would want. The complementary position (that he does not) is also quite clear:

> *Jim:* Feeling that sex was kind of dangerous. If you had sex, it meant that you were committed in some way and I didn't want that. Also that if you *just* had sex without a relationship, it was a pretty shitty thing to do to have one part of it without the other.

The permissive discourse

The sexual practices of the participants in my study (aged on average around 30 in 1980) cannot be understood without recourse to a third discourse: the 'permissive' discourse. In this, the principle of monogamy is explicitly challenged, as is illustrated by this comment from the Student Christian Movement in 1966 speaking, predictably, from within the have/hold discourse: 'The teaching of the Christian church that sexual intercourse should be confined to marriage is frequently attacked as a theory and ignored in practice' (Sex and Morality, p. 4). In assuming that sexuality is entirely natural and therefore should not be repressed, the permissive discourse is the offspring of the male sexual drive discourse. Similarly it takes the individual as the locus of sexuality, rather than looking at it in terms of a relationship.[6] In one important respect it differs from the male sexual drive discourse: it applies the same assumptions to women as to men. In other words it was – in principle at least – gender-blind. In 1968, a reviewer of Vance Packard's book *The Sexual Wilderness* summed up the characteristics of the permissive society in the following terms: 'On the whole the young of *both sexes* believe that they have a right to express their sexuality in any way they choose so long as nobody is hurt' (my italics). Women could now be subjects of a discourse in a way which meant active initiation of a sexual relationship based on the idea that our natural sexual drives were equal to (or the same as) men's. However, gender difference in sexuality was not suddenly transformed. That this was not the case demonstrates the importance of recognizing the historically specific nature of discourses, their relation to what has gone before and how practices – such as the one-night stands of the permissive era – are not the pure products of a single discourse.

The differences between men's and women's positions in the traditional discourses were never banished in permissive practices. Beatrix Campbell sums up what is commonly recognized now by women in the Women's Movement (many of whom were believers in the equality of sex in permissive practices at the time):

> [the permissive era] permitted sex for women too. What it did not do was defend women against the differential effects of permissiveness on men and women. . . . It was about affirmation of young men's sexuality and promiscuity; it was indiscriminate, [so long as she was a woman]. The very affirmation of sexuality was a celebration of *masculine* sexuality. (Campbell, 1980, pp. 1–2)

In the following extract Jo describes why permissive sex was alienating for her:

> *Jo:* I've fantasized it [the quickie] yes, but it's never functioned like that – even when that person was a complete stranger. Afterwards I just looked at that stranger and felt completely alienated from what I'd just done with him. I mean, really uncomfortable in the extreme. Why did I do it? I think in that situation I'd almost never come, because I'd just be too guarded. You know, there was too much, which I'm just not going to let go – with a complete stranger. . . .
> *Colin:* Isn't that just the point? – Why the attraction? It's the fact that it's a stranger. It's nothing to do with the rest of your life. There's no damage that can be caused, you know, and all that kind of thing.
> *Piera:* Yes, you don't have to have a relationship with that person.
> *Jo:* But I don't think I can have sex without having a relationship. So if I haven't got one, it feels alienated, because to me, sex is expressing whatever the relationship is, and is going to be, and what can be built and how I feel with that person, and if it doesn't I really do feel awful. I do feel that if all I want is a quickie – that is some sexual tension released – then I'm much happier masturbating.
> *Colin:* I don't think that's the nature of a quickie, though.

The meanings of sex for Jo are inconsistent with the permissive discourse and therefore the practice which it promoted felt wrong. In contrast Colin's statements emanate from the assumptions of the permissive discourse. His account of the attraction of the quickie casts light on what Jim said above. In contrast to the have/hold discourse, the permissive discourse did not imply any commitment or responsibility. Had Jim been able to position himself by means of the permissive discourse rather than the have/hold discourse, sex would not have seemed so dangerous.

However, as I shall argue in the fourth part of this chapter, the meanings of sex are more contradictory than that.[7]

The practices that a discourse re-produces are not neutral. The liberating effects of the permissive discourse were particularly contradictory for women. Certainly the discourse enhanced men's powers (men's 'rights') to a heterosexual practice without emotional bonds. Later I shall return to the question of why men had more invested in this than women.

Summary and restatement of the approach

My treatment of these three discourses makes several points which are theoretically significant for the use of a discourse analysis to understand the relation of gender difference, subjectivity and change.

(1) Discourses make available positions for subjects to take up. These positions are in relation to other people. Like the subject and object[8] of a sentence (and indeed expressed through such a grammar), women and men are placed in relation to each other through the meanings which a particular discourse makes available: 'the female who yields and submits' to the man (Storr, quoted on p. 231).

(2) Because traditional discourses concerning sexuality are gender-differentiated, taking up subject or object positions is not equally available to men and women. (Try out Storr's formulation in reverse: 'the man who yields and submits to the woman's aggressive pursuit'.) The same applies to practices understandable in terms of gender-differentiated discourses. For example it's virtually impossible for women to put themselves in the position of subjects in the male sexual drive discourse when it comes to practices such as bottom-pinching or wolf-whistling.

(3) The positions are specified for the category 'man' or 'woman' in general. None the less particular men and women fill these positions. Their practices in relation to each other are rendered meaningful according to gender-differentiated discourses.

(4) Practices and meanings have histories, developed through the lives of the people concerned. These histories are not the product of a single discourse (though, depending on the hegemony of one discourse, meanings may be more or less homogeneous).

(5) Because discourses do not exist independently of their reproduction through the practices and meanings of particular women and men, we must account for changes in the dominance of certain discourses, and the development of new ones (for example those being articulated by feminists) by taking account of men's and women's subjectivity. Why do men 'choose' to position themselves as subjects of the

discourse of male sexual drive? Why do women continue to position themselves as its objects? What meanings might this have for women? How do the contradictions between the have/hold and male sexual drive discourses produce the practices of a particular heterosexual relationship? Do the practices signify differently for women and men, because they are being read through different discourses? Why and under what past and present circumstances are women more likely to read a sexual relationship through the have/hold discourse than men?

(6) By posing such questions, it is possible to avoid an analysis which sees discourses as mechanically repeating themselves – an analysis which cannot account for change. By showing how subjects' investments, as well as the available positions offered by discourses, are socially constituted and constitutive of subjectivity, it is possible to avoid this deterministic analysis of action and change.

How can we understand gender difference in a way which can account for changes? If we do not ask this question the change of paradigm from a biologistic to a discourse theory of gender difference does not constitute much of an advance. If the concept of discourses is just a replacement for the notion of ideology, then we are left with one of two possibilities. Either the account sees discourses as mechanically repeating themselves, or – and this is the tendency of materialist theory of ideology – changes in ideology follow from changes in material conditions. According to such a use of discourse theory people are the victims of certain systems of ideas which are outside of them. Discourse determinism comes up against the old problem of agency typical of all sorts of social determinisms.

Foucault's genealogies – because they are based on empirical historical data – do not register the stasis of discourses, but rather their changes. However, there is a gap in the theory which he uses to account for such changes. He stresses the mutually constitutive relation between power and knowledge: how each constitutes the other to produce the truths of a particular epoch (see Introduction to section 2, pp. 115–18). Rather than power being equated with oppression and seen as a negative thing, which can be got rid of come the revolution, power is seen as productive, inherently neither positive nor negative: productive of knowledges, meanings and values, and of certain practices as opposed to others. He still does not account for how people are constituted as a result of certain truths being current rather than others. The advantage of the idea that current at any one time are competing, potentially contradictory discourses (concerning for example sexuality) rather than a single patriarchal ideology, is that we can then pose the question, how is it that people take up positions in one discourse rather than another? If the process is not a mechanical positioning, why is it that men take up the subject position in the discourse of male sexual drive? What's in it for them? Under what conditions do men cease to do this? What accounts for the differences between some men and others? These questions require that attention is paid to the histories of individuals in order to see the recursive positioning in certain positions in discourses. It also requires a question concerning the *investment* in that position.

I have had considerable difficulty finding a good term here. 'Motivation' connotes biologically determined drives or alternatively individual needs (*qua* Maslow (1968), see chapter 1, p. 31). 'Drive' gets its meaning from psychoanalytic theory and reduces to 'instinct'. The terms all express concepts which are subject to the weaknesses of dualism. They are also subject to the related problem of accounts of agency. For when the forces propelling people's actions have not been theorized as reducing to biology or society, they have been seen as a product of rational decision-making. Yet, following our critique of the rational subject, a term like 'choice' does not convey the complexity of causes for action. I have chosen 'investment' because it appears to avoid most of these problems. In addition it was the German word for 'investment', *Besetzung*, which Freud chose to refer to what in English has been translated as 'cathexis'. As the two uses share some important emphases, it is a potentially productive meeting of paradigms. By claiming that people have investments (in this case gender-specific) in taking up certain positions in discourses, and consequently in relation to each other, I mean that there will be some satisfaction or pay-off or reward (these terms involve the same problems) for that person. The satisfaction may well be in contradiction with other resultant feelings. It is not necessarily conscious or rational. But there is a reason. In what follows, I theorize the reason for this investment in terms of power and the way it is historically inserted into individuals' subjectivity. (See chapter 6 for an account of the early emergence of subjectivity in these terms.)

Boys' and girls' entry into masculinity and femininity

In this part I will try to give an account – albeit schematic – of boys' and girls' developing relation to sexuality through the available discourses. Any analysis which focuses on subjective positioning in discourses requires an account of the investment that a person has in taking up one position rather than another in a different discourse. Of course some discourses are more hegemonic and thus carry all the weight of social approval. But successful positioning in these discourses is not automatic, else there would be no variations. But to assume the mechanical reproduction of discourse requires asking how it got to be like that in the first place. And that question is in danger of throwing theory back into answers according to the terms of biological, Oedipal, or social and economic determinisms. (Chapter 6 tries to address the question of the emergence of subjectivity in young children without falling into these determinisms.)

The point that I have been at pains to stress is that discourses coexist and have mutual effects and that meanings are multiple. This produces choice, though it may not be simple or conscious. Consequently we have to account for what investments a boy or girl has in taking up a particular position in discourses by relating in certain ways with the other.[9] What accounts for the different investments produced historically in people of the same gender? Clearly other major dimensions of social difference such as class, race and age intersect with gender to favour or disfavour certain positions. However, as well as recognizing cultural regularities it is also necessary – without resorting to essentialism – to account for the uniqueness of individuals. Lacanian theory does so by stressing the somewhat anarchic character of desire: desire as a motive force or process is common to all significations (although it is contentious whether it is universal). Although the significations which it occupies may be quite idiosyncratic, I try to show that they are not arbitrary. Significations are a product of a person's history, and what is expressed or suppressed in signification is made possible by the availability and hegemony of discourses. Positions available in gender-differentiated discourses confer relative power by enabling the suppression of significations which would be undermining of power.

Growing up properly for a boy

For Jim girls were essential to 'growing up properly'

> *Jim:* I remember very young – before twelve – feeling a pressure to have a girlfriend and not having a clue. I remember hanging around a local cinema thinking that might be how something happened. But it was like an abstract pressure – I just felt that I should in order to show I was growing up properly. It didn't have any connection with the rest of my life, it was just something that I felt I should take on.

What did having a girlfriend mean that it signified 'growing up properly'? It positioned Jim as a 'proper man'; in other words it afforded him a gender-appropriate position:

> *Jim:* I did feel the onus always to actually be pushy, to see how far it was possible to go with somebody, to see how far they were actually *into* me.

> *Wendy:* What did you want?
> *Jim:* Well just an obvious sign of . . . as a way of showing I was into them – well in a way showing I was a proper man.

The sexual (or protosexual) practices he engaged in enabled him to be positioned as subject in the male sexual drive discourse ('being pushy'). He was not the victim of a natural drive (though the girl concerned probably read it that way). His interest was to do with gender not sex. His successful masculine positioning depended on a girl being 'into him' and the proof of this would be that she let him get sexual with her.

'Being attractive' for a girl

The same principle is illustrated in Clare's account of her adolescent feelings about boys. The available positions are different however. Where Jim had to be pushy, Clare had to be attractive. There is a chain of assumptions running through the account: being attractive . . . (means) . . . being attractive to boys . . . (means) . . . engaging in sex (or protosex) with boys . . . (means) . . . having a boyfriend.

> *Clare:* I can see from the photographs that I went from being a child who was quite pretty to an early adolescent who – I felt myself to be fat and ugly, and desperately lacking in confidence. I suspect I lacked confidence because I had had ways of dealing with people, which were to do with being an attractive child. They didn't work any more, because I wasn't one. When I was fourteen or fifteen I went on a diet – and I went down from being quite big to seven stone. It was an absolutely wonderful thing. It had a lot for me, to do with sexuality. I remember I thought I would be more confident, I thought I would be more attractive to boys.
> *Wendy:* Were you more confident?
> *Clare:* In a way, yes. I was quite good at school, though but certainly – when I lost weight, it seemed like the resolution of a set of contradictions. Having lost weight, I was no longer destined to be the 'ugly, clever type'. It would be alright because I was actually quite attractive as well. The more I dig deep, the more I think of the hurt – there's a hell of a lot of hurt around not being attractive enough and particularly about not having boyfriends. I remember, kind of, going out with anybody who asked me. I was so pleased to be asked, that I would have gone with anybody.
> *Wendy:* When you did go out with them, what did you think of them?
> *Clare:* Not a lot. I thought it was all a bit of a joke. Most of them were fools.

Adolescent girls' sexual practices gain them the reputation of being either slags or drags (Cowie and Lees, 1981) – a contradiction which is a logical product of women's contradictory positions in the male sexual drive and have/hold discourses. Yet girls do not on the whole feel free to forego relationships with boys, for the reasons that Clare illuminates. Her identity as an attractive girl is at stake. According to McRobbie (1978) adolescent girls' main goal is 'to attract and keep a boy'. There are ostensibly few pay-offs and plenty of risks: the danger of being called 'slags' (Cowie and Lees, 1981), no enjoyment of the kind of sex that boys practise, the experience that the boys are fools anyway. Their investment is in their own identities. Boys are necessary simply because in the only discourse in which being attractive can be understood, being attractive means being attractive to the opposite sex.

Attractiveness and femininity

It is within the practices of gender-differentiated discourses concerning sexuality that girls' and womens' gender identity is re-produced. In the following quote, Clare explores why she felt in a weak position later on when she did get involved in a long-term relationship with a man:

> *Clare:* I mean, with Phil he was very loud and domineering, and I was very quiet and weak. He was strong, and I was weak. I think that was the main thing. And I was more feminine.
> *Wendy:* What did that involve?
> *Clare:* Looking pretty. I think it relates back to when I said that when I was little I was the good, pretty little girl. It's to do with – the fear – being frightened of not being attractive enough.
> *Wendy:* To keep him?
> *Clare:* Mmmm.

Attracting a man is the defining feature of Clare's femininity. Keeping him, according to the male sexual drive discourse, means continuing to be attractive to him. This is the crucial recurrent interest in Clare's take-up of the object position in the male sexual drive discourse. In order to feel herself as gender-appropriate, she thus feels driven to be in a couple relationship with a man. These practices re-produce certain sexual and couple practices, and re-produce both gender difference and the inequality of women's position in the dominant discourses concerning sexuality.

I have shown that the practice of heterosexual couple relations (including sexual relations) is a site where different discourses concerning sexuality are available to produce different knowledges or meanings through which practices are mediated. Within this general usage of discourse analysis what is of particular significance is how the gender-differentiated nature of these discourses affects women's and men's powers and therefore the investment they have in taking up gender-appropriate positions and practices. Girls and women actively engage in certain heterosexual practices in order to re-produce their gender identity.

Heterosexual practice and the construction of women's sexuality

However, the investments of those participating in sexual relations are no more unitary than the powers conferred on them through their positions in discourses. In the following extract, Clare indicates that her sexuality was completely subordinated to the need to be attractive:

> *Clare:* I think my understanding of my own sexuality when I was an adolescent was about zero. I mean it felt like doing this thing which meant you had to attract boys – to be attractive to them. There wasn't anything else. But even later, when I began fucking men, it was actually an extension of that.

That this need to be attractive produced her as passive in heterosexual sex is illustrated below. Clare and I discover the similarities in the way that our sexuality and gender was reproduced in the practices which were a product of the male sexual drive. The take-up of a position as object in the discourse of male sexual drive, motivated by the interest in being attractive, constructs the practice of heterosexual sex:

> *Clare:* Well, I don't know, the term 'sexuality' means something quite different now. I don't think I felt I had a sexuality.
> *Wendy:* I was never actually aware of having a spontaneous desire, that somehow seemed to be initiated by me, which I could then act out.
> *Clare:* Right, yes. That's it.
> *Wendy:* . . . Except the desire to attract a man, and follow it through.
> *Clare:* Right. It was that which was powerful for me.
> *Wendy:* Although, if I was attracted to a boy, and we went out together, or something, I was always – y'know, wanting kisses and cuddles, and fumbles, and . . . I don't know – the kind of things that would signify that it was getting more intense.
> *Clare:* Yes, but I think that was because of what it signified, rather than because I actually liked it.
> *Wendy:* Yes, and even that had a kind of genital goal. Because even though I didn't know at that point what we did, I knew that that was the most risky place.
> *Clare:* Yes – I knew that. But I can't say that I enjoyed it. But then I didn't enjoy screwing very much either. I didn't know that I didn't, even. I feel very ashamed – I feel it's an awful admission. I actually

had my first orgasm with Ken. I mean, I was sleeping with men for that long, and I never had one. I mean, I didn't think I was, and I wasn't sure, and for the life of me I wouldn't ask. It took me a long time to realize – well that I had masturbated and reached orgasm. I didn't know it was the same thing. I just thought it was something rather peculiar. I did masturbate when I was younger but I associated it – not one iota – with sex. I suppose later it was a certain kind of confidence which I had, which meant that I was more determined to get what I wanted. Even though I wasn't quite sure what that was. I mean, I think I was probably very passive.
Wendy: That passivity thing – I think is tied up with confidence. Er, with me, in short relationships, where I didn't actually . . . know a man very well, I never trusted the man enough for me to be active. Or, another way of putting it would be – to show myself as someone who had . . . desires.
Clare: I think that's right – for me. I was passive – because I didn't know how to express myself and also because I didn't know what to do. And because I felt judgements were being made of my sexual competence. And I had no idea, whether or not I was doing it right.
Wendy: The criterion that I evolved – of doing it right or not, was . . . um . . . ministering right to a man's needs, to what turned him on. If he seemed to enjoy it. And it was all about his sexuality.
Clare: Yes. Right.
Wendy: . . . I mean, that's how I learned to be sexual.
Clare: . . . Doing things that men liked. Yes.
Wendy: And in that sense I was quite active – I took initiatives.

The suppressed in discourse and the multiple significations of sex

So far it might appear that men and women are so positioned by these different discourses that gender difference is well established and successful in producing men and women whose subjectivity is a unitary product of them. Is it not rather surprising, then, that men often stay in couple relationships – even hang on to them when the woman wants out – and find immediate replacements when a relationship ends? (I'm not saying women don't too, but this is consistent with women's positioning in discourses and inconsistent with men's.)

The meaning of sex is no more unitary than the discourses which compete to define the practice of sex. In this section I want to show how suppressed significations coexist with those expressed. Rather than seeing what is suppressed as something which is directly reducible to the Oedipus Complex, or as invisible in the sense that the suppressed meanings have no effects (that is tantamount to the suppressed being non-existent and meaning being unitary), I will show how for men there are continued investments – to do with power – in defining women as subjects of the have/hold discourse, thereby suppressing their own wishes to have and to hold. One participant in my research wrote the following about the man she was in a relationship with:

> If he's saying he has no expectations, no needs, then I can't let him down. If I can't let him down, he has more power. He has the power to hurt me, but I don't have the power to hurt him.

Her observation is a beautifully clear recognition of the relation between knowledge (discourses) and power. As long as she and not he is positioned as the subject of the have/hold discourse, unequal power is the consequence.

What does a man want?

It's obvious to men who have achieved a minimum of insight into their feelings that men's wants are not made explicit in sexist discourses. One of the men who participated in my research expresses needs more in keeping with women's as they are articulated in the have/hold discourse, at the same time as being aware of the contradictions:

> *Sam:* The thing that has caused me the most pain, and the most hope is the idea of actually living with Jane. And that's in the context of having tried to live with three other women before. And each time the relationship's been full of possibility. I don't want to live on my own. There's too many things all wrapped up in coupling. There's too many needs it potentially meets, and there are too many things it frustrates. I do want to have a close, a central-person relationship, but in the past, the negative aspects outweighed the positive aspects dramatically. Or my inability to work through them has led me to run.

What happens to men's needs for a 'close central-person relationship' as Sam put it? The negative aspects, which occupy the other side of Sam's contradiction, are not to do with free sexuality (although in the extract below he specifically refers to that discourse in order to gainsay it):

> *Sam:* I'm very frightened of getting in deep – and then not being able to cope with the demands that the relationship's making. You see, a lot of these things aren't really to do with sexuality. They're to do with responsibility.

In this quotation from Sam, there is an elision between getting in deep[10] and responsibility. This occurs through the lack of clarity about whether

Sam was frightened of getting in deep himself, or of the women doing so. In the following extract from Sam, the effect of the woman's position in the have/hold discourse is to protect Sam's own deep feelings. It is a further illustration of the relation between power and knowledge – the effect of discourse in action. It shows the idea of women requiring commitment being reproduced as a result of men's projected fears.

> *Sam:* I'll tell you something – which I don't know what it means but I'll say it anyway. When I say to somebody, who I'm making love to – I'm close to, when I say, 'I love you, I love you' it's a word that symbolizes letting go. The night before Carol went away, she was saying it, and then I started saying it to her, when we were making love. What frightens me is that word, it's an act of commitment. Somebody suddenly, expects something of me. They've said something, that's the first word in a long rotten line towards marriage. That when you fall in love, you're caught up in the institution. And it's been an act of principle for me, that I can love somebody, and feel loved, without feeling any responsibility. That I can be free to say that I love somebody if I love them. Be free to feel. I can feel it quite unpredictably. It can hit me quite unexpectedly. And I think I worry about it because I can be quite sentimental.

The power of the meaning 'I love you' for Sam was that he felt close to someone and it was a 'letting go' of his emotions. This is dangerous because of the power it confers on someone else; the other in the sexual relationship. As soon as Sam has said this, the signifier 'letting go' is suppressed by its capture in the discourse which positions women as requiring commitment. The fear which is generated because this can 'hit me quite unexpectedly' is sufficient to produce its repression, its falling to the level of the signified. Thus gender difference in the discourse 'women requiring commitment' is reproduced.

However, there is a contradiction which remains: men still have needs for the intimacy of a heterosexual relationship. A man writing in *Achilles Heel* (an anti-sexist men's magazine) suggests that this is the only place where men can get these needs met:

> For men (heterosexual) sex works out as a trap because it's the only place where men can really get tenderness and warmth. But they have no skills to evoke these things because there is nothing in the rest of our lives that trains us to do this. So we come into this where we want warmth and intimacy and we don't know how to get it. But it's the only place it exists so there's this tremendous tension for men, getting into bed with women. (*Achilles Heel*, 2, 1979, p. 9)

This quotation again illustrates that sex can be a cover for men's need for intimacy to be met. The reproduction of women as subjects of a discourse concerning the desire for intimate and secure relationships protects men from the risk associated with their own need (and the consequent power it would give women). Their own simultaneous position as object of the have/hold discourse and subject of the male sexual drive discourse enables them to engage in the practice of sex, and thus get what they want without recognizing those needs or risking exposure. 'Sex' as male drive therefore covers for the suppressed signification of 'sex' as intimacy and closeness. Because the practice itself does not require verbalization, the suppressed signification is not necessarily recognized. These significations (not necessarily conscious) are completely woven in to the practices of sex, suppressed as they are with the aid of the male sexual drive discourse. This is illustrated by Sam's immediate association when asked how a woman makes him feel: 'It's a closeness, isn't it . . . going to sleep, cuddling close. Feeling – I mean, I don't worry about burglars. I think I feel a lot more secure.'

Unlike a reply from within the discourse of male sexual drive, such as 'it turns me on', Sam's response captures significations normally suppressed through projection: closeness and security.

A man's fear of 'getting in deep' requires theorization in its own right. What are the strong feelings that are evoked by women with whom they have – or want – sexual relationships, which are invested in suppressing their own emotions and projecting them on to women?

Desire for the Other, power relations and subjectivity

In the following extract, Martin describes forcefully what happens to him when he feels a little attracted to a woman.[11] The account imposes on my analysis the question of the irrational in couple relations.

> *Martin:* People's needs for others are systematically denied in ordinary relationships. And in a love relationship you make the most fundamental admission about yourself – that you want somebody else. It seems to me that that is the greatest need, and the need which, in relationship to its power, is most strongly hidden and repressed. Once you've shown the other person that you need them, then you've made yourself incredibly vulnerable.
> *Wendy:* Yes, I agree. But I think there's a question about – how much you show yourself to be vulnerable.
> *Martin:* But you do, just by showing that you're soft on somebody. It seems to me when you've revealed that need, you put yourself in an incredibly insecure state. You've before managed by not showing anyone what you're like. By showing them only what is publicly acceptable. And as soon as you've shown that there is this terrible hole in you – that you want somebody else – then you're in an absolute state of insecurity. And you need much more than the

> empirical evidence that somebody likes you. . . . You become neurotically worried that you're not accepted. Now you've let them see a little bit that's you. It'll be rejected. It's not so bad when a false exterior is rejected. The insecurity gives someone else power. I don't mean any viable self-exposure. I just mean any little indication that you like the other person.

Martin's experience of attraction leaves us with a pressing question: what is it that provides us with the irrational charge in sexual attraction? It is the quality of this experience which precipitates Martin's vulnerability and resistance. I call this experience 'desire for the Other',[12] and by the use of this concept, link in to psychoanalytic theory for an explanation: desire for the mother is repressed but never extinguished. It reasserts itself in adult sexual relations.[13]

I want to stress the effects of this subjective experience. Martin's 'desire for the Other' produces a feeling of intense vulnerability which in turn motivates him to exercise whatever powers he can muster in relation to women to whom he feels attracted. Sexist discourses serve this precise function. By reading himself as object of the have/hold discourse he can suppress the recognition of his dependence on a relationship with a woman. As long as he reads the woman as subject of the have/hold discourse he can camouflage his desire. If he succeeds, he can sustain the relationship and meet some of his needs while both remain unaware of them. That this has power effects, even when its suppression is not total, is illustrated in the following account by Martha, the woman with whom Martin has a relationship:

> *Martha:* All these things that we've been talking about hand such power to people. Martin and I go up and down like a see-saw. There are days when he's in another city, and needing me, and suddenly I'm powerful and can dictate terms. We're back here, and I'm wanting a close, reciprocal, warm, working-out relationship, and suddenly he's powerful, because he doesn't want to give it. It really is dynamite . . . every day of our lives. It really is working less and less well. This business of having needs is so humiliating, because it makes one vulnerable.
>
> *Wendy:* And shifts the power.
>
> *Martha:* And shifts the power – exactly.

Her experience of the effects again bears witness to the way sexist discourse is productive of power – for men.

In the following extract Martha refers to the more general oppressive effects of Martin's resistance to the power he experiences her having in the relationship:

> *Martha:* I put up with it, rather than saying, 'No, this is not the way I want to be treated'. I want to be treated as a complete person,

> someone who has feelings and ideas and intuitions that are actually worth taking notice of. No room is allowed for me to be myself, fully because it might be too powerful an intrusion on his actions. To be accepted one hundred per cent means that the other person has to be strong enough . . . to keep their own integrity in the face of you being one hundred per cent yourself. It's so hard to find men who might be committed to taking those risks.

Her moving testimomy to the effects on her of Martin's power is a specific example of the experience of gender difference: it points to the psychological characteristics which are consistent with – and reproduce – sexist discourses where woman is the inferior 'other'.

Misrecognition of men

When men behave warily and defensively, women do not necessarily read it as stemming from their vulnerability or dependence. This is because women too are subject to the production of meanings through dominant discourses. The available assumptions about men are that they are, for example, powerful, rational, autonomous, in control and self-confident. These features are, by definition, positively valued in sexist discourses. The effect is to foreground men's qualities and conceal their weaknesses and to do the opposite for women. Positioned within such discourses women misread themselves as easily as men. Clare's account of her relationship exemplifies this misrecognition:

> *Clare:* That guy, I didn't even know he was so dependent on me.
> *Wendy:* That's so often the way men play it. But it's also so often the way that women read it.
> *Clare:* Oh, it's two-way. Precisely. His behaviour was very stereotypical, really. I thought he was a competent person – but he didn't think he was at all. He was outwardly confident – domineering – which actually made me feel incredibly oppressed.
> *Wendy:* How long did it take you to realize that?
> *Clare:* Oh, a long time. I didn't realize he was dependent on me, till I left him, I had no idea. That's the extent we both managed to keep this from each other. And when I look back on it, I realize that I should have known. It's always the same set of signs that I misread. The very signs that I took to signify confidence, were, for him – well, he actually used it as displays of confidence, but they were, actually, exactly the signs of his lack of confidence, like – talking too much . . . being opinionated and things that I couldn't bear. And when I read it back as lack of confidence, I could see. . . . He was so insecure inside – and I didn't know. Quite a lot of things changed in our relationship. When I first met him, he had a Degree, and I had a

Certificate and I wanted a Degree and he encouraged me. But I mean, not only did I do that . . . but I actually got far higher qualifications than he did. So that also made him feel unconfident. And I hadn't realized that either. We did things like . . . both applying for Open University teaching. I got it, and he didn't. It didn't occur to me it was a problem. Of course it was a problem for him.

It was possible for Clare to understand this as misrecognition because the process was uncovered when she left him. However, it is relevant to point out that this kind of misrecognition does not simply cease to operate through a rational process of learning by experience. The irrationality of women's desire for the Other also demands analysis:

Wendy: What you said – about not being able to read his dependence on you – I think that's true of you and Ken.
Clare: Um, yes, I've been told that before, but I still don't know how to know it.
Wendy: Yes, it's the kind of thing, y'know, when like, somebody kind of breaks, and expresses themselves on a different level. Like Phil did when you left – like Jeremy did when I left. He actually felt like a different person.
Clare: Yeah. Phil felt like a different person. Why is it then that I can't get hold of that knowledge about Ken? Why can't I see it? 'Cause I can't. Um . . . it's very silly 'cause I know where my power lies.

Desire and the signifier 'woman'

Misrecognition of the Other of desire, when it is an opposite-sexed Other, is not explicable simply by the existence of gender-differentiated discourses. I will argue, through analysing Jim's account, that the way in which 'woman' signifies for him has a history going back to his desire for the mother. The argument is an illustration of Lacan's slogan 'the desire for the Other is the desire for the mother' (Lacan, 1977, p. 286).

Like Sam, Jim is aware that he is frightened by strong emotions. Again like Sam, there is an elision between his own and the woman's emotions:

Wendy: And was it that the girls wanted to be more intimate?
Jim: Yeah – I was frightened of making that kind of commitment, that kind of involvement, 'cause I thought I'd be let down, because of what happened the first time, when I was so unreserved about how I felt. I think that really affected my life incredibly, that first time I fell in love.
Wendy: Why was having a relationship with her such a burden?
Jim: She was very strong and very emotional – that's pejorative,

> but I mean she had strong reactions, so that I didn't actually feel safe that I wasn't going to be knocked out, or sucked in by her.

It transpires that Jim's fear of her strong emotions was a projected fear of his own.[14] He feared them because it felt unsafe to feel so strongly for a woman. As many men experience with their first sexual relationship – particularly if it is with an older woman – their lack of defences leave them painfully hurt when the relationship ends. As I have argued above, this constitutes the investment in reading the woman as the subject of the have/hold discourse.

What does Jim want that he's so afraid of losing that he can't have it in case he loses it?

> *Wendy:* What was it that you wanted out of a stable relationship with Jeanette?
> *Jim:* Well, I think support. Knowing that there was somebody who was going to be on my side, that I could talk about things that were affecting me and they would more or less automatically be important to her. And that she would be able to give me strength in that way. Very classic. Like my parents' relationship. But it was me who set the agenda, and she fitted in, and in a way that's what I wanted. Someone who wouldn't actually challenge me. There's a gaze of uncritical, totally accepting love that I find really attractive. 'I'll love you forever, whatever,' – is really a powerful gaze. And that's a mother's gaze.

I have considered in greater detail elsewhere (Hollway, 1982) the implications and theorization of this mother/Other link. Here I will give one further instance of the way that seemingly unimportant day-to-day relationships are suffused with meanings which must be explicated in terms of 'desire for the Other' and how the woman of the relationship is linked to the mother. Another woman Jim had a relationship with said:

> I was feeling preoccupied with other things, so I suppose not paying him much attention. Jim got at me twice – about tiny things, in a way that felt antagonistic. When I pointed it out we tried to do some work on it. Blank. Then he came up with the word 'oranges', as if from nowhere. When he thought about it a bit he said it had something to do with his relations with women. If a woman peeled an orange for him, it showed that they cared for him. Then he said that his mother used to do it for him, even when he could do it for himself.

Desire has a history through its occupancy of certain significations – in this case, who peeled oranges. It does not express itself through the rationally accessible layer of meaning – it couldn't be included in the definition of oranges. But when it comes up in the practice of peeling oranges this meaning is there as a presence. For Jim it is part of a wider set of significations around proof of loving and caring through women doing things for him. It is consistent with the common experience of women in relationships with men that men get them to do things for them when they are 'objectively' unnecessary. The suppressed signification is 'I'll do it for you because I love you'. The signifying chain from mother to Other is historically unbroken for men, although, according to Freudian theory, savagely repressed.[15]

Implications for changing gender difference

In this part I have shown that the positions which are available in discourses do not determine people's subjectivity in any unitary way. Whilst gender-differentiated positions do overdetermine the meanings and practices and values which construct an individual's identity, they do not account for the complex, multiple and contradictory meanings which affect and are affected by people's practices. Specifically, men's sexuality is not plausibly accounted for by their positions as subject in the discourse of the male sexual drive and object in the have/hold discourse. 'Sex' signifies in many ways at once. The fact that a man succeeds in reading his sexual practices according to such sexist positions – locating the woman in the complementary positions – only means that the discourse provides the means whereby other significations can be suppressed. Yet 'desire for the Other' is present through the metaphoric axis (see p. 214) and affects practices. Thus the knowledge produced by the male sexual drive discourse confers power on men which, in a circular way, motivates them recurrently in taking up that position. This is a specific example of the power–knowledge relation that Foucault theorizes (see Introduction to section 2, pp. 115–18). If the woman is unable to resist her complementary positioning by having access to an alternative discourse and practice, or if her investment in being so positioned is paramount,[16] the couple will reproduce the discourse and thus the existence of gender difference in practices and subjectivity.

What makes this analysis different from one which sees a mechanical circulation of discourses through practices is that there is an investment which, for reasons of an individual's history of positioning in discourses and consequent production of subjectivity, is relatively independent of contemporary positions available. According to my account this is an investment in exercising power on behalf of a subjectivity protecting itself from the vulnerability of desire for the Other. Otherwise power could only be seen as a determined feature of the reproduction of gender-differentiated discourses, which would be left untheorized or reduce to a biological or economic determinism. Instead I have tried to show by concrete example that the interest is specific and part of the history of men and women (in different ways).

I believe that the heterosexual couple relationship (or sexual relationship) is a crucial site for the reproduction of gender difference because of 'desire for the Other'. In chapter 6, it is suggested that the vulnerability of subjectivity and the consequent interest in exercising power is true in some measure of all relations. An analysis of race or class difference could follow many of the same principles but it could not rely in quite the same way on the concept of 'desire for the Other'. This issue raises the question of the relation between desire and 'desire for the Other' in psychoanalytic theory (see Introduction to section 3, pp. 215–16).

The analysis is of political importance because it indicates the nature of the problem involved in changing gender difference. It is not only the social division of labour. We have indicated that there are problems with the Oedipus Complex as an explanation (see Introduction to section 3, p. 215). Furthermore, it is not a problem to be addressed at the level of discourses alone, critical as that is. The reproduction of gender-differentiated practices depends on the circulation between subjectivities and discourses which are available. The possibility of interrupting this circle is contained in a grasp of the contradictions between discourses and thus of contradictory subjectivities. While one set of desires may be suppressed, along with their signification, by the dominant sexist discourses, the contradictions are never successfully eliminated. They are the weak points in the stronghold of gender difference: taking up gender-appropriate positions as women and men does not successfully express our multiple subjectivities.

In the final part of this chapter I shall argue that gender difference is maintained, that is re-produced in day-to-day interactions in heterosexual couples, through the denial of the non-unitary non-rational, relational character of subjectivity.

Splitting the differences

The following introductory extract describes splitting between a gender-differentiated pair of characteristics: expressing feelings and giving support. The exclusion, through projection, of one 'side' of this pair is made possible by the way their meaning already contains a specification of what is gender-appropriate. The difference is re-produced in the subjectivities of each member of the heterosexual couple.

> *Jim:* The thing got specialized, as it were polarized, where one person does the feeling. My relationship with Jeanette, who I lived with for many years, developed in such a way that she was responsible for doing the feelings – she was the one that got upset, and I

> was the one who was coping, providing support, kindness, et cetera. And so what that meant was that I didn't get to express any feelings and she didn't get to express any support. And so what that means is that both sides are completely prevented from experiencing what the other person's 'job' is. Which means that you get a completely shrivelled – a completely incomplete – idea of what's going on.

Two important points emerge from this comment. First – and most obviously – the content of the split is predictable from discourses specifying gender difference: it was the woman whose job it was to do the feeling.[17] Our common-sense experience of this split is through the naturalistic assumption that it is part of women's natural make-up. In consequence, this characteristic of their relationship was not read as a relational dynamic, it was read as aspects of their personalities. Jim said that at the time he firmly believed that he was just not a 'feeling person'. Whereas traditionally this would have been considered a positive characteristic, in the humanist and feminist climate of the post-1960s, he felt that it was a lack. None the less, the effect of the denial, through projection of these feelings, was experienced as part of his 'personality', that is as something fundamental and unchangeable. Clearly then, it is vital to understand the mechanisms whereby gender-differentiated characteristics – such as expressing feelings – are located in one member of a heterosexual couple. By focusing on the mechanisms, I am able to avoid seeing the effect as a once-and-for-all accomplishment of sex-role socialization. Instead I am seeing it as a dynamic which is constantly being re-produced in day-to-day couple relationships. I shall illustrate this in due course.

The second point emerges from the opposition which is implied between expressing feelings and giving support. This is not a logical pair of opposites, but you probably took it for granted when you read it (which illustrates the power of gender-differentiated discourses to construct our assumptions). The value which we are obliged to accept in order to make sense of this opposition is that people, usually women, who express feelings need support because expressing feelings is a weakness. 'Doing the feelings' is equated with 'getting upset'. Conversely the person, usually a man, who gives support is thus obliged to position himself as someone who is strong enough not to have feelings. The logic of the opposition is not contained in the meaning itself, but rather in the judgement attached to it. In our society, the judgement is a sexist one: expressing feelings is weak, feminine and in contradistinction to men's rationality. With the value – which is indeed inextricable from the meaning once it is seen as inserted into the discourse – comes power difference. Men can support women who are subject to the unfortunate bane of feeling and thus men are superior. As I have already argued, this constitutes a substantial investment in taking up such a position recurrently in relations. I have already shown how it can be the fear of their own feelings, signifying weakness, which is concealed by the manoeuvre. Now I shall show how splitting, through projection and introjection, operates as a defence. This accounts for the mechanism whereby gender-differentiated positions in discourses are reproduced.

This splitting is contradictory. Giving support implies not being able to ask for support, as I shall demonstrate in the example of Beverley and Will below. (Again there is not a logical opposition involved – support can in principle be mutual.) In this part I therefore want to clarify two issues raised by the idea of characteristics being split through gender difference into women and men. First, the interpersonal dynamic must be theorized – and this is where psychoanalytic theory's non-unitary, non-rational subject and the unconscious and its ability to theorize relations come into play. Second, the space for movement in the gender-differentiated content of these splits must be specified. Here, the contradictory subject positions offered by coexisting and inconsistent discourses, and the consequent production of multiple meanings and powers, offer the necessary theoretical perspective.

Repression and rationality

How does this mechanism of splitting work? In the following extract, I look at an example in detail and link it to my concept of investment. Will is describing an occasion when he became aware of his feelings, and how they were related to a change in Beverley's position. One of the methodological (and theoretical) questions raised by the use of the concept of splitting is that – by definition – it is not observable while it is in operation. It feels like the natural state of affairs in a relationship, what personality psychology would deal with under the rubric of 'individual differences'. Here Will is able to describe it because for 'one and a half minutes' the splitting dynamic was ruptured:

> *Will:* In a relationship for me, this 'frozenness' of certain feelings is really terrible. Much more of the time than I would like, we're doing this specialization job. There's maybe a split second in which I feel in touch with the set of feelings that I'm not normally responsible for, and that I don't particularly avow. And I don't even know if I feel them. And I think, 'Shit I actually felt that'. For two or three weeks I don't feel anything about it again, and I have to say, 'Well, at the moment I don't feel anything, but I do remember.' I mean at one stage, Beverley said [sighs], 'Well, maybe we should have an abortion,' and I suddenly burst into tears. Now it was very peculiar, because I'd actually been the person who'd been saying, 'You really should think about having an abortion,' you know, I was giving all

the excellent reasons, 'cause normally – and this might be the Catholic thing – she has always said, 'No, an abortion is *terrible.*' And for me, it's just a matter of convenience. If she wants one. If it interferes with her studies, then we'll certainly wait two or three years. So I felt quite knowledgeable about it all, and there was no problem.
Wendy: Yes, this is Will, being the rational, reassuring side of the relationship.
Will: Yes, that's right. So it's my job to make her think about it. And then she actually thought about it, and she decided, maybe she would. And I burst into tears, which was completely unexpected for me. And I felt terribly depressed. And for that split second – it lasted about one and a half minutes – I knew that I actually did not want her to have an abortion. I mean, one of the things she's actually said to me is, 'I don't know whether you want to actually have this child or not' and I've said, 'Of course I want to have this child.' And at one level that's certainly true. But I didn't actually feel it in the same way. And I had to hold on to that feeling, because it went very quickly. A breakdown of that division or specialization is quite rare, and it's difficult to break out of that type of role – that division of labour. So I had to hold on to those moments of knowledge.
Wendy: What you said about Beverley saying, 'I don't know what you feel about having this baby' – at one level you knew that this was absurd: you'd said a hundred times, 'I'm into having this baby,' but you'd repressed a lot of the feelings – [Will: Mmm] – for fear that you might be disappointed. So actually, she's right. Because apart from those moments, the feelings that you have about it aren't coming over and that's the information that is so lacking.

Will describes the rational arguments that he put forward in a way which exemplifies how they were devoid of his own desires. The experience of the issue is summarized by his comment, 'I felt quite knowledgeable about it all'. The effect is summed up as 'there was no problem'. His position in relation to Beverley shows what he was not taking on himself: 'It's my job to make her think about it.' Will's account of what happened next illustrates the usefulness of the idea of positions in discourses. Beverley resisted the 'gender-appropriate' position. Rather than remaining the receptacle of all the non-rational feelings about abortion, Beverley adopted the position that Will had been occupying: 'She actually thought about it and she decided, maybe she would.' Will's ability to repress his feelings of wanting a baby were conditional on positioning Beverley so that she would want it (despite rational considerations, which he, not she, was representing). When this unconscious strategem failed, the effect was 'completely unexpected'. His defence against strong feelings that he wanted a baby – the mechanism of projection – had broken down. It did not, however, break down for long. This demonstrates how the evanescence of feelings is the result of their repression by the defence mechanisms.

Defence mechanisms and social relations

The importance of this extract is that it illustrates the link between psychodynamics on the one hand, which affect (in this case) a man's experience of an issue and his understanding of his identity, and on the other the effects on social relations and gender difference. Will's repression was not just an intrapsychic matter. A theory of the unconscious is not just about personal well-being and individual treatment. Repression is a dynamic with social and political effects. However, the effects are not comprehensible if we stay within the framework of psychoanalytic theory. The latter has had a tendency to concentrate on processes and structures (the processes of splitting, defence mechanisms, identification and the structures of the unconscious, conscious and desire). Ignoring content, the conclusion – erroneous in my view – which psychoanalysis tends to draw is that the content of desire is inserted in infancy (most likely to be theorized as at the Oedipal stage). The political implications are thus not dissimilar from socialization theory: the continuous changes which characterize the social domain and are not linked to generational change are left out of the picture because there is no account of how these changes in content are produced in subjects' positions in multiple discourses; of what is suppressed and expressed; and of the content of splits. Discourse analysis provides a way of understanding the content of the split: what in this case Will calls 'being in charge of patriarchal reassurance' because 'somebody else's needs or fears or anxieties are greater than mine'.

Why did Will believe that he was the stronger of the two?[18] I have illustrated how the availability of a position in discourse which is positively valued and which confers power must be accompanied by a mechanism at the level of the psyche which provides the investment to take up this position. I have also argued that the investment in these positions is produced in the individual's history. Will's history is no exception:

> *Will:* Women are developing strength, which is in a way what I wanted, because when I was at school – I mean, women were nothing and I hated it. Because I couldn't think of them as equals. I felt them as people with whom I could only have a false relationship. I felt really bad about that. And I used to read novels in which there were strong women, with whom I could talk because actually the women I found around were not like that.

Will experienced and positioned women through sexist discourses. He despised women for being weaker than him. The effect of the discourses was mysogny. Women were associated with weakness and consequently negatively valued. The following extract shows how these feelings about strength and weakness produce and are re-produced by Will's own contradictory subjectivity. He is responding to a woman who has been saying how she feels uneasy about being powerful with other women.

> *Will:* Yeah but you feel that. Now you see I feel that in spades. If I fight, I fight from the wrong side. So I am constantly feeling like an elephant walking around with lots of eggshells, and I hate people for being eggshells. And I hate myself for being an elephant. I really fight feeling very kind to lots of people. When people were kind to me in that way, I used to lap it up, and hate me for needing it. And them.

Will's discomfort is with his own weakness: needing other people. If he can't accept this in himself, it is no wonder that he cannot accept it in women. In this respect he wanted women to be equally strong. There is a contradiction between this and the effects of splitting which means that he will position women as weaker because of his investment in being strong, the effect of which is to project the unwelcome feelings of weakness. The following extract illustrates this dynamic. Will is continuing the account of their decision whether to have a baby:

> *Will:* We were having a conversation about something which at the moment I've repressed. Oh yes, it was about the small matter of pregnancy and having a child. I can't imagine how I forgot about that. [Laughs] And I was in a sort of reassuring mood. And what she said was she was very worried about it – it was at the end of quite a long conversation – and she'd been saying how she felt and I'd been doing my reassuring bit. It sounds so ludicrous but it wasn't at all. I said, 'In my mind, I'm prepared for every eventuality.' Right, and this was some way of saying, 'If you want an abortion, we'll have an abortion, and if you don't want an abortion, we won't have an abortion.' And she said quite sharply, and nastily, 'You mean we could have the child and then strangle it immediately afterwards!' And I burst into tears, because what her saying that meant was, 'You've been talking in a completely abstract way without any feeling whatsoever.' And that got me out of my reassuring general thing. I'd actually felt all that, yet I'd also felt quite distant. I felt I was the reassuring one, y'know, I was feeling anxious for myself, yes, but she was much more anxious and therefore I had to say we were prepared for every – blah blah. And that sharp remark – it just tore away that sheath over my emotions. That sheath of being in charge of patriarchal reassurance. The point is that if anything makes me feel – and it's incredibly easy for me to feel – that somebody else's

> needs or fears or anxieties are greater than mine I immediately shift into this caring thing.
> *Sarah:* Yeah but, can you stop there a minute? Because do you really feel that theirs is greater than yours?
> *Will:* I don't know whether it's true, I always tend to think that other people's needs to talk or needs to work things out are greater than my own. Because in a sense I have this fantasy of myself as quite strong.

Several important relational dynamics are illustrated in this part of the chapter.

(1) The abstract mode is perfectly exemplified by Will's statement 'In my mind I'm prepared for every eventuality.' One important effect of this abstract mode of talking is that it purports to give people information, but the information it denies the other person is what really matters. It conceals value, importance, desire, the person's commitment to an issue or position. Beverley reflects this problem when she points out that despite the fact that Will says 'I want to have this child' her feeling is 'I don't know whether you want to have this child or not'. The effect of the abstract mode is that the information that comes over is not dependable: it leaves unsaid what is most important. In contrast, when Will burst into tears, Beverley told me that she got more information of the kind that she needed in order to make the decision than from Will's rational statements.

(2) The abstract mode is not simply 'rational' (by implication, desirable). It is invested. The effect of not providing the information that counts is not an arbitrary by-product. It protects Will's vulnerability. Suppression of feelings enables Will to occupy a powerful position of not minding, disguising his strong wishes to have a baby and protecting him from the vulnerability which would follow due to the fact that Beverley might decide against it.

(3) Repressed desires do not go away. The defence mechanisms of introjection and projection – the means through which they are expressed in displaced ways – are interpsychic, that is they are relational. This means that they are dependent on the participation of another. This other represents needs which are opposite, rather than just different. The opposition is a product of the principle that positive and negative value is imbricated in the meanings. What is projected onto another person represents the material which is unacceptable because of contradictions in the one who is doing the projecting. What is repressed is not just material whose repressed status is isolated from subjectivity. Freud maintained that repression was always related to a desire and vice versa, so that there is a principle of opposition. Repression of contradiction is thus a highly

complementary mechanism to the principle of opposition which is fundamental to gender difference. Hence, Will suppresses his feelings because of his vulnerability. They are more likely to be introjected by a woman because discourses have already conferred on her a position of doing the feelings.

(4) The successful completion of the splitting still requires that Will can take up a position of rational reassurance (note that it is gendered: 'patriarchal reassurance'). The extract illustrates how this is made possible by the way he reads himself as stronger through sexist, gender-differentiated discourses. As he himself acknowledges, his deflection from his own feelings is through reading the other person as having greater needs, fears, anxieties than his. The discourse and the mechanism of projection work hand-in-glove: he is uncomfortable with his own needs. They don't go away. Rather he projects them. The moment he feels stronger than the other person, he can't help but shift into 'this caring thing'. His 'fantasy of himself as quite strong' is both the condition and effect of this dynamic: condition because it invests him in that position (already differentially available to him as a man because of sexist discourses); effect because he can project his own weaknesses and thus his feelings of relative strength are reproduced. The continuity of Will's reproduction of his position as stronger requires a historical perspective: it is an investment which is inserted into his subjectivity.

(5) Will's gendered subjectivity is articulated not in isolation but in relation to a woman: he wants her to be equally strong, not least because he can also get support and not take all the responsibility.[19] On the other hand, he ends up positioning himself as stronger because of suppression and projection of the negatively valued character of feelings of vulnerability. It is important to recognize such contradictions because they challenge the smooth reproduction of gender difference.

A complementary production of this contradiction is evident in many women in heterosexual relations who feel that they want a man to be stronger than they are. Consistent with their history of positioning they too reproduce themselves as needing support. Their investment, while not so clear cut as for men, is in getting looked after and being required to take little responsibility.[20] Yet because connotations of weakness and inferiority are carried along with their need for support, it contradicts their feelings of effectiveness and their experience of being strong enough to provide support.

The circle of reproduction of gender difference involves two people whose historical positioning, and the investments and powers this has inserted into subjectivity, complement each other. When there remain contradictions in each person's wants of the other, there is ground for an interruption of its reproduction. These contradictions are the products of social changes. It is through the kinds of social changes that I outlined at the beginning of this chapter that alternative discourses – for example feminist ones – can be produced and used by women in the struggle to redefine our positions in gender-differentiated practices, thus challenging sexist discourses still further. Changes don't automatically eradicate what went before – neither in structure nor in the way that practices, powers and meanings have been produced historically. Consciousness-changing is not accomplished by new discourses replacing old ones. It is accomplished as a result of the contradictions in our positionings, desires and practices – and thus in our subjectivities – which result from the coexistence of the old and the new. Every relation and every practice to some extent articulates such contradictions and therefore is a site of potential change as much as it is a site of reproduction.

Notes

1 Heterosexual relations seemed the most powerful site for the reproduction of gender difference, based as they are on the biological difference which over-determines individuals' positionings, both historically and in present interaction. Couple or sexual relations add the extra dimension of 'desire for the Other' (see Introduction to section 3, pp. 215–16) which I believe makes salient the power relations. In lesbian and homosexual relations too, this desire and power can produce gender-differentiated positionings. While in this chapter, I have not space to discuss this, chapter 8 of my thesis (Hollway, 1982) takes such an example and shows how – even with the variable of biological difference controlled (to use the terminology of psychological experiments) gender difference is produced: difference of positions in gender-differentiated discourses and thus powers and practices associated with them.

2 The same phenomenon occurs with colonized peoples. For example, Gustav Jahoda (1961) quotes Ghanaian blacks generalizing in a derogatory manner about 'blacks', calling them superstitious, lazy, etc., in other words reproducing the racist discourses with which whites position them. Frantz Fanon (1968) addresses the same phenomenon in his analysis of black identity. He was one of the first to emphasize the importance of consciousness for political change and to use psychoanalytic theory alongside a radical political analysis of colonialism, to theorize the contradictions in the identities of black people in colonized countries.

3 Lewis Nkosi illustrates the same principle when talking about his experience of his Africanness in South Africa: 'I know that in my case I first discovered my Africanness the day I learned that I was not only black but non-white. . . . From that day onwards I began to regard this prefix *non* with absolute hostility. Everywhere I went in public places notices shouted at me 'non-whites only' and every time I read the message it vividly brought to mind the crude fact that in the eyes of the world my life represented something negative, something 'non'. In that small prefix put before the word *white* I saw the entire burden

and consequence of European colonialism: its assault on the African personality; the very arrogance of this assumption' (Nkosi, 1983, pp. 44–5).

4 I think this partly accounts for why the vast majority of transsexuals are man to woman.

5 The classic and oft-quoted demonstration of this contradiction is the experiment by Broverman *et al.* (1970). Clinicians judged what was considered 'mentally healthy' for adults, for men and for women. Traits which represented a normally healthy male and a normally healthy adult were highly correlated. Traits characterizing a normally healthy female were significantly different and, predictably, not highly valued.

6 *Forum* magazine's emphasis on technique reflects this focus. The sexual partner is supposedly necessary 'to take part in reciprocal stimulation that will provide the maximum intensity of voluptuous sensations at coming off' (1971). The individualism of this discourse is characteristic of the epoch generally (see Introduction to section 1).

7 The contrast between Jim's and Colin's positions demonstrates that men's positions and thus the meanings of sexual practices, are not determined even for men of similar age and background.

8 By my use of 'subject' and 'object', I mean to emphasize the difference of position which is expressed in the grammatical differentiation between subject and object. In this use, subject is not equivalent to our general use of the term (see Introduction, pp. 2–3). Subjects occupy both positions in discourses, in that sense. Neither is object equivalent to the use made in some feminist theory, as in 'sex-object'. There it tends to imply that the position affords no agency and no power. As my analysis makes clear, I do not hold with this implication.

9 While a fair amount of feminist work has been done concerning girls (McRobbie, 1978; Nava, 1982, Cowie and Lees, 1981) it is difficult to find work on boys which challenges dominant assumptions. However, see Willis (1978) and Wood (1982) for descriptions of working-class boys' relations to girls.

10 This is the first instance of several sexual metaphors used by men in these accounts: getting in deep, letting go (p. 244), soft on (p. 246) and sucked in (p. 250). All refer to the danger of strong positive feelings for a woman and the metaphors all reflect a man's position in heterosexual sex. The unselfconscious use of these metaphors supports my argument that the significations of sex are closely bound up with the contradictions involved in 'desire for the Other'.

11 Martin does not speak of himself directly, but this is typical of his style and the phenomenon of protection that I am illustrating. Generalizing is a way of distancing oneself from the risk associated with what one is saying. As there is no commonly accessible discourse which says what he is expressing here, I am confident that Martin is speaking about his own experience.

12 See note 10.

13 The feelings are likely to be similar whether the person in receipt of them is same or 'opposite' sex. So the choice (compulsion might be a more accurate word) concerning the gender of the loved object is a very important phenomenon to account for. Psychoanalytic theory does provide an account which answers these questions about desire, love and the irrational. However, in its present form, it emphasizes desire as a process at the expense of the meanings it occupies (and thus the social content). Lacan's theorization of the metaphoric

axis sees the chain of signifiers which desire has occupied as contained within the meaning of a word such as 'woman'. This historical chain runs from mother (the first Other) to woman/Other. The positions occupied in discourses in relation to a man – whether occupied by mother or woman – clarify how this historical chain of signification is produced. See pp. 250–1 for an illustration of this claim.

14 This is not to claim that these feelings weren't the woman's as well. It is the fear of them which indicates his own projection. Another person is a suitable vehicle for a projection precisely when they are subject to the same feelings themselves.

15 The account of (heterosexual) women's desire for the Other represents a further theoretical problem: how and to what extent does the girl transfer her desire for the Other from mother, where it is originally located, to father and thence to a man? In the Freudian account, for the girl unconscious meanings (what Lacan would call the metaphoric axis) slip from wanting to 'be' the penis (that is on identification with the father and continuing desire for the mother) to wanting to 'have' it and give the father a gift of a baby. I cannot enter into a detailed critique here. However if we see psychoanalytic theory as itself being subject to defence mechanisms operating in its (predominantly male) authors and reproducing sexist discourses, we can hypothesize that this formulation may be a reversal. The valorization of the penis would be a compensation for the power of the mother/woman to give birth and be reproduced through men's investment in this position in discourse. The process is similar to my analysis of Jim's and Sam's accounts (pp. 245 and 249–50) who accomplished a reversal through projection.

16 For a more detailed consideration of women's contradictory investments and powers in sexist discourses see Hollway (1983).

17 In this context, Jim means that his coping and strength were in response to Jeanette getting upset. Jim equates 'doing the feeling' with getting upset. Clearly there are other feelings like anger which are more associated with men. However, the slippage in Jim's usage is a common one. The question of who 'gives support' in heterosexual couple relationships is a good deal more complicated than this and is traditionally divided into gender-appropriate areas. For example it was clear from the earlier extract from Jim (p. 250) that Jeanette provided a great deal of emotional support for him. Between Beverley and Will, another couple in my research (see pp. 257–8), support was explicitly gender-differentiated: Beverley's was called 'mothering' and Will's 'patriarchal reassurance'.

18 It is particularly clear in Beverley's case that weakness is not a feature of who she 'is'. By this I mean a dynamic and a positioning which she unintentionally re-produces in new relationships and not her 'personality', as psychology might account for it. In a previous relationship she was not so positioned and her experience in this relationship is more recognizable as a relational dynamic: 'I feel like when I'm around you I lose all resolve. I feel completely weak and helpless. I don't know why it happens, why I let it happen.'

19 I have not developed or illustrated this claim here, but see Hollway (1982), chapter 7.

20 This may not be the case in practice, but if the investment has been inserted historically (a history of desire eventually linking back to the mother) it is not simply conditional on a rational view of the outcome. This is one reason why my use of investment in no way slides into a learning-theory explanation.

6

Power relations and the emergence of language

Cathy Urwin

Introduction

It is not unusual for psychologists to use children's development as a testing ground for more general theoretical propositions. One of the most frequent debates focuses on the relative importance of nature versus nurture, inbuilt as opposed to environmental factors, or other versions of this familiar see-saw. Representing a particularly clear example of the individual–social dualism which we have criticized, at the core of this view of development is an implicitly or explicitly assumed unitary subject which knows and exists outside of, or prior to, its entry into the social world. This assumption is particularly evident in the study of language development, where there is a marked if not universal tendency to view language as an object outside the child, its acquisition depending on its interaction with internal cognitive structures and/or pre-existing communication systems. The nature of these, of course, may be more or less specified.

This chapter presents an alternative account of the development of language, one which both decentres language *per se* as the object of investigation, and presupposes a radically different account of subjectivity. It is based on a reworking of Lacan's (1949) account of the formation of subjectivity through the entry into language and on certain ideas critically extracted from Foucault's work. These have been discussed in a preliminary way in the Introduction to this section and elaborated with respect to a particular area in the last chapter. Here, the aim is to show that, on the one hand, redefining the problematic in this way enriches, extends or even overturns the terrain which traditional approaches can cover, making accessible what is usually hidden. At the same time it puts forward a reading of what may go on between parents and children which illuminates the processes involved in the production of human subjects, not as unitary points of origin, but as contradictory, irrational as well as rational, capable of assertion, yet constantly in the play of relations of power.

The first part of this chapter illustrates the ubiquitousness of the assumption of the unitary subject in language development research and how it constrains the questions which can be asked, even in approaches which emphasize the 'social context' of language development and which are politically committed to understanding the implications of cross-cultural and subcultural differences, for example in applications of socio-linguistics within education. It then presents a fuller account of Lacan's view of development, discusses inherent problems and proposes some major modifications. These modifications are taken into the study of parent–child relationships in the final part of the chapter. There, unless otherwise stated, the examples are drawn from my own study of mother–infant and infant–infant communication, currently under way. The study involves twelve infants followed longitudinally through a large part of the first two years. It was preceded by an interview study of forty mothers at home with small children, and I have also included some of this material.[1]

Language development in social context

The implicit dualism in prevailing approaches

The decade following the end of the 1960s saw an explosion in child language research which was quite unprecedented. An analysis of why the utterances of little children should have promoted such interest at this time is beyond the scope of this chapter (but see Urwin, 1984). However we have already indicated some contributing factors, in discussing the relation between radical shifts in psychology and the new liberalism of the period in the Introduction to section 1. It was as the cognitivism of the 1960s began to challenge the hegemony of behaviourism that the theory of language put forward by Chomsky (1957, 1965) caught the imagination of a number of psychologists. Amongst other things, this promised that the study of language could shed light on the quintessentially human, the properties of mind, the familiar terrain of innate ideas (see Slobin, 1971).

In Chomsky's explicitly rationalist, though hypothetical, account of language development it is particularly easy to see both the assumption of the unitary cognate subject and its effects on the questions asked about developmental processes. Here the task of language development was assumed to involve 'testing' innate knowledge of language structure against a relatively garbled or unstructured 'input' through a 'language acquisition device'. Despite its sophistication, this theoretical construct, with neurological correlates in the child's brain, has all the essential properties of a homunculus. Following Chomsky's emphasis on the priority of grammatical structure, the account produced a whole generation of research which concentrated almost exclusively on writing grammars of children's utterances in order to plot the emergence of syntactic structures. These were presumed to emerge in an ordered sequence of developmental stages. There was little or no room in the account for communicative or interpersonal functions of language, or for variability; variations could occur in rate of development, but not in route.

Chomsky's theory of transformational grammar is now less influential on child language research than it was. Nevertheless an explicit or implicit dualism is retained in all subsequent approaches. So, too, is the tendency to produce universalized, and normalized, accounts. For instance, the emphasis on syntax was followed by a shift in focus onto semantics (see, for example, Schlesinger, 1971; Slobin, 1973), and the idea that children's grasp of meaning relations provided the key to their acquisition of language structure. Now the task became one of grafting aspects of the speech 'input' onto pre-established cognitive schemes, such as the particular concepts which Piaget proposes are established by the end of the second year, as in Brown's (1973) influential formulation. It was also now recognized that the ways in which adults actually speak to young children may be a good deal more 'helpful' than in Chomsky's hypothetical account (see, for example, Snow and Ferguson's collection of studies of mothers' speech to children (1977)). None the less, the direction of development is still determined by properties of children's minds and, like Chomsky's account, it focuses attention on producing a sequence of universals.

Now any account which prioritizes the content of children's minds in this way puts necessary constraints on how the development of language may be conceived. For instance, there is a logical barrier to theorizing the contribution of language to the development of thinking, rationality or 'consciousness', subjects of perennial debate within psychology, if cognitive processes are already pregiven as determining processes, or relied on implicitly. Similarly, if the account privileges a universal sequence, then a study of the significance of, say, cross-cultural class or gender differences will tend to reduce to comparisons of positions on a hypothetical norm. Obviously, too, an account which hangs development on an inbuilt capacity for rationality, or which privileges logic over and above other forms of thinking, is incompatible with an attempt to explicate what we have argued for in previous chapters: irrationality, or contradiction as experienced by individuals, and the possible role of language in this. It is of course true that Piaget includes both affective and social processes in his account (see, for example, Piaget and Inhelder, 1969). But as Ingleby (1980a) points out, the relation is entirely functional. Affectivity provides the 'energetics', and social interaction can speed up the developmental process. But they do not enter into the structuring of cognition itself. In consequence affect and emotion by-pass cognition, preserving the ubiquitous split which we have criticized, and, to all intents and purposes, specific content is omitted.

Given Chomsky's explicit rationalism and Piaget's allegiance to a particular biological tradition, discussed in chapter 4, it is hardly surprising that, from our point of view, a major problem with these accounts is that they give little or no room for questions of social formation. It is perhaps more surprising that very similar constraints emerge in sociolinguistics and in recent work in parent–child communication. Indeed sociolinguistics initially flourished through its opposition to formal linguistics, in reaction to the inability of Chomsky's account to deal with what were being felt in the 1960s and 1970s as pressing social issues, the under-achievement of working-class children and the problem of integrating children from different racial backgrounds into mainstream education (see, for example, Hymes, 1974; Labov, 1970; Rosen, 1972 and 1977). Much of this work has been invaluable, particularly in challenging crude notions of 'verbal deprivation' as an explanation for school failure. But this sociolinguistic tradition is none the less constrained by the fact that, like Chomsky's theory, it retains de Saussure's (1974) distinction between *langue* and *parole*; or a universal and fundamental 'competence' plus an additional component which accounts for or encompasses variaability, 'performance' in Chomsky's theory. As suggested in chapter 3, situating the work historically, de Saussure's universal competence is rooted in the notion of a unitary subject and a common core rationality, which can be viewed as independent of specific social processes. In consequence, by drawing on the same tradition, the sociolinguistic work aimed at opposing Chomsky's framework at best complements it and recreates the same dualism and fundamental problems. For instance, if a fundamental core competence or rationality is built into the account, then it is difficult, if not impossible, to see variations in language use as having anything but superficial implications for thought processes, since the core itself is left untouched. (For further discussions of the problems with this sociolinguistic tradition and the 'equal but different' political position which has promoted it, see Adlam and Salfield, 1980; Urwin, 1984).

Though not dissimilar, the problems in parent–child communication research come from other sources. Beginning in the early 1970s in reaction to Chomsky's exclusive preoccupation with the structure of language as opposed to its use, this work stresses that language is, first and foremost, a social process, and that its development is rooted in children's relationships with other people. Not surprisingly, this tradition's relation to formal linguistics is far less comfortable than sociolinguistics' and the theoretical frameworks are diverse. For example, some approaches have focused on the development of conversational skills, such as 'turn taking' and adjusting the form and content of utterances to the listener's requirements (see, for example, the collections edited by Ervin-Tripp and Mitchell Kernan, 1977, and Ochs and Schieffelin, 1979). Many studies have been markedly influenced by ideas drawn from the philosophy of language and the speech-act theories of Austin (1962) and Searle (1969) in particular. Here the emphasis is on the speaker's intentions to bring about specific effects in the listener, such as getting something done through making a request, and on the conventions through which communicative intention is regulated. (See, for example, Bates, Camioni and Volterra, 1975; Bruner, 1975 and 1978; Dore, 1975 and 1978.) Another, though less dominant, line of approach comes through the functionalist tradition in linguistics, epitomized in the work of Halliday (1975).

One of the most interesting aspects of this work is that, through various theoretical routes, it has now provided fairly convincing evidence for some kind of continuity between the ways in which babies may communicate before they begin to speak, through non-verbal vocalization and gesture, for example, and their first communications with words. For instance, with or without distinguishing intonational patterns, gestures of demand or indicative pointing may persist as accompaniments to children's first single-word utterances, and it is these communicative procedures which enable them to communicate differentially whether they want a particular object or are merely drawing the other person's attention towards it. It has been argued that early communicative functions such as these are prototypical of later language functions or speech-acts, such as 'requesting', 'declaring' or 'referring' (Bates *et al.*, 1975; Bruner, 1975).

This work challenges the assumption that language emerges *sui generis*, independent of other communicative and developmental process, as Chomsky's position implied, and raises the possibility that developmental studies could shed light on relations between language and human action in general. By focusing on the emergence of language, it foregrounds the possible significance of children's first relationships. There are obvious problems, of course, in moving beyond the identification of a functional similarity between the single-word utterances of 1 year olds and the grammaticalized utterances of adults to proving a developmental continuity. But, more immediately, what accounts for the emergence of these quasi-ritualized communicative procedures in the first place?

Despite an emphasis on language as a 'social' process, there has been a rapid shift in focus onto the individual, with a consequent limitation in the questions which can be asked. For example, the predominant explanations are either maturational (Carter, 1974), hence implying predetermination in accordance with properties of individual physiological structure, or they envoke underlying cognitive capacities, such as Piagetian sensorimotor schemata. Thus Bates and her colleagues argue that such diverse communicative means as 'reaching in demand', 'indicative pointing' and 'offering objects', all depend on infants' reaching a particular developmental stage in Piaget's account of means–end relationships (Bates *et al.*, 1975). Again the separation between affect and cognition in Piaget's theory by-passes the question of what actually motivates children's communications; and the universalist paradigm, through which a variety of communicative procedures gets reduced to the same underlying cognitive structure, renders the study of systematic differences in development inaccessible within the account.

Nevertheless, the existence of differences which may be related to different types of qualities of social relationships is indicated by other studies. One of the most influential of these is that of Nelson (1973), who distinguished between children whose first words are predominantly about objects and those whose speech is dominated by social words and phrases, or a 'referential' versus 'expressive' orientation. Though the distinction is an oversimplification and there are conceptual and methodological problems with the study itself (see, for example, McShane, 1980), similar kinds of differences in bias or style have been described in other studies, for instance by Dore (1975). Both Dore and Nelson conjecture that these differences reflect differing characteristics of parent–child interaction established prior to the emergence of speech itself. As interesting, given the tendency towards simple determinist models of causation within psychology, Nelson also describes cases of 'mismatch' between what she calls children's language-acquisition 'strategies' and the strategies used predominantly by their parents, 'mismatch' being associated with relatively slow progress in language development. But neither she nor Dore probes how the more usual congruence comes about, and the emotional implications of 'mismatch' between children and their parents are left unexplored. It is true that some researchers have recognized that emotionality plays a crucial role in language development, and that studying individual differences should illuminate more general processes (Lieven, 1980). But thus far this has not moved much beyond the assertion that there are many routes to the same end, again retaining the notion of language as a universal object.

Part of the problem with the above studies is that, despite the emphasis on communication, they have concentrated exclusively on children's communicative repertoires. On the other hand, the approaches of Bruner (1975 and 1978) and Lock (1978 and 1980) give more attention to the contribution of the people with whom the children interact, in a way which could, in principle, contribute to our understanding of how differences are produced. Immediately or indirectly influenced by the work of Mead and Vygotsky and by Shotter's (1974a and b and 1978) humanistic psychology, discussed in the Introduction to section 1, these investigators emphasize the significance of early negotiations and shared activities and the part played by adults in consistently interpreting their children's behaviour. This process is taken to enable the children to discover the meaning of their behaviour (Lock, 1978; Shotter, 1974b), and to provide a 'scaffold' for mastering the execution of socially appropriate action (Bruner, 1975).

This line of approach appears to provide the beginnings of an account of the social formation of communicative intention and specific action procedures, and to root children's entry into language in interactional processes. It clearly moves several steps nearer to viewing language as a social process and I will be using some of the descriptions generated by these empirical studies later, though reading them differently. However, theoretically the approach is constrained by its adherence to the work of Mead and Vygotsky. As we have discussed in the Introduction to section 1, each of these accounts is overly deterministic and leaves the infant's contribution as an empty space. As Ingleby (1980b) points out, there is no room for tension in mother–child relationships in this account, or for the possibility of conflict or contradiction. It would be unable to explain the kinds of 'mismatches' described by Nelson, for example. By leaving the infant's contribution unspecified, the position rapidly falls back onto the assumption of an originatory individual subject. It is perhaps for this reason that these investigators have been unable to encompass the question of cognitive change within the same account, recreating the perennial split between social interaction and something inherent in the child. For example, the problem of the contribution of cognitive development to language is regarded as part of a separate endeavour (Bruner, 1978; Lock, 1980), or one which has yet to be solved (Newson, personal communication). Alternatively uneasy references to Piagetian schemes are tagged on afterwards (Bruner, Roy and Ratner, 1979). And since looking at the preverbal period has not solved the problem of where language structure comes from, it is simple to reinvoke Chomsky's theory to account for this as the residual (Dore, 1978). Ironically, this work is back where it started; communication is added to predetermined language structure.

Apart from these problems, much of this preverbal communciation work must be criticized for what Denise Riley (1978a) describes as a 'desert-islanded' view of mother–child relationships, which pre-empts any examination of material conditions, ideology and questions of power. As the social has collapsed into first the interpersonal and then the individual, and videotapes of mother–infant dyads are analysed for turn-taking skills, attention-monitoring devices, interpretative responses and scaffolding strategies, it is as if, Riley suggests, mother and babies have been watched at their communicatings in a bell-jar. Taking Riley's criticisms further, one might add that this work is itself contributing to a normalization of what mother–child interaction consists of, and a new orthodoxy in what constitutes the role of the mother. It is my impression that this is already having effects within the practice of health visitors, for example, as mentioned in the Introduction to section 1 (see also Bradley, 1983).

In that social class is forefronted and questions of ideology are opened, one approach to language which is strikingly different from those I have disussed so far is Bernstein's (1971) account of Elaborated and Restricted codes. Not only does his emphasis appear to break away from the universalist tradition within sociolinguistics, but he also presents arguments for why, historically and contemporaneously, middle-class and working-class cultures might privilege one mode of language usage over another, and offers an explanation for variations in parental style. These he sees in terms of control systems operating at the familial level. Thus the approach appears to articulate a relationship between language development, parent–child relationships, and wider sociopolitical systems. However, the account is overly deterministic, constrained both by its functionalist view of social class, provided by orthodox sociology (see, for example, Sinha, 1977), and by a view of language–thought relationships, derived from the work of Whorf (1956) and Vygotsky (1962). As discussed here and in the Introduction to section 1, these approaches which involve the 'outside' getting 'inside' via language fix individuals over-deterministically, at the same time leaving open an empty space, to be filled by default with the unitary, rational subject.

Some of these problems re-emerge in the functionalist account of Halliday (1975), who explicitly acknowledges his debt to Bernstein, in producing what is perhaps the 'most social' of current approaches to the emergence of language. In contrast to the studies which take speech-act theory and the individual child as starting points, Halliday aims to locate his account firmly and squarely in the social world. For example, in discussing how we are to understand the significance of particular language functions which a child may discover, he argues:

> If, for example, language is used from an early stage to regulate the behaviour of others . . . this assumes some general framework of social structure and social processes in terms of which a function such as 'regulatory' would make sense. More particularly . . . it presupposes a concept of cultural transmission within which the role of language in the transmission process may be highlighted and defined. Here the concept of meaning, and of learning to mean, is in the last analysis interpreted in sociological terms, in the context of some chain of dependence such as: social order – transmission of the social order to the child – role of language in the transmission

> process – functions of language in relation to this role – meanings derived from these functions. (Halliday, 1975, p. 5)

However, this assumption remains at the level of an assertion. In taking the social order as given and by invoking the concept of 'transmission' Halliday, in fact, by-passes the question of *how* the social domain is reproduced at the level of the speech of the individual child. Of course he resists a simple determination from the culture downwards. Instead he concentrates on charting the appearance of particular language functions in his son's preverbal and early verbal expressions. We are left with a picture of the impulsion to language coming entirely from within the child, and as such we are back with the assumption of a pregiven individual subject.

Redefining the problematic

A serious consideration of what children contribute to the emergence of language which does not involve having to posit a homunculus will need both a different view of human subjectivity and a way of articulating its relation to language as it is manifested in particular social practices through which children grow up. I have already indicated areas where traditional approaches not only leave problems unanswered but render them inaccessible, such as the contribution of affective relations to language development and the political significance of differences. By implication then, a new approach must include within the same account both affectivity and the production of differences in a way which neither trivializes them nor inevitably reduces them to variations on a common theme.

Before putting forward the beginnings of an approach which is addressed to these issues, it is useful to consider two further examples of problem areas which the conceptual schemes available within contemporary developmental research cannot deal with satisfactorily. Again, the question of affectivity and the significance of differences are central.

First, as mentioned in chapter 4, there is now a large body of work which demonstrates the powerful effects of context on how children reason (for example, Donaldson, 1978), and on the language which they produce. The 'neglected situation' (Goffmann, 1964), for instance, or in this case the context of the classroom, was one of the main criticisms mounted against work used to support crude notions of 'verbal deprivation' in the late 1960s and early 1970s, a controversy which I briefly mentioned earlier (p. 267). Indeed, the most convincing attack on this concept came through Labov's (1970) demonstration that using a black rather than a white interviewer, or promoting a relaxed atmosphere, would produce a very different reading of a black child's linguistic ability from what would be obtained through standard testing. Similarly Cole (1978) and his colleagues have demonstrated that children are much more verbally expansive with peers in the school playground than they are with teachers in the classroom, and Tizard has again argued for the importance of 'contextual factors' in discussing the fact that middle-class and working-class nursery school children may produce very different language in the school setting, whereas measurements of productive language in the home indicate relatively few differences (Tizard, Hughes, Pinkerton and Carmichael, 1982).

But nothing has been explained by asserting the importance of context. First, a theory of context is not part of any theory of language acquisition thus far proposed. The appeal is based merely on demonstrating covariations between settings and performances. Of course, the researchers can speculate that there is something about the settings, or the way that language is used in these settings, which affect children from particular groups differentially. But these speculations fall outside the scope of the theoretical frameworks actually used. Second, the appeal to context not only fails to explain; it also conceals. As Walkerdine (1981a) points out, this kind of account puts the context outside the child, who is viewed as a point of origin which interacts with or is affected by external factors. As a consequence the relation between the situation and the process of production is left out of the account. So, too, is the child's motivation or power to speak.

Similar issues are raised by the relationship between language and gender. There is now a large body of work, both historical and contemporaneous, which argues that certain modes of speaking or forms of language are 'man made' (Spender 1980) and that women face particular difficulties in speaking in public, or in 'finding a voice' more generally. This argument proposes a relation between the power of men within particular institutionalized sites, and specific forms of language used to maintain and regulate it. (See, for example, Bassnett and Hoskin, 1982; Spender, 1980; Selby, in preparation; Steedman, Urwin and Walkerdine, 1984.) There is a tendency for much of this work to confuse the issue of whether it is the 'language' which is gendered, again treating it as an object, or something about its conditions of production which can affect men and women differentially. Nevertheless, given the considerable weight of opinion, it is extremely surprising that work on language development in children has produced relatively little evidence for this kind of relationship between gender and the acquisition process. Indeed the differences that have been demonstrated tend to go in the opposite direction, as many girls are initially more 'advanced' in language development than boys, the differences tending to 'disappear' as the children get older (Maccoby and Jacklin, 1975).

One explanation, of course, is that there are no differences of the sort described in the so-called acquisition period; they emerge in adulthood or adolescence. But it is as likely that no differences have been found because existing frameworks do not tell us how and where to look. That is the significance of gender for the process of production in relation to specific situations would need to be theorized within the same account.

A delightful example suggesting a very early relationship between the significance of gender within social relationships and the language children produce in specific situations is given by Ervin-Tripp (1977) in another context. This obliges us to consider the importance of the child's social–emotional relationships and the power relations operating within and on the family. In an analysis of request forms and 'politeness' rules in young children, Ervin-Tripp cites Lawson's (1967) study of a 2 year old who was 'duped' into producing quite different language with her mother as compared to her father. In a deliberate test, this child's milk glass was set at her place, empty, next to a bottle of milk. Normally her milk was poured before she arrived. To her mother she simply demanded: 'Mommy, I want milk.' When her father only was present, she was more ingratiating, or as Ervin-Tripp puts it, the child 'beat about the bush'.

> 'What's that?' 'Milk.'
> 'My milk, Daddy.' 'Yes, it's your milk.'
> 'Daddy yours. Yours Daddy?' 'OK yours. OK it's mine.'
> 'It's milk Daddy.' 'Yes it is.'
> 'You want milk Daddy?' 'I have some thank you.'
> 'Milk in there Daddy?' 'Yes.'
> 'Daddy, I want some please? Please Daddy, milk?'
> (after Ervin-Tripp, 1977, p. 184)

Ervin Tripp discusses this as evidence of young children's sophistication in reading social situations on the basis of expectations, and their sensitivity to the listener's requirements. The importance of this child's expectations is not in doubt. But what this account leaves out is the crucial question of this child's relationships with her mother and father; the how and the why behind her deferential behaviour towards the latter, and the opposite tendency shown to her mother. Does the example not also suggest that there may be a relationship between this child's developing gender identity and the different positions she takes up in language, in relation to her mother and father? In the one case she assumes, or fights for, control over her mother; in the other case, her desire to please her father, to cater for *his* wants, perhaps, seems to undercut her demanding for herself. Is it not also possible, then, that in learning to manage interpersonal situations in accordance with what is allowed or expected, the production of language may itself enter into the production of culturally prescribed and proscribed aspects of masculinity and femininity?

This question presupposes a new view of the relation between language development, situations and expectation and individual children's identities viewed neither as unitary points of origin, nor simply determined by the context outside. I have already indicated the need to cut across the usual individual–context distinction in order to encompass the process of production and the power to speak. The example also forces us to consider the production and nature of this little girl's desires. It is both because it challenges the unitary subject of traditional psychology, and because it gives motivations and tensions a central role in the development of language, that, of theoretical schemes currently available, the work of Lacan holds most promise.

The promise of Lacan

As we have discussed in the Introduction to this section, what is potentially useful about Lacan's account is that his problematization of what psychology usually takes for granted enables us to shift the axis through which we pose our questions. To recapitulate, Lacan continually asserts that the 'I' of the cogito, or the unitary rational subject, is illusory and forever unattainable. Instead his account prioritizes the 'symbolic order', or an order of signs and meanings which pre-exists the infant's birth and through which he or she must pass in order to become an effective member of the community. According to Lacan it is only through entering into the symbolic order as a speaking subject that full consciousness, or autonomy over the immediacy of current events, is possible at all. And, in consequence, for Lacan language acquisition is the central process whereby conscious subjectivity is produced, to be continually reproduced every time we use language, whether as adults or children.

From this perspective, examining the processes involved in language development is vital to the theorization of subjectivity. In emphasizing that language is essential to both cultural regulation and the production of consciousness, Lacan's account is at first sight remarkably similar to Mead's. This similarity is not accidental since both theorists were at various times strongly influenced by the phenomenologists and the philosophy of Husserl in particular. However Lacan's account differs from Mead's in crucial respects. First, though Mead's 'mind' is socially produced (see Introduction to section 1, pp. 16–18), it becomes relatively autonomous and self-determining. Lacan, on the other hand, emphasizes that, though we may have a sense of our own identity and feel that we are the source from which our thoughts emanate, these experiences are far from constant and cannot necessarily be captured at will; we continually struggle to find a continuity to our being. Second, this different view of ourselves is in part due to Lacan's account being psychoanalytic, hence following Freud's view that we are only partly rational, and to the distinction between conscious and unconscious mental processes. Third, this contributes to differing views of developmental processes. As we have discussed, Mead's account of the social formation of the self involves taking on board or internalizing social descriptions of the self, the mechanisms responsible for this being largely unspecified. In following Freud, not only does Lacan provide an account of motivation but, as we shall see, processes of identification rather than internalization move to the forefront.

Lacan's account of development

Lacan's account of the period before the emergence of language itself follows Freud's theory of psychosexual development extremely closely. However he has modified it crucially through the addition of the 'mirror stage' (Lacan, 1949). This is inserted into Freud's (1914b) account of narcissism, which asserts that a period of self-love precedes object-love and the resolution of the Oedipus Complex. For Lacan it is conceptually necessary in order to account for how the process of identification and the splitting of the subject begins. Like Freud, Lacan assumes that immediately after birth the infant is unable to distinguish between things associated with his or her own body and the external world, and that a predominant sensation is one of fragmentation. For Lacan a critical change in this state occurs at around 6 months with the onset of the 'mirror stage', as the infant catches sight of and identifies with a 'mirror' image of a complete unified body. Here Lacan uses Charlotte Buhler's (1930) observations of children's behaviour in front of a mirror to illustrate how, at this age, they will joyously perform to their images which capture their every movement. Marking the infant's first conscious recognition of a distinction between his or her own body and the outside world, this experience provides the infant with a first glimpse of wholeness or unity, and the identification serves as a point of purchase for all future identifications.

But this identification is nevertheless based on an illusion, or a misrecognition, since the infant is not yet capable of distinguishing between the form he or she identifies with and the self. Moreover, it is essentially alienating, since the infant is in fact subordinated to the image, as controlled by it as he or she is capable of controlling it. Nevertheless, the mirror phase is vital for introducing the child into what Lacan calls the order of 'imaginary relations', and for precipitating structural changes in the mother–child relationship, putting the infant in a position to experience separation from the mother in a new way. Though based on an ideal, the mirror episode gives the child an imaginary experience of what it must be like to be whole, and to be in control of his or her own body and needs – able to control their satisfaction. Simultaneously, it provides a primitive experience of the self as an object. Following Freud, the mother is regarded as being the primary source of satisfaction in Lacan's account, and in consequence the infant is now in a position to both want the mother, to control her and hence satisfaction, and to want to be what the mother wants. Though at this stage the relation is a narcissistic one, it is here, in the mirror stage, that the process of establishing desire for the Other, discussed in the Introduction to this section, begins. Hence Lacan asserts that desire for the Other is ultimately rooted in desire for the Mother (a connection illustrated in the previous chapter, pp. 250–1).

It is in the mirror phase that the child begins to acquire language, as he or she attempts to come to terms with the experience of the presence and absence of satisfaction. Both the absence of satisfaction itself and fear of loss of the source of satisfaction create anxiety in the child. Like Freud, Lacan sees the attempt to master this anxiety, and ultimately to control desire, as the impetus behind the acquisition and use of language. This shift into language is epitomized in the *Fort-da* game, an example given by Freud (1920) which involved an 18-month-old boy child who was apparently finding it difficult to cope with repeated separations from his mother. According to Freud, these problems were resolved as the child invented or utilized a game with a cotton-reel, a game which symbolized his control over the mother's appearance and disappearance. Holding a thread attached to the reel, the child would throw it away crying *Fort*, (the German for 'gone'), drawing it back crying *Da* ('there'). This example of Freud's has been extremely influential in child analysis, providing the basis of the idea that play is a crucial medium through which we can gain access to children's unconscious mental processes, and children themselves can master anxiety. However, Lacan's interpretation adds another dimension. For Lacan, in this moment captured by the game, the infant is 'raising his desire to a second power' as he struggles to find a new position in relation to it. This movement is achieved through two operations. First, the infant, through the use of the cotton-reel, symbolically annihilates the mother and controls her return; second, through his alternating use of the linguistic contrast (*Fort*, *Da*) to accompany the disappearance and reappearance of the reel, he marks his own control over the experience. In this process the child transforms his relation to the object of his desire, and to himself at the same time (Lacan, 1953).

The cotton-reel game illustrates how language allows the child some detachment from immediate sensation and the pain of separation, providing a relative increase in autonomy. But at first children's use of language is still bounded by the imaginary identifications of the mirror stage. This is illustrated by young children's tendency to confuse the pronouns 'I', 'you', and 'she' or 'he', or to refer to themselves by their own names, as they reproduce the language which their parents use to talk about them, and from which they are still excluded. For Lacan, it is only through the resolution of the Oedipus Complex, when children resolve problems associated with desire for the mother or father by identifying with the same-sexed parent, that they are able to communicate within the same terms of reference as adults, and hence on a more equal footing. In

Lacan's account this resolution simultaneously enables children to take alternative positions, implied by the appropriate use of personal pronouns, and to become aware of themselves as distinct entities. In consequence, for Lacan, the I–you dialectic is the cornerstone of conscious subjectivity, providing a point of purchase from which ordered thought can progress.

Thus it is through the entry into language that the child is constituted as a subject, able to take an independent place within the family and wider community. But despite the gains in autonomy and relative authority, as the child steps into the position from which to speak and think, the entry into language has not been achieved without a struggle, or without cost. First, because of the essentially narcissistic nature of the preverbal child's relation to the mother, her symbolic annihilation in the cotton-reel game has also marked an annihilation of part of the self which must be renounced in order to achieve independence or status as a separate subject. Furthermore the game did not, in fact, produce control over the mother's presence and absence. For these reasons Lacan stresses that the infant's attempt to come to terms with the mother's absence creates an ever-open gap in psychic structure, or a fundamental splitting or discontinuity in being. Since desire is constructed retrospectively around this, it is essentially unfulfillable, to be constantly replayed in human language. Ironically, too, in entering into language, the child's own thought is now inevitably regulated through cultural laws. As Lacan (1953) puts it with respect to the male child attempting to master Oedipal relations, the child's desire for the mother has already become the desire of another – the father – with whom he is now in competition by virtue of having entered into the same terms of reference.

Some problems with Lacan's account

Now there are many problems with Lacan's account, and we have already argued that, for our purposes, we cannot take it over as it stands. First, the inbuilt phallocentricism and universalism is incompatible with theorizing the production of subjectivity in a way which accounts not only for how the processes may occur under existing patriarchal social relations, but would also allow that things could be otherwise. As we have discussed, despite the shift of emphasis onto signification as opposed to biological differences between men and women, and the production of subjectivity in accordance with cultural laws, the phallus as the sign of difference remains, for Lacan, the 'signifier of signifieds'; and, following Lévi-Strauss's emphasis, universals of culture are taken as inevitables. This produces a simple deterministic reductionism, so that any discussion of the possibilities of change has to operate outside the terms of reference of the account itself.

Second, to these inbuilt inevitabilities in Lacan's account as grounds for pessimism, one might also add that many people are put off by his constant emphasis on 'gaps' and unfulfillable desires. Lacan (1953) himself has criticized ego-psychology, a branch of psychoanalysis which flourished in America between the wars, for its emphasis on self-determination and the rational powers of the individual. This, he says, is a misreading of Freud's emphasis, which represents the 'American dilemma', or the preoccupation of Americans during this phase in the development of American capitalism. But one might equally well point out that Lacan's emphasis on narcissism and its counterpart, paranoia, also depends on an accentuation of one aspect of Freud's theory, and that Lacan's account emerged in the wake of French existentialism. It is from this tradition that Lacan takes his emphasis on the fundamental lack of being in the subject, which hence should be situated historically.

For us the attraction of Lacan's work is the theorization of subjectivity as non-unitary, rather than the emphasis on the unfulfillability of desire. Nevertheless, we have argued in the Introduction to section 3 that our aim is not to avoid the problem of desire, or its possible unfulfillability. Moreover, any attempt to use psychoanalysis as a starting-point must, I feel, accept as basic the inevitability of pain. But it is also true that some wishes *are* fulfilled, that we do achieve 'satisfaction', are capable of change and, under certain circumstances, demonstrate considerable powers of assertion. How does this fit within Lacan's account?

A third problem with Lacan's account, which we have briefly mentioned in the Introduction to section 3, is the precise sense in which the unconscious, produced through entering the symbolic order as a speaking subject, is 'structured like a language'. The implication that the unconscious is therefore to be comprehended entirely through the rules of spoken discourse has been questioned (see, for example, Thom 1981). From our point of view, this raises additional problems in that Lacan's account relies heavily on tenets drawn from structural linguistics.

Finally, as far as the entry into language and development in infancy is concerned, it is important to recognize that a psychoanalytic account cannot be immediately translated into empirical predictions, and possibly not even into directly observable phenomena. Nevertheless the fact that Lacan leaves the initial 'recognition' in the mirror episode unexplained leaves us wondering if there is not, after all, a concealed point of origin.

Some preliminary solutions

Solutions to some of these problems have already been suggested, here or in related articles. First, in the Introduction to this section, we have proposed that, instead of prioritizing the symbolic order with its universalist and timeless implications, we might prioritize instead the discursive order or particular discourses, viewed in their historical specificity. Following the post-structuralist emphasis on the production of modern subject forms through social apparatuses, here we are focusing on the ways in which language is implicated in the production of particular regimes of truth, associated with the regulation of specific social practices – such as the practices of the home, the family, the school, the hospital, the world of science, and so on. Implicit in this viewpoint is the claim that the production of particular discourses is associated with the production of particular forms of rationality, 'scientific thinking', for example. But here our emphasis departs from the post-structural tradition. As we have argued, if we wish to explain how the discursive enters into the production and reproduction of particular ways of thinking on the part of individuals without invoking a simple determinism (see Introduction to section 3 and chapter 5), the account must include an analysis of subjectivity; one which recognizes both subjective continuity and contradiction, and what we have described as the 'investments' associated with particular subject positions within particular discourses (see chapter 5).

Chapter 5's analysis of adult relationships has shown that Lacan's account of the non-unitary, non-rational subject can be retained to this purpose, in spite of shifting the emphasis onto discursive relations as opposed to a pregiven symbolic order. With respect to children's development, the possibilities have been illustrated by Walkerdine and Corran (1979) in their analysis of children learning mathematics in school. In contrast to most psychological approaches to this problem, which tend to follow Piaget in viewing the task as one which requires children to graft mathematical notions onto previously established, action-based concepts, such that the specific social experiences are excluded, Walkerdine and her colleagues emphasize that children are required to enter into a new signifying practice which produces rather than translates relations of meaning. The mathematical discourse is, of course, at first remote to young children, and here they have broadened Lacan's notion of 'metaphor' to refer to the ways in which a teacher will make new signifying relations accessible by setting them in relation to some other frame of reference in which children are already able to take up the position of subject. Notions of number, for example, are introduced through encouraging the children to pretend to do the shopping. Secondly, the teacher uses the written test itself to focus the children's attention on the 'metonymic' axis, or on the relations which operate between the numerical signs themselves. Here Walkerdine (1982b) argues that the actual production of written signs, in which metaphoric connections are now suppressed, provides a productive 'distancing', eventually enabling the child to reflect on and reproduce mathematical rules. In the process, a new subjective position is produced, and with it a new form of rationality.

More recently Walden and Walkerdine (1981), in a study of girls' relative under-achievement in mathematics, have used the notion of identification in exploring why it is that, contrary to popular myth, many girls are extremely 'good' at mathematics in the primary school period compared to boys, a notion which points towards the origins of particular investments and their reproduction. They propose that in primary school the successful girls are aided both by the particular frames of reference used to set up mathematical notions, such as playing shops, and by their willingness to identify with, or help out, the teacher, who is generally female and often insecure about her own relation to mathematics. At this time there appears to be no contradiction between being 'good' at mathematics and being female. By adolescence, it appears, other aspects of the cultural construction of femininity are exerting their pull (see for example, Brewster, 1980).

Walden and Walkerdine's study illustrates the complex relationship between gender and rationality, which cannot be considered as fixed once and for all through some single determining process. Like Walkerdine and Corran's work, it differs markedly from approaches offered by traditional psychology, in that, by prioritizing the workings of signifying practices and the positioning of subjects in relation to them, the approach cuts across the usual dichotomies between 'language' and 'thought', 'social' and 'cognitive', or the 'child within' and the 'context' outside, illustrated in the first part of this chapter.

But a shift in emphasis onto the discursive order does not resolve all the problems, as becomes particularly clear in dealing with prelinguistic children. In working with school-aged children in a school setting, Walkerdine and her colleagues were able to use a particular discourse, mathematics in this case, as the axis of their account, using the fact that these children were already using language as a basis for exploring links to other discursive practices. While we do not wish to claim that, because they do not speak, babies exist outside discursive relations, the question of how to use the notion of discourses in analysing their development is far from clear. Furthermore, we still have to account for the transitional processes through which infants' subjectivity is constituted in the first place.

This raises the question of the applicability of Lacan's account of the mirror stage. A major attraction of this account is that it suggests a formulation of the problematic of language development which allows affectivity and emotionality to enter into the acquisition process, rather than running alongside it, or outside the account altogether, as in the approaches discussed in the first part of this chapter. But again, we cannot rely totally on the explanatory mechanisms offered by Lacan. Apart from the idealism which I have suggested can be read into the account, both because he relies on Freud's theory of psychosexual development and because the resolution of the Oedipus Complex is the key developmental moment through which conscious subjectivity is produced, gender is built in as an irreducible determinant. In consequence we face the same implications of inevitability as before.

What is needed, then, is an orientation which retains Lacan's emphasis on the non-unitary nature of subjectivity and its relation to emotional processes, which avoids an idealist collapse and which allows the significance of gender to be investigated without viewing it deterministically. We also need to show how, in principle, relations between the discursive order, infants' development and the particular positions young children first take up as speaking subjects can be articulated.

Modifying Lacan's account of the mirror stage

I suggest that the necessary modifications may be achieved in two stages, each having several implications for what might be examined empirically and theoretically. First, instead of prioritizing the symbolic order or even the discursive as such, I propose to prioritize the social practices which occur frequently and regularly in particular infants' lives, such as feeding, bathing and other care-taking operations, greetings and farewells, certain forms of regularized play and games and so on. To those familiar with child-language research, this prioritization may appear similar to Bruner's (1975) focus on 'formats', or forms of interaction which occur regularly and thus provide optimum conditions for mutual expectations to become established and intentions negotiated. It may also appear similar to the notion of 'scrips' (Schank and Abelson, 1977) which Nelson (1980) has taken from artificial intelligence work in attempting to develop a socially based account of representation underlying language, and even to Mead's emphasis on regularized action, an emphasis which has, of course, itself influenced each of these approaches.

However, the emphasis I intend is different from all three orientations. Whereas Bruner and Nelson emphasize these events because they occur frequently and relatively predictably in the infant's life, here they are additionally emphasized because they are bounded by adult sanctions or constraints, or systems of belief about how things ought to be. Moreover, these systems of belief are not fixed, static nor orchestrated from above. They are productive, and as such bear a particular relation to truth. It is at this juncture that a relation between regularized action and discourses regulating that action is produced.

Consider, for example, 'table setting' or 'nappy changing'. Neither of these are discourses as such; they are social practices. But there may well be a good deal prescribed or written about both of them, in books on etiquette or child-care, for example. Here, the coherence between the actions regulating the social practices of table setting or nappy changing and the production of discourses about these practices depends on their being regulated through the same regime of truth, in accordance with the same law. That is, they are produced through power–knowledge relations.

From this perspective, the task for the child is not one which involves mapping language onto cognition or action, or even representations of action, however 'socially based', as in Nelson's account. Nor does it involve internalizing, in any simple sense, the social prescriptions of others. Rather, it requires that the child enters into this productive relationship through taking up a position from which the course of action and language can be appropriately conducted and ordered. This positioning is achieved in the first instance through identifying with some Other, such as a particular mother, from whom the source of meaning and regularity apparently comes. Imagine, for example, 2-year-old children who in pretend play 'set the table', insistently announcing 'need spoons', 'need forks', 'want beans' and so on. From the present perspective these children are not rehearsing the event, nor simply expressing or 'representing' their knowledge of the social practice, as some psychological accounts of pretend play would argue. Nor are they simply mastering some previous, emotionally significant event. Rather, by taking up subjective positions, which were previously occupied by significant adults, in fantasy they are actually controlling the regularities of the event and producing its truth themselves.

But would we now wish to say that these children are taking up subject positions within a particular discourse? In this example, changes in the children's use of language and their ability to take up positions of control within a particular regulated activity occurred simultaneously, a co-occurrence which is very frequent, if not general, in development. Yet although these children are using language, at this point it is still bounded by the particular social practice rather than being produced with reference to systems of knowledges or discourses about the practices themselves. This step, I suggest, requires a level of reflection on and through language which these children have yet to reach. For this reason I shall use the term *discursive frame of reference* to refer to the intermediary ground between social practices and discourses in which young children are able to take up subjective positions.

Using regulated social practices as a focus cuts across the individual context distinction, as in Walkerdine and her colleagues' analysis. In principle it would allow us to examine how particular discourses, such as those through which child-care or home-management are regulated, enter into the production of subjectivity via parent–child relationships. One could consider, for example, how the mother was positioned through those discourses which contribute to defining and regulating motherhood which we referred to in the Introduction to section 3, and the implications of the reproduction of this positioning through the child's identifications.

But how are we to characterize the development of children's participation within these practices, and what of the production of subjectivity itself?

Here a second modification in Lacan's account is needed. Processes of identification remain crucial, as we have seen. So, too, does the emphasis on the production of subjectivity and the unconscious through signifying relations, though these are now interpreted more broadly (see the Introduction to section 3, p. 220). But the modification is already implicit in the shift from the symbolic to the discursive order, and follows from our emphasizing, after Foucault, that power–knowledge relations are integral to the production and reproduction of discourses. If, as we have argued, an adequate account of the functioning of the discursive must include an account of subjectivity, then taking up a subjective position also marks a relation of power with respect to the particular discourse in operation.

Now there is ample evidence suggesting that, consciously or unconsciously, young children make use of power relations very early. For example, in the studies of language and context discussed on p. 267 the differential effects of black as opposed to white interviewers, the home setting as opposed to the school, or the peer group as opposed to teachers as interlocutors, all imply an intimate link between power relations and the language children produce in particular situations. But how are we to understand that link? We have rejected as too simple and overly deterministic the position which sees power as a property or force imposed from above, in the hands of individual teachers, for example, onto children as blank slates. We have argued that power is not a property of individuals *per se*, but a relation, and that its directionality depends both on the particular discourse in operation and the positioning of individuals within that discourse (see Introduction to section 2, pp. 116–18).

A particularly vivid example, which illustrates both that individuals are not positioned, once and for all, as powerful or powerless, and that their relative power depends on the discourse through which their behaviour is read, is given by Walkerdine (1981a). She describes how a group of small boys reduced their teacher, who one assumes would have normally held a powerful position in relation to them, to a state of near helplessness by producing a slow, repetitive chant based on explicit references to 'cunts', 'wee wees' and 'bums'. On the basis of an interview with the teacher afterwards, Walkerdine suggests that the teacher's relative powerlessness was due to the fact that, in accordance with her training, she read their behaviour through the child-centred discourse (discussed in chapter 4), which stresses that young children's 'natural' aggression and interest in sexuality should not be repressed. As Walkerdine points out, if she had been in a position to read the behaviour as sexist, for example, she might have coped with the situation rather differently.

But power relations are not confined to children's interactions with adults. For instance, Walkerdine (1982b) has also illustrated how, in play with their peers, nursery school children may themselves switch the discursive frame of reference, and in doing so turn the situation to their advantage. For example, she describes how a little boy's attempts to manage the proceedings were firmly thwarted by a little girl's turning the game into a domestic situation. Here, in the position of the mother and manager of the home, she could put the little boy, as dependent husband or young child, firmly in his place.

There are uncanny similarities between the discourse switching and repositionings produced by nursery school children and the conscious and unconscious repositionings and splittings produced by the adults described in chapter 5. There, relations of power were shown to be implicated in both the particular discourses called into play – discourses which themselves have different implications for men and women – and in the ways in which individuals were positioned within them. Like the little boy in the above example, a man could be positioned as dominant or dependent, for example. In chapter 5, too, a number of examples suggested that the management of power relations, or the search for a point of assertion, authority or security and so forth, was inextricably related to the workings of desire, though the relation was not one of simple determination.

Taken together, these examples imply that power relations interpenetrate the production and reproduction of subjectivity throughout children's development. The examples from adults also suggest a developmental relation between power and desire. This possibility was also raised in discussing the example cited by Ervin-Tripp, on pp. 274–5. Lacan's account, of course, focuses on the production and workings of desire. But if it could be modified to emphasize power relations, then the resolution of the Oedipus Complex would lose its centrality as the necessary determinant of human subjectivity. At the same time we would be free to investigate the significance of gender as one amongst many possible sites for the reproduction of power.

Though presupposing a different starting point, in my view an articulation of the relation between power and the production of subjectivity is already implicit in Lacan's account of the mirror phase. Returning to it again, it becomes apparent that there are in fact several functions served by the mirror. First, it provides a point outside the self through which the self is recognized. Second, it provides the infant with his or her first experience of corporeal unity, albeit an illusory one. This stands as an ideal of some future developmental state, contributing to the third function; the introduction of the infant to an order of imaginary relations. Mediated by the mirror image, or the 'imago', this is born from the split between a glimpse of perfect unity and the infant's actual state of fragility and non-integration. But at the same time the mirror also substantiates the infant as a locus of control, both affecting changes in the self and in the outside world. In Lacan's account both the perfection of this control and the imagined unity support and pre-empt the infant's narcissism and sense of omnipotence.

The convenience of the mirror metaphor for serving all these functions is clear. But conflating them within a single moment as Lacan has done, in order to make what is, in his account, a structural distinction, also conflates several possible readings of their relative centrality. For Lacan it is the ideal of corporeal unity which is prioritized. I propose to prise open Lacan's conflation by, first, replacing the somewhat solipsistic child described by Lacan with a child in relations with others who are themselves positioned through power–knowledge relations, and secondly, shifting axis of the account to emphasize the mirror's function in providing the infant with an illusion of perfect control. It is this focus which will allow development in infancy and the emergence of language to be read in terms of relations of power.

I have already argued, by discussing the development of congenitally blind infants, that we do not take the 'mirror' in Lacan's account literally, and that Lacan's preoccupation with visual imagery is as unnecessary as it is constraining (Urwin, 1982b). There I argued that we can regard functions of the mirror as being, in part, served by significant adults in the child's life, as they carry out various caretaking operations, respond to signs of distress by providing comfort or reassurance, or to the child's smiles by smiling in kind, and so on, within social practices which may become increasingly regularized. In particular one might include what recent developmental studies describe as characteristic ways in which adults 'adjust' their behaviour, expectations and demands to their babies' capabilities, behavioural repertoires and what has already been established between them. Particularly striking amongst these 'adjustments' are the use of exaggerated grimaces, mock gestures, and high-pitched speech, all of which appear to be particularly attention-getting to very young infants, and result in behaviour which is paradoxically very like the infants' own (see, for example, Bruner, 1975; Stern, 1974; Sachs, 1977; Sylvester-Bradley and Trevarthen, 1978; Trevarthen, 1975). While I shall take this caring and communicative behaviour as functioning like a mirror for babies, this is not simply because there is often a behavioural correspondence. Rather, through drawing attention to a relation between the babies' actions and those outside themselves, it produces their sense of control and simultaneously provides a point external to themselves from which their powers as effective originators of communication can be recognized.

Later I shall illustrate how, by emphasizing the relations which it produces and how it may articulate with the positioning of the parents, this mirroring can be read without implying a concealed point of origin. But for Lacan the mere reflection of the infant in the mirror is not the total process; there must be a disjunction which introduces the child into the order of imaginary relations and eventually into language. In Lacan's account, this disjunction is produced through the gap between the image ideal and the infant's actual state of fragmentation and dependence, the disjunction itself having consequences for his or her relationship with the mother. Here I will emphasize the illusory nature of the infant's control, in the sense that in actuality the recognition of his or her communicative efforts depends on adult interpretation and willingness to respond and to make concessions to the infant's relative immaturity. I shall argue that the recognition of *this* disjunction by infants is a crucial motive force, first in initiating changes in their relations with significant adults, and second in precipitating them into language. Eventually this takes place through identification, as they attempt to resolve the imbalance of power which results from their dependence on adults for the completion of their communications. Three major consequences follow from this. First, since these communications are already socially produced through the mirroring function, *preverbal* communication enters into the production of unconscious processes, a view not articulated by Lacan. Second, in principle an analysis of the subjective positioning of the parents is part of the same account. Third, the emergence of language is from the outset constituted through relations of power; these enter into the emotional investments underlying the child's positionings in particular discursive frames of references, and the structuring of subjectivity itself.

Summary

In this part of the chapter I have proposed two major modifications to Lacan's account of the mirror stage. The first involves emphasizing specific social practices which become relatively regularized in a particular infant's life. The second involves reorienting the axis of Lacan's account to emphasize power relations. Though presented here in a general way, this analysis should be taken as applying to specific processes and practices through which particular infants are precipitated into language and are simultaneously produced as subjects.

Neither of these modifications undercuts the stress on emotionality and the role of unconscious processes fundamental to the psychoanalytic tradition. We are left with a view of language development in which the child no longer contributes from a unitary point of origin, nor is the production of language simply determined by the context outside him or her. At the same time, language *per se* has lost its centrality as the object to be acquired. By recasting the terms of reference, many of the gaps or questions left unanswered by the current approaches to language development, discussed in the first part of the chapter, now become accessible. For example, just as for older children, Walkerdine and her colleagues' emphasis on the positioning of subjects with respect to particular discourses provides a way of cutting across the usual cognitive–social distinction, here the focus on regularized social activities and changes in infants' relative powers of assertion within them provides a basis for integrating social and cognitive development within the language-acquisition process. Since their emotional relationships now play a constitutive role, this transformation affords us a handle on motivational aspects of children's communications. And because the approach hinges on relations between subjectivity, language and power with respect to particular social practices, it points directly at the psychological concomitants of speech/silence. Finally, by focusing on what particular practices are at issue for particular children, and on variations in how their powers of assertion and identification are produced or promoted within them, it can be extended to encompass the production of differences, such as those described by Nelson (1973), or those related to gender or class. At the same time, linking the ways in which the parents contribute to their infants' development through what I have loosely called the 'mirror' function to their own positioning in the discussive order, suggests a way of breaking from the typical 'desert islanded' view of parent–child relationships characteristic of most studies of mother–infant interactions, as discussed in the first part of the chapter (pp. 270–1).

In principle, an analysis focusing on particular discursive practices, power relations and subjective positioning can be developed for looking at the language produced by children of any age, for instance, to shed light on the relation between the language of home and school. In the next part of this chapter, however, I shall concentrate on making tangible the modified account of the mirror stage itself. I will illustrate the kind of view of development it presents and the questions which it raises comparing and constrasting it with what is offered by some of the existing theoretical frameworks used to approach infant development, such as those of Lock (1980), Bruner (1975 and 1978) and Piaget (1951, 1953 and 1955). For reasons of space, I shall concentrate on the preverbal period and the initial entry into language, roughly comparable to the emergence of the *Fort-da* game in Lacan's account, presenting the account in very general terms. However, I shall give some indication of possible sites for the production of differences, and illustrate how one might consider what underlies the parents' investment in relating to their baby, and the implications of particular discourses which position them and regulate their actions. I shall begin with a brief discussion of how to circumvent the idealism implicit in Lacan's account of the mirror stage, in a way which at the same time takes account of the neurological equipment of newborn babies.

The mirror phase and the illusion of control

The status of young infants' 'abilities'

Earlier I suggested that the idealism implicit in Lacan's account is due to his leaving out what might explain the initial recognition in the mirror. But it is not, of course, true that he makes no assumptions about what happens in development before this. As I have mentioned, Lacan holds to the traditional psychoanalytic view that the infant's state at birth is fragmented, unintegrated, or fused with the surroundings, a view held by most psychologists until comparatively recently. Piaget's theory, for example, proposes a fundamental 'adualism' or lack of differentiation between the self and the outside world (see for example, Piaget and Inhelder, 1969). His account takes as its starting-point the exercise of simple reflexes, such as grasping, sucking and looking. Through 'interaction' with the environment these reflexes gradually become co-ordinated, looking with grasping, for example, to form more complex schemata which underlie a new developmental stage. Recently, however, the assumption of an initial state of 'adualism' or 'fragmentation' has been challenged by fairly convincing evidence that newborn infants are far more sophisticated or organized than these assumptions imply (see, for example, Bower 1974; Trevarthen, 1975). This includes evidence for an inbuilt co-ordination between different sensorimotor systems, thus apparently contradicting Piaget's assumptions. Newborn infants will turn their heads to a source of sound, for example, (Wertheimer, 1961), and very young infants will reach out for and grasp objects which they have not touched previously (Bower, Broughton and Moore, 1970), an activity which would seem to be quite impossible if there was no differentiation between the infant and the 'outside world'.

Such evidence must be taken seriously in theorizing the starting-point within the present account. However, since it is almost invariably discussed in terms of particular 'capacities', 'competences', 'abilities' or 'knowledge' inherent *in* the child, it rapidly reduces once again to the assumption of an inbuilt subjectivity as point of origin. Here I shall accept that the behaviour produced in the studies used to support these claims actually occurs, but at the same time indicate an alternative reading which cuts across these rationalistic assumptions. First, in line with our arguments concerning the production of scientific knowledge developed in section 2, I shall point to particular circumstances through which the evidence has been produced. Second, rather than hypothesizing pregiven constructs in the child's head, I shall concentrate on relations between the infant's body and actions and aspects of the animate and inanimate environment, and on the processes of signification which mediate them. From this perspective, what develops or changes is always situated in a relational patterning rather than in a construct, schema or hypothesis in the child's head, and development itself becomes definable in relational terms.

Such a framework can be developed for looking at all aspects of so-called infant competence, including the examples mentioned above which are usually discussed in terms of cognitive functioning. Here, however, I shall concentrate on evidence which is particularly important to the present perspective. This is the work, discussed briefly in the Introduction to section 1, which proposed that very young infants respond differently to 'people' and 'things' (Richards, 1974c; Trevarthen, 1975), or are particularly sensitive to the properties of other people, and that they show early evidence of 'intentions' to communicate (Trevarthen, 1975 and 1977). Particularly intriguing and theoretically crucial is evidence which demonstrates that 2-week-old infants can 'match' or imitate another person's movements, such as sticking out the tongue, even if this involves moving parts of their bodies which they cannot perceive directly (Meltzoff, 1976).

This work challenges psychoanalytic theory both because it implies an early distinction between 'self' and 'other' and because, as Ingleby (1980b) has rightly pointed out, no psychoanalytic account has seriously reckoned with the implications of the mediation of preverbal communication between mother and infant. It also mounts a powerful challenge to Piaget because his theory aims to account for the infant's knowledge of people through the same processes as knowledge of objects, the same principles of action and interaction, for example. This is one reason why social interaction does not enter into the contents of cognitive structure in Piaget's account, as mentioned in the first part of this chapter. Of course, similar principles or processes must be involved in establishing both kinds of knowledge, in so far as people are a special class of material objects, and objects gain meaning within social relations. But Piaget's position masks the implications of the fact that there are also inescapable differences between people and things, which imply different kind of relations, and different consequences for development. These include the fact that people can adapt to a baby in a way that objects cannot. They can enable a baby to establish particular expectations, for instance, which they may then break themselves, as is particularly evident in playful teasing. Moreover, in so far as other people have body parts which are similar to the baby's, they can respond in a way which approximates the baby's own actions. Third, at their own initiative other people can provide comfort, food and security in times of distress, and they, too, have anxieties, fears and wishes which distinguish them from inanimate objects. Fourth, particularly important to the present account and implicated in all the above, in so far as other people are already positioned within the culture, their interactions with the baby are always mediated through a grid of signification.

The pertinence of the latter claim, and the importance of the processes which Piaget's account conceals, will be illustrated later. But to assert that there are differences between people and things does not explain the implication of these for development. Nor does the fact that confronting the infant with an inanimate object as opposed to an animated person (Trevarthen, 1975) will, under certain circumstances, engender different kinds of behaviour in the infant, support any claims about what the baby 'knows'. As far as very young infants' apparent 'protosociability' is concerned, the evidence used to support this assumption includes the demonstration of specific movements of the mouth and gesture-like movements of the limbs – dubbed 'prespeech' by Trevarthen (1975) – produced by 2-month-old infants in highly intense, playful interactions with their mothers, and other signs of animation and excitement in the other's company, which seem to indicate that the infants are courting their mothers' attention and attempting to assert some control over them (see, for example, Stern, 1974). But again, there has been a rapid slippage from the demonstration of this, admittedly very appealing, behaviour to the claim that it indicates that an intersubjective process is inbuilt, or that infants have innate knowledge of other people, or particular predispositions which facilitate their becoming social (see, for example, Richards, 1974c; Trevarthen, 1975).

This reading, of course, ultimately or immediately collapses into the notion that subjectivity itself is pregiven. This conclusion is not given 'directly' in the behaviour. Rather, it already presupposes particular rationalistic assumptions, which have entered into the production of the evidence used to support it. Here, for example, we might point to the particular conjunction of events through which psychologists become preoccupied with the quintessentially human at the beginning of the 1970s, as discussed in the Introduction to section 1. It is within this conjuncture that producing any differences between infants' behaviour with people as against things attained such enormous significance. We might also indicate, as Bradley (1983) and Riley (1978a) have done, the particular historical and political circumstances through which so many resources have been focused on mothers' interactions with their tiny babies, and the view of the mother's role which this research presumes and perpetuates. We might point, too, to the highly selective nature of the material which has been used to support such strong claims about 'human nature'. Most of this data, if not all, comes from laboratory studies in which mothers have been specially recruited and asked to 'chat to' or 'play with' their babies. We do not know when and how often the ways of relating described in the early social interaction studies occur under more usual circumstances.

But taking the infant studies as they stand, the problem now is how to read the behaviour without explicitly or implicitly assuming pregiven subjectivity. Rather than beginning by hypothesizing abilities in the infant, this may be achieved by focusing on relations between the infant and aspects of the environment, which in this case includes the mother, as they are manifested in the particular circumstances of the experiment. By defining what is being observed and produced in relational terms, we can still contend with infants' neurological sophistication, but in a way which does not involve a collapse into idealism. We may acknowledge, for example, the obvious fact that the neurological equipment of infants is similar to that of adults in crucial respects; this is part of what is meant by being in the same species, and contributes the material constraints on development. We may also allow that the neurological equipment of very young infants enables them to produce and adduce regularities in their relationships with aspects of the inanimate environment where they are apparently particularly sensitive to the breaking of expectations (see, for example, Papousek, 1969). But it also allows them to establish correspondences and produce relationships between their actions, affects and moods and those of other people. This is partly suggested by the early imitation experiments of Meltzoff, cited on p. 290. But in so far as the processes of action, expectation and correspondence are now by definition relational ones, and hence do not function independently of specific circumstances, we no longer have to presume that infants are born with knowledge of other people which they then apply to the world outside.

Looking again now at the social-interaction studies in this light, the descriptions produced by these studies make it clear that the promotion of the infant's engaging behaviour and appealing range of expressions depends crucially on subtleties in phasing, timing and action on the part of the mother, and that range of 'adjustments' which I referred to earlier (p. 288) (Newson, 1977; Schaffer, 1977; Trevarthen, 1975 and 1977). We may now recognize that 'protosociability' is not a property of the infant; it is a relation produced through the mother's support, which itself is produced through her positioning within the situation.

Later, in line with the modified account of the mirror stage presented previously, I shall provide a more precise account of these relations which involves reading parent–infant interaction in terms of power relations, and the infant's participation in terms of what may loosely be called his or her relational positioning and relative powers of assertion as these change over time and from one situation to another.

However, before describing the kinds of processes which mediate changes in the infant's positioning en route to language, it is important to ask: what holds the mother's attention to the baby, besides, in this case, the obvious constraints of the laboratory? Particularly interesting from the present perspective, the kinds of 'adjustments' required of the mother to produce the infant's sociability seem to indicate 'mirroring' *par excellence*.

I have already drawn attention to the fact that her behaviour as she supports the infant may include exaggerated grimaces and 'gestures' like the baby's own, high-pitched speech, baby-talk which 'matches' the baby's mood, as well as a marked tendency to imitate (Pawlby, 1977). But it would be misleading to view the mother as simply copying or following the baby as a mechanical object. Analyses of mothers' baby-talk in these situations, for example, show that, although they may be oriented to the babies' facial expressions, the enterprise is more about trying to work out what their babies may be wanting, feeling, needing, than a reflection of what they know automatically. Consistent with this, it is apparently characteristic of mothers to produce a high proportion of questions in their speech to very young infants, whether this is recorded in the home or in the laboratory. These are questions of the sort, 'Are you tired?' 'Is that nice?' 'Who's smiling at me?' 'Who's beautiful?' and 'Don't you like me?' (Snow, 1977b; Sylvester-Bradley and Trevarthen, 1978).

A mother's baby-talk, then, is both selective and productive of meaning. It may tell us more about what she reads into the baby, hopes to find out, needs to know, or feels about her own situation than it does about the baby's actual mood, and what she says will often indicate how particular discourses help to define the nature of her responsibility as caregiver. As Walkerdine (1982b) has illustrated, the process of responding to a baby's cry, for instance, cannot be understood as a simple automatic triggering of the mother's response to the baby's need. Her decisions are regulated through culturally based assumptions, professional dogma and received wisdoms, all of which have a productive effect on child-rearing itself.

But although a mother's interaction with her baby is always mediated through signification, it is, of course, also a highly emotional process. And given that her questions cannot be answered, one wonders: to whom are they directed?

Here Lacan's account of the mirror stage potentially offers an analysis of parenting which in many ways complements the analysis of infant development.[2] Although the parents' own subjectivity has, of course, been produced through entering culture as a language user, Lacan also proposes that the kind of imaginary identificatory processes operating for infants in the mirror stage, when the baby identifies with an ideal image, are never entirely lost. This process, I suggest, is reactivated in adults relating to babies. Mediated through imaginary relations, in which there is an interchangeability of positions, or in Lacan's terms, a lack of differentiation between the image ideal and the self, these interactions call into play that position and imagined perfection which has been partially suppressed in moving to adulthood. From the present perspective, to this we may add that these playful interactions also provide the adult with occasions for playing with power and control, producing the baby as all powerful one minute, and perhaps undercutting this the next, through breaking the baby's expectations, for example. In some instances the interactions may be highly erotic or sexualized. Here one would anticipate that the sex of parent and infant would produce differences, though not altogether predictable ones. The mother, for example, may conjure in fantasy the potential lover who controls or entices her, or project herself as the passive recipient of the desires of another, or as active and potent, a positioning which may not be available elsewhere. As for the baby in the mirror stage, these kinds of interactions act as a support to the adult's own narcissism. This is one of the reasons why relating to babies can be so pleasurable.

Power and positioning through the first six months

Given the preponderance of mirroring by adults and the apparent control shown by very young infants themselves in the videotape studies it seems tempting to ask: is this Lacan's mirror stage beginning at a younger age than he proposed? Here it is important to stress that I am not intending a normative 'stage' account, and age *per se* is of relatively little significance. Rather, I shall describe a series of shifts in the infant's relation to familiar adults through certain distinctions which indicate changes in the baby's relative positioning and powers of assertion within particularly regulated social practices. However, in general terms changes do occur over time, distinguishing younger babies from older babies. Here it is convenient to compare the performances of infants in the early social interaction studies which I have just described with what one is likely to observe a few months later, to clarify how I am using the relational notions of power and positioning.

In the heightened play exchanges between mothers and 2 month olds I suggest that, in spite of the infants' apparent precocity, it is their mothers who create conditions for their manifest powers of assertion in these circumstances, through their phasing, timing and preparedness to make concessions to the babies' developmental level. Directly related to this, there are corresponding limitations in the infants' relational positioning. This is supported first, and most obviously, by the fact that the positions of mother and baby are not interchangeable. The interaction sequences cannot run in both directions, for example; this would be indicated by infants following, supporting or imitating their mothers. Though there is evidence that imitation can occur in 2 week olds, in actuality it is very rarely produced under usual circumstances and is difficult to elicit in very young infants, even though they may be highly engaged when someone imitates them (Trevarthen, 1975). As yet, then, these infants have a limited model of other people, and of how their bodies work, and of the differences as well as the similarities between themselves and others.

Second, the descriptions of these interactions show that infants may repeat action patterns consecutively in order to reproduce pleasurable effects produced through the adult's responses. It is this goal-directedness which has been used as an argument for 'infant intentionality' (Trevarthen, 1977). But there are no indications that these actions stand for their effects, or that particular action procedures have any persistence for the baby over time or across different situations. That is, they have yet to acquire a significatory value for him or her. Third, the breaking of expectations may produce considerable distress in a very young infant, when the relation between his or her actions and the adult's is disrupted or transformed in some way, by using videotape to desynchronize the mother's contribution, for example (Murray, 1980). But there is no indication that the infant's distress is based on recognition of some agreement having been broken. Rather, the experiments suggest that the infant's distress may be a reaction to the loss of anticipated pleasure or control in the here and now.

But by six months or thereabouts, changes will have generally occurred along all these dimensions; so, too, will changes in infants' motoricity. For example, many babies will be sitting upright by this age, which will change their relation to the environment, which itself will contribute to changes in body image generally. More particularly, infants may now show evidence of utilizing the significance of particular action procedures, which mediate or stand for goal-directed activity and its effects. These will have some relative stability over time, though this is still limited to the particular situation which produced them.

This phenomenon may occur in both object play and interpersonal interaction, where there are implications for the relative control shown by the infant in relation to the adult, thus marking a shift in both relative power and relational positioning. For object play, Piaget (1953) provides numerous examples of the phenomenon in discussing what he calls 'secondary circular reactions' or the 'use of procedures to make interesting sights last'. For instance, he describes his own daughter Jacqueline somewhat superstitiously pulling the strings of her bassinet in the vain attempt to reactivate a variety of objects which were, in fact, held by her father some way away from her (1953, Observation 113, p. 202). In interpersonal situations the phenomenon is seen particularly in the way infants begin to exploit the signalling properties of crying, as a call for attention (e.g. Bates *et al.*, 1975), and in the emergence of social games or rituals. These may be more or less idiosyncratic to any particular adult–child pair, often evolving in care-taking situations. In the following example, Thomas controls his mother's participation through the use of a procedure produced within the situation. In signalling the specific effects the baby anticipates, it also specifies what, in particular, is required of the adult by way of response; it is this that marks a change in the baby's relative power of assertion.

1 Thomas. 0.5.1 [five months, one week]. *Home observation*

Thomas quietened fairly quickly on his mother's lap and started to laugh when she began to play a game with him. She lifted him up and jiggled him from side to side. He squealed with delight. She put him on her lap and lifted him up again. Again he squealed. After a few times Thomas started to squeal in a forced fashion, with a deliberateness which I had not seen before. His mother used this squeal as the signal to lift him up again, so that he was 'controlling' the game.

In these highly affective situations one is likely to see infants showing more inclination to imitate adults, indicating a shift towards interchangeable positions, as parents themselves produce behaviour which is relatively well established in their infants' repertoires. This is again illustrated in an example from Thomas, a few weeks later.

2 Thomas. 0.6.2. *Home observation*

Thomas, who had just learned to sit upright, slipped sideways. His mother propped him up. He coughed and spluttered. 'Oh what a cough you've got', his mother said, and imitated him. He laughed and forced out his cough again. The sequence was repeated, mother and baby imitating each other.

For Piaget, these phenomena, in which the procedure represents part of the original action, mark the beginnings of voluntary control; the child is now experimenting with acting on objects and/or controlling events, though, in Piaget's terms, the ritual quality of the action procedure indicates that the baby's knowledge still remains centred in the self. Clearly these infants are now experimenting with what objects and people can be made to do. But in Piaget's account, all the examples are subsumed under the same explanation and are discussed in the same terms as 'secondary circular reactions'. This inevitably conceals crucial differences between babies in relations with other people as opposed to inanimate objects. In the examples of Thomas, while the production of the procedure in the first instance involved the mother's seeing the baby's behaviour as significant, its subsequent effectivity depended on the fact that she was prepared to concede control to the baby; in one sense she was disguising her own relative power by putting herself at the baby's disposal. There are also interesting similarities or points of comparison between the two examples which are concealed by Piaget's account. It is interesting, for example, to compare the position of the mother in the first example with the position which Piaget was taking in relation to his little daughter as he attempted to observe her 'objectively'.

Here I propose that the distinctions which the first example of

Thomas illustrates bring the infant to a position which, within the revised account, is directly comparable to the onset of Lacan's mirror stage. Like the mirror in Lacan's account, interaction sequences such as these, in which communicative procedures specify the actions required of the other, provide the baby with the illusion of perfect control. However, there are crucial shifts in emphasis. First, while the mirror image in Lacan's account provides a 'point' outside the self from which the 'self' is recognized, the mirror image serving as a mediating link here, not only is the shift defined in relational terms, but the mediation is provided by a communicative procedure. This has itself been socially produced through adult concessions, that is, through a relation of power. Second, Lacan's account emphasizes the disjunction between the ideal of wholeness and unity and the infant's actual state of uncoordination and physical immaturity. Here, what is significant is the gap between the infant's apparent control and the fact that his or her power of assertion is still heavily dependent on the adult to produce it; it is in this sense that the 'perfect control' is illusory. Finally, while Lacan's mirror stage introduces a distinction between an asocial imaginary and a reality whose nature is not specified (see Introduction to section 2, pp. 108–14, for discussion of the problem of defining the 'real'), here it is the production of a specific communicative procedure, such as Thomas's deliberate coughing, which distances the infant from the particular situation which produced it. In this disjunction we are already seeing the contribution of power relations to the formation of unconscious processes. But just as in Lacan's account the onset of the mirror stage changes emotional aspects of the child's relation to the mother, here the production of the disjunction and the introduction of the illusion of perfect control changes the infant's position in relation to the mother, and his or her own use of power. This sets preverbal communication on a new plane.

The emergence of ritualized procedures and communicative intention

In very general terms the products of this shift may be seen particularly clearly over the last quarter of the first year, as infants' use of quasi-conventionalized communicative procedures for specifying what is required of the other gets off the ground. For example, from the preverbal communication studies discussed in the first part of the chapter, they may begin to take more active control in actually initiating social games, to use gestures such as indicative pointing and reaching-in-demand, to show and offer objects, and to deliberately court adult attention by repetitively playing give-and-take games (Bates *et al.*, 1975).

Infants, of course, vary in how early or extensively they engage in this kind of behaviour, even amongst the rather narrow range of home backgrounds from which children studied intensively are usually drawn. They also vary in the particular procedures which they employ, procedures which are often highly idiosyncratic. Though it is limited, there is sufficient evidence to suggest that this specificity is due to the fact that these communicative procedures originate in forms of interaction which occur particularly frequently and regularly in the infant's life, persisting for long enough to ensure their consolidation.

However, sheer familiarity is unlikely to produce a sufficient explanation. We need to account not only for why particular procedures are produced and consolidated, but also for the infant's emotional investment in using them. Apart from the fact that the social practices described in these studies, such as care-taking, games and greetings, would seem likely to produce highly affective situations, it has been argued that adults themselves play a far more specific role in the developmental process (for example, Bruner, 1975; Lock, 1978; Newson, 1978; and Shotter, 1978). As discussed in the first part of this chapter and in the Introduction to section 1, this work has been directly or indirectly influenced by G. H. Mead. Consistent with this, much has been made of mothers 'interpreting' their babies' actions as if they signalled specific intentions or carried a particular meaning as an explanation for related changes in the babies' communications. From the present perspective it is clear that the significance of babies' actions for their particular parents is crucial. But by itself interpretation carries no magical properties. First, as we have argued, posing the problem in terms of meaning outside getting inside by-passes the issue of the infant's contribution. Second, from the present perspective one would anticipate that adults would normally show more inconsistency, ambivalence, or contradiction than these studies seem to presume. For example, competing demands on the mother, her conscious and unconscious desires, will affect her subjective positioning and hence the particular discourse through which she reads the baby's behaviour at any one time.

Nevertheless, given that there are regularities which become significant to infants, it is possible to interpret descriptions generated by some of these studies in terms of power relations and changes in the infants' positioning. In particular, one might consider Bruner and his colleagues' studies of social games, joint action on objects, and picture-book reading, and some of my own observations on blind children, all of which present examples extending from the middle of the first year well into the second (Bruner, 1975; Ninio and Bruner, 1978; Bruner, Roy and Ratner, 1979; and Urwin, 1978). What is illuminating about these studies is that they suggest how, within these regularized social activities, changes in the child's relative positioning relate to changes in the adult's contribution.

Within particular regulated activities, these studies describe how, as in the example of Thomas, the adult's early relation to the infant provides the groundwork for the mirror function, through producing the infant's assertive power, which he or she perceives through the adult's reactions. This is achieved, initially, by the adult following and capturing the infant's attention, by her imitating the infant, and/or by her showing signs of pleasure or heightened affectivity in her own demeanour. The ways in which the adult marks correspondences between her actions and the child's own and the concessionary nature of the process is easiest to perceive in social games like 'pat-a-cake' or 'round and round the garden'. Here, as I suggested earlier, part of the pleasure for the mother is that she, too, plays with the illusion of control. This is particularly evident in teasing. But similar principles operate in situations in which objects are involved, such as spoon-feeding or book-reading. Here links to discourses which position and regulate the mother are more apparent. Of course the mother's presentation of the object and the task is geared initially to the kind of actions the infant is currently able to perform. But it is at the same time based on her conceiving a potential relation between what the infant is doing and how these actions eventually ought to be performed. What particular practices become regularized, in accordance with what regimes of truth, is an obvious source of variability contributing to differences produced between infants. But differences may also be produced according to the mother's own subjective positioning. For example, in one case the mother may persist in doing things for the infant because of her own investment in being a caregiver, or in the infant's dependence on her. This positioning is not simply a result of her own past history, but may be produced or reproduced as a partial resolution to current conflicts and contradictions, for example the lack of opportunities for assertion in other social practices such as paid work. In other cases, the mother may, consciously or unconsciously, foster the infant's initiative in conducting the situation.

Consider, for instance, a family in which intellectual activity is enjoyed and highly valued. In such a case the mother's attempts to support her small baby's 'book reading' may initially appear wish-fulfilling in the extreme. Bruner's data, for example, are rife with instances in which enthusiastic comments on the baby's interest and achievement give way to such statements as 'Oh, you're eating it! Poor book!' On the other hand, in such a case the baby may fairly rapidly respond to the mother's pleasure produced in response to the baby's initial interest. This affective marking on the adult's part both links the baby's relation to the inanimate object with his or her relation to the mother and enters into the production of the baby's assertion. Initially, of course, it is the mother who creates conditions which regulate book-reading as an ordered activity; through her presentation of the book, her comments on what the baby attends to and her enthusiasm and praise, she provides a framework through which the baby learns what 'reading a book together' is all about, and what responses from the mother are to be anticipated. By the time that the baby is eagerly pointing to the pictures and looking up in expectation of a confirmation, such as 'Yes, that's the duck, isn't it?', this predictability and the mother's emotional investment have produced in the baby the illusion that he or she is the source of this activity, as the one who is in control.

Here we see how the emotional investment underpinning the positioning of the mother in relation to particular discursive practices, in this case those concerned with academic achievement, may begin to be reproduced in the child. But at this point the baby's position is inherently unstable. Rapidly the baby's illusory control is undercut by changes in the mother's reading of the situation. The descriptive studies suggest that, whether in situations involving games or social performances or more task-oriented activities like book-reading, adults themselves begin to make more demands on their babies, asserting their own authority and social appropriateness in response to relatively clear-cut communicative initiatives on the babies' part, and to evidence that they now know more about the regularities of the event. The mother may insist that the baby wait, or she will wait herself until the baby has produced a clear communicative action, anticipating 'please'. Or she may flout the baby's expectations, or introduce conflict, by breaking the procedural regularity herself. Alternatively she may take advantage of the fact that the baby is getting the point of the exercise, and is matching his or her increasing assertion by showing more inclination to imitate an adult model, by demonstrating what the baby is supposed to do, marking the correspondence between the baby's body parts and her own.

Thus adults themselves contribute both to the baby's recognition of the disjunction between their illusion of control and their dependence on adults for the completion of these communications, and at the same time they promote the infant's repositioning in more adult directions. By the end of the first year, for many infants, there is no doubt that their communicative behaviour is 'intentional'. We infer this from the specificity of the behaviour and the babies' persistence, as they are prepared to repeat actions again and again, often, apparently, simply for the sake of gaining and manipulating adult responses. From the peculiarities of demands, for example, we can see that not only the communicative procedure but 'what the child needs' has been produced through a specific and extensive, relational history. The former is not a simple reflection of underlying cognitive activities. The latter is not a simple extension of biological needs. By the end of the first year, compared to the position of Thomas at 6 months, there has clearly been a shift in the balance of power in the infant's relation to adults.

There is a striking sense of omnipotence and autonomy in 1 year olds, as the world revolves around them, as it were, which is admirably captured in the painting *His Majesty the Baby*, cited by Freud (1914b) in his paper on the theory of narcissism. Yet, despite this apparent autonomy of 1 year olds and the persistence with which they make their demands, the period is a paradoxically fragile one. It is over the same period of development that stranger and separation anxieties emerge. These anxieties are sometimes acute and, though varying in intensity, they are seldom resolved immediately. There are, of course, many accounts of these phenomena, ranging from cognitive approaches (for example, Schaffer, 1971) to the attempt to use the associated behaviour patterns, such as crying and clinging, as indicators of the strength of underlying 'bonds' (e.g. Ainsworth, Bell and Stayton, 1974). None of these accounts is entirely satisfactory. The cognitive account, for example, by-passes the problem of how anxiety is produced, why it is shown more intensively with personal as opposed to inanimate objects, and why it is shown inconsistently in particular children. (For empirical and conceptual problems with the Attachment account, see, for example, Bernal, 1974.)

The present perspective provides an alternative reading of these anxiety phenomena. I suggest that crucial reasons for their being particularly evident over this period are, first, that the experience of a misfit between strangers and people who would confirm the infants' initial glimmers of themselves in positions of assertion, controlling the world in predictable ways, is intensely persecuting in the psychoanalytic sense. This is not simply a question of distorted feedback from a strange adult who fails to understand the baby's idiosyncratic messages, a position put forward by Bower (1977). Rather, like the mirror in Lacan's account, which is as controlling as it is controllable (see p. 276), here the illusion of control has as its counterpart the illusion of total subjugation. (It is for this reason that narcissism and paranoia are juxtaposed in Lacan's reading (1948) of Freud.) Second, over this time infants are beginning to discover for themselves their dependence on adults, a dependence which has changed in its nature through the disjunction produced through the entry into preverbal communication. That is, adults are no longer simply acting on assumptions about infants' physical or emotional needs; adults are now necessary to interpret and complete the infants' own communicative initiatives. These are, of course, already distanced from the situations in which they were produced. Within this constellation the infant's investment in the mother becomes pivotal, as a support for his or her sense of autonomy. In consequence of this, separation is experienced as annihilating. Yet the discovery of separation itself sets the baby in a new relation to the mother. The baby may show considerable anger towards her, through screaming, biting and rejection, for example, because of her control projected onto her through the baby's fantasy; or because the baby fears abandonment. But at the same time, the baby may want to please her; her pleasure and affection has produced the baby's power of assertion, and it continues to be necessary to sustain his or her position of control. In Lacanian terms, the baby wants to be that object which the mother most desires. These ambivalent and contradictory feelings in babies show how inadequate are accounts of 'mothering' which presume that this task is simply a question of meeting the baby's 'needs'. For the baby, the complexity of the struggle is further amplified by the fact that, with the onset of mobility, adults may be obliged to take advantage of how much more infants understand of regularized events, and markedly increase their use of social sanctions and prohibitions over the same period. This conflicts with the infant's imagined control and self-determination, and in my own study I have found that temper tantrums are particularly frequent around the end of the first year.

The second year: the discovery of power differences and their partial resolution

It is in the second year that we generally see infants making tremendous gains in discovering the potential effectiveness of their own behaviour and their ability to manipulate other people. In doing so they themselves make increasing use of the regularities in their own lives, taking up positions from which they apparently order the proceedings. But they are also obliged to discover limits in their powers of assertion, and how their resources and positions differ from those of adults. Wanting to be independent will in consequence often come into conflict with a wish to be dependent, so that infants will frequently oscillate between the two; here the pathos is that the gaining of one implies the loss of the other. Ultimately a partial resolution to this contradiction is achieved through repositionings within discursive relations which enable the child to act in more 'adult' ways, a process which, as I shall illustrate, involves suppressing the position of the dependent infant.

Illustrative of increasing assertiveness, in our culture, it is very common for infants to begin the second year with a period of showing off. This may take the form of seductive exhibitionism, or endless pointing and ejaculations of 'ooh!' or 'der!' directed towards objects which are, in fact, familiar and located in predictable places. By this time most infants are aware of social sanctions. But they may also show evidence of making use of the relation of power which that implies, turning it back on their mothers. In the following examples, Linette and Paula wilfully tease their mothers. By showing that they anticipate rebuke, they put their mothers in a position from which they are unable to assert their authority.

3. Linette. 1.0.2. *Home observation*

Linette swaggers towards the television set, reaches for the knob and turns to smile at the mother. 'You know, don't you?' Linette laughs, reaches for the knob again, and holds her hand hovering over it. She taunts her mother, repeatedly; by her manner she 'dares' her mother to tell her off. Yet she also makes it plain that she has no intention of actually touching the knob, so that the mother is 'caught' as to whether or not she should utter the rebuke.

4. Paula. 1.1.0. *Home observation*

Paula's mother has closed the door firmly, making it clear that Paula is not to go out. Shortly afterwards, Paula crawls to the door and reaches towards the knob. She turns and smiles at her mother. 'Paula, no.' Paula slowly raises her arm again, watching her mother from under her arm. 'No, Paula.' Paula teases her again. Her mother is caught. 'No' is to no avail and the child is not really leaving. Yet she persists in her teasing. No course of action is available to the mother, since getting up and removing the child would be an indication that, in one sense, the baby had 'won'. It would also contradict the emphasis on self-discipline and control which she is trying to encourage. In the end the mother gets up and offers an attractive toy.

In these examples, the infants are putting their mothers into a classic double bind, made possible through the use of communicative procedures which are already distanced from the situations which produced them (Bateson, 1973). We may note, too, that both mothers were also partly trapped by being positioned within a particular mothering discourse which stresses the importance of avoiding conflicts with young children. The events are precisely about playing with power, and there are striking similarities with Walkerdine's example of the teacher and small boys, cited on p. 284.

Yet, at the same time, infants show real attempts to please their mothers. The following example shows the counterpart to fantasies of omnipotence, as the child over-reacts to the mother's rebuke.

5. Linette. 1.0.2. *Mother's report*

We were at a friend's house the other day, and Linette made a puddle on the carpet. I was a bit embarrassed and I said, rather carelessly, 'Oh Linette!' She burst into tears! And all I'd done was say 'Oh Linette.' I never thought she'd be that sensitive!

Nevertheless, the desire to control the mother, to have and hold her attention, is persistent and can appear to be positively manipulative. For example,

6. Paula. 1.1.2. *Home observation*

Paula would sit beside the toy box, pointing into it and demanding things which she could not reach. 'Ergh. Ergh.' Sometimes she would

> go through the entire box of toys, rejecting everything in turn, before the mother realized that the child was, for its own sake, exploiting her power to direct.

At a somewhat older age in a play setting which was now relatively familiar to them both, Roger directs a telephone game with his mother. It is he, now, who defines the constraints of the game. Assertively, he allocates his mother a position which is comparable or interchangeable with his own. Although his mother colludes in this, her ambivalence about his apparent control is suggested by her final comment.

> 7. Roger. 1.4.0. *Video recording in standard play setting*
>
> Roger and his mother are positioned around the play table. Roger picks up the receiver of the toy telephone, 'speaks' into it, and hands it to his mother indicating that she should do likewise. He then demands it back again. He directs his mother to get another, identical telephone from the side, and smiles when she obliges. The mother engages in a mock conversation with Roger, which he breaks by demanding the mother's phone. She concedes. Roger sits down on one of the two small chairs, gets off, and indicates to his mother that she is to sit on it. He gets on the other himself. He points to one of the telephones, indicating that they are to play telephones again. The mother does as bid, commenting 'Gosh, you are a little tyrant.'

In the same session, the intensity of Roger's domination and apparent self-assertion was marked by the acuteness of his distress and anger when his mother left the room, crying inconsolably for several minutes before he settled to play. This indicates particularly poignantly the position of the infant grappling with the limitations in his or her position in relation to adults (though we may note the similarity in the behaviour of adults). In other children, or the same child at a different point, the contradiction may be expressed in different ways. For example, children will often oscillate between performances which demonstrate their independence, or which are aimed at maintaining adult approval, and an exasperating reluctance to reveal what they are capable of, sliding into babyishness. Their behaviour may take the form of appeals which indicate 'Mummy do it for me', even though the task is something which on other occasions they manage very adequately, or an exaggerated insistence on being held, comforted, cuddled and so on. Alternatively, some children may show their anger with their mothers more openly, as in the following example of a little girl 'splitting'.

> 8. Kate. 1.2.0. *Mother's report*
>
> When one of her mother's women friends, whom Kate knew well, came to visit, Kate would regularly take her into the bedroom and

> slam the door, shutting her mother out, and giving her pleasure and attention to the woman friend.

The availability of another adult temporarily solves a problem for this child: that the need for autonomy and her growing mastery over the world are still bounded by her dependence for completion on adult support. Ultimately, this problem can only be resolved for infants through taking the positions of adults, from which they themselves can apparently regulate the course of action, increasing their relative powers of assertion. This will be achieved through identification as they themselves become like their mothers. Alternatively they may identify with others whose position they perceive as powerful relative to their mothers and/or themselves, such as their fathers, or, as in the above example, close friends who have taken care-taking responsibilities. But these resolutions are only partial ones. First, taking the position of adult necessarily involves suppressing the position of dependence, and the crucial aspect of the relation with the mother which has produced the baby's illusion of perfect control, and of his or her own perfection. Second, although significant adults in the infant's life may be powerful relative to the infant, in actuality as individuals they are not the source of power; their positioning is produced and regulated through discursive relations, which set constraints on the infant's subsequent positioning.

These adults, though, may themselves take steps to faciliate their child's coping with separations and taking on adult roles. At the same time the child's separation anxiety can be as much of a problem for the mother as for the child, because the child's distress can engender considerable distress in the mother, and because of her own separation anxieties. This may be particularly so if child-care has been her major occupation for several months. For many mothers, leaving the child becomes a real issue. I take as an instance Mrs Z, who participated in my interview study. Here she is talking about leaving the baby as one of the major problems which she had had to contend with.

> I realized afterwards that it was the first time I'd left her, apart from the odd evening. I thought I'd get so much done. But I felt absolutely bereft, wandering round the shop, not being able to buy anything, and not really even looking.

Consciously a mother may feel caught in a contradiction between, on the one hand, believing that distress may damage the infant and that it is wrong to leave the baby in someone else's care and, on the other, not wanting a clinging child, itself a source of social condemnation. This is a clear example of how discourses on child-care which define appropriate action on the mother's part are contradictory.

A particular mother's ambivalence may at times appear in the way she herself plays with her baby. More generally, many well-known games are based around separation, as the mother hides her face in 'peek-a-boo', for example, or conceals objects in 'hide and seek'. Like the *Fort-da* game described by Freud (see p. 277), many of these traditional games are admirably suited to promoting the baby's control over the disappearance and reappearance of objects and/or the mother herself. Here, they contribute to the baby's repositioning, and perhaps facilitate the mother's own preparation for separation. The fascination which children show in playing these games with people is complemented in their own play, which often includes a large amount of throwing things away, going to fetch them, and throwing again, sometimes in anger. This is often preceded by, or alternates with, demanding that the mother retrieve them, in a similar fashion to the management of the mother shown by Paula, in example 6 above.

Parents may also use more obviously task-oriented forms of co-operative play, like building towers of bricks, or reading books to encourage adult-like behaviour. The principles of adult participation described for the first year extend into the second, though the adult may now be more likely to assert the appropriate functions of objects or to use more demonstration, in encouraging the infant's management of the proceedings. In these situations, the mother is using the fact that the baby is now motivated to control the proceedings by taking up the position of the mother herself. Changes in the baby's position in the direction of interchangeability with adults may appear in significant action procedures, which now mark the socially appropriate function of the object and/or specify the action required of the other, such as how the telephone is to be held. Some indication of these changes can be obtained by comparing examples 6 and 7, of Paula and Roger.

Structured play between adults and infants has been studied particularly intensively in psychological research, and one must assume that parents vary both in the extent to which they engage in these kinds of activities and when. Other occasions when adults deliberately or unconsciously foster the children's ability to take up adult positions may occur through the course of the day, when the mother, say, is trying to combine doing housework with looking after the child, or the child is encouraged to 'help Daddy'.

Both the kinds of play and ways of 'helping' which adults make available to infants are an obvious place to look for the implications of gender for the production of differences. However, I suspect that this is not simply a question of whether or not children are exposed to sex-stereotyped toys (dolls versus cars and trains, for example). The processes are much more complex. They may involve the extent to which the infant's sex enters into how the mother positions him or her within a particular activity, as 'dependent' on her, for instance, or as 'authoritative', as in the example of Roger, or as 'like me'. In the latter case the mother herself stresses comparability and correspondences between positions. I will give examples of these positioning processes below after illustrating children's own identifications, as they take up positions of power hitherto held by adults by being as adults themselves. We can gain access to these processes through their symbolic play and language itself.

Pretend play emerges much earlier than is usually believed and intensive studies suggest that, in the initial stages at least, it is based on particularly highly significant regulated events in the child's life. Often, though not invariably, these involve things done to the child by an adult so that the re-enactment puts the child in the position of the significant other doing the action.

9. Linette. 1.0.2. *Home observation*

Linette spreads a tissue on the floor, lies on it, pulls it up between her legs, gets up and wipes her bottom.

At the same age she uses her toothbrush to clean the teeth of her teddy bear and rabbit.

Taking the part of the significant other, though in fantasy, marks a shift in the child's power in relation to the mother within these particular activities. In these examples Linette is also simultaneously looking after herself as the little baby, the position which must eventually be suppressed.

In the following example of Clare, at an older age, initially the mother creates the conditions for the child's control, such that she can do things as her mother for her mother.

10. Clare. 1.9.0. *Video recording in standard play situation*

Clare and her mother are sitting at the small table with a toy tea-set. 'Ergh!' Clare reaches for a cup. 'Is Clare going to pour Mummy a cup of tea?', pushing the teapot close. 'Pour?' Clare lifts the teapot and shakes it. 'Yeah. You pretend there's some tea in it. Put your cup down,' taking it and putting it on the table. 'And pick this up, and pour Mummy some tea,' pointing to the teapot and cup. Clare picks up the teapot and pretends to pour. 'That's right. Can Mummy have one?', as she points out another cup. Clare carefully mock pours. 'Oh, *thank* you,' as Clare passes the cup over, beaming. 'Mmmm! Lovely cup of tea,' the mother says pretending to drink.

By the end of the sequence Clare moves from marking the correspondence between herself and her mother, to a position in which her pleasure is very much about managing the regulated activity and, in somewhat omnipotent fashion, apparently reversing the positioning in relation to her mother.

Clare deftly pours another cup. 'Mine, mine,' looking at her mother. 'Yes, that's yours.' Clare lifts up the cup and saucer and pretends to drink, quickly putting it down again and taking the mother's cup away. 'All gone.' 'Yes, it's all gone.' 'All gone,' says Clare, now pointing to her own cup. 'Is yours all gone?' Clare nods and begins pouring again. 'Now what shall we do?' The mother suggests giving a cup of tea to the doll. But Clare ignores her. She pours out two more cups, pointing to one saying 'Mummy.' 'Oh, I'm having another one now?' Clare hands it over. She points to the other cup saying 'Mine.' 'That's yours, is it?' Clare looks at her own cup, and at her mother's, and drinks from her own. The mother drinks from hers. Clare puts hers down, takes the mother's away, and begins pouring yet again. 'Oh dear, I don't think I shall be able to hold it all!'

For Jeremy, on the other hand, it is his relation with his father, or being like Daddy, which is at issue. Again, the mother initially sets up the game, using language to mark the parts and praise to punctuate steps of the procedure.

11. Jeremy. 1.10.0. *Video recording in standard play setting*

Jeremy is investigating the tool set. His mother suggests, 'What are you going to build? Are you going to fix something? Are you going to fix the trolley?' 'Yeah.' 'Why don't you take the screwdriver and go and fix the trolley?' She pulls it close. 'Where are the screws on the trolley?' Jeremy points to the screws through the wheel axis, smiling. '*That*'s right. Very good. And can you see the nuts and bolts? Like you see in a tool box?', pointing to a nut and bolt in the tool set. Jeremy looks round to see. He turns the nut and bolt and says, 'Turn.' 'That's right. It turns.' Jeremy bangs the bolt with the hammer. 'Oh you're fixing it? Very good.'

But the mother soon gives way to the child's direction, again using praise to confirm his assertion.

Jeremy gets out the screwdriver and begins working at the nut on the trolley with it. 'It goes on this side really Jeremy,' the mother points to the bolt head. 'In fact, it's a little big for this screw.' The mother demonstrates using the screwdriver on one of the plastic screws in the tool set. 'Do you want to try screwing them?' Jeremy snatches the screwdriver and begins working with it. 'That's right. Straight up. That's *perfect*. You finish it. Very nice.' Jeremy works persistently. 'You've got it. Very good, Jeremy. Good boy.'

By this time, Jeremy has made his own links between his current position in relation to this regulated activity, the significance of this activity, and the position of his father. The mother both confirms this correspondence, and encourages the child's assertion and his fantasy. He, as it were, can be just as good as his father.

> Jeremy reaches for the hammer, bangs, screws some more, vocalizes, and reaches for the bolt on the wheel of the trolley. He says, 'Dadda. Daddy!', looking up at the mother and smiling 'Daddy!' He puts the screwdriver to the wheel. The mother comments, 'Daddy has screwdrivers? Daddy can fix that?' Jeremy vocalizes then points to another wheel, and says, 'Da two.' 'Mmm. *Jeremy* has screwdrivers and *he* can fix it.' Jeremy goes to the bolt on the second wheel, bangs it with the plastic hammer, goes back to the tool set, and so on.

Finally, the mother confirms the child's male gender, and reproduces recursively (see chapter 5, pp. 227–38) her own position of exclusion.

> The mother has sat back by now, and is looking around the room. 'Jeremy, Jeremy,' whispering, and pointing. 'Look. There's a doll sleeping. Covered up under the blanket.' Jeremy looks. 'Would you like to go and play with that?' 'No.' Jeremy goes back to the tool set. The mother laughs. 'I didn't think you would.' Jeremy turns a screw in the tool set. 'Daddy. Daddy!'

Thus regulated play activities such as these, which are already linked through signification to discursive practices of the adult world, provide frameworks in which the child is produced in a position of control, apparently ordering the regularity of the event. Yet at the same time this position is itself ordained through the power relations operating within and on the family.

The emergence of language

It is over the same period that language emerges. From the foregoing, we would anticipate that, just as they enter into the formation of the child's first intentional communicative procedures and the repositionings worked in fantasy, the specifics of the social regularities in the child's life would emerge in the content of early linguistic expressions. For example, referring to the child-language research discussed at the beginning of this chapter, on a crude level, we would expect that activities such as book-reading, co-operative play with objects, and so on, might contribute to the marked bias towards talking about 'things' which Nelson (1973) called a 'referential' orientation. On the other hand, a child for whom care-taking has constituted a major regulated activity and/or whose position in the family constellation has been consistently emphasized, might show the bias in using social words and phrases or names of familiar people which Nelson characterized as 'expressive'.

But it is not simply a question of the relative frequency of different kinds of events in the child's life. It is the issue of relative control which matters, and the shifts in position which enable the child to move from preverbal communication to language via particular identifications. Moreover, as I pointed out in the first part of this chapter, one also has to account for the possibility, in Nelson's terminology, of a 'mismatch' between the child's orientation and the parental 'strategy'. In each case, questions of emotionality come to the fore.

Taking the issue of 'mismatch' first, this forces us to recognize that children are not simply constituted as direct copies of their parents. We have already seen how contradictory are the processes involved, particularly as infants begin to struggle with the conflict between independence and the wish to maintain adult approval, which will often occur with the production of the first words. In addition, a baby's resistance to separating from the mother can result in a temporary loss of interest in inanimate objects, or a reluctance to produce well-established social performances, in spite of parental exhortations to the contrary. Given the emotional implications of infants' clinginess, bolshiness or exuberant omnipotence for parents, and/or the threat of separation to themselves, there is no reason, of course, to expect them to be entirely consistent either.

More generally, I have pointed elsewhere to the highly affective nature of the child's first verbal expressions (Urwin, 1982b). These productions have been described as 'pure performatives' (Greenfield and Smith, 1976; McShane, 1980), as the child uses them to gain adult attention or acknowledgement, or in the execution of a simple demand, the words being accompanied by communicative procedures which indicate what specific effects the child intends. I have already argued that these procedures are produced through particular regulated social activities, like greetings, feeding situations or social games. But one also finds that first words themselves, such as 'up', 'Teddy', 'look' and 'oh dear', can generally be traced to the same specific activities, in which the child has already gained some measure of active control over the outcome and the other's response. For example, discussing the somewhat tedious regularities in her own care-taking practice which influenced her daughter's language acquisition, Ferrier (1978) describes how she would habitually stop halfway up the stairs when taking the baby to bed, and show her the geraniums. The child would eventually point these out herself, looking to the mother for approval and confirmation. The mother would show her pleasure with her comments. These consistent comments provided the basis for one of the child's first verbal productions, 'pretty' accompanied by the pointing procedure.

But this is not a question of the word being grafted onto a pre-established communicative procedure, in the way research on the transition from preverbal communication to language has implied. Rather, from the present perspective, even the first words mark, and make possible, a shift in the infant's position relative to the adult within specific regulated activities. Through entering into the common language the specificity of what the child wants is now being made explicit, defining more precisely the response required of the other from within the same terms of reference.

Yet early word usage is notoriously unstable. Some early acquired words rapidly disappear, and whether the child's range of application of a particular word is sufficiently like adults' to justify the claim that they are operating within the 'same language' is generally questioned. From the present perspective, the fact that young children apparently acquire words and then fail to use them is unsurprising. We have seen that over the same period children are grappling with the costs (as well as the gains) of entering adults' frames of reference. As far as the child's use of words itself is concerned, psychological literature has given much attention to the phenomena of 'under extension', 'over extension', and 'over generalization'. This refers to the fact that some early words may at first be used restrictively, so that they remain tied to the original situation of production; 'up' being confined to requests to be lifted, for example. Alternatively the child may extend the word into new situations which bear some relation to the original one, or to situations in which the word has subsequently been applied. This often results in usages which are inappropriate in adult terms, such as calling all men 'Daddy'.

There are many accounts of these phenomena, several of which use children's 'errors' with the aim of supporting one or other general theory of semantic storage or word meaning. The 'word' thus becomes the focus, and the child's relation to the situation of production, and how this itself may be affected by the use of language, is totally discounted. Alternatively, a predominant approach views children's over or under extensions as evidence of the relatively inferior cognitive status of younger infants as opposed to older children who are using words within the 'appropriate' range of application. That is error is assumed to be a reflection of what the child does not yet know. Again, virtually no attention is given to the emotional significance of the process of extension itself. For example, from a Piagetian perspective, Bloom (1973) discusses the relative commonality of 'function' words like 'more', 'gone', 'all gone', 'there' and 'no' in terms of cognitive changes taking place through the infancy period. The child's cognitive level is supposed to determine what aspects of the environment are particularly salient to him or her. 'More', for example, used to refer to recurrent objects, is assumed to depend on the child's knowledge of objects as distinct entities, and 'no', 'gone' or 'all gone', used to refer to absent things, have been said to require the achievement of object permanence, or the ability to mentally represent objects across space and time. This development is generally placed somewhere between 18 and 24 months.

Apart from the fact that empirical evidence does not entirely support such a view (Corrigan, 1978), the present framework suggests another explanation for children's preoccupations. Words like 'more', used initially in requests for a repeat of a game, or for another mouthful of food, and 'all gone', used ritualistically at the termination of a meal, are precisely those which are particularly likely to mark the child's own control within predictable social practices. Similarly, the preoccupations with using 'there!' to indicate familiar things, or their appearance where anticipated, and with marking similarities with 'more', are themselves hallmarks of the contribution of expectations and social regularities. 'No' is often used initially in protesting or resistance, as the child is beginning to deal with the implications for repositioning implied by the use of parental sanctions by appropriating the parental term. But 'no' is not only used in protesting by young children; they refer to absent objects and events far earlier than the object permanence model presumes. Here it is in relation to some predictable event or frame of reference that something absent becomes significant; the child may comment on part of a toy which is lost, for example. Alternatively, the predictable framework becomes the platform from which the child refers to something which is absent or wished for. Requests for food which is concealed, for example, may be handled by pointing to the biscuit tin, or out into the kitchen, where food is normally kept, or where the mother goes to prepare it.

These early requests may be motivated, of course, as much by the wish to control the adult as by the wish for food itself. But young children's early use of words is not confined to their interactions with adults, as the words are taken over and produced as accompaniments to their own play. Here, they may take positions of control over their own toys, marking the completion of activities and seeking and reproducing regularities.

But 'taking control' must be set in relation to the shift in position relative to others which it implies. Over this period, of course, children are also working through the conflicts engendered by separation. Earlier, I mentioned how themes involving 'making things disappear', sometimes in anger, are dominant in the play of many young children. On the other hand, other children, or the same children at different points, become preoccupied with what goes with what, where and when, finding parts to complete objects, or pieces that make things whole again. Reflecting what ought to be the case, in terms of the social regularities of the particular child's life, this searching is often tinged with anxiety. However, once the child begins to use words such as 'gone', 'all gone' or 'no' to mark control over absence, this control is regulated through the adult system within which the child is beginning to take up a position of assertion. No longer is it the dependent infant who must cope with the threat of annihilation which results from the loss of the mother. Rather, the use of language both distances the child from the pain of separation, and in taking on board the adult terms of reference, the child marks his or her own control over the experience.

In this light, consider the following example in which Jeremy makes links between a piece of jigsaw which is missing and necessary to complete it, and the absent mother, using language to mark his own control over absence.

12. Jeremy. 1.9.0. *Home observation*

> Jeremy's mother has recently been absent from home more than usual, having taken a temporary part-time job. His mother felt that Jeremy had reacted by becoming 'more clinging' but that things were now settling down again.
>
> Jeremy and his mother are playing with an inset jigsaw which contains five pieces to fit into five spaces. One piece is missing. Jeremy searches obsessively. 'Gone. Gone.' 'Where's it gone, Jeremy?' At first the mother helps him. 'Never mind, Jeremy, we can do it as it is.' 'Gone. Gone.' Jeremy persists. 'It doesn't matter. Look, Jeremy.' 'Gone. Gone.' Jeremy carries on. Eventually he finds it amongst other toys. Smiling broadly, his tone indicating that he intends to label it, he says 'Mummy!' The mother comments, 'Is that Mummy? Thanks very much! It looks like a pig to me!'

In searching for order, as things should be, this child is also searching for a position from which he may ordain it, and at the same time regulate the mother. By entering into the adult system his relative dependence on her has been displaced. The mother's comment suggests, perhaps, that she is sensitive to the implications of this shift, revealing her own ambivalences about having left the child, as he makes her presence redundant in the immediate situation.

Given the preponderance of both themes of separation and the words 'gone' and 'there', one is immediately reminded of Lacan's account of the *Fort-da* game, discussed on p. 277, in which a child symbolized his control over his mother's disappearance, yet introduced an inevitable distance between himself and the object of his desire at the same time. It is appropriate to ask how far this epitomizes what is at issue for children moving into language, and what are the implications of the shifts in emphasis in the present account.

According to Lacan, the *Fort-da* example demonstrates both the inevitable costs of entering language and the processes through which desire is produced as unfulfillable. Here, the move into language involves renouncing or suppressing the position of the infant whose powers of assertion are produced by the attentive adult; in addition, the appropriation of words will introduce a further distancing in the child's relation to immediate events. In consequence, as in Lacan's account, the entry into language will involve a double cost. However, by beginning with parent–infant communication within particular social practices rather than, say, with the position of the nursing infant, the notion of 'satisfaction' is far broader than in psychoanalytic theory. This implies that the motivation underlying language development is not necessarily dependent on the presence and absence of the particular mother. Rather, this gains its relative centrality as the mother becomes a focus for supporting the infant's illusory control and omnipotence, to which separation is one amongst many possible threats. This means, for example, that the consistent availability of more than one caretaker will influence how, when and how extensively infants will show separation anxiety, and there will be considerable variations between infants in the relative dominance of separation themes in their play and language. Moreover, I have illustrated how the child's wish to control the mother is produced through relations of power. This implies that desire itself is produced through power relations as they operate in particular social practices. These are themselves regulated discursively. This means, then, that rather than assuming that desire is governed by a universal symbolic order, we can look at the implications of the child's repositioning through the appropriation of words for his or her relative power within particular social practices. Here there are gains as well as costs. Consider what the following example suggests concerning the relation between early word production, the child's repositioning via identification within particular discursive frames of reference, and his relative powers of assertion.

13. Jack. 1.2.0. *Video recording in a standard play setting*

> Jack's mother has been asked to read a book for five minutes, and to ignore the baby's overtures as far as possible. While his mother is not attending to him, Jack picks up a round baby mirror. Holding it in two hands, he looks at himself and says 'baby'. He moves the mirror from side to side, and says 'brrm brrm'. He then lowers the mirror, looks round, and reaches out for a toy truck, some way away from him. He pushes it along the ground, going 'brrm brrm', repeating this several times, with exuberance.

'Brrm, brrm' has been in Jack's vocabulary for some weeks, associated with pushing things along, with toy cars, and with pointing out real cars in the street. The connection between holding the mirror and saying 'brrm, brrm' is either mediated by the action of steering, the roundness of the mirror, the way he is sitting, or a mixture of these. According to his mother, Jack has very recently been allowed to sit in the driver's seat of the car, so long as she is beside him, when the family has been out together and the father has stopped the car in order, say, to go into a shop. Up to this point, then, driving has always been associated with taking the place of the father.

Within traditional psychology, this example might be discussed in terms of whether it indicates generalization based on function, perceptual features, or prototypes (see, for example, Nelson, 1974; Clark, 1973; Rosch, 1975). But here what is significant is the emotional dynamic underlying the pattern of associations, and the chaining process itself. In Lacan's terms we are seeing the formation of a metaphoric axis. One might speculate, for instance, that the word 'baby', produced when the mother was not available to the infant, provides a link to the lost object. As the word replaces the image of himself in the mirror, introducing a disjuncture through language, he recognizes himself from the position of another. As the infant's association moves from 'baby' to 'brrm, brrm', simultaneously we see the process of displacement, from the recognition of himself as a baby from the position of another, to taking up an imaginary position driving a car, the position occupied by his father.

In Lacan's account this identification marks a shift in the child's positioning in the symbolic order. Since for Lacan all movement in language is ultimately governed by desire (see p. 215), it is the child's desire to control the mother from the position of the Other which underlies the movement in the above example. From the present perspective, however, it is simultaneously possible to read this movement as being governed by the child's searching for a position of relative assertion. This itself is what is made possible through the use of language. Words are not simply extended into new contexts according to properties of action or objects. Rather, they enable the child to make connections across different fields of action or discursive frames of reference within which, through identification with others, the child may take up more powerful positions. Within this perspective, it is still possible to regard the metaphoric axis, which is always idiosyncratic, as that which provides continuity to the subject, as in Lacan's account (see Introduction to section 3, p. 215). Now, however, this is not rooted in the loss of the mother *per se*, but in the specific processes and constellations in which the individual child's illusion of control is produced and regulated, and reproduced recursively, via identification across different spheres of action.

The example of Jack illustrates again how, in signifying practices and discursive relations of the adult world, play activities provide sites for the child's repositioning in discursive relations through particular identifications. But in Lacan's terms, this child's identifications are still bounded by the imaginary relations of the mirror stage. From the present perspective, it is not yet appropriate to speak of him as positioned as a speaking subject within the discursive order. Jack's relative powers of assertion are limited by the fact that he has yet to achieve that interchangeability of position which is only possible through the mastery of the adult system. By the end of the one-word stage he will have moved considerably nearer to this, both through further processes of identification, and through the entry into language itself, as words gain meaning not simply through their relation to particular situations, but as they enter into relations with other words. These relations may be metaphoric, making links to positionings obtained in other discursive frames of reference. Alternatively the relations may be ones of contiguity, or metonymic (see Introduction to section 3, p. 214). Here words in combination order the regularity operating within a particular practice.

Of course, the child is now beginning to produce structured speech. By the time this occurs many children are able to sustain short conversations about events remote from the here and now, relying solely on verbal connections. The content of these conversations is not arbitrary. Significantly, they are generally about salient past or habitual events and familiar people, as in conversations of the 'Daddy's gone to work' variety. Here these children are both controlling and reproducing the truth of these events themselves. This is what Halliday (1975) calls the 'true dialogue' function of language, as the child uses language not only to get beyond the here and now, but to convey information to someone who does not already have it. In contrast to the conversations of younger children, where they must rely on adults' understanding of their implicit intentions, and where the aim of the conversation is often to obtain confirmation and attention rather than to convey information, now from the position of the speaking subject the child is able to mark explicitly both an interchangeability of positioning with those of others, and the fact that the positions of others' are separable from his or her own.

But the subject produced in this way is neither fixed nor static. Nor has he or she simply obtained possession of an increased power to assert. This power, of course, remains relational, depending on the particular discursive frame of reference in operation. That is, the possibilities opened to the child through entering into language are not, simply, those of an increasing effectivity within particular frames of reference. Rather, the entry into language facilitates the child's switching from one discursive frame of reference to another, thereby increasing the child's options within relationships to take up alternative positions. Some positions, of course, may be relatively more powerful than others. Returning to the example of Jack, although this child is only using one word at a time, I suggest that the movement through language from the position of 'baby' to the position of 'father' is analogous to the switching of the discursive reference which Walkerdine's examples suggest is evident by pre-school age (p. 285), and which, consciously or unconsciously, is used by adults as they take up positions which effectively increase their powers of assertion within relationships (see chapter 5, pp. 242–3).

Yet taking up relatively powerful positions is not unproblematic. Considering these particular examples, it is a moot point whether taking a relatively assertive position within a discourse which itself implies women's subordination is necessarily to the advantage of an individual woman. For instance, in Walkerdine's example, is it advantageous to the little girl to attain power over the little boy through a domestic activity? The following example of two same-aged children who play together regularly illustrates particularly poignantly the gains made possible to the child through entering into the terms of reference of the adult system, but also the constraints which follow from this.

> 14. Marie and Christopher. 2.0.0. *Video recording in a standard play setting*
>
> This is the children's first visit to the University playroom. Their mothers are out of the room, watching through the one-way mirror. Both children have been playing with a tea-set. Marie sees a tool-set and goes over to play with it. Christopher goes over too and reaches to take it away. Marie resists initially. But then she pauses, '*Boy* have it,' she says, and gives it to him. She looks at the camera, smiles, and goes back to the tea-set.

Afterwards Marie's mother said that she was amazed at Marie's 'good' behaviour, and that normally she, rather than Christopher, wins all the fights when they play in either of the children's homes. She thought that the demands of the novel situation had made Marie produce her very best behaviour.

But did Marie lose on this occasion? She gave up the toy and yielded to the little boy's pressure. Yet she did not have the appearance of one who had lost a fight. Rather, she seemed very pleased with herself for having acted, in her mother's absence, in a thoroughly grown-up way. In this situation, in taking an adult position she is in an assertive position relative to the little boy and to her mother, and it is here that her pleasure lies. Yet at the same time, of course, in entering into the terms of reference of the adult system, her positioning is regulated by accepted definitions of what is appropriate, which correspond to taken-for-granted positions of men and women in the adult world; tool-sets are for boys. Moreover, it may be that she is already denying her own wishes and putting those of the boy first, as I suggested in discussing the example cited by Ervin-Tripp (p. 274). 'Giving way' to the little boy, then, marks an increase in her relative powers of assertion, but also advances her own oppression.[3]

Concluding discussion

I began this chapter by illustrating how the ubiquitous assumption of the unitary rational subject has constrained psychological approaches to language development, resulting in certain impasses and paradoxes. These are most evident in dealing with the relations between affective, cognitive and social development, and in accounting for the actual production of language and the power to speak within particular situations. I also pointed to a general tendency for language development research to produce normative accounts of development, such that differences are trivialized or their significance diffused.

In previous chapters we have indicated that understanding the production of differences is a political necessity (see, for example, chapters 2 and 5). We have also emphasized how the effectivity of regulatory apparatuses described by Foucault and Donzelot depends on the appropriation of production of normative accounts and techniques. For example, in chapter 4, it was shown how the insertion of Piagetian theory into primary education has produced an almost exclusive emphasis on 'the stages' of cognitive development. Elsewhere, I have proposed that within medicine, social work, health visiting, and other practices particularly pertinent to pre-school children, the aspects of developmental psychology which are most readily taken up are those which prioritize 'the normal' course of development (in infant testing, for instance), and which present normative accounts of the role of 'the mother' (Urwin, 1982b). This implies that, at the very least, we should examine the implicit assumptions and processes through which such acounts are produced. It is equally necessary to produce alternative readings.

A major aim of this chapter, then, has been to move towards an account of the emergence and early development of language which would render accessible processes which are concealed by traditional psychological approaches and which would also counteract their normative tendencies. But at the same time, in basing this account on certain concepts developed from Foucault's work and on a modified reading of Lacan's theory, the chapter has also aimed to use children's development as a site for developing theoretical assumptions and for evaluating their adequacy. Following our recognition of the potential value of psychoanalytic concepts to our theorizing subjectivity, as discussed in the Introduction to section 3, here I have reworked Lacan's account of the mirror stage theoretically (pp. 279–87) and have illustrated how some of the inherent problems may be circumvented. For instance, by focusing on relations rather than inbuilt capacities in the infant, I have attempted to avoid an idealist collapse. By emphasizing the discursive order and its historical specificity, I have displaced the particular universality and the inevitable subordination of women which Lacan's account implies. In retaining basic tenets of psychoanalytic thinking I have none the less emphasized as fundamental the role of emotionality, fantasy, identification, the significance of separation and the production of desire, processes as important to parenting as they are to children's development. Now, however, both the production of particular desires and the material of fantasy are viewed as being produced through particular power–knowledge relations, and processes of identification operate with respect to particular mothers in social practices, which are themselves regulated through discursive relations.

The analytic tools sketched here may, in principle, be extended to encompass how children of any age are positioned in power–knowledge relations and the implications of this for their use of language. However, it is important to stress that the focus on language *per se* has shifted. That is, a major implication of the present analysis is that answers to questions concerning, say, situational effects and the production of differences will not be found by looking at language alone. Focusing here on the preverbal period and the emergence of language, the reworking of Lacan's account has produced a reading of what may go on between infants and parents which differs markedly from what prevailing psychological approaches have offered. For instance, compared to the smooth passage suggested by the accounts drawing on G. H. Mead, here we have seen the costs and struggles for the child, as well as the pleasures, involved in the transitions from infancy to language use, and processes normally regarded as peripheral now become central. We have seen considerable conflict, not only between infants and adults over adult-imposed sanctions, but contradiction produced in infants themselves, as they are caught between an illusory autonomy and a wish for adult approval and confirmation. We have seen that babies can get angry and reject their mothers, and the delightful if provocative way in which they can use power relations to turn a situation to their advantage. Yet we have also seen considerable distress and vulnerability, and the extent to which themes of separation appear in the play and language of many young children. These problems are not resolved simply or quickly. Children oscillate, showing variations from one occasion to another, and between practices. Though for convenience I have used age periods in organizing the examples, some children will show these phenomena earlier than I have noted, or later, or more or less extensively. It is not an account of developmental stages.

Apart from presenting a different view of infant development, this account has also opened the possibility of an alternative view of mothering. As we have noted in the Introduction to section 3, normative tendencies in certain branches of psychoanalysis have contributed to a particular stress on the role of the mother and the idea that 'good' mothering involves reading and meeting the baby's needs accurately. Here I have attempted to show how inadequate it is to assume that the mother's contribution could, or should, involve simply meeting the baby's needs. Not only are the mother's initiatives and responses always mediated, but the question of what the baby needs is problematized. The disjuncture processes through which babies enter into social relations introduces an inevitable distancing and, babies are contradictory. For instance, they may want incompatible things at any one time, as indeed may the mother herself. Though I have not dealt with how the mother's contribution can be encompassed within the same account thoroughly here, I have indicated the interplay between the mother's own desires and conflicts and her positioning within particular discourses which enter into the constitution of her role. One of the implications of the account is that the mother's positioning, like the infant's, is mediated through the unconscious or conscious search for a position of relative power. This may contribute to the particular decisions taken by individual mothers (such as whether or not to leave the baby), in the face of competing demands, material constraints and discourses which are themselves often contradictory. As in the example of the little girl with the tool-set, or the child in the nursery described by Walkerdine, the positionings resulting from these decisions may imply both gains and costs.

There are many unanswered questions and issues which I have not touched on. First, the observations presented in this account have been restricted to the kinds of infants and parents who participate in intensive psychological studies in western society. Though I have indicated the considerable variation within this narrow band, pointing to processes involved in the production of differences, it is important to recognize both the historical specificity of the particular processes and practices which I have illustrated and to acknowledge both the limitations and productivity of the research methodology. Second, in largely confining the account to the preverbal period and the one-word stage, I have stopped short of a thorough examination of the implications, of gender. That is, taking Lacan's account as the point of departure, I have not examined whether or not there are observable concomitants to a 'resolution' of the Oedipus Complex which affect children's positioning in language. In Lacan's account this resolution is marked simultaneously with the appropriate use of 'I' and 'you' (see p. 278). Moreover, in focusing on mothers and infants, I have not explored fully the impact of the father, or a third term, in the infancy period. Though from the examples given it is clear that effects of gender are evident very early, in what sense Oedipus remains as 'the big fixer' for human subjectivity must thus remain an open question.

However, it is possible to speculate. The present account makes it clear that the achievement of a gendered identity is preceded by a period in which infants actively engage in relations of power. In the first instance these crystallize around their gaining attention to themselves through socially produced communicative procedures, in exploiting crying, for instance. But infants may react very early to being in competition with others. For example, many young infants show considerable upset when they perceive another infant being given adult attention (Urwin, 1983), and when emotional exchanges take place between the parents. It is possible that, within what is the pre-Oedipal period in Lacan's account, the disruption of what I have called the illusion of control can take place through the presence of a third party. In so far as they perceive power relations operating between themselves and their parents, they may also perceive those operating between the parents. (This is witnessed in the tendency to play one parent off against the other, for example, or to reject one in favour of the other.) It may be that the infant's perception of these enters into the relative costs and gains involved in identifying with the same-sexed parent, producing subjective contradictions which may take different forms in boy and girl children. In the short term, this perspective implies that changing power relations operating between men and women in the home, through shared care-taking, the availability of alternative positions of effectivity for women, for example, would have consequences for the production of subjectivity in children.

These consequences, however, would not be entirely predictable, nor would they be without contradictions, and from the present perspective particular aspects of psychic life remain inevitable. From this position, power relations interpenetrate human subjectivity. This is not because of some innate urge for power, but it is an inevitable consequence, in the first instance, of the prolonged period of relative immaturity and dependence on adults within a society regulated through systems of signification. This implies that we are produced as capable of assertive action, yet also fragile and acutely vulnerable, as we have seen in the descriptions of adults in chapter 5. Both the fear of this vulnerability and the search for what I have loosely called positions from which we may maximize our relative powers of assertion contribute to our ineffable tendency to adopt positions which are not in other ways advantageous, to seek safety in what is familiar, to hark back to the past; it is why change is so difficult.

Compared to the promise of personal liberation, this position may appear pessimistic. But this is not entirely so. First, we have argued the political necessity at the present time of acknowledging resistance to change, and the vital need to understand it further. Second, the kind of account of the production of subjectivity I have sketched through looking at developmental processes is not one of determination. It is one which moves towards an understanding of recursive positioning. Moreover, it does not preclude the possibility of change, nor does it predict the future, any more than does the psychoanalytic tradition on which it was based. Theoretically, we have now moved beyond psychoanalysis to a position in which the workings of desire are produced through power relations, though the relationship is not a simple reductive one. We now have tools for examining relations between the social processes which regulate us and the psychic functioning of individuals. In contrast to what psychoanalysis can offer, these processes are in principle ones to which we can all gain access. They are the stuff of our daily lives; they are material for struggle.[3]

Notes

1 The mothers were predominantly, though not entirely, middle-class women, who applied to an advertisement in a local newspaper asking for volunteers for a research project on friendships between same-aged babies. The interview included questions on the kind of support they had received from professionals, relatives and friends, questions concerned with their ideas about child-rearing and development, and where they thought these came from, and what they felt about working outside the home, and their hopes and plans in this direction.

2 The psychoanalyst, Winnicott (1967), has also used a notion of mirroring on the mother's part which he acknowledges he has taken from Lacan. However, Winnicott's account shifts the emphasis by assuming an unbroken unity between mother and baby, as part of the process of maternal preoccupation which enables her to read and meet the baby's needs. In Lacan's account, however, the mirror relation is mediated in imaginary relations. The implications of this difference and problems with Winnicott's account have been discussed briefly in the Introduction to section 3. (See also Adams, 1983.)

3 In addition to the other authors, I am also grateful to Jane Selby for her very helpful comments and support through the preparation of this chapter.

Bibliography

Abercrombie, J. (1838) *Inquiries Concerning the Intellectual Powers and the Investigation of Truth*, London, John Murray.

Adams, P. (1982) 'Family affairs', *m/f* 7, 3–14.

Adams, P. (1983) 'Mothering', *m/f* 8, 41–52.

Adlam, D., Henriques, J., Rose, N., Salfield, A., Venn, C. and Walkerdine, V. (1977) 'Psychology, ideology and the human subject', *Ideology and Consciousness* 1, 5–56.

Adlam, D. and Salfield, A. (1980) 'The diversion of language: A critical assessment of the concept "Linguistic Diversity"', *Screen Education* 34, 71–86.

Adorno, T. W., Frenkel-Brunswik, E., Levinson, D. J. and Sanford, R. N. (1950) *The Authoritarian Personality*, New York, Harper.

Ainsworth, M., Bell, S. and Stayton, D. (1974) 'Infant–mother attachment and social development: socialisation as a product of reciprocal responsiveness to signals', in Richards, M. P. (ed.) *The Integration of a Child into a Social World*, Cambridge, Cambridge University Press.

Albury, D. and Schwartz, J. (1982) *Partial Progress*, London, Pluto Press.

Allport, G. W. (1954) *The Nature of Prejudice*, New York, Addison-Wesley (page references to 1958 abridged edn, New York, Anchor Books).

Althusser, L. (1970) *Reading Capital*, London, New Left Books.

Althusser, L. (1971) *For Marx*, London, Allen Lane/The Penguin Press.

Althusser, L. (1971) *Lenin and Philosophy and Other Essays*, London, New Left Books.

Anastasi, A. (1979) (2nd edn) *Fields of Applied Psychology*, New York, Macmillan.

Andreae, V. (1619) *Christianapolis*.

Armistead, N. (ed.) (1974) *Reconstructing Social Psychology*, Harmondsworth, Penguin.

Austin, J. (1962) *How to Do Things With Words*, Cambridge, Mass., Harvard University Press.

Back, K. (1979) 'The small group: tightrope between sociology and personality', *Journal of Applied Behavioural Science*, 283–94.

Bannister, D. and Fransella, F. (1971) *Inquiring Man*, London, Penguin.

Banton, M. (1965) *Roles*, London, Tavistock.

Barker, M. (1981) *The New Racism: Conservatives and the Ideology of the Tribe*, London, Junction Books.
Barnes, B. (1974) *Scientific Knowledge and Sociological Theory*, London, Routledge & Kegan Paul.
Barnes, D., Britton, J. and Rosen, H. (1971) *Language, the Learner and the School*, Harmondsworth, Penguin.
Bassnett, S. and Hoskin, K. (1982) 'Textuality/sexuality', unpublished manuscript, School for Comparative Literature, University of Warwick.
Bates, E., Camioni, L. and Volterra, V. (1975) 'The acquisition of performatives prior to speech', *Merrill Palmer Quarterly* 21, 205–26.
Bateson, G. (1973) 'A theory of play and phantasy', in *Steps to an Ecology of Mind*, London, Paladin.
Bayton, J. A. (1941) 'The racial stereotypes of Negro college students', *Journal of Abnormal Social Psychology* 36, 97–102.
de Beauvoir, S. (1972) *The Second Sex*, Harmondsworth, Penguin.
Bell, D. (1961) *The End of Ideology*, Glencoe, Ill., Free Press.
Bennett, F., Coward, R. and Heys, R. (1980) 'The limits to "financial and legal Independence": a socialist feminist perspective on taxation and social security', *Politics and Power* 1, 185–202.
Bennett, N. (1976) *Teaching Styles and Pupil Progress*, London, Open Books.
Benton, T. (1977) *Philosophical Foundations of the Three Sociologies*, London, Routledge & Kegan Paul.
Berg, L. (1969) *Risinghill: Death of a Comprehensive School*, Harmondsworth, Penguin.
Bernal, J. (1974) 'Attachment: some problems and possibilities', in Richards, M. P. M. (ed.) *The Integration of a Child into a Social World*, Cambridge, Cambridge University Press.
Bernstein, B. (1971) *Class, Codes and Control*, vol. 1, London, Routledge & Kegan Paul.
Beveridge, M. (ed.) (1982) *Children Thinking Through Language*, London, Arnold.
Bhaskar, R. (1978) *On the Possibility of Naturalism*, Brighton, Harvester Press.
Billig, M. (1978) *Fascists: A Social Psychological View of the National Front*, London and New York, Harcourt Brace Jovanovich.
Billig, M. and Tajfel, H. (1973) 'Social categorization and similarity in intergroup behaviour', *European Journal of Social Psychology* 3 (1), 27–52.
Bland, L. (1981) 'The domain of the sexual: a response', *Screen Education* 39, 56–68.
Bland, L. and Hollway, W. (n.d.) 'Turning off what turns you on? The problem for feminism of biological accounts of sexuality and sexual desire', unpublished manuscript.
Bloom, L. (1971) *The Social Psychology of Race Relations*, London, George Allen & Unwin.
Bloom, L. (1973) *One Word at a Time: The Use of Single Word Utterances Before Syntax*, The Hague, Mouton.
Bloor, D. (1976) *Knowledge and Social Imagery*, London, Routledge & Kegan Paul.
Bogardus, E. S. (1925) 'Measuring social distances', *Journal of Applied Sociology* 9, 299–308.
Bonnet, C. (1769) *Contemplation de la nature*, Amsterdam.

Bower, T. (1974) *Development in Infancy*, San Francisco, Freeman.
Bower, T. (1977) *A Primer of Infant Development*, San Francisco, Freeman.
Bower, T., Broughton, J. M. and Moore, M. K. (1970) 'Demonstration of intention in the reaching behaviour of neonate humans', *Nature* 228, 5272.
Bowerman, M. (1978) 'The acquisition of word meaning', in Waterson, N. and Snow, C. E. (eds) *The Development of Communication*, Chichester, Wiley.
Bradley, B. (1983) 'The neglect of hatefulness in psychological studies of early infancy', unpublished manuscript, University of Cambridge.
Braverman, H. (1974) *Labour and Monopoly Capital: The Degradation of Work in the Twentieth Century*, New York, Monthly Review Press.
Brewster, P. (1980) 'School days, school days', in Spender, D. and Sarah, E. (eds) *Learning to Lose*, London, The Women's Press.
British Psychological Society (1966) *Psychological Tests: A Statement by the BPS*, London: British Psychological Society.
British Society for Social Responsibility in Science (1981) *The Question of Race: The Case against including any Question on Race or Ethnic Origin in the 1981 Census*, London, BSSRS.
Broverman, I. *et al.* (1970) 'Sex role stereotypes and clinical judgements of mental health', *Journal of Consulting and Clinical Psychology* 34 (17).
Brown, R. (1965) *Social Psychology*, New York, Free Press.
Brown, R. (1973) *A First Language: The Early Stages*, Cambridge, Mass., Harvard University Press.
Bruner, J. S. (1975) 'The ontogenesis of speech acts', *Journal of Child Language* 2, 1–19.
Bruner, J. S. (1978) 'From communication to language: a psychological perspective', in Markova, I. (ed.) *The Social Context of Language*, Chichester, Wiley.
Bruner, J. S. (1980) *Under Five in Britain*, London, Grant McIntyre.
Bruner, J. S., Roy, C. and Ratner, N. (1979) 'The development of requests', in Nelson, K. (ed.) *Children's Language*, vol. 3, New York, Gardner.
Buhler, C. (1930) *The First Year of Life*, New York, Day.
Burns, A. (1948) *Colour Prejudice*, London, George Allen & Unwin.
Burt, C. (1940) *The Factors of Mind*, London, London University Press.
Campanella, T. (1622) *The City of the Sun*.
Campbell, B. (1980) 'A feminist sexual politics: now you see it, now you don't', *Feminist Review* 5, 1–18.
Canguilhem, G. (1975) *Etudes d'histoire et de philosophie des sciences*, Paris, Vrin.
Canguilhem, G. (1977) *Idéologie et rationalité*, Paris, Vrin.
Carter, A. (1974) 'The development of communication in the sensorimotor period: a case study', unpublished doctoral dissertation, University of California at Berkeley.
Carter, A. (1978) 'From sensori-motor vocalisation to words: a case study of the evolution of attention-directing communication in the second year', in Lock, A. (ed.) *Action, Gesture and Symbol: The Emergence of Language*, London, Academic Press.
Cattell, J. M., Eber and Matsuoka (1970) *Handbook for the 16PF*, Columbia, IPAT.
CCCS (Centre for Contemporary Cultural Studies Education Group) (1981) *Unpopular Education*, London, Hutchinson.

CCCS (Centre for Contemporary Cultural Studies Race and Politics Group) (1982) *The Empire Strikes Back*, London, Hutchinson.

Chetwynd, J. and Harnett, O. (eds) (1978) *The Sex-role System*, London, Routledge & Kegan Paul.

Chodorow, N. (1978) *The Reproduction of Mothering*, Berkeley, University of California Press.

Chomsky, N. (1957) *Syntactic Structures*, The Hague, Mouton.

Chomsky, N. (1965) *Aspects of the Theory of Syntax*, Cambridge, Mass., M.I.T. Press.

Clark, E. (1973) 'What's in a word? On the child's acquisition of semantics in his first language', in Moore, T. E. (ed.) *Cognitive Development and the Acquisition of Language*, New York, Academic Press.

Clarke, C., Critcher, C. and Johnson, R. (eds) (1977) *Working Class Culture*, London, Hutchinson.

Clavelin, M. (1974) *The Natural Philosophy of Galileo*, Cambridge, Mass., and London, M.I.T. Press.

Coard, B. (1971) *How the West Indian Child is Made Educationally Subnormal in the British School System*, London, Beacon Books.

Cole, M., Dore, J., Hall, W. and Dowley, G. (1978) 'Situation and task in young children's talk', *Discourse Processes* 1, 119–76.

Collins, H. M. (1981) 'Stages in the empirical programme of relativism', *Sociological Studies of Science* 11 (1), 3–10.

Consultative Committee of the Board of Education (1926) *On the Education of the Adolescent* (Hadow Report), London, HMSO.

Consultative Committee of the Board of Education (1931) *The Primary School* (Hadow Report), London, HMSO.

Consultative Committee of the Board of Education (1933) *Infant and Nursery Schools* (Hadow Report), London, HMSO.

Corran, G. and Walkerdine, V. (1981) *The Practice of Reason*, vol. 1: *Reading the Signs of Mathematics*, London, University of London Institute of Education.

Corrigan, R. (1978) 'Language development as related to stage 6 object permanence development', *Journal of Child Language* 5, 173–89.

Coward, R. and Ellis, J. (1977) *Language and Materialism*, London, Routledge & Kegan Paul.

Cowie, C. and Lees, S. (1981) 'Slags or drags', *Feminist Review* 9, 17–32.

Crick, F. and Mitchison, G. (1983) 'The function of dream sleep', *Nature* 304 (5922), 111–14.

Crollius (1624) *Traite des signatures* (trans.), Lyons.

Cronbach, L. J. and Meehl, P. E. (1955) 'Construct validity in psychological tests', *Psychological Bulletin* 52, 281–302.

Danziger, K. (1971) *Socialization*, Harmondsworth, Penguin.

Darwin, C. (1837–9) 'Transmutation notebooks', in Gruber, H. E. and Barrett, P. H. (1974) *Darwin on Man*, London, Wildwood House.

Darwin, C. (1887) 'A biographical sketch of an infant', *Mind* 7.

Deleuze, G. and Guattari, F. (1977a) *Politique et psychoanalyse*, Paris, Des Mots Perdus.

Deleuze, G. and Guattari, F. (1977b) *Rhizome*, Paris, Editions de Minuit.

Delphy, C. (1974) *The Main Enemy*, London, Women's Research and Resources Centre.

de Lissa, L. (1918) *The Making of the Teacher for Young Children*, London, Longman.

de Lissa, L. (1939) *Life in the Nursery School*, London, Longman.

Derrida, J. (1972) *Positions*, Paris, Editions de Minuit.

Descartes, R. (1637) *Discourse*.

Descartes, R. (1641) *Meditation*.

Dickson, D. (1979) 'Science and political hegemony in the 17th century', *Radical Science Journal* 8, 7–37.

Dollard, J. L., Doob, N. E., Miller, D. H., Mowrer, D. H. and Sears, R. R. (1939) *Frustration and Aggression*, New Haven, Yale University Press.

Donald, J. (1979) 'Green paper: noise of crisis', *Screen Education* 30, 13–49.

Donaldson, M. (1978) *Children's Minds*, London, Fontana.

Donzelot, J. (1979) *La Police des familles*, Paris, Editions de Minuit.

Donzelot, J. (1980) *The Policing of Families*, London, Hutchinson.

Dore, J. (1975) 'Holophrases, speech acts and language universals', *Journal of Child Language* 2, 21–40.

Dore, J. (1978) 'Conditions for the acquisition of speech acts', in Markova, I. (ed.) *The Social Context of Language*, Chichester, Wiley.

Du Boulay, J. (1974) *Portrait of a Greek Mountain Village*, Oxford, Clarendon Press.

Dunnette, M. D. (1976) *Handbook of Industrial and Organizational Psychology*, New York, Rand McNally.

Easlea, B. (1973) *Liberation and the Aims of Science*, London, Chatto & Windus.

Easlea, B. (1980) *Witch-hunting, Magic and the New Philosophy*, Brighton, Harvester Press.

Ehrlich, H. J. (1973) *The Social Psychology of Prejudice*, New York, Wiley.

Eichenbaum, L. and Orbach, S. (1982) *Outside In, Inside Out*, Harmondsworth, Penguin.

Eiser, J. R. and Stroebe, W. (1972) *Categorization and Social Judgement*, London, Academic Press.

Elliott, A. G. P. (1976a) 'Fakers: a study of managers' responses on a personality test', *Personnel Review* 5 (1), 33–7.

Elliott, A. G. P. (1976b) 'The effect of a 16PF response set on Assessors' judgement', *Journal of Occupational Psychology* 49, 249–52.

Ellis, T. *et al.* (1976) *William Tyndale: The Teachers' Story*, London, Writers' and Readers' Co-op.

Elms, A. C. (1975) 'The crisis in confidence in social psychology', *American Psychologist* (October), 967–76.

Ervin-Tripp, S. (1977) 'Wait for me, roller skate', in Ervin-Tripp, S. and Mitchell Kernan, C. (eds) *Child Discourse*, New York, Academic Press.

Ervin-Tripp, S. and Mitchell Kernan, C. (1977) *Child Discourse*, New York, Academic Press.

Fanon, F. (1968) *Black Skin, White Masks*, London, Paladin.

Fechner, G. T. (1860) *Elemente der Psychophysik*, Leipzig, Breykipf & Hartel.

Ferrier, L. (1978) 'Some observations of error in context', in Waterson, N. and Snow, C. E. (eds) *The Development of Communication*, Chichester, Wiley.

Feyerabend, P. (1975) *Against Method*, London, New Left Books.

Finkle, R. B. (1976) 'Managerial assessment centers', in Dunnette, M. D. (ed.)

Handbook of Industrial and Organizational Psychology, New York, Rand McNally.
Firestone, S. (1972) *The Dialectic of Sex: The Case for Feminist Revolution*, London, Paladin.
Fletcher, C. and Williams, R. (1976) 'The influence of performance feedback in appraisal interviews', *Journal of Occupational Psychology* 49, 75–83.
Foucault, M. (1966) *Les Mots et les choses*, Paris, Gallimard.
Foucault, M. (1971) *L'Ordre du discours*, Paris, Gallimard.
Foucault, M. (1972) *Histoire de la folie*, Paris, Gallimard.
Foucault, M. (1973) *Birth of the Clinic*, trans. A. M. Sheridan, London, Tavistock.
Foucault, M. (1975) *Surveiller et punir*, Paris, Gallimard.
Foucault, M. (1976) *Histoire de la Sexualité*, vol. I: *La Volonté de Savoir*, Paris, Guallimard.
Foucault, M. (1977) *Discipline and Punish*, London, Allen Lane.
Foucault, M. (1979a) *The History of Sexuality*, vol. I: *An Introduction*, London, Allen Lane.
Foucault, M. (1979b) 'On govermentality', in *Ideology and Consciousness* 6, 5–21.
Foucault, M. (1982) 'The subject and power', *Critical Inquiry* 8 (4), 777–89.
Freud, A. (1968) *The Ego and its Mechanisms of Defence*, London, Hogarth Press.
Freud, S. (1900) *The Interpretation of Dreams*, London, Hogarth Press.
Freud, S. (1914a) *On the History of the Psychoanalytic Movement (1914): Collected Papers*, London, Hogarth Press (1949).
Freud, S. (1914b) *On Narcissism: An Introduction*, Standard Edition, vol. XIV, 73–102, London, Hogarth Press.
Freud, S. (1920) *Beyond the Pleasure Principle*, Standard Edition, vol. XVIII, 7–64, London, Hogarth Press.
Freud, S. (1926) *Inhibitions, Symptoms and Anxieties*, Standard Edition, vol. XV, 87–178, London, Hogarth Press.
Freud, S. (1930) *Civilization and its Discontents*, London, Hogarth Press.
Gergen, K. (1977) 'The social construction of self-knowledge', in Mischel, T. (ed.) (1977) *The Self: Psychological and Philosophical Issues*, Oxford, Blackwell.
Giddens, A. (1979) *Central Problems in Social Theory*, London, Macmillan.
Glaser, B. G. and Straus, A. L. (1967) *Grounded Theory: Strategies for Qualitative Research*, Chicago, Aldine.
Goffman, I. (1964) 'The neglected situation', *American Anthropologist* 66 (6), 133–6.
Golembiewski, R. T. (1980) 'Organisation development in industry: perspectives on progress and stuckness', in Smith, P. B. (ed.) (1980) *Group Processes and Personal Change*, London, Harper & Row.
Goodman, J. and Novarra, V. (1977) 'The Sex Discrimination Act, 1975 – a role for psychologists', *Bulletin of the British Psychology Society* 30, 104–5.
Gramsci, A. (1971) *Prison Notebooks*, London, Lawrence & Wishart.
Greenfield, P. and Smith, J. (1976) *The Structure of Communication in Early Language Development*, New York, Academic Press.
Greer, G. (1971) *The Female Eunuch*, London, Paladin.
Gruber, H. and Voneche, J. J. (1977) *The Essential Piaget*, London, Routledge & Kegan Paul.
Habermas, J. (1971) *Toward a Rational Society*, London, Heinemann.

Hacking, I. (1975) *Why Does Language Matter to Philosophy?*, Cambridge, Cambridge University Press.

Hacking, I. (1981) 'How should we do the history of statistics?', *Ideology and Consciousness* 8, 15–26.

Hall, C. (1984) 'Private persons and public someones: class, gender and politics in England 1780–1850', in Steedman, C., Urwin, C. and Walkerdine, V. (eds) *Language, Gender and Childhood*, London, Routledge & Kegan Paul (in preparation).

Hall, G. S. (1883) *The Contents of Children's Minds on Entering School.*

Hall, S. (1980) 'Recent developments in theories of language and ideology: a critical note', in Hall, S., Hobson, D., Lowe, A. and Willis, P. (eds) *Culture, Media, Language*, London, Hutchinson.

Hall, S. (1982) 'The lessons of Lord Scarman', in *Critical Social Policy* 2 (2), 66–72.

Hall, S., Hobson, D., Lowe, A. and Willis, P. (eds) (1980) *Culture, Media, Language*, London, Hutchinson.

Halliday, M. D. K. (1975) *Learning How to Mean*, London, Arnold.

Hamilton, D. (1981) 'On simultaneous instruction and the early evolution of class teaching', mimeo, University of Glasgow.

Hampshire, S. (1959) *Thought and Action*, London, Chatto & Windus.

Harré, R. (1977) 'The self in monodrama', in Mischel, T. (ed.) (1977) *The Self: Psychological and Philosophical Issues*, Oxford, Blackwell.

Harré, R. (1979) *Social Being*, Oxford, Blackwell.

Harré, R. and Secord, P. (1972) *The Explanation of Social Behaviour*, Oxford, Blackwell.

Heath, S. (1982) *The Sexual Fix*, London, Macmillan.

Henriques, J. F. (1977) 'The struggles of the Zimbabweans: conflicts between the nationalists and with the Rhodesian regime', *African Affairs* 76 (305), 495–518.

Henriques, J. F. (1980) 'Perception, cognition and group relations: a critique of cognitive social psychology', unpublished manuscript.

Henry, P. (1977) *Le Mauvais Outil*, Paris, Klincksieck.

Herriot, P. and Rothwell, C. (1981) 'Towards an attributional theory of the selection interview', *Journal of Occupational Psychology* 54, 165–73.

Hindess, B. (1979a) *Philosophy and Methodology in the Social Sciences*, Brighton, Harvester Press.

Hindess, B. (1979b) 'Critique of social phenomenology', *Economy and Society* 8 (1), 59–97.

Hirst, P. and Woolley, P. (1982) *Social Relations and Human Attributes*, London, Tavistock.

Holland, R. (1977) *Self and Social Context*, London, Macmillan.

Hollway, W. (1981) '"I just wanted to kill a woman." Why? The Ripper and male sexuality', *Feminist Review* 9, 33–40.

Hollway, W. (1982) 'Identity and gender difference in adult social relations', unpublished PhD thesis, University of London.

Hollway, W. (1983) 'Heterosexual sex: power and desire for the Other', in Cartledge, S. and Ryan, J. (eds) *Sex and Love: New Thoughts and Old Contradictions*, London, The Women's Press.

Horkheimer, M. and Adorno, T. (1979) *Dialectic of Enlightenment*, London, Verso.

Hymes, D. (1974) *Foundations of Sociolinguistics: An Ethnographic Approach*, Philadelphia, University of Pennsylvania Press.

Incomes Data Services (1979) *A Review of Job Evaluation Schemes*, London, IDS.

Ingleby, D. (1974a) 'The psychology of child psychology', in Richards, M. P. M. (ed.) *The Integration of a Child into a Social World*, Cambridge, Cambridge University Press.

Ingleby, D. (1974b) 'The job psychologists do', in Armistead, N. (ed.) *Reconstructing Social Psychology*, Harmondsworth, Penguin.

Ingleby, D. (1980a) review of Lock, A. (ed.) *Action, Gesture and Symbol: The Emergence of Language*, London, Academic Press, in *European Journal of Social Psychology* 10, 319–28.

Ingleby, D. (1980b) 'Freud and Piaget: the phoney war', unpublished paper presented at the 1st World Congress on Infant Psychiatry, Cascais, Portugal.

Isaacs, S. (1930) *Intellectual Growth in Young Children*, London, Routledge & Kegan Paul.

Isaacs, S. (1933) *Social Development in Young Children*, London, Routledge & Kegan Paul.

Jacob, F. (1970) *La Logique du vivant*, Paris, Gallimard.

Jahoda, G. (1961) *White Man: A Study of the Attitudes of Africans to Europeans in Ghana before Independence*, Oxford, Oxford University Press.

Jakobson, R. and Halle, M. (1956) *Fundamentals of Language*, The Hague, Mouton.

Jones, G. (1980) *Social Darwinism and English Thought*, Brighton, Harvester Press.

Jones, J. M. (1972) *Prejudice and Racism*, Reading, Mass., Addison-Wesley.

Jones, K. and Williamson, J. (1979) 'Birth of the schoolroom', *Ideology and Consciousness* 6, 59–110.

Kamin, L. (1974) *The Science and Politics of I.Q.*, New York, Erlbauer.

Katz, D. and Braly, K. (1933) 'Racial prejudice and racial stereotypes', *Journal of Abnormal and Social Psychology* 30 (1935), 175–93.

Katz, J. H. (1978) *White Awareness*, Norman, University of Oklahoma Press.

Keenan, A. (1977) 'Some relationships between interviewers' personal feelings about candidates and their general evaluation of them', *Journal of Occupational Psychology* 50, 275–83.

Kelly, G. A. (1955) *The Psychology of Personal Constructs*, New York, Norton.

Kerner, O. (1968) (chairman) *Report of the National Advisory Commission on Civil Disorders*, New York, Bantam Books.

Kilty, J. (1978) 'Self and peer assessment', unpublished paper given at 4th International Conference on Higher Education, University of Lancaster.

Kleiman, L. S. and Faley, R. H. (1978) 'Assessing content validity: standards set by the court', *Personnel Psychology* 31, 701–13.

Klein, L. (1976) *A Social Science in Industry*, London, Gower Press.

Klein, M. (1932) *The Psychoanalysis of Children*, London, Hogarth Press.

Kleiner, S. A. (1979) 'Feyerabend, Galileo and Darwin: how to make the best of what you have – or think you can get', *Studies in History and Philosophy of Science* 10 (4), 285–309.

Kline, M. (1953) *Mathematics in Western Culture*, London, George Allen & Unwin.

Knorr, K. (1977) 'Producing and reproducing knowledge: descriptive or constructive?', *Social Science Information* 16 (6), 669–96.

Kristeva, J. (1969) *Recherches pour une semanalyse*, Paris, Seuil.

Kristeva, J. (1974) *La Révolution du language poétique*, Paris, Seuil.
Labov, W. (1970) 'The logic of non-standard English', reprinted in Giglioli, P. (ed.) *Language and Social Control*, Harmondsworth, Penguin.
Lacan, J. (1948) 'Aggressivity in psychoanalysis', reprinted in Lacan, J., *Ecrits*, trans. A. Sheridan, London, Tavistock (1977).
Lacan, J. (1949) 'The mirror stage as formative of the function of the I as revealed in psychoanalytic experience', reprinted in Lacan, J., *Ecrits*, trans. A. Sheridan, London, Tavistock (1977).
Lacan, J. (1953) 'Function and field of speech and language', reprinted in Lacan, J., *Ecrits*, trans. A. Sheridan, London, Tavistock (1977).
Lacan, J. (1966) *Ecrits*, Paris, Seuil; trans. A. Sheridan, London, Tavistock (1977).
Lacan, J. (1977) *Ecrits: a Selection*, London, Tavistock.
Laplanche, J. and Pontalis, J.-B. (1973) *The Language of Psychoanalysis*, London, Hogarth Press.
Lawrence, E. (1982) 'In the abundance of water the fool is thirsty: sociology and black "pathology"', in Centre for Contemporary Cultural Studies Education Group, *The Empire Strikes Back*, London, Hutchinson.
Lawson, C. (1967) 'Request problems in a two year old', unpublished manuscript, Berkeley, California.
Le Doeuff, M. (1974) 'Operative Philosophy: Simone de Beauvoir and Existentialism', *Ideology and Consciousness* 6, 47–58.
Lefebvre, G. (1973) *The Great Fear of 1789*, London, New Left Books.
Lemaire, A. (1977) *Jacques Lacan*, London, Routledge & Kegan Paul.
Lewin, K., Lippitt, R. and White, R. (1939) 'Patterns of aggressive behaviour in experimentally created social climates', *Journal of Social Psychology* 10, 271–99.
Lieven, E. (1980) 'Different routes to multiple word combinations?', unpublished manuscript, paper presented at Stanford Child Language Conference, April 1980.
Likert, R. (1932) *A Technique for the Measurement of Attitudes*, New York.
Lindsay, P. H. and Norman, D. A. (1977) *Human Information Processing*, New York, Academic Press.
Livy, Brian (1975) *Job Evaluation: A Critical Review*, London, George Allen & Unwin.
Lock, A. (1978) *Action, Gesture and Symbol: The Emergence of Language*, London, Academic Press.
Lock, A. (1980) *The Guided Reinvention of Language*, London, Academic Press.
Loevinger, J. (1957) 'Objective tests as instruments of psychological theory', *Psychological Reports* 3, 635–94.
Lowenfeld, M. (1935) *Play in Childhood*, London, Gollancz.
Maccoby, E. E. and Jacklin, C. N. (1975) *The Psychology of Sex Differences*, Stanford, Standford University Press.
McCormick, E. J., Jeanneret, P. R. and Mecham, R. C. (1972) 'A study of job characteristics and job dimensions as based on the Position Analysis Questionnaire (PAQ)', *Journal of Applied Psychology*, Monograph 56 (4).
McDougall, W. (1912) *Psychology: The Study of Behaviour*, London, Williams & Norgate.
McGregor, D. (1960) *The Human Side of Enterprise*, New York, McGraw-Hill.

McKinnon, D. W. (1975) *An Overview of Assessment Centers*, Technical Report, I, New York, Center for Creative Leadership.

MacMurray, J. (1957) *The Self as Agent*, London, Faber & Faber.

McRobbie, A. (1978) '*Jackie*: An ideology of adolescent femininity', *Working Papers in Cultural Studies*, SP53, Birmingham Centre for Contemporary Cultural Studies.

McShane, J. (1980) *Learning is Talk*, Cambridge, Cambridge University Press.

Maier, N. R. F. (1958) 'Three types of appraisal interview', *Personnel* (March–April), 27–40.

Manier, E. (1978) *The Young Darwin and His Cultural Circle*, Boston, Reidel.

Marcuse, H. (1964) *Eros and Civilization: A Philosophical Inquiry into Freud*, London, Routledge & Kegan Paul.

Maslow, A. H. (1968) *Towards a Psychology of Being*, 2nd edn, Princeton, Van Nostrand.

Mathematical Association (1955) *The Teaching of Mathematics in Primary Schools*, London, Mathematical Association.

Mayo, E. (1933) *The Human Problems of an Industrial Civilization*, New York, Macmillan.

Mayo, T. (1838) *Elements of the Pathology of the Human Mind*, London, John Murray.

Mead, G. H. (1934) *Mind, Self and Society*, Chicago, University of Chicago Press.

Meltzoff, A. (1976) 'Imitation in early infancy', unpublished PhD thesis, University of Oxford.

Merleau-Ponty, M. (1947 and 1969) *Humanism and Terror*, trans. J. O'Neill (first appeared as *Humanisme et Terreur*), Paris, Gallimard.

Messick, S. (1975) 'The standard problem: meaning and values in measurement and evaluation', *American Psychologist* (October), 955–66.

Miller, G. H., Galanter, E. and Pribram, K. H. (1960) *Plans and Structure of Behaviour*, New York, Holt, Rinehart & Winston.

Milgram, S. (1977) *Obedience to Authority*, London, Tavistock.

Mischel, T. (ed.) (1977) *The Self: Psychological and Philosophical Issues*, Oxford, Blackwell.

Mitchell, J. (1974) *Psychoanalysis and Feminism*, London, Allen Lane.

Mitchell, J. and Rose, J. (eds) (1982) *Feminine Sexuality*, London, Macmillan.

Moi, T. (1982) 'Jealousy and sexual difference', *Feminist Review* 11, 53–69.

Montessori, M. (1912) *The Montessori Method*, London, Heinemann.

Mort, F. (1980) 'The domain of the sexual', *Screen Education* 36, 69–84.

Moscovici, S. (1979) 'A rejoinder', *British Journal of Social and Clinical Psychology* 18, 181.

Murray, L. (1980) 'The sensitivities and expressive capacities of young infants in communication with their mothers', unpublished PhD thesis, University of Edinburgh.

Nava, M. (1982) '"Everybody's views were just broadened": a girls' project and some responses to lesbianism', *Feminist Review* 10, 37–60.

Neisser, U. (1966) *Cognitive Psychology*, New York, Appleton-Century-Crofts.

Nelson, K. (1973) 'Structure and strategy in learning to talk', *S.R.C.D. Monograph* 149 (38), nos 1–2.

Nelson, K. (1974) 'Concept word and sentence: interrelating in acquisition and development', *Psychological Review* 81, 267–85.

Nelson, K. (1980) Paper presented at the British Psychological Society Developmental Section Meeting, Edinburgh.
Newson, J. (1977) 'An intersubjective approach to the systematic description of mother–infant interaction', in Schaffer, H. R. (ed.) *Studies in Mother–Infant Interaction*, London, Academic Press.
Newson, J. (1978) 'Dialogue and development', in Lock, A. (ed.) *Action, Gesture and Symbol: The Emergence of Language*, London, Academic Press.
Ninio, A. and Bruner, J. S. (1978) 'The achievement and antecedants of labelling', *Journal of Child Language* 5, 1–15.
Nkosi, L. (1983) *Home and Exile*, 2nd edn, London, Blackwell.
Oakley, A. (1981) 'Interviewing women', in Roberts, H. (ed.) *Doing Feminist Research*, London, Routledge & Kegan Paul.
Ochs, E. and Schieffelin, B. (1979) *Developmental Pragmatics*, New York, Academic Press.
O, Void (1973) 'The 16 PFffft . . .', *Humpty Dumpty* 2, 2–5.
Owen, R. (1813) *A New View of Society: Or Essays on the Principles of the Formation of the Human Character*.
Ozment, S. E. (1971) *The Reformation in Medieval Perspective*, Chicago, Quadrangle Books.
Packard, V. (1968) *The Sexual Wilderness*, London, Pan.
Papousek, H. (1969) 'Individual variability in learner responses in human infants', in Robinson, R. J. (ed.) *Brain and Early Behavior: Development in the Fetus and Infant*, New York, Academic Press.
Paracelsus, T. in Koyre, A. (1933) and reprinted in Ozment, S. E. (1971) *The Reformation in Medieval Perspective*, Chicago, Quadrangle Books.
Pasquino, P. (1978) '*Theatrum politicum*. The genealogy of capital – police and the state of prosperity', *Ideology and Consciousness* 4, 41–54.
Pasquino, P. (1980) 'Criminology: the birth of a special savoir', *Ideology and Consciousness* 7, 17–32.
Pasquino, P. (1981) 'Introduction to Vonstein, L.', *Economy and Society* 10 (1), 1–6.
Patterson, S. (1963) *Dark Strangers*, London, Tavistock.
Pawlby, J. (1977) 'Imitative interaction', in Schaffer, H. R. (ed.) *Studies in Mother–Infant Interaction*, London, Academic Press.
Pearn, M. (1976) 'Race relations legislation and the role of the occupational psychologist', *Bulletin of the British Psychology Society* 29, 300–2.
Pêcheux, M. (1975) *Les Vérités de la police*, Paris, Maspero.
Perkins, T. E. (1979) 'Rethinking stereotypes', in Barrett, M., Corrigan, P., Kuhn, A. and Wolff, J. (eds) *Ideology and Cultural Reproduction*, London, Croom Helm.
Petty, W. (1672) *Essays on Political Arithmetick*.
Piaget, J. (1915) 'Mission of the idea', in Gruber, H. and Voneche, J. J., *The Essential Piaget*, London, Routledge & Kegan Paul.
Piaget, J. (1918) 'Biology and war', in Gruber, H. and Voneche, J. J., *The Essential Piaget*, London, Routledge & Kegan Paul.
Piaget, J. (1920) 'Psycho-analysis and its relations with child psychology', in Gruber, H. and Voneche, J. J. (1977) *The Essential Piaget*, London, Routledge & Kegan Paul.
Piaget, J. (1951) *Play, Dreams and Imitation*, London, Routledge & Kegan Paul.

Piaget, J. (1953) *The Origin of Intelligence in the Child*, London, Routledge & Kegan Paul.
Piaget, J. (1955) *The Child's Construction of Reality*, London, Routledge & Kegan Paul.
Piaget, J. (1972) *Insights and Illusions of Philosophy*, London, Routledge & Kegan Paul.
Piaget, J. and Inhelder, B. (1969) *The Psychology of the Child*, London, Routledge & Kegan Paul.
Popper, K. (1957) *The Poverty of Historicism*, London, Routledge & Kegan Paul.
Popper, K. (1972) *Objective Knowledge*, Oxford, Oxford University Press.
Porta, G. (1650) *Magie Naturelle*, Rouen.
Porter, L. W., Lawler, E. E., and Hackman, J. R. (1976) *Behavior in Organizations*, New York, McGraw-Hill.
Preyer, W. (1881) *The Mind of the Child*.
Pym, D. (1966) 'Effective managerial performance in organizational change', *Journal of Management Studies* 3, 73–84.
Pym, D. (1973) 'The politics and ritual of appraisals', *Occupational Psychology* 47, 231–5.
Randell, G. (1973) 'Performance appraisal: purposes, practices and conflicts', *Occupational Psychology* 47, 221–4.
Reeves, F. (1982) 'The concept of prejudice: an evaluative review', *SSRC Research Unit on Ethnic Relations, Working Paper* no. 17, 1, Birmingham, SSRC.
Reich, W. (1972) 'Dialectical materialism and psychoanalysis', in *Sexpol*, New York, Vintage.
Richards, G. (1982) 'James and Freud: two masters of metaphor', unpublished paper presented at 'Changing Language of Psychology' Symposium, NELP.
Richards, M. P. M. (1974a) 'The biological and the social', in Armistead, N. (ed.) *Reconstructing Social Psychology*, Harmondsworth, Penguin.
Richards, M. P. M. (1974b) *The Integration of a Child into a Social World*, Cambridge, Cambridge University Press.
Richards, M. P. M. (1974c) 'First steps in becoming social', in Richards, M. P. M. (ed.) *The Integration of a Child into a Social World*, Cambridge, Cambridge University Press.
Riley, D. (1978a) 'Developmental psychology, biology and Marxism', *Ideology and Consciousness* 4, 73–92.
Riley, D. (1978b) 'War in the nursery', *Feminist Review* 3, 82–108.
Roberts, B. (1977) 'Mead's social philosophy', *Ideology and Consciousness* 2, 81–108.
Rogers, C. R. (1951) *Client-Centred Therapy: Its Current Practice, Implications and Theory*, Boston, Houghton.
Rogers, C. R. (1961) *On Becoming a Person*, London, Constable.
Rosch, E. (1975) 'Cognitive representations of semantic categories', *Journal of Experimental Psychology* 104, 192–233.
Rose, N. (1979) 'The psychological complex: mental measurement and social administration', *Ideology and Consciousness* 5, 5–68.
Rose, N. (1982) 'The pleasures of motherhood: discussion of Elizabeth Badinter "The Myth of Motherhood: an historical view of the maternal instinct"', trans. Roger DeGaris, *m/f* 7, 82–6.

Rose, E. J. B., Deakin, N., Abrams, V., Peston, M., Vanags, A. H., Cohen, B., Gaitskell, J. and Ward, P. (1969) *Colour and Citizenship*, London, Oxford University Press.

Rose, S. and Rose, H. (eds) (1976) *The Political Economy of Science*, London, Macmillan.

Rosen, M. (1972) *Language and Class*, Bristol, Falling Wall Press.

Rosen, M. (1977) 'Out there or where the masons went', in Hoyles, M. (ed.) *The Politics of Literacy*, London, Writers and Readers Publishing Cooperative.

Rosenberg, B. G. and Sutton Smith, B. (1972) *Sex and Identity*, New York, Holt, Rinehart & Winston.

Rosenthal, R. (1966) *Experimenter Effects in Behavioral Research*, New York, Appleton-Century-Crofts.

Rotman, B. (n.d.) 'Mathematics: an essay in semiotics', unpublished manuscript, Department of Mathematics, University of Bristol.

Rowan, J. (1979) 'Mail survey of occupational psychologists', unpublished paper (for the Working Party on the future of Occupational Pyschology of the British Psychological Society) given at Occupational Psychology Conference, January 1980.

Rowe, K. K. (1964) 'An appraisal of appraisals', *Journal of Management Studies* 1, 1–25.

Sachs, J. (1977) 'The adaptive significance of linguistic input to prelinguistic infants', in Snow, C. E. and Ferguson, C. A. (eds) *Talking to Children: Language Input and Acquisition*, Cambridge, Cambridge University Press.

Sartre, J.-P. (1960) *Critique de la Raison Dialectique*, Paris, Gallimard.

Saussure, F. de (1974) *Course in General Linguistics*, London, Fontana.

Sayers, J. (1982) 'Psychoanalysis and personal politics: a response to Elizabeth Wilson', *Feminist Review* 10, 91–5.

Scarman, Lord (1981) *The Brixton Disorders, 10–12 April 1981*, Cmnd 8427, London, HMSO.

Schaffer, H. R. (1971) *The Growth of Sociability*, Harmondsworth, Penguin.

Schaffer, H. R. (ed.) (1977) *Studies in Mother–Infant Interaction*, London, Academic Press.

Schank, R. and Abelson, R. P. (1977) *Scripts, Plans, Goals and Understanding: An Enquiry into Human Knowledge Structures*, Hillsdale, Erlbaum.

Schlesinger, I. M. (1971) 'Production of utterances and language acquisition', in Slobin, D. (ed.) *The Ontogenesis of Grammar*, New York, Academic Press.

Searle, J. (1969) *Speech Acts: An Essay in the Philosophy of Language*, London, Cambridge University Press.

Selby, J. (n.d.) PhD dissertation, University of Cambridge (in preparation).

Select Committee on Race Relations and Immigration, Session 1977–8, *First Report, Immigration*, Vol. I, Hoc Paper 303–1, London, HMSO.

Selleck, R. J. W. (1972) *English Primary Education and the Progressives, 1914–1939*, London, Routledge & Kegan Paul.

Sharp, R. and Green, A. G. (1975) *Education and Social Control*, London, Routledge & Kegan Paul.

Sherwood, R. (1980) *The Psychodynamics of Race: Vicious and Benign Spirals*, Brighton, Harvester Press.

Shotter, J. (1974a) 'What is it to be human?', in Armistead, N. (ed.) *Reconstructing Social Psychology*, Harmondsworth, Penguin.

Shotter, J. (1974b) 'The development of personal powers', in Richards, M. P. M. (ed.) *The Integration of a Child into a Social World*, Cambridge, Cambridge University Press.

Shotter, J. (1978) 'The cultural context of communication studies: theoretical and methodological issues', in Lock, A. (ed.) *Action, Gesture and Symbol: The Emergence of Language*, London, Academic Press.

Silverman, D. and Jones, J. (1976) *Organizational Work*, London, Collier Macmillan.

Simon, B. (1965) *Education and the Labour Movement, 1870–1920*, London, Lawrence & Wishart.

Simon, B. (1974) *The Politics of Educational Reform 1920–1940*, London, Lawrence & Wishart.

Sinha, C. (1977) 'Class, language and education', *Ideology and Consciousness* 1, 77–92.

Sinha, C. and Walkerdine, V. (1978) 'Children, logic and learning', *New Society* (12 January 1978).

Sivanandan, A. (1976) 'Race, class and the state: the black British experience in Britain', *Race and Class* 17 (4), 347–68.

Sivanandan, A. (1981) 'From resistance to rebellion: Asian and Afro-Caribbean struggles in Britain', *Race and Class* 13 (2/3), 111–52.

Slobin, D. (1971) *Psycholinguistics*, Glenview, Ill., Scott Foreman.

Slobin, D. (1973) 'Cognitive prerequisites for the development of grammar', in Ferguson, C. and Slobin, D. (eds) *Studies of Child Language Development*, New York, Holt, Rinehart & Winston.

Smith, M., Hartley, J. and Stewart, B. (1978) 'A case study of repertory grids used in vocational guidance', *Journal of Occupational Psychology* 51, 97–104.

Smith, P. B. (ed.) (1980) *Group Processes and Personal Change*, London, Harper & Row.

Snow, C. (1977a) 'Mothers' speech research: from input to interaction', in Snow, C. and Ferguson, C. (eds) *Talking to Children: Language Input and Acquisition*, Cambridge, Cambridge University Press.

Snow, C. (1977b) 'The development of conversation between mothers and babies', *Journal of Child Language* 4 (1), 1–22.

Snow, C. and Ferguson, C. (eds) (1977) *Talking to Children: Language Input and Acquisition Research*, Cambridge, Cambridge University Press.

Southey, R. (1829) *Colloquies on the Progress and Prospects of Society*.

Spender, D. (1980) *Man Made Language*, London, Routledge & Kegan Paul.

Steedman, C. (n.d.) 'The mother made conscious: the development of a primary school pedagogy' (in preparation).

Steedman, C., Urwin, C. and Walkerdine, V. (eds) (1984) *Language, Gender and Childhood*, London, Routledge & Kegan Paul (in preparation).

Stern, D. N. (1974) 'Mother and infant at play: the dyadic interaction involving facial, vocal and gaze behaviours', in Lewis, M. and Rosenbaum, L. (eds) *The Effect of the Infant on its Caregiver*, New York, Wiley.

Stewart, A. and Stewart, V. (1976) *The Identification and Development of Management Potential*, London, Institute of Personnel Management.

Stewart, A. and Stewart, V. (1979) 'How to spot the high fliers', *Personnel Management* 11 (9), 28–31.

Stewart, D. (1829) *The Works of Dugald Stewart*, 7 vols, Cambridge, Hilliard & Brown.

Stewart, W. A. C. (1972) *Progressives and Radicals in English Education 1750–1970*, London, Macmillan.

Storr, A. (1971) *Human Aggression*, Harmondsworth, Penguin, quoted in *The Observer* (24 May 1981).

Student Christian Movement (1966) *Sex and Morality: A Report Presented to the British Council of Churches*, London, SCM Press.

Sulloway, F. (1980) *Freud, Biologist of the Mind*, London, Fontana.

Sylvester-Bradley, B. and Trevarthen, C. (1978) 'Baby talk as an adaptation to the infant's communication', in Waterson, N. and Snow, C. E. (eds) *The Development of Communication*, Chichester: Wiley.

Tajfel, H. (1972) 'Experiments in a vacuum', in Israel, J. and Tajfel, H. (eds) *The Social Context of Social Psychology: A critical assessment*, London, Academic Press.

Tajfel, H. (1974) 'Intergroup behaviour, social comparison and social change', Katz Newcamb Lectures, mimeo, University of Michigan.

Tajfel, H. (1978) 'The structure of our views about society', in Tajfel, H. and Fraser, C. *Studies in Intergroup Behaviour*, London, Academic Press.

Tajfel, H. (1979) 'Individuals and groups in social psychology', *British Journal of Social and Clinical Psychology* 18, 183–90.

Tajfel, H. and Brown, R. J. (1975) 'Inadequate social identity in an anticipated superordinate goal situation', unpublished manuscript, University of Bristol.

Tajfel, H., Flament, C., Billig, M. and Bundy, R. P. (1971) 'Social categorization and intergroup behaviour', *European Journal of Social Psychology* 1 (1), 149–78.

Tajfel, H. and Turner, J. (1976) 'An integrative theory of intergroup conflict', unpublished manuscript, University of Bristol.

Taylor, D. and Brown, R. (1979) 'Towards a more social social psychology', *British Journal of Social and Clinical Psychology* 18, 989–1016.

Taylor, F. W. (1911) *The Principles of Scientific Management*, New York, Harper.

Taylor, R. (1966) *Action and Purpose*, New York, Prentice-Hall.

Thom, M. (1981) 'The unconscious structured like a language', in McCabe, C. (ed.) *The Talking Cure: Essays in Psychoanalysis and Language*, London, Macmillan.

Thompson, E. P. (1978) *The Poverty of Theory*, London, Merlin.

Thurstone, L. L. (1927) 'Attitudes can be measured', *American Journal of Sociology* 33, 529–54.

Thurstone, L. E. and Chave, E. J. (1929) *The Measurement of Attitude*, Chicago, University of Chicago Press.

Tizard, B., Hughes, M., Pinkerton, G. and Carmichael, H. (1982) 'Adults' cognitive demands at home and at nursery school', *Journal of Child Psychology and Psychiatry* 23 (2), 105–46.

Treble, S. (1972) 'The development of shape perception in young children', unpublished PhD thesis, University of Nottingham.

Trevarthen, C. (1975) 'Early attempts at speech', in Lewin, R. (ed.) *Child Alive*, London, Temple-Smith.

Trevarthen, C. (1977) 'Descriptive analyses of infant communicative behaviour', in Schaffer, H. R. (ed.) *Studies in Mother–Infant Interaction*, London, Academic Press.

Trevarthen, C. (1979) 'Communication and cooperation in early infancy' in Bullowa, M. (ed.) *Before Speech: The Beginning of Interpersonal Communication*, Cambridge, Cambridge University Press.

Trevarthen, C. (1982) 'The primary motives for cooperative understanding', in Butterworth, G. and Light, P., *Social Cognition: Studies of the Development of Understanding*, Brighton, Harvester Press.

Turkle, S. (1979) *Psychoanalytic Politics*, London, Burnett Books.

Urwick Orr and Partners (n.d.) *Job Evaluation – the Profile Method*, London.

Urwin, C. (1978) 'The development of communication between blind infants and their parents', in Lock, A. (ed.) *Action, Gesture and Symbol: The Emergence of Language*, London, Academic Press.

Urwin, C. (1982a) 'Developmental psychology and child rearing practices: some problems with prescriptions', paper presented at BPS Developmental Section Conference, Durham, September 1982.

Urwin, C. (1982b) 'On the contribution of non-visual communication systems and language to knowing oneself', in Beveridge, M. (ed.) *Children Thinking Through Language*, London, Arnold.

Urwin, C. (1983) 'Observations of aggression between same-aged infants', unpublished paper presented at World Infant Psychiatry Conference, Cannes, April 1983.

Urwin, C. (1984) 'Making the evidence: language development as a "normal" process', in Steedman, C., Urwin, C. and Walkerdine, V. (eds) *Language, Gender and Childhood*, London, Routledge & Kegan Paul (in preparation).

Venn, C. (1982) *Beyond the Science–Ideology Relation*, unpublished PhD thesis, University of Essex.

Venn, C. and Walkerdine, V. (1978) 'The acquisition and production of knowledge: Piaget's theory reconsidered', *Ideology and Consciousness* 3, 67–94.

Vygotsky, L. S. (1962) *Language and Thought*, Cambridge, Mass., M.I.T. Press.

Walden, R. and Walkerdine, V. (1981) 'Girls and mathematics: the early years', *Bedford Way Papers* 8, London, Heinemann.

Walkerdine, V. (1981a) 'Sex, power and pedagogy', *Screen Education* 38, 14–21.

Walkerdine, V. (1981b) 'Gender and rationality: telling the truth about girls', unpublished paper presented at the British Sociological Association Annual Conference.

Walkerdine, V. (1982a) 'Collected papers: a report to the SSRC', unpublished report, London, Social Science Research Council.

Walkerdine, V. (1982b) 'From context to text: a psychosemiotic approach to abstract thought', in Beveridge, M. (ed.) *Children Thinking Through Language*, London, Arnold.

Walkerdine, V. (n.d.) 'Women teachers and the pedagogy of love', *Girls and Mathematics Unit*, mimeo, London, University of London Institute of Education (in preparation).

Walkerdine, V. (1983) 'It's only natural: beyond child-centred pedagogy', in Wolpe, A. M. and Donald, J. (eds) *Is There Anyone Here From Education?*, London, Pluto Press.

Walkerdine, V. (1984) 'Some day my prince will come', in Nava, M. and McRobbie, A. (eds) *Gender and Generation*, London, Macmillan.

Walkerdine, V. and Corran, G. (1979) 'Cognitive development: a mathematical experience?', unpublished paper presented at BPS Developmental Section Conference on Social Cognition, Southampton, September 1979.

Walkerdine, V., Walden, R. and Hayward, M. (n.d.) *Women and Education: Mathematics, a Case Study* (in preparation).

Wallis, D. (1980) 'Sex discrimination and the law', *Bulletin of the British Psychology Society* 33, 1–5.

Weinreich, H. (1978) 'Sex-role socialisation', in Chetwynd, J. and Hartnett, O. (eds) *The Sex-role System*, London, Routledge & Kegan Paul.

Wertheimer, N. (1961) 'Psychomotor co-ordination of auditory visual space at birth', *Science* 134, 1692.

Whitehead, A. N. (1929) *The Aims of Education*, London, Williams & Norgate.

Whorf, B. (1956) 'Science and linguistics', in Carroll, J. (ed.) *Language, Thought and the School*, Cambridge, Mass., M.I.T. Press.

Williams, S. and Shuard, H. (1974) *Primary Mathematics Today*, London, Longmans.

Willis, P. (1978) *Learning to Labour: How Working-Class Kids Get Working-Class Jobs*, London, Saxon House.

Wilson, G. (1979) 'The sociobiology of sex differences', *Bulletin of the British Psychology Society* 32, 350–3.

Winnicott, D. W. (1956) 'Primary maternal preoccupation', in *Collected Papers. Through Paediatrics to Psychoanalysis*, London, Tavistock (1958).

Winnicott, D. W. (1967) 'Mirror-role of the mother and family in child development', in Lomas, P. (ed.) *The Predicament of the Family: a Psychoanalytic Symposium*, London, Hogarth Press and the Institute of Psychoanalysis.

Wood, J. (1982) 'Adolescents', *New Socialist* 5, 41–3.

Young, R. M. (1977) 'Science *is* social relations', *Radical Science Journal* 5, 65–129.

Name index

Subject index